Christm

Dear Rome, Diara +
Rita,

This is a work for
the 3 of you to share.
It was published this
year + includes an essay
on the philosophy of creative,
synthetic learning which I
wrote. I also include a
follow up lecture regarding
the implementation of the theory
which is submitted to the
Chinese Ministry of Education. Ron

Alfred North Whitehead
on Learning and Education

Alfred North Whitehead
on Learning and Education:
Theory and Application

edited by

Franz G. Riffert

Cambridge Scholars Press

Alfred North Whitehead on Learning and Education: Theory and Application,
edited by Franz G. Riffert

This book first published 2005 by

Cambridge Scholars Press

15 Angerton Gardens, Newcastle, NE5 2JA, UK

British Library Cataloguing in Publication Data
A catalogue record for this book is available from the British Library

ISBN 1-904303-57-9

Table of Contents

II. APPLICATION

II.1. WHITEHEAD'S EDUCATIONAL THOUGHT IN THE FIELD OF MANAGEMENT

II.2. WHITEHEAD'S EDUCATIONAL THOUGHT AND ITS APPLICATION TO COLLEGES

II.3 EVALUATION - A WHITEHEADIAN TURN

Introduction: Via Negativa – Whitehead's Critique of Traditional Concepts of Learning and Instruction

Franz Riffert

1. The Contemporary Situation in Education

During the last decades the educational system of the USA has been severely criticized. This criticism was – and still is – based on "statewide skill-based testing and the poor performance of American students in international comparison" (Dick 1991, 43). According to the Cognition and Technology Group at Vanderbilt (1992, 77) "[o]ne source of concern about the need to teach thinking stems from poor national test scores, especially on tasks involving problem solving and reasoning". (See also: Schoenfeld 1992; Jones & Idol 1990; Carpenter et al. 1983; NAEP 1983;) Nickerson (1988) summarized his analysis of the test results by maintaining: "In the aggregate, the findings from these studies force the conclusion that it is possible to finish 12 or 13 years of education in the United States without developing much competence as a thinker" (1988, 5; see also CTG 1991, 34). More or less the same situation is revealed by the international performance tests in many European nations. Especially in Germany 'educational shock' was widespread after the results of the PISA 2000 study were published about three years ago.

There have been calls for fundamental reform of the educational system in many places. But where to go? Simply being shocked by national and international test results does not lead to a better educational system. A first step, certainly, is an analysis of possible explanations of the bad results. Human cultures and their social subsystems are very complex, and so are the educational systems, the school cultures, and even the multifaceted processes going on between a teacher and say 20 to 30 students in one single class of 50 minutes. Problem analysis is difficult – certainly – but it is not impossible. No detailed analysis can be given here; but there is one aspect which is frequently thought to be crucial: "[A] major cause of poor performance on tasks that require the generation of relevant sub-problems, arguments, and explanations is that most curricula emphasize the memorization of facts and the acquisition of relatively isolated sub-skills that are learned out of context and hence result in knowledge representations that tend to remain inert (e.g., see Brown, Collins & Duguid 1989; Cognition and Technology Group at Vanderbilt, 1990; Resnick & Klopfer 1989)." (Cognition and Technology Group 1992, 78)

According to Jerome Bruner it should be just the other way round: "A method of instruction should have the objective of leading the child to discover for [her]himself. Telling children and then testing them on what they have been told inevitably has the effect of producing bench-bound learners whose motivation for learning is likely to be extrinsic to the task – pleasing the teacher, getting into the College, artificially maintaining self-esteem. The virtues of encouraging discovery are of two kinds. In the first place, the child will make what [s]he learns [her] his own, will fit his discovery into the interior world of cultures that [s]he creates for [her]himself. Equally important, discovery and the sense of confidence which it provides is the proper reward for learn-ing" (Bruner 1971, 123f).

But we may ask further: Why do we teach isolated context-free contents? One among many answers directs attention to the curricu-lum. Curricula encouraging, if not forcing, teachers to present isolated scraps of knowledge are based on associationist-behaviorist assump-tions. These assumptions themselves rest on a mechanist-substantialist neo-positivist epistemology and its, often only implicit, metaphysics: "There is no question that the major principles of instructional design have been derived from Skinnerian psychology and Gagne's conditions of learning [1965]. These theories have been integrated, along with other principles, into systematic models for designing instruction." (Dick 1991, 41) According to this line of argumentation instructional manuals which rest on neo-positivist/behaviorist assumptions lead to inert knowledge.

The term 'inert knowledge' was coined by Alfred North Whitehead (see for instance 1967, 32) when describing the failure of the school system of his day, i.e., the beginning of the twentieth century. The term was taken up by the Cognition and Technology Group at Vanderbilt decades later and since then appears frequently in the discussion between traditionalist and constructivist educators. It was one of Whitehead's major intentions to provide teachers and school authorities with an outline of an educational concept, based on a new learning theory, which avoids the production of inert knowledge. This alternative learning theory and educational theory is based on an alternative epistemology and even metaphysics. Only with this fundamental shift can we hope to found educational reform on a better basis. Alfred North Whitehead has offered a philosophical alternative to the mechanistic, neo-positivist view on which behaviorism was founded.

2. Whitehead's Critique of Traditional Views on Learning and Education

In this book a number of scholars undertake adventurous expeditions into Whitehead's theory of learning and teaching. Whitehead is known less for his educational ideas than for his work in the fields of formal logic, mathematical physics and metaphysics. Nevertheless, he also developed creative ideas on such topics as learning and teaching on the basis of his challenging process metaphysics. In his days, and even today, these ideas have to be termed bold. They leave behind many of the traditional concepts and propose a radically new approach.

While the authors in this book focus attention on the positive side of Whitehead's approach, I will take the *via negative* in this introductory section and present Whitehead's criticism of those *insufficient, if not harmful, principles* underlying traditional curriculum and teaching in his day. Unfortunately, these principles still operate in our day as well. In doing this, I hope to improve the understanding of Whitehead's novel ideas.

(a) According to Whitehead, probably the most severe mistake is the sometimes implicitly held conviction that students "progress in a steady, uniform advance from the elementary stages of the subject to the most advanced level which the student attains, a movement containing no changes in the kind of progress and no changes in pace." (Dunkel 1965, 109)
Whitehead put it this way: "The pupil's progress is often conceived as a uniform steady advance undifferentiated by change of type or alteration in pace. [...] I hold that this conception of education is based upon

a false psychology of the process of mental development which has gravely hindered the effectiveness of our methods." (1967, 17) It issues from a mechanist-associationist psychology (and its underlying epistemology and (tacit) metaphysics): single disconnected ideas are mechanically associated in a more or less random way. This is the way learning takes place according to the behaviorists: steadily adding bit by bit of new (isolated) building blocks of knowledge. But Whitehead warns: "It must never be forgotten that education is not a process of packing articles in a trunk. Such simile is entirely inapplicable." (1967, 33) Instead Whitehead promotes a dynamic cyclic theory of learning (descriptive theory) and of teaching (prescriptive theory) which will be presented and elaborated later in this book.

(b) Intimately linked to the first point of critique, Whitehead directs our attention to the obvious fact that pupils "must be continually enjoying some fruition and starting afresh"; i.e. "We should banish the idea of a mythical far-off end of education." (1967, 17) Such far-off aims are hardly reachable and therefore easily lead to frustration and demotivation. This position is intimately connected to his concept of cyclic education. Each educational cycle issues in a termination or satisfaction and thereby motivates the student to start a new cycle. Linear, non-cyclic education ends up in failure because it is undertaken "without rhythm and without stimulus of intermediate success and without concentration." (1967, 20)

(c) Whitehead also criticizes modern compartmentalization of the subjects. Such absolute divorce of subjects neither is good in research nor in education. The basic gap underlying this compartmentalization is what Whitehead had termed the "bifurcation of nature" (see: Whitehead 1920). This bifurcation has its origin in the radical independence ascribed by Descartes to the bodily substances and mental substances. The introduction of two completely separate types of entities: *res cogitans* and *res extensa* created two mutually exclusive and therefore absolutely distinct 'worlds': a world of quality including subjectivity, values and consciousness opposed to a world of mere quantitative extension. Such bifurcation of nature is mirrored by a "bifurcation of education: the splitting of education into the Arts and Humanities [...] versus the Sciences (usually including technology)" as Pete Gunter (1994, 11f) has correctly pointed out. This dissatisfying situation of two separately existing 'cultures' of learning, "unconcerned with each other if not antithetical" (Gunter 1994, 12) and its unfortunate implications have been thoroughly discussed by C. P. Snow in his famous book *The Two Cultures*. It was Whitehead who had long before pointed out the negative implications of such a radical separation; and it was his intention to overcome this conceptual bifurcation. He attempted to do this by the construction of his one-type (type-monist) metaphysics. Although nowhere in his books and articles does he dwell further on the implications of this metaphysical bifurcation of nature to the field of education, we may conjecture that he thought that a re-union at the metaphysical level would also result in the break down of the bifurcation in education. Besides this fundamental bifurcation, the splitting up of the sciences into diverse and unrelated fields of research and teaching is another characteristic of the modern world which has to be overcome. This scatteredness of the diverse sciences is another factor contributing to what Whitehead has termed "inert knowledge" (1967, 34) Inert knowledge is what traditional education mainly produces, and therefore it is necessary "to eradicate the fatal disconnection of subjects which kills the vitality of our modern curriculum." (1967, 6). According to Whitehead, in agreement with John Dewey, "[t]here is only one subject-matter for education, and that is Life in all its manifestations. Instead of this single unity, we offer children – Algebra, from which nothing follows; Geometry, from which nothing follows; Science from which nothing follows; a Couple of Languages, never mastered; and lastly, most dreary of all, Literature, represented by plays of Shakespeare, with philosophical notes and short analyses of plot and character to be in substance committed to memory." (1967, 7)

(d) Whitehead also warns us not to teach too many subjects. (1967, 2) This point of criticism again is linked to the point of criticism just mentioned. The danger here is that teaching too many subjects will necessarily – simply because of lack of time – lead to a presentation of "small parts of a large number of subjects" (1967, 2) and "the passive reception of disconnected ideas not illuminated with any spark of vitality." (1967, 2)

(e) Further, Whitehead criticizes behaviorist (mechanist) assumptions concerning learning: "It must never be forgotten that education is not a process of packing articles in a trunk. Such simile is entirely inapplicable. It is, of course, a process completely of its own peculiar genus. Its nearest analogue is the assimilation of food by a living organism: and we all know how necessary to health is palatable food under suitable conditions." (1967, 33)

So learning is not a mere passive, mechanical process of adding simple units on a 'tabula rasa' and so piling up a heap of isolated bits of knowledge. On the contrary: learning is an active process of assimilation, i.e., of actively integrating new elements into pre-existing dynamic (cognitive) structures. In this way the structures themselves, as well as the newly assimilated elements, are altered (accommodated to one another). "Education must essentially be a setting in order of a ferment already stirring in the mind: you cannot educate mind in *vacuo*." (1967, 18). This position closely corresponds to Piaget's genetic-structuralist theory of learning. Piaget (see: 1968) maintained that human intelligence is the expression of a general tendency toward endogenous reconstruction (by new variations and 'interselection') of unstable, exogenous acquisition.

(f) Whitehead also stresses the fact that, when learning, students "must be free to think rightly and *wrongly*" (1967, 93 italics added). This means that making mistakes should not be conceived as a disaster, which should be hidden or explained away. On the contrary, it should be conceived as a unique opportunity and an additional source for gaining new knowledge. As Daniel Dennet, a well known cognitive psychologist, put it: "Mistakes are the key to making progress [...] they are, in an important sense, the *only opportunity for learning something truly new*." (Dennett 1986, 137 italics added) This attitude towards mistakes is a consequence of Whitehead's radical concept of learning as a genuinely adventurous and endless process of research. "[L]earning should begin in research and end in research." (1967, 37)

(g) Whitehead, in addition, rejects the principle that "easy subjects should come first and harder ones should only follow these easier ones!" He agues that under natural circumstances sometimes the contrary is the case "because nature so dictates" and because some of the more difficult tasks "are essential to life," (1967, 16) He refers to the fact that infants have to cope with the highly ambitious task of acquiring spoken language. "What an appalling task, the correlation of meanings with sounds!" (1967, 16) So, according to Whitehead, there is no need of "postponing the harder subjects." (1967, 16) Of course the environmental conditions under which hard tasks are presented are crucial and must be very carefully selected.

(h) Finally, Whitehead also rejects the principle of 'necessary precedence'. Although this principle rests on firmer ground and has some obvious instances of application, it "dissolves under scrutiny." (1967, 16) The problem with this principle is that it is almost a "necessary truth, and that it is applied in another sense for which it is false." (1967, 16) Certainly, one cannot start reading difficult texts, before one can read at all. But on the other hand, Whitehead points to the fact that the old songs of the Greeks, Homer's Iliad for instance, were sung to children well before they were able to read.

This list of eight shortcomings of the traditional concepts of learning and education urges us to turn to Whitehead's alternative theory of learning and education, to elaborate it, and to examine how it can be implemented in everyday educational work. This task is undertaken by the authors of this book.

Bibliography
Brown, J. S., Collins, A. & Duguid, P. (1989): Situated cognition and the culture of learning. *Education Researcher* 18, 1, 32-42.
Bruner, J. (1971): *The Relevance of Education.* New York: Norton.
CTG (Cognition and Technology Group at Vanderbilt) (1990): Anchored instruction and its relation to situated cognition. *Educational Researcher* 20, 2-10.
CTG (Cognition and Technology Group at Vanderbilt) (1991): Some thoughts about constructivism and instructional design. In: T. M. Duffy & D. H. Jonassen (Eds.) *Constructivism and the Technology of Instruction: a Conversation.* Hillsdale: Erlbaum, 115-119.
CTG (Cognition and Technology Group at Vanderbilt) (1992): Technology and the design of generative learning environments. In: T.M. Duffy & D. H. Jonassen (Eds.): *Constructivism and the Technology of Instruction. A Conversation.* Hillsdale: Erlbaum, 77-89.
Cognition and Technology Group at Vanderbilt (1992): Emerging technologies, ISD, and learning environments: critical perspectives. *Educational Technology Research and Development*, 40, 1, 65-80.
Carpenter, T. P., Lindquist, M. M., Matthews, W., & Silver, E. A. (1983): Results of the third NAEP mathematics assessment: Secondary school. *Mathematics Teacher* 76, 9, 652-659.

Dennett, D. C. (1995): How to Make Mistakes. In: J. Brockman and K. Matson (Eds.): *How Things Are.* New York: William Morrow and Company. 137-144. (also available online: URL: http://ase.tufts.edu/cogstud/papers/howmista.htm (access: 26.01.2005).

Dick, W. (1991): An instructional designer's view of constructivism. In: T. M. Duffy & D. H. Jonassen (Eds.): *Constructivism and the Technology of Instruction: a Conversation,* Hillsdale: Erlbaum, 91-98.

Dunkel, H. B. (1965): *Whitehead on Education.* Columbus: Ohio State University Press.

Gunter, P. (1994): Education, Modernity, and Fractured Meaning (Education, Modernite et Fragmentation de Sens). Colloquium on the Rhythms of Education in the Philosophy of Whitehead, Universite Catholique de Lille. paper available from the author.

Jones, B. F. & Idol, L (1990): *Dimensions of Thinking and Cognitive Instruction.* Hillsdale: Erlbaum.

NAEP (National Assessment of Educational Progress) (1983): *The Third National Mathematics Assessment: Results, Trends, and Issues.* (Report No. 13-MA-01). Denver: Educational Commission of the States.

Nickerson, R. S. (1988): On Improving Thinking Through Instruction. *Review of Research in Education* 15, 3-57.

Piaget, J. (1968): *Six Psychological Studies.* New York: Random House.

Resnick, L. B. & Klopfer, L. E. (1989): *Toward the Thinking Curriculum: Current Cognitive Research.* Alexandria, VA: ASCD.

Schoenfeld, A. H. (1992): Learning to think mathematically: problem solving, metacognition, and sense-making in mathematics. In: D. Grouws, (Ed.). *Handbook for Research on Mathematics Teaching and Learning.* New York: MacMillan, 334-370.

Whitehead, A. N. (1967/1929): *The Aims of Education and Other Essays.* New York: Free Press.

Whitehead, A. N. (1920): *The Concept of Nature.* Cambridge: Cambridge University Press.

Part I

THEORY

PART I.1

THE CYCLIC NATURE OF LEARNING AND EDUCATION

Education and the Phases of Concrescence

John B. Cobb, Jr.

Abstract
Whitehead's book on education (1967) has been extensively discussed. Interest has centered on his analysis of the three phases of learning: romance, precision, and generalization. There have been useful efforts to correlate what he says on these points with his later technical description of the phases of concrescence of actual occasions. Still more can and should be done along these lines.

I am proposing to supplement this approach by a move in the opposite direction. I want to begin with his discussion of phases of concrescence and move from them to a consideration of teaching and learning. I will focus on what Whitehead says about propositions and propositional feelings, but I will discuss other phases of concrescence also.

It should be recognized at the outset that the phases of concrescence cannot in fact be separated. The physical feelings of the conformal phase, to which I turn first, actually exist only as part of the whole concrescence and its satisfaction. Teaching and learning concern this totality as a totality. Nevertheless, it is possible to accent the contribution to this totality of distinct elements within it. A teacher who is aware of these diverse contributions can direct the learner into activities that emphasize one or another of them.

1. The Conformal Phase

The conformal phase of an occasion is its 'physical pole'. It consists in physical feelings or causal feelings. The content of the conformal phase is determined by the actual world of the occasion. It is the way that actual world enters into the new occasion.

In the analysis of a single actual occasion, this phase is determined by the past, and for this reason it seems irrelevant to a discussion of teaching and learning. But it is, in fact, far from irrelevant. What an occasion becomes is largely determined by its actual world, and for that reason influencing in one moment what the actual world will be in future moments plays a very large role in teaching.

If a teacher encourages students to close their eyes, the actual world of those students will change. The role of some of the stimuli that are important when their eyes are open will be dramatically reduced when their eyes are closed. This leads to other stimuli playing a larger role in the new concrescence and perhaps having the chance to rise to the level of consciousness. Alternately, if a teacher encourages students to concentrate on their sensory experience of touch or smell, students will become aware of what they are touching and smelling as they are not when the teacher asks them to concentrate on their multiplication tables. Or if a teacher takes the students on an outing, their experiences will arise out of a quite different actual world.

Much of the educational process directs attention to the supplementary phases of concrescence dominated by conceptual feelings. This is, perhaps, as it should be. For human beings the life of the mind is of immense importance. However, failure to attend to what is concretely given impoverishes experience. Some of this awareness is of one's own body. Instead of ignoring one's body or controlling it, one may be encouraged to attend to its role in constituting experience. Some of the awareness is of physical feelings is of one's emotions as they flow into the present from the past. Some of the awareness is of the wider world as it impinges upon the concrescing occasion. Some of the awareness may be of the feelings of other people or nonhuman creatures. Some of the awareness may be of the divine.

Attending to physical feelings is more likely to be encouraged in the context of religious meditation than in the typical secular classroom. Some Buddhist traditions have been particular effective in getting people to attend to what is, just as it is, allowing more of it to be consciously noticed. In Whitehead's terms, this is attention to the data of the physical feelings constituting the conformal phase. From a Whiteheadian point of view, it is not possible to separate these entirely from the supplementary phases, but the role of the latter can certainly be reduced.

Some Christian traditions concentrate on awareness of the divine. In Whitehead's view, God is felt in the conformal phase as a lure to attain what 'strength of beauty' is possible in the concrescence itself while contributing to such beauty also in subsequent occasions. Orienting oneself to conforming to that lure is a spiritual discipline.

Despite the religious character of much of the attention to the conformal phase, this is not excluded from secular education. An emphasis on this phase of the occasion can also be nurtured in the classroom without religious language. Such an emphasis is most likely to occur in the context of instruction on the arts, which, unfortunately, are often regarded as a nonessential part of the curriculum.

The lack of attention to this grounding in the given reality is a serious limitation of most formal education. It both results from, and is a major contributor to, the dualistic sensibility that plays so large a role among educated people and leads to the deep cultural alienation from the natural world. Without a widespread reconnection of humanity with its physical ground, ecologically responsible behavior is not likely to become dominant. Unless this is encouraged in public education, prospects for it are bleak.

I pass on from this topic quickly, not because it is unimportant, but because it has been ably discussed by one of the leading Whiteheadian philosophers of education, Robert S. Brumbaugh, in his book, *Whitehead, Process Philosophy, and Education* (1982), points out that if education "is to be realistic, it must rest on a correct notion of reality. If Whitehead's philosophy is right, that has not been the case for three hundred years and is not the case now." (1982, 1-2)

Brumbaugh's point is that for Whitehead the world *is* as it is given in physical feeling, not as it is projected in presentational immediacy or imagined in intellectual feelings. Consciousness, however, focuses first on presentational immediacy, and secondly, on propositions. Physical feeling, or perception in the mode of causal efficacy, is essential to the symbolic reference that is our basic awareness of the world. But the philosophical theories that have shaped our thought in the modern world have consistently abstracted from these physical feelings that constitute the conformal phase of the occasion. This has resulted in the loss of a sense of being part of the very real natural world. As Western thinkers have recognized and stressed the enormous role of the later phases of concrescence in ordering the content of our consciousness, they have so emphasized this role of creativity as to forget that it arises out of a real world and passes back into that world. Education that leads us thus away from the true reality does more harm than good. Nothing could be more important in the process of education than bringing our physical feelings back into play. And Brumbaugh has many concrete suggestions about how educators can and should do this.

2. Propositional Feelings

To turn from physical feelings to a focus on propositional feelings is not to abandon the former. Physical feelings are an essential component of propositional feelings. Much of what Brumbaugh discusses with respect to our experience of the real physical world actually belongs to the sphere of propositional and intellectual feelings, accenting the neglected physical feeling component. Similarly, the physical feelings are in fact, in our conscious experience, integrated into intellectual feelings. As noted in the introduction, to treat any phase of the concrescence as if it existed apart from the whole is erroneous. Nevertheless, as long as we remember the element of abstraction involved, it is also useful.

A propositional feeling is, obviously, the feeling of a proposition. Unfortunately the usual connotations of 'proposition' lead to deep misunderstanding of Whitehead's meaning. The problem is that most people suppose that a proposition is a verbal statement. It can, of course, be defined in that way. But logicians also use the term to mean that to which verbal statements refer, and this is Whitehead's use.

In this understanding of propositions, a variety of verbal statements in different languages can intend the same proposition. Indeed, in a single language there can be a variety of verbal expressions of the same proposition. On the other hand, no verbal expression is completely unambiguous. Hence, every verbal statement, simply as such, refers to diverse propositions. The context in which the statement is made, written or oral, usually narrows the range of propositions considerably, but absolute univocity is nonexistent.

Whitehead is unusual among logicians in going beyond this to analyze the ontological status of what is intended in verbal statements, that is, of propositions. Often it is assumed that a more careful and precise verbal statement can function as a surrogate for the proposition. But for Whitehead, this cannot be the case. Language is inherently vague. He speaks of the fallacy of the perfect dictionary. For him, the proposition must be nonlinguistic.

His proposal is that the proposition is the unity of something physically felt and an eternal object. Eternal objects are the objects of conceptual feelings. They are potentials for participation, Whitehead says 'ingression' in the world. But in and of themselves they lack any relation to the actual world. Such a relation is established by the integration of a conceptual feeling and a physical feeling. One physically feels a stone and one conceptually feels a certain shade of gray. The propositional feeling integrates these two feelings. Its datum is that stone as having that color.

There is, however, another important step in the definition of a proposition. The term 'stone' as used above already says a lot about the object being indicated as the logical subject of the proposition. It implies that that object is stony. In other words, identifying the object as a stone already involves a proposition. The proposition, accurately formulated, has as its logical subject some particular entity, physically felt, but abstracted from all qualifications, that is, devoid of any eternal objects. It might be designated as 'this'. Whitehead usually speaks of the logical subject of a proposition as 'it', insisting of course that it is a very specific 'it'.

For this reason, when we formulate statements that more directly refer to propositions, we do not begin with 'The stone as gray.'. We begin, instead, with 'It as stony.' We can then move on to the more complex statement – 'It as stony and gray.'.

The use of 'as' instead of 'is' is also important for our understanding of Whitehead. Propositions are proposals about how things may be. They prepare for another phase of concrescence, intellectual feelings, in which judgments can be made about the truth or falsehood of a proposition. But the initial feeling of the proposition does not include such judgments. It is simply a feeling of how something in the world may be. Something may be a person and angry. Something else may be stony and gray.

Of course, these statements are vague and may refer to any number of propositions of which some may be true and some false. No matter how much we work at it, language will never unequivocally denote one particular eternal object, simple or complex. It is also very difficult for language to specify a particular actuality.

Consider the case of something that may be a person and angry. This is about as simple a proposition as can be found. But what is being indicated as the logical subject? A psychophysical organism?

Where is the boundary located? Does it include all the actual entities within that boundary? Or just selected ones? If so, which? Just those that make up the psyche? The psyche at one moment or through some period of time? Just what period of time?

Exactly what quality of feeling is denoted by 'angry'? Is the intention that anger is the dominant quality of feeling in the entity identified? If this is not required, must the anger still be conscious? Or is the entity to be described as angry if this feeling plays any role whatsoever in its subjective form, however minor or unconscious?

Difficulties with respect to anger are minor in comparison with those associated with personhood. What constitutes a 'person'? These days there are extensive and irresolvable debates about when a fertilized human egg becomes a person. There are also debates relating to when personhood ends. Does it end with death? When does that occur? Does a disembodied person exist thereafter or does personhood require embodiment? Or may personhood end before physical death if the capacity for interaction with others has ended, for example? Or should we say that some members of the species never become persons at all because of severe brain damage or because they are raised by members of other species? Or shall we extend the term 'person' to nonhuman creatures as well if they meet certain standards? What standards?

The situation is far more complex with respect to something being stony and gray. I will not review the ambiguities of language in this case, since a quick look in the dictionary will suffice in this regard. But there is an added difficulty. Whereas something may feel anger quite independently of it being perceived by another, there is nothing in the entity being indicated that is in itself 'gray', if we mean by 'gray' a specific eternal object that sometimes qualifies human visual experience. The society of occasions constituting the stone is not enjoying any such visual experience. As a whole it has no feelings of its own. Assuming that the molecules that make it up do have feelings, there *may* be some analogy between those feelings and the subjective form of the human feeling of gray. This is an interesting hypothesis. Is this possibility the one that is being raised by the proposition? Or does the proposition really mean that when the light is right, it is reflected from that entity in such a way that human beings with normal eyesight, and looking in the appropriate direction, have an experience of grayness in that region occupied by the entity identified as the logical subject?

Despite these complexities, many of which rarely play a role in books on logic, language often functions adequately for purposes of the needed communication. If I am driving and am told that the pavement ahead is rough, the ambiguities, which are numerous, are usually unimportant in comparison with the evocation of attention and care. The propositional feelings evoked in me may not be identical with those that the speaker or the creator of the sign intended, but the overlap of the propositions involved suffices for the practical purposes at stake.

The same is true if I am told that the date of the American Declaration of Independence was July 4, 1776. I will be led to understand why July 4 is a holiday in the United States, and if I am an American, I am likely to participate in events on that day that accentuate my patriotism. I will also be able to understand something of the relation of that Declaration to the Revolutionary War.

If someone says to me that I am angry, the propositions intended by the speaker may be quite numerous. In fact, some may be false and some true. I may dispute the assertion because of those that are false. But often I recognize that enough of them are true to be forced to acknowledge and deal with my feelings.

Obviously, this is not always the case. The propositions evoked in me by a sign stating that there is rough pavement ahead may not be the same as those intended. I may over-react or under-react. For example, I may suppose that the pavement quickly becomes very rough and slam on my brakes quite unnecessarily. Or I may suppose that being 'rough' is a minor problem that need not slow me down, when in fact if I do not slow down, I will damage the car.

Whitehead also calls propositions 'impure potentials' in contrast with eternal objects, which are 'pure potentials'. They are impure because they tie the pure potential to an actuality. They remain 'potentials' because they describe what may be rather than what necessarily is. Whitehead also calls them 'theories'. They are hypotheses about the actual.

For our purposes here, the most interesting definition of propositions given by Whitehead is "lures for feeling" (1978, 25). Our actual world in every moment consists of innumerable actual entities. According to Whitehead, we feel them all. He explains in some detail how most of them are felt in vague collective ways rather than individually. My point here is only that these actual entities are not 'lures for feeling'. They exercise causal efficacy in each concrescence by imposing themselves in that concrescence as givens.

However, just how they will be objectified by the concrescing occasion is not determined by the entities themselves. That depends on integrations of the physical feelings of these entities with conceptual feelings. The eternal objects felt in these conceptual feelings are often just those that are derived from the physical feelings, but they are not limited to those.

The differences are not minor. The actual entities making up the stone reflect light that impinges on the eye and through the eye and nerves reaches the occipital globe. In presentational immediacy the colour gray is projected on the region occupied by the stone. One may theorize that there is a real connection between the feelings in the stone molecules and the subjective form of perception of the stone in the mode of presentational immediacy. But there is certainly a great difference between the color gray and anything that is occurring in the stone independently of being perceived.

Again, the situation is far more complex than this. Whitehead believed that the feeling of that entity as gray was at the same time a feeling of it as not black or white or yellow or green. Without the penumbra of other theories about the color of that region of space in presentational immediacy, there could be no consciousness of its grayness. If we consider that in ordinary experience there is not only vision but also hearing, touch, bodily feeling, memory, and much else, we can see that a huge number of propositions are being felt with varying degrees of intensity. No doubt many others are being excluded from feeling altogether, or, in Whitehead's language, being negatively prehended.

To summarize, the logical subjects of propositions are the data of physical feelings stripped of the eternal objects that in fact characterize them. Whitehead calls the feelings that give us these data 'indicative feelings'. The predicative pattern of the proposition is given in a conceptual feeling. The propositional feeling is the integration of the indicative and conceptual feelings. The proposition, as the datum of the propositional feeling is the potential togetherness of the actual entity and particular eternal objects.

Although we have approached propositions from the side of human experience and logic, their ontological status does not depend on human experience. Much less does it depend on any effort to express the proposition in language. They exist as potentials for being felt, whether that potentiality is actualized or not. As noted, they are 'impure potentials', since their existence does depend on the actuality of the entities that are their logical subjects. They are defined, as we saw, as 'lures for feeling' rather than as the data of propositional feelings. The latter are a subset of the former.

This background enables us to understand what occurs in human communication. What I say to others is designed either to call attention to propositions they already feel so as to heighten their efficacy or to introduce new propositions into their experience. If I think a companion is paying too little attention to where she steps, I may try to get her to be more attentive. I may also give her news about the engagement of a mutual friend.

Again, this is far too simple. Often the purpose of the exchange has more to do with influencing the subjective feelings of the companion, what Whitehead calls the subjective form of feelings. I may remind my friend about the behavior of a political candidate, providing no new information but presenting what is already known in a negative light and with a particular tone of voice. My intention is then to change the subjective form of the propositional feelings already entertained by my friend. Of course, in the process I may also introduce some new propositions. Often, I present these propositions as if they are true, whether I believe them or not, but I *may* offer them only as possibilities, so as to arouse doubts and uncertainties.

In general, then, much communication is for the purpose of introducing propositions, heightening the importance of some in the experience of the hearer, and influencing the subjective form of the feeling of particular propositions. Other communication may be for the purpose of amusement, of reassurance, of bonding, or even of causing pain. I am making no effort to be exhaustive. The point relevant here is that most of the content of communication consists in the evoking of propositions in the hearer and influencing the subjective form of the propositional feelings.

3. The Role of Propositions in Teaching

Sometimes it seems to be thought that there are just two basic ways of teaching. One is the communication of information. The other is the evocation of already given understanding. Both surely play an important role. Clearly, they also need each other. There are marked limits to what can be evoked from one who has had very limited life experience or exposure to the knowledge of those who are better informed. On the other hand, simply communicating information leads to what White-head calls 'inert ideas'.

Without belittling either of these approaches, I propose that we re-think them, and the teacher's role in general, from the perspective of propositions as lures for feeling. The teacher's task is to decide which lures for feeling are best introduced and accented at what time and place. In general the teacher will introduce and accent lures for feeling by making statements. However, the making of such statements, when understood as evoking propositional feelings in students, is no longer to be understood primarily as the impartation of facts.

This approach to teaching is one in which students are invited to consider possibilities. What may be the best explanation of observed phenomena? What is most likely to have actually occurred at a particular point in the past? Why do current leaders take the positions they do? The propositions the teacher seeks to evoke are hypotheses about such matters.

These hypotheses should be plausible ones. Propositions that are too far removed from what the teacher knows to be probable might direct the imagination of the students in fruitless and even dangerous directions. Propositions that are too far removed from what the student already knows will evoke very little response. The teacher tries to evoke propositions that are closely related to those already entertained by students but that will expand the student's world a little and in ways that will be supported by experience and further reflection.

The statements used to direct attention to propositions are not presented for students to memorize. They are presented to evoke interest. Once the interest of students is evoked, they will develop other hypotheses. Most of these will be closely related to the hypotheses offered by the teacher for consideration, but sometimes they will be quite different. If students want others to take the new propositions seriously, they may explore matters on their own seeking support or perhaps arriving at new theories.

How directive should the teacher be? If students start down paths that the teacher is convinced are dead ends, the teacher should usually point the student to the evidence most inconsistent with the hypotheses being tested. But from a Whiteheadian point of view, the teacher must be hesitant to block the students' lines of thought. This is for two reasons.

First, the orthodoxies of one generation are regularly overthrown in later generations. It is too easy for teachers to be convinced of the current orthodoxy into which they have been socialized in their own education. Even if the students are quite wrong in their present explo-rations, teachers should not discourage them from challenging estab-lished assumptions.

Second, there is no sharp boundary between facts and theories. Facts are well- established theories. But well-established theories are never finally-established theories.

An important part of education is to learn this, not as a fact, but as a stance. Obviously, for the most part, each individual must appropriate from the past the well-established theories that constitute 'knowledge'. No individual can question and challenge sensibly in more than a few areas. But individuals can be brought to understand not only that one should be respectful of received knowledge, but also that one should be supportive of those who challenge it responsibly even in fields with which one is not personally conversant. To communicate this sensibili-ty means to encourage imaginative ideas, recognized as imaginative, but just for that reason productive of fresh thought about what is, in every generation, too easily regarded as 'fact'.

More than once Whitehead pointed out that it is more important that a proposition be interesting than that it be true. This should not be hard to understand. If a true proposition arouses no interest, it is likely to be forgotten, and unlikely to generate much thought. A false propo-sition that does arouse interest will not simply be accepted and filed away. It will evoke some testing against other ideas and in terms of im-plications and consequences. Hopefully, in the process the errors will become apparent.

Whitehead goes on to say that truth adds to interest. A grossly false proposition will soon appear too disconnected from other beliefs to sustain interest. A true proposition of which one was not previously aware can correct and connect existing beliefs and lead to new discovery. Truth is certainly not unimportant.

The problem is that truth and falsehood are not so neatly distinguishable in the statements that a teacher can use in the evocation of propositions. All statements are vague and ambiguous. The propositions in the mind of the teacher will not be just those evoked to awareness in the students. Indeed, it is unlikely that any two students will focus on exactly the same propositions. In many cases, some of the propositions evoked will be true and some false, or if pressed hard, all may be false to varying degrees. If the initial statements of the teacher evoke propositions that are sufficiently interesting, it may be possible to sort out some of these issues. Where there is little interest, this will prove a tedious matter indeed!

In general conversation, often the focus is as much on influencing the subjective form of propositional feelings as on heightening attention to propositions or introducing new ones. This is surely important in the classroom as well. But it poses a particular problem for the teacher who wants students to think independently. To make statements in a way that too greatly influences the subjective form associated with the propositions that are brought to attention may block the student's own critical thinking. On the other hand, much of the interest of propositions is determined by the subjective form of their reception. If statements are made in ways that imply that the teacher has little emotional investment in the propositions evoked, these propositions are unlikely to have much interest to students.

In general it is better for teachers to show in their speech their sense of the importance of the propositions evoked rather than their judgment about their truth and falsity. On the other hand, students have a right to know what their teachers believe as well as what they think to be important. This can be shared more in order to help the students to understand the particular perspective of the teacher than to impose that perspective on the students.

But there are beliefs so important to the teacher, or to the culture and society the teacher represents, that the teacher's task is more socialization than simply opening up possibilities for consideration. Education is in part transmission of cultural values. Sheer neutrality is neither possible nor desirable. For example, that students allow other students to speak and respond to them respectfully is essential for healthy discussion and learning. It is not simply a possibility to be presented neutrally for individual consideration.

The teacher also needs to present propositions in such a way as to express respect for each student. Again, it is the subjective form of the propositions evoked in the student that are crucial. A major part of the teacher's task is to communicate confidence and self-respect to students, not just about their academic work, but also about themselves.

Nevertheless, the major contribution of Whitehead's idea of propositions to reflection about teaching has to do with the content that is taught. The primary task of the teacher is not to increase the number of facts known by the student but to expand the student's horizons of thought. The introduction of new propositions to the student's awareness, propositions that are appropriate to the student's present level of understanding, requires skill. The result is to generate fresh understanding and imagination. This is the expansion of vision that often endures even when memorized information is forgotten.

4. Judgments

Propositional feelings are integrated with physical feelings, and the result is intellectual feelings. It is these that are conscious. In the previous section propositional feelings were presented as if they existed in themselves. In fact they exist only in their unity with physical feelings in the higher phases of concrescence. Nevertheless, it is worthwhile to consider propositions and propositional feelings in terms of what they contribute to the whole.

Notice that physical feelings play a triple role in the concrescence. First they introduce the past world into the conformal phase of the occasion. Second, stripped of their eternal objects, they constitute the logical subjects of propositions. Third, they are compared with the propositions whose logical subjects they have been. For example, I feel another person. What I feel conformally in the first phase of concrescence is that person as he or she is. In the propositional phase, I entertain the idea that that person is friendly, or rather that *that* is both a person and friendly. Finally I compare that proposition with the initial conform feeling. At that point I may make a judgment. I may judge that the proposition corresponds with what I physical felt, or I may judge that there is some error involved in the proposition. On the other hand, I may decide to leave the matter undecided. Of course, there are degrees of confidence associated with both positive and negative judgments. Also, if the judgment is that the proposition is not to be affirmed, that may be because of a very subtle error or of a major one.

The discussion of propositions above emphasized that in themselves they are lures for feeling, not facts. The acceptance of them in that role leads to far more suspended judgments. But this does not mean that students should live primarily in a state of neutrality with respect to the truth and falsity of propositions.

With respect to many propositions, one can recognize that one does not *know* that they are true, and indeed one suspects that at best they are true only with qualifications that one cannot specify. Yet one also recognizes that it is best to treat them as true for purposes of further inquiry until and unless there is some reason seriously to doubt this. On this basis one can build from one hypothesis to another, testing them along the way, while remaining open to revision at any and every stage.

The testing is partly in terms of coherence and partly in terms of adequacy to new relevant data. Often in relation to such data, some revision of the existing theory is required without abandonment of its general nature. The anticipated but unknown qualifications are uncovered.

5. Conclusions

There are, of course, many questions about good teaching and effective learning that are not touched on in these comments. Nevertheless, I believe that close attention to Whitehead's analysis of concrescence leads to important insights. In conclusion, I lift up just three points, one from each of the phases I have discussed.

First, education too often fails to ground students in the concrete immediacy of their experience of the world. In the West it has tended to replace this foundational groundedness in a reality independent of ourselves with a world constructed by the human mind. The destructive consequences of the resulting alienation from the natural world are being actualized psychologically, spiritually, socially, and ecologically. Teachers have an enormous responsibility to keep students grounded in what is.

Second, propositions are too often identified with statements in such a way that language is taken to be the inclusive horizon of experience. This often leads to the supposition that teaching is primarily the communication of linguistic information or socialization into a cultural linguistic system. Whitehead shows that the function of language is to evoke a heightened awareness of what may be the case with the actual world. The question is not simply whether what may be actually is. Equally important is the possibility that the possibility envisioned is desirable, or, alternately, very much to be overcome or prevented. Further, the awareness of what may be can lead to theories or hypotheses to be tested. Or possibilities may be simply enjoyed as such as in fiction.

Third, judgments are also important. One cannot live without them. But students need to learn to make judgments and act upon them without supposing that they are incorrigible. The awareness that judging is essential, but that alternative judgment made my others can contribute to the health and vitality of the ongoing discussion, can place judgment in the right perspective and contribute much to personal life as well as to the well being of society.

Bibliography
Brumbaugh, R. S. (1982): *Whitehead, Process Philosophy, and Education.* Albany: SUNY.
Whitehead, A. N. (1967/1929): *The Aims of Education.* New York: Free Press.
Whitehead, A. N. (1978/1929): *Process and Relaity.* (Corrected Edition) New York: Free Press.

The Rhythm of Learning
and the Rhythm of Reality

William J. Garland

Abstract
Whitehead claims that education must possess a rhythmic
character in order to attain its goals effectively. This rhythmic
character contains three distinct stages, which he calls romance, precision, and generalization. My essay explores
Whitehead's views about the rhythm of learning and examines
his claim that we should pattern our educational practices after
this rhythm. I show how Whitehead's views about learning
reappear in his metaphysical account of the three main phases
in the concrescence of actual entities, which constitute his
basic units of reality. I argue that the initial phase corresponds
to romance, the responsive phase corresponds to precision, and
the integrative phase corresponds to generalization. Accordingly, Whitehead's views about education find metaphysical
support in his account of the development of actual entities. I
use Whitehead's theory of learning to suggest ways to enhance
the teaching of introductory philosophy courses, and I raise
one critical question about the applicability of his theory to all
learning processes.

1. Introduction

In *The Aims of Education*, Whitehead puts forth the provocative thesis
that education must possess a rhythmic character in order to attain its
goals effectively. This rhythmic character manifests itself in cycles,
and each cycle contains three main stages, which he characterizes as
romance, precision, and generalization. Whitehead grounds this thesis
about education upon his claim that these three stages also characterize
the process of human learning. Whitehead's claims about learning and
education are thus distinct but intertwined: human learning naturally

occurs in the stages outlined above, and education should pattern itself after these natural stages of learning if it is to be effective and beneficial.[1] My paper examines the import of these claims and the way in which Whitehead uses them to criticize traditional systems of education. I show how Whitehead's views about learning reappear in his metaphysical account of the three main phases in the concrescence of actual entities, which constitute his basic units of reality. I then use Whitehead's theory of learning as a guideline for suggesting ways to enhance the teaching of introductory philosophy courses. Finally, I raise one objection to Whitehead's view of learning.

1.1 The Stages of Learning

Let us first examine Whitehead's view that learning takes place in three distinguishable but interrelated stages – romance, precision, and generalization. How does Whitehead characterize each of these stages? The stage of romance is the stage in which we first become interested in exploring a new area. This is the stage of intellectual excitement:

> The subject-matter has the vividness of novelty: it holds within itself unexplored connexions with possibilities half-disclosed by glimpses and half-concealed by the wealth of material. In this stage knowledge is not dominated by systematic procedure. Such system as there must be is created piecemeal *ad hoc*. (Whitehead 1967, 17-8)

The stage of romance is the stage of investigation and discovery, of asking questions and looking for answers, of seeking and savoring a wealth of new experiences. The stage of romance is disorganized, but it has a disorganization that calls out for systematic codification. This

---

[1] A previous (and much shorter) draft of this paper was read at the 1991 Summer Conference of the Association of Process Philosophy of Education, Cornell University, Ithaca, New York. Another version, entitled "Romance, Necessity, and Education," was presented at the International Colloquium on Whitehead's Philosophy of Education, Universite Catholique de Lille, Lille, France, April 1994. This version is scheduled for publication in French as 'Romance, Necessite, et Education' in an upcoming volume from Ontos Verlag.

stage thus naturally leads to its antithesis, the stage of precision.[2]

The stage of precision is the stage of discipline and systematic organization. In this stage, the multitude of facts and possibilities from the stage of romance are classified and placed within conceptual frameworks. This is the stage of exact formulation and careful analysis. It is where techniques are mastered and applied to materials we have encountered in the stage of romance. Whitehead remarks that the stage of precision is one most familiar to educators because this is the stage which is emphasized in most systems of education. He also calls attention to the way in which young minds can be irreparably damaged when the discipline of precision is imposed before the stage of romance has been allowed to run its full course. Yet it should be made clear that Whitehead thinks that the stage of precision is the natural successor to the stage of romance. The mind craves order, system, clarity, and exactness so that it will not wander aimlessly amidst the wealth of materials it has encountered in the stage of romance. The craving for the discipline of precision is just as natural as the craving for the freshness of new experience. In fact, learning things for which you presently have little inclination can be valuable in character development. As Whitehead wisely remarks, "[I]t is necessary in life to have acquired the habit of cheerfully undertaking imposed tasks" (Whitehead 1967, 35).[3]

The third and final stage in learning is the stage of generalization. This is the Hegelian synthesis of the stage of romance with the stage of precision. As Whitehead puts it, "It is a return to romanticism with added advantage of classified ideas and relevant technique. It is the fruition which has been the goal of the precise training" (Whitehead 1967, 19). This is the stage in which both power and style can emerge. We gain power from the mastery of a subject matter because we now have the relevant habits and techniques for increasing our knowledge rapidly and without much conscious effort. We gain style because we can act efficiently, without any waste of effort or imagination. As

---

[2] The stage of romance provides the 'aesthetic appreciation' of concrete experience that Robert Brumbaugh considers of central importance to Whitehead's philosophy of education. See Robert S. Brumbaugh, 'Why Whitehead?', *Process Studies*, 20 (1991), 72-7.

[3] It is clear from the text that by "imposed tasks" Whitehead means "tasks that are imposed upon you by *someone else* [such as a school-teacher]". Earlier he calls these imposed tasks "allotted tasks". (Whitehead 1967, 35).

Whitehead puts it, "Style is the ultimate morality of mind" (Whitehead 1967, 12). It provides a moral restraint on the exercise of power by directing it to beneficial goals.

1.2. Observations

Now let me make some observations about Whitehead's theory of the three stages of learning. First, I think that Whitehead is making a *descriptive* claim when he holds that there are three main stages in the process of learning. He is claiming that human beings naturally go through these three stages when they confront a new subject-matter, whether in school or in everyday experience. In fact, Whitehead often compares the acquisition of knowledge with the ingestion of food; for example, he says, "[T]he ordered acquirement of knowledge is the natural food for a developing intelligence" (Whitehead 1967, 30). Note that if the 'food' is not acquired in the proper manner, the mind may reject it altogether. Whitehead expresses this point in a picturesque way: "When you have put your boots in a trunk, they will stay there till you take them out again; but this is not at all the case if you feed a child with the wrong food" (Whitehead 1967, 33). Second, Whitehead does not hold that these stages are mutually exclusive; instead, an element of each stage is present throughout the process of learning. Whitehead explains that his distinction is merely a distinction of emphasis, or what he calls "pervasive quality" (Whitehead 1967, 28); each stage of learning contains some of the qualities that characterize the other stages. Nonetheless, one of these qualities predominates in each respective stage of this process, and it is this alternation which constitutes the rhythm of learning.

1.3. The Stages of Education

So far, we have mainly spoken of Whitehead's theory of learning, not his theory of education. However, this preliminary work has been necessary because Whitehead grounds his theory of education on his theory of learning. Moreover, I would contend that these two theories have different philosophical standings in Whiteead's thought. As I mentioned earlier, Whitehead sees his theory of learning as a *descrip-*

tive theory – he claims that he is describing the natural course of human learning. His claims about education, however, are *normative*; he holds that education must model itself after the rhythm of the learning process in order to be effective and beneficial. Whitehead further contends that traditional educational systems have *not* modeled themselves after this natural order of mental development. Instead, past educational systems have concentrated on the stage of precision and have virtually ignored the preceding stage of romance. The result is that the minds of the students have been crammed with facts in which they have little interest and have been fettered with procedures and techniques that lack direct relevance to their lives. Such a system of education dulls the minds of the students and leaves them with 'inert ideas' – that is, ideas which they have passively received from their teachers or their books and which they will soon forget. Whitehead holds that this kind of education is not only useless; instead, it is positively harmful. As he says in his preface to *The Aims of Education*, his book is one long protest against inert ideas.

1.4. Freedom and Discipline

Whitehead discusses the relative importance of freedom and discipline at each stage of education. His main claim is that freedom should predominate in the stages of romance and generalization while discipline should predominate in the stage of precision. Students should be free to explore a new subject-area as much as possible so that they do not lose their sense of wonder and adventure. Nonetheless, Whitehead recognizes that the teacher has a responsibility for furnishing guidance even at the stage of romance. First, the teacher should ensure that students are surrounded by materials that can stimulate their minds and excite their imaginations. Here Whitehead cites with approval the Montessori system of education. As he puts it, "Its essence is browsing and the encouragement of vivid freshness." (Whitehead 1967, 22). Second, the teacher should point out salient features of the new subject-area and direct the attention of the students to the beauty inherent in that area of investigation. This is how a certain degree of discipline accompanies the freedom that predominates in the stage of romance.

The way in which discipline is salient in the stage of precision is relatively straightforward. The stage of precision is the stage in which the teacher actively instructs the students in the rules and techniques of the subject-matter in question. At this stage, the techniques of drill, repetition, and memorization are all appropriate because "there are right ways and wrong ways [of proceeding], and definite facts to be known." (Whitehead 1967, 34). Whitehead admits that the discipline of precision inevitably takes a toll on the interest and adventure inherent in the stage of romance. Yet he encourages teachers to preserve as much romance as possible within the necessary stage of precise training. This is because students need the spirit of romance provide them with a reason for submitting to the discipline of precision. As Whitehead puts this point, "The organism will not absorb the fruits of the task unless its powers of apprehension are kept fresh by romance." (Whitehead 1967, 34).

Whitehead claims that freedom should predominate again when we reach the stage of generalization; here the wonder and adventure of romance are rekindled and provide additional stimulus for honing of the tools of preision. However, it might be more accurate to say that the stage of generalization involves synthesis of freedom and discipline. The discipline acquired in the stage of precision enables a student to act with style and efficiency, and the freedom gained from the rekindling of wonder and adventure gives him or her a reason to do so. This is the stage in which 'active wisdom' can be achieved. Wisdom is achieved when our grasp of general principles enables us to understand the particular events in our experience as instances of these principles. The 'active' part of wisdom lies in the molding of our future actions in accordance with the insight these general principles provide.[4]

1.5. The Relevance of Whitehead

Whitehead developed his theory of learning by reflecting upon his experience with British education, particularly during the first two decades of the twentieth century. He was also directing his criticism of educational practices to the British educational system. Yet I would contend that Whitehead's views about learning and teaching are just as relevant today as they were in the early decades of the twentieth

---

[4] What Brumbaugh calls 'concrete appreciation' reappears at the stage of generalization, but this time in the mode of savoring accomplishments rather than in the mode of delighting in new facts and new possibilities (which is the mode appropriate to the romantic stage).

century. They are also just as relevant to education in the United States and Europe as they were (and still are) to education in Britain. In support of this claim, I refer the interested reader to Robert Brumbaugh's proposals for reforming contemporary education in his *Whitehead, Process Philosophy, and Education* (1982). Here Brumbaugh argues that the modern world needs an educational theory that is grounded upon a theory of reality such as Whitehead's that emphasizes process rather than static endurance. Moreover, he endorses Whitehead's claim about the three main stages of learning, and he urges educators to recognize and cultivate the stage of romance, which he also calls 'concrete appreciation', before embarking upon the stage of precision.[5]

2. The Metaphysical Counterpart

My next task is to show how Whitehead's views about the rhythmic nature of learning are reflected in his metaphysical account of the coming-into-being of actual entities, which constitute his basic units of reality. Here I will argue that there is a close parallel between the rhythm of learning and the rhythm of reality. Moreover, the existence of such a parallel offers metaphysical support for Whitehead's normative claims about education. Whitehead correctly sees that process rather than substance is the fundamental category for interpreting the nature of reality, and the cogency of his process orientation provides additional confirmaion for his views about education.

Whitehead's views about the primacy of process receive their most systematic and comprehensive statement in the *magnum opus* of his metaphysics, *Process and Reality*. He expresses his fundamental claim about reality in his first Category of Explanation, which asserts "[t]hat the actual world is a process, and that the process is the becoming of actual entities" (Whitehead 1978, 22). Actual entities are 'units'or 'chunks' of the process that Whitehead sees as the essence of reality: they are momentary events that come into being and then 'perish' into the fixity of the past. An example of an actual entity would be a momentary event in human experience; for instance, my act of striking the keyboard would be an actual entity for Whitehead. Whitehead is con-

---

[5] See Robert S. Brumbaugh, *Whitehead, Process Philosophy, and Education* (Albany: State University of New York Press, 1982), 4-5, 16-7, 117-20.

vinced that atomism is the correct metaphysical stance; the basic particulars in his universe are actual entities, and new actual entities are
constantly coming into being. As Whitehead puts it, "The final facts
are, all alike, actual entities; and these actual entities are drops of experience, complex and interdependent" (Whitehead 1978, 18). By contrast, the enduring objects that we see around us are composites that
arises from the interrelations of these actual entities. In technical terms,
Whitehead calls ordinary macroscopic objects 'societies' of individual
actual entities.

2.1. Concrescence

I will focus on Whitehead's account of the concrescence of a single
actual entity, since he distinguishes a three-fold rhythm in concrescence that has striking parallels with his view of the rhythm of learning. The term 'concrescence' comes from the Latin verb *crescere*,
which means 'to spring forth, to come into existence, or to grow',
along with the prefix *con*, which means 'together'. Thus, concrescence
is the growing together of many different entities in order to produce a
novel actual entity. More generally, it is the process through which a
new actual entity comes into existence. Whitehead also claims that
concrescence takes place in various 'stages' or 'phases'. Nonetheless,
we must be careful not to take this distinction into stages too literally.
Whitehead holds that concrescence embodies a whole 'quantum' of
time, a quantum which cannot be divided into different temporal slices.
Thus, when we distinguish different stages in concrescence, we must
remember that this distinction expresses an order of logical presupposition, not one of temporal development.

Thomas Hosinski (1993) provides us with a strategic way for thinking about the main phases in concrescence. He proposes that we look at
the simplest case of concrescence and see what phases are present
there. He discerns three phases in such a concrescence, which he terms
the initial phase, the responsive phase, and the integrative phase. Once
we have examined the nature of each of these phases, we can see weth-

er Whitehead's account of the higher phases of experience will fit into this general structural pattern[6].

2.2. The Phases of Concrescence

The initial phase of concrescence constitutes the new actual entity's reception of causal influence from the past actual world. Sometimes Whitehead says that the new actual entity *inherits* the material for its process of concrescence from the settled facts of the past. He also says that the initial phase provides the new actual entity with the *initial data* for its concrescence. The new actual entity passively receives this data as the basis for its own process of self-formation. The reception of this data signifies the compulsion or the 'causal efficacy' of the past.

Whitehead puts this point into technical terms by saying that the initial phase consists of physical prehensions of the actual entities in the causal past (and God). 'Prehension' is another term Whitehead takes over from Latin, in this case from the verb *prehendere*, which means 'to seize' or 'to grasp'. When an actual entity prehends another entity in the universe, it grasps or seizes it in order to incorporate it into (or exclude it from) its own process of self-development. A physical prehension is the prehension of another actual entity; Whitehead also calls physical pehensions 'feelings'. The initial phase of concrescence is one in which the new actual entity's feelings conform to the feelings of the actual entities in its causal past. This conformity of feeling expresses the compulsion that the past exerts on the new process of concrescence.

The second phase of concrescence is known as the supplemental phase or the responsive phase. The term 'responsive' is especially appropriate because this is the phase in which the new actual entity responds creatively to the data it has received from the past. The responsive phase constitutes the new actual entity's valuation of the stubborn facts that it has confronted in the initial phase. This is the stage in which novelty can emerge into the actual world. Whitehead

---

[6] My discussion of the three main phases of concrescence has been influenced by Thomas E. Hosinski's comprehensive discussion of this topic in chapters 3-5 of his *Stubborn Fact and Creative Advance* (Lanham, Maryland: Roman and Littlefield, 1993).

expresses this point in his technical vocabulary by saying that the responsive phase gives rise to conceptual prehensions of alternative possibilities, which he calls 'eternal objects'.

Here I should explain what Whitehead means by an 'eternal object' by examining the contrast between eternal objects and actual entities. The stubborn facts of the past are composed of actual entities, which are Whitehead's basic particulars. Once an actual entity has come into being, it is a perfectly definite fact with a determinate position in the space-time continuum that pervades the universe. There is no hint of ambiguity or possibility concerning the stubborn facts of the past; each of these facts is fully determinate and particular. By contrast, an eternal object is a bare possibility; it has an inherent nature of its own, but its nature does not indicate where or when it might appear in the actual world. An example of an eternal object would be some particular shade of color, such as scarlet. This shade of color can characterize objects in the actual world; for example, the robes of the Cardinals are tradition-ally scarlet. However, we can think about the color scarlet in abstrac-tion from the particular objects that have this color. This is scarlet as an eternal object, or what Peirce calls a 'may-be'; it is scarlet as it is in it-self, quite apart from its realization in the world of actual entities.

An actual entity grasps eternal objects with its conceptual prehen-sions, just as it grasps other actual entities with its physical prehen-sions. The differences is that our conceptual prehensions are concerned with what might be the case, whereas our physical prehensions relate us to what has actually taken place. For this reason, our conceptual prehensions afford a measure of freedom from the causal efficacy of the past. Whitehead's account of just how this occurs would take us too far into the technical intricacies of his philosophy. For our purposes, it is sufficient to say that an actual entity's conceptual prehensions deter-mine just how much emphasis the new actual entity will give to each datum it has received from the past actual world. The responsive phase is the phase of individual freedom and autonomous development. It is the phase of final causality in contrast with the efficient causality that operates in the initial phase.

The final phase in concrescence is what Hosinski calls the 'inte-grative phase'. This is the phase in which the new actual entity inte-grates its physical prehensions and its conceptual prehensions into a fully determinate feeling that terminates its process of becoming. This fully determinate feeling is what Whitehead calls the 'satisfaction.'

The satisfaction is the aesthetic synthesis that establishes exactly how the new actual entity is related to every other entity in the universe. It represents the creative stamp of 'decision' concerning what character the new actual entity will finally exhibit. The satisfaction completes the process of the actual entity and determines how it will affect the concrescences of the actual entities that lie in its causal future.

2.3. The Higher Phases of Experience

Now let us see whether we can use this tripartite framework to interpret the processes of concrescence for all actual entities. It is clear that the simplest cases of concrescence involve only the three stages we have discussed; for example, these are the phases that we can distinguish in the concrescence of the actual entities that make up a physical object. These actual entities integrate their physical feelings with their conceptual feelings into a determinate satisfaction which 'closes up' the process of concrescence. Whitehead does distinguish two additional phases within the concrescence of high-grade actual entities, such as those that constitute the conscious experience of human beings. He calls these the phase of simple comparative feelings (such as propositional feelings) and complex comparative feelings (such as intellectual feelings). However, I would argue that these additional phases can be fruitfully seen as distinctions within the integrative phase. This is because these sub-phases merely serve to prolong the process of synthesis that leads to satisfaction. For example, the distinguishing mark of propositional feelings is that they do not directly lead to satisfaction. Instead, they 'lure' the new actual entity forward into a more complex experience by suggesting novel possibilities for its consideration. Nonetheless, propositional feelings eventually lead to satisfaction as well; they themselves become part of the data that the new actual entity integrates to 'satisfy' its creative urge. Thus, we can place propositonal feelings within the general rubric of the integrative phase.

3. Concrescence and Learning

We will now examine the parallels between Whitehead's theory of the phases of concrescence and his theory of learning. There are noteworthy similarities between the initial phase of concrescence and the stage of romance in learning. The initial phase is the influx of data from numerous actual entities in the past actual world and from God. It is the phase in which the settled hand of the past confronts the new actual entity. Likewise, the stage of romance puts the learner into direct contact with numerous facts and possibilities in the novel area of investigation. The first stage in learning is not a stage of critical evaluation; instead, it is the stage in which we receive and appreciate the welter of data we have encountered in our new field of inquiry. Nonetheless, there are some differences between the stage of romance and the initial phase of an actual entity's concrescence. Whitehead emphasizes the freedom involved in the stage of romance; the learner should be allowed to explore the new facts and possibilities with relatively little guidance from the teacher. By contrast, the initial stage of concrescence embodies the compulsion of the past; it contains the necessity of causal efficacy, not the freedom of spontaneous activity.

The responsive phase of concrescence has strong parallels with the stage of precision in learning. The responsive phase is the actual entity's valuation of the multitude of data it has encountered in the initial phase. This phase constitutes a creative response to the material thrust upon the new actual entity from the past actual world. Likewise, the stage of precision is the stage in which we organize and analyze the multitude of data we have absorbed in the stage of romance. In both the responsive phase and the stage of precision, the emphasis is upon conceptual and emotional evaluation of material that was originally received in a non-critical way. Nonetheless, there is a difference between the two. The stage of precision is the stage of discipline and systematic organization, in contrast with the novelty and freedom inherent in the stage of romance. By contrast, the responsive phase of concrescence is precisely the phase of spontaneity and novelty, in which the actual entity entertains and evaluates alternative possibilities.

Finally, the phase of integration in concrescence displays a remarkable resemblance to the stage of generalization in learning. The phase of integration is a phase of synthesis, in which the actual entity achieves a harmonious coordination of the physical prehensions of the initial phase and the conceptual prehensions of the responsive phase. This phase represents the 'embodied wisdom' of the new actual entity. Likewise, the stage of generalization is a synthesis of the facts and possibilities of romance with the techniques and rubrics furnished by precision. It embodies the wisdom appropriate to the subject matter in question. In the stage of generalization, the learner's knowledge of details can grow exponentially because he or she has mastered the techniques for organizing and systematizing novel facts. Moreover, these new facts are now embraced with the wonder and adventure of romance. This stage of generalization accordingly exemplifies the 'satisfaction' inherent in learning.

4. Metaphysical Issues

My next step is to argue that Whitehead's theory of reality provides metaphysical support for his views concerning the education. This is due in part to the parallel I have been articulating between the rhythm of reality and the rhythm of learning. However, there is a larger issue at stake, and this is the inherent correctness of Whitehead's theory of reality. First, Whitehead accurately sees that process rather than substance is the basic category for interpreting the nature of the universe. Second, Whitehead provides a cogent account of the underlying structure of each process of concrescence. My first claim is a general claim about the validity of the process perspective, while my second claim is a specific claim about the pattern exhibited by the individual processes that make up the actual world. I will now examine some ways of defending each claim.

4.1. Rescher's Argument

The first claim goes to the heart of Whitehead's process philosophy, and I cannot support it adequately within the scope of this paper. Fortunately, there is an excellent book by Nicholas Rescher, *Process Metaphysics* (1996), which gives a spirited defense of process philosophy (and by extension of Whitehead as one of its major representatives). Here Rescher contends that the category of process is more fundamental than the category of perduring things. This is evident from the way in which we ordinarily think about processes and substantial things. There are clearly some processes that represent the activities of things – the growing of the grass, the growling of a dog, the singing of a choir. However, there are also what Rescher calls "unowned processes" – some of his examples are "the cooling of the temperature, the change in the climate, the flashing of lightning, the fluctuation of a magnetic field" (Rescher 1996, 42). These are clearly events which take place in the world but which do not represent the activity of any particular substances. This point is significant because it shows that the realm of processes is more extensive than and independent of the realm of substantial things. Moreover, Rescher claims that process philosophy can account for the presence of enduring objects by interpreting them as clusters of processes that possess a functional unity over time. Accordingly, process philosophy can do justice to our commonsense view that the world contains numerous enduring objects that stand in causal relationships to each other.

Rescher concludes his book with a synoptic view of the value of the process way of understanding the world:

> The paramount value of process metaphysics, however, lies in its providing [...] a distinctive and illuminating window on the world. For this approach has an importantly true-to-reality aspect. It invites us to regard what we see when we look about us, not in the light of an aggregation of perduring things but in that of a vibrant manifold of productive activity. It pictures the world not as a museum where objects are displayed but as a show where things happen – a theater, as it were, in full productive stir. (Rescher 1996, 174)

Here Rescher draws our attention to what is fundamentally correct in Whitehead's metaphysical perspective: its portrayal of the creative and dynamic nature of reality. This passage captures the intuitive meaning behind Whitehead's technical doctrine "[t]hat the actual world is a process, and that the process is the becoming of actual entities" (Whitehead 1978, 22). This is what I have termed Whitehead's 'general claim' about the validity of the process perspective, and Rescher forcefully defends this claim throughout his book.

4.2. A Journey Through Paris

I now turn to my more specific claim that Whitehead has correctly discerned the basic structure of each process of concrescence. To support this claim, I will argue that Whitehead's account of the structure of concrescence does justice to the nature of *human* experience.

The particular experience I wish to analyze is that of finding one's way around in an unfamiliar city. Suppose I am visiting Paris for the first time and know enough French to read the street signs and get some directions from the local residents. I also have a map of Paris that I can use to get my bearings. My evening project is to get from my hotel to the Louvre. The first phase of my experience consists of the numerous sensations and observations that I have upon leaving the hotel. Here a multiplicity of perceptual data confront me from my surroundings – the sights of Paris at night, the sounds of a bustling city, the smell of freshly baked bread, and so forth. This phase would correspond to the initial phase of concrescence, which is the physical prehension of the facts in the actual world. The next phase of my experience consists of my conceptual response to these many sense-perceptions. In this phase, I turn my attention to the Paris map to orient myself in relation to my surroundings. This project would correspond to the responsive phase of concrescence. The lines and street names on the map indicate possible routes from my hotel to the Louvre, and I am able to recognize these possibilities through my conceptual prehensions of these patterns. The final phase of my experience involves the integration of my sense-perceptions with the possible routes suggested by the patterns represented on the map. In this phase, I use the conceptual apparatus provided by the map to systematize and organize my many sense-perceptions in a meaningful way. The most satisfying result would be to find a route that leads me quickly and directly to the Louvre. This phase of my project would correspond to the integrative phase of concrescence. It is appropriate that Whitehead uses the term 'satisfaction' to characterize the culmination of this final phase of process.

Of course, this account only establishes an *analogy* between the phases of concrescence within an individual actual entity and a practical endeavor in the macroscopic realm of human experience. Whitehead's actual entities merely last a split-second of time, and the trip I have described within Paris would consist of a very large number of actual entities related to each other in intricate ways. Furthermore, the first two phases of the exploration of Paris could be interchanged without significant problems. I could always look at the map before I embark on my journey and encounter the multitude of sense-perceptions from the streets of Paris. Nonetheless, my account of the Paris adventure does show that Whitehead's metaphysical theory can be plausibly applied to the time-frame appropriate to everyday human experience. Surely the journey within Paris is a process with an integrity of its own, and as such it can provide us with an intuitive grasp of the microscopic process that Whitehead discerns within the concrescence of an individual actual entity. As Rescher remarks, "What renders the idea of process preeminently accessible to us is the processual nature of our own experience." (Rescher 1996, 48).

4.3. Application to Learning

Whitehead's metaphysical categories, then, can be used to illuminate ordinary human experiences, such as the experience of finding one's way around in an unfamiliar city. But the process of learning something new bears a striking resemblance to the experience I have just described; we could just as easily say that I *learned* how to get from my hotel to the Louvre. Accordingly, this example gives us some reason to think that Whitehead's metaphysical categories will also apply to learning in the academic sense of that term. Moreover, I have already shown that Whitehead's descriptive account of the process of learning provides support for his normative claims about how educational practices should be conducted. Thus, there is some reason to think that Whitehead is offering us good prescriptions concerning educational reform. This, incidentally, is the most Whitehead himself claims for his views about the rhythm of education; these viewpoints are correct in their broad outlines, although not necessarily in their details (see Whitehead 1967, 27). This is another example of the extraordinary humility of Whitehead's mind.

5. Teaching Philosophy

My next project will be to apply Whitehead's theory of education to the question of how to teach introductory philosophy in a college or university. In particular, I will put forth some suggestions about how to cultivate the stage of romance in an introductory philosophy course. Philosophy is usually thought of today as a discipline with numerous technical terms and well-defined methods of argumentation. Accordingly, it is hard to resist the temptation to teach philosophy almost exclusively at the stage of precision. This is not just a temptation for analytically inclined philosophers; philosophers of a more speculative inclination face this temptation, too. For example, suppose a speculative thinker is teaching introductory students about Plato's theory of Forms. She does not merely want her students to learn *that* Plato developed a theory of Forms to account for certain puzzles in the world of everyday experience. Instead, she usually wants her students to come to see exactly *what* the Forms are and exactly *why* Plato thinks the Forms exist. The temptation to emphasize precision is one that besets us all.

This leads me into my main question: How can we cultivate the stage of romance when we teach introductory philosophy? How can we cultivate an atmosphere of discovery and excitement in our classrooms? Sometimes we do not have to start from scratch; many students who enroll in introductory philosophy already have a natural curiosity about philosophical questions. Here is a sample list of these questions: (1) What are the basic constituents of the universe? (2) Does God exist? (3) Does life have a meaning? (4) Are moral values objective or subjective? The challenge for the teacher is to build on this initial interest instead of stifling it by insisting on precision too soon.

5.1. Historical Dramas

I have three proposals for keeping the spirit of romance alive in our introductory philosophy courses. First, we can make use of the drama that is already present in the history of Western philosophy. My first example is Plato's account of the life, the trial, and the death of Socrates. Here is a drama in preserving one's integrity that Plato has crafted with literary genius. Students who read the *Apology*, the *Crito*, and the relevant parts of the *Phaedo* almost always gain an appreciation for the courage and steadfastness of Socrates, even if they do not share Socrates' conviction about the value of examining our most basic beliefs. My second example is drawn from Descartes' *Meditations*. Here we also find drama, although it is not the drama of a man willing to die for his convictions. Yet Descartes embarks on a remarkable adventure when he casts aside his former beliefs in search of an absolutely certain first principle. This sense of adventure is most prominent in Meditations I and II, and I find that these are precisely the Meditations that

capture most student interest. The challenge for educators is to cultivate an appreciation of the drama and excitement within these historical narratives.

5.2. Active Learning

My second proposal is that we should use teaching methods that encourage students to be active rather than passive. This is also a
proposal that Whitehead would endorse, since he constantly stresses
the active nature of the mind. One unfortunate result of the lecture
method is that it can encourage passivity in students. Students do not
have to read the assigned material if they know that the main points
will be covered in the lectures, and they can take notes with a minimal
amount of intellectual activity. I do not intend to condemn the lecture
method altogether. It can be an effective way to convey background
information, and it can provide synoptic overviews and suggest lines of
critical questioning. Yet I think that it must be employed together with
other methods which involve the students more actively. The method I
favor consists of dividing the class into small discussion groups with
three or four students in each group. Each group is then assigned a
topic to discuss and asked to prepare a short report to present to the
class as a whole. When used skillfully, this method forces the students
to take an active role in analyzing the reading material and in making a
report to the class. This method has the further advantage of encouraging the students to talk to each other and not just to the
instructor.[7]

5.3. Tolerance of Imprecision

My final proposal is perhaps the one that is most controversial. I claim
that, as instructors, we must be tolerant of and even receptive to imprecision in the way our introductory students state and defend philosophical positions. To put this point another way, we should not insist

---

[7] Here I am indebted to Anthony Weston's observations in his 'Uncovering the
'Hidden Curriculum': A Laboratory Course in Philosophy of Education', *APA
Newsletter on Teaching Philosophy*, 90 (1991), 36-42.

on precision when our students are struggling to understand new thinkers and to deal with new issues. Instead, we should allow a certain inexactness of expression. Let me now defend what seems to be a counterintuitive claim.

First, this claim is based on the assumption that we want to cultivate the spirit of romance in our introductory students; we want them to see philosophy as an intellectual adventure that involves inquiry and discovery. Yet it is part of the nature of an adventure that we do not know the outcome yet, and we may not even know exactly what goal we are seeking. In a word, adventure involves inexactness and imprecision just as much as it involves inquiry and discovery. Second, insisting on precision too soon stifles initiative and imagination. It inhibits students from responding to philosophical arguments and positions from their *own* points of view, which are usually quite different from that of a professional philosopher. There is also a third advantage to being open to imprecision in the way in which our students state and defend their positions. A position that is stated imprecisely has room for development; it provides an opening for further dialogue and discussion. By contrast, a position that is stated too precisely is fixed and settled; as a result, it may block the road to further inquiry.

I must add a caveat at this point. I do think that precision and exactness are desirable qualities, and I do not want my remarks to be construed as a sanction for sloppy thinking. My point is that we should not insist on precision when such an insistence threatens to undermine the stage of romance. As Whitehead puts it, "Undiscriminating discipline [i.e., precision without any hint of romance] defeats its own object by dulling the mind" (Whitehead 1967, 32, explanation added)

6. Critical Reflections

So far, I have been explicating Whitehead's theories of learning and education, arguing for their plausibility, and illustrating some of their implications for teaching introductory philosophy. Now I will raise one critical question about an assumption Whitehead makes about the nature of learning. This is the assumption that learning always takes place in the three-stage process of romance, precision, and generalization. I have called this a *descriptive* claim because Whitehead thinks that it describes the natural course of human learning. This descriptive claim is a crucial premise for Whitehead's *normative* conclusion that education should be structured in the same three stages. But is Whitehead's claim about learning true? There is one important case in which I think it is not.

Romance is not always the first stage in a natural process of learning. Instead, the first stage may be what I will call *necessity*. Remember that we are speaking of learning in general, not just learning in school. In everyday life, necessity sometimes forces us to learn things in which we have little initial interest and for which we have little inclination. Furthermore, necessity can be just as effective as romance in teaching us lessons that we do not forget.

6.1. The Role of Necessity

Let me draw an example here from my own experience. Once I began my teaching career and exchanged the cramped quarters of graduate housing for a three-bedroom house with a lawn, one of my first acquisitions was that typical suburban machine, the lawn mower. When I first bought a lawn mower, I knew very little about it; my interest in it was confined to its effectiveness in cutting the grass. All of this changed suddenly one summer when the grass was high and the lawn mower would not start. At this point I was compelled to read the instruction booklet to find out what to do. Necessity had forced me to learn something about the machine that I had previously taken for granted.

This experience was the beginning of a learning process that has taught me things about lawn mowers that are still with me today. My project of cutting the grass is not longer thwarted by a lawn mower that refuses to start. When my lawn mower will not start today, I know about certain procedures to follow that will (hopefully) reveal the problem. I check to make sure that there is gas in the tank, that the oil is at its proper level, that the air filter is clean, and (especially) that the spark plug is clean. If the spark plug is dirty, I have learned that cleaning it with sand–paper will usually work until I can purchase a new one. I have also learned how to clean the air filter, how to change the oil, and how to take further maintenance precautions. Furthermore, I know why these procedures are important to the proper operation of the mower.

Now I cannot say that thirty-five years of experience with various lawn mowers has led me to an abiding interest in the nature of internal combustion engines. In this sense, we can say that I learned only as much about lawn mowers as I needed to learn in order to keep my machine in working order. But it is easy to imagine another person (say Smith) who begins with an experience similar to the one I have described and then goes on to develop a lasting interest in internal combustion engines. Smith's original experience (occasioned by necessity) leads her to investigate the nature of small engines and to gain a precise knowledge of their operation and repair. Eventually she gains the deep understanding of internal combustion engines which Whitehead calls 'generalization'. Moreover, Smith finally decides to put her knowledge to practical advantage; she opens up her own 'small engine shop' and earns a good living from selling and repairing small engines. Here romance and precision (and ultimately generalization) have been generated by an initial stage of necessity.

My point in this example is that necessity can form the initial stage of a process of learning just as easily as can romance. Necessity usually imparts an unpleasant quality to experience, but it can sometimes generate a learning process that has beneficial results. But if this point is granted, then doubt is cast upon Whitehead's claim that the *natural* process of learning is romance-precision-generalization. Necessity – romance/precision – generalization[8] may be just as natural and just as effective as a pattern of learning. Thus, Whitehead's three-stage cycle does not capture *all* the natural ways in which human beings can learn.[9]

---

[8] Here I entitle the second stage 'romance/precision' because this stage seems to involve an intimate blending of the qualities of romance and precision. In terms of my example, Smith became *interested in* the operation of small engines and also gained *precise* knowledge of their operation. However, *some* precise knowledge (occasioned by necessity) generated her initial interest, which in turn led to additional precision in knowledge and technique.

[9] Whitehead does recognize that necessity can play a role in the development of "inventive genius", but he expresses serious reservations about its educative value: "Again, inventive genius requires pleasurable mental activity as a condition for its vigorous exercise. 'Necessity is the mother of invention' is a silly proverb. 'Necessity is the mother of futile dodges' is much nearer to the truth" (Whitehead 1967, 45). However, my counterexample here shows that necessity may well be the impetus to learning, if not the impetus to invention.

6.2. Thinking Beyond the Box

What implications does my claim about necessity have for education? This is a complex question, and I can only suggest the outlines of an answer here. The main implication seems to be that it is appropriate at times to challenge our students in ways which will force them to go beyond the boundaries of their previous knowledge. That is, the imposition of necessary tasks has a legitimate place even in a broadly Whiteheadian system of education. I do not think that especially difficult readings, assignments, or exams are appropriate at the beginning of an introductory course. Here I stand by my earlier view that it is important to cultivate romance at that time. But challenging projects later in the course may be a way of enlisting necessity to further the aims of education. My best example for this comes from an introductory logic course that I usually teach each year. Most of the exercises I assign as homework are based upon the presentation in the preceding section of the logic text. Students who study the section carefully and attend class on a regular basis usually have no trouble working these exercises. But halfway through the course I sometimes give a lecture on 'problem-solving' (a topic which is *not* covered in the text) and then assign five or six 'problem-solving' exercises as homework. These exercises are difficult to work, in spite of the fact that I outline a method for approaching them. Many students complain that they spend several hours on the homework and accomplish little. Yet some students are always so challenged by the problems that they complete the assignment and ask for more exercises at the end of the next class. Necessity has forced them to transcend their previous mind-sets. It has also generated a genuine interest in problem solving.

The point here is that romance does not always have to be the initial stage in an effective process of learning (and, by implication, teaching). Instead, students can learn new materials and techniques when they are forced to do so under the constraints of necessity.[10] Of course, we might still maintain that the romance-precision-generalization process is the *ideal* way to learn something new. Certainly it is

---

[10] At least, *some* students can learn in this manner. It is important to notice in my example that most students in the class did *not* learn how to work the problem-solving exercises when they were challenged to do this through the initial assignment. Most students in the class eventually learned how to work these problems, but I cannot say that they developed much 'zest' for them.

better to begin a learning process with the pleasure of romance, not the pain of necessity. But necessity can *sometimes* be enlisted in the service of education, and it can *sometimes* produce results just as effectively as romance.

Bibliography
Brumbaugh, R. S. (1982): *Whitehead, Process Philosophy, and Education.* Albany: SUNY.
Hosinski, T. E. (1993): *Stubborn Fact and Creative Advance.* Lanham: Rowman & Littlefield.
Rescher, Nicholas (1996): *Process Metaphysics.* New York: State University of New York Press.
Whitehead, A. N. (1967/1929): *The Aims of Education and Other Essays.* New York: Macmillan.
Whitehead, A. N. (1978/1929): *Process and Reality.* (Corrected Edition) New York: Free Press.

Whitehead's Modes of Experience and the Stages of Education

George Allan

Abstract

This essay explores the homologies between Whitehead's well-known three phases of education – romance, precision, generalization – and the basic features of his epistemology developed in *Symbolism: Its Meaning and Effect*. Romance is explicated in terms of symbolic reference and the modes of perception. Precision is taken to be the educational analogue to conceptual analysis, which involves the critique of symbolic reference and its enhancement through the development of conceptual schemes of interpretation. Whitehead's notion of symbolically conditioned action is then seen as analogous to generalization in learning, where the focus is upon developing life-defining habits of critiquing the symbols crucial to the meanings that create social solidarity, thereby fashioning a social order of distinctive individuals who are able to live in harmony by continually reforming their shared symbols.

1. Preliminary Expectorations

Whitehead's 1922 essay on 'The Rhythm of Education' and his essay a year later on 'The Rhythmic Claims of Freedom and Discipline', published as the second and third chapters of *The Aims of Education and Other Essays* (1967), run to a total of only 26 pages. Yet they develop what is probably the most frequently mentioned of all his ideas – that education has a rhythmic structure to which teachers should be sensitive.

In the first essay, Whitehead cites the "truism" that "different subjects and modes of study should be undertaken by pupils at fitting times when they have reached the proper stages of mental development" (1967, 15), then parses the fitting times as having to do with "rhythmic" stages of a pupil's "mental growth." He organizes these stages into a "threefold cycle," which he likens to Hegel's thesis-antithesis-synthesis, labeling them as the stages of romance, precision, and generalization.

Education, Whitehead argues, "should consist in a continual repetition of such cycles" (1967, 19). He then applies these cycles of stages to infant and adolescent learning, and makes some comments about university education. He concludes with a warning that the stages are not linear but concurrent: each stage marks merely "a distinction of emphasis, of pervasive quality" – an "alternation of dominance" – in a process where all three are "present throughout" (1967, 28).

In the second essay, Whitehead elaborates these same points with a few minor differences. He characterizes the three stages as marked respectively by "freedom, discipline, and freedom" (1967, 31). He then emphasizes how these stages recur cyclically, as "minor eddies" in ever wider contexts, "running their course in each day, in each week, and in each term" (1967, 38) as well as composing the way by which a formal educational curriculum should be organized and, indeed, a person's whole life structured. "Education," Whitehead concludes, "is the guidance of the individual toward a comprehension of the art of life" (1967, 39).

Romance, precision, and generalization. They are Whiteheadian notions that have taken on a significance all out of proportion to the few oracular pages in which they are discussed. I suspect that this disproportionate interest is a function of their vagueness, their utility as a way to name a wide variety of views about the dynamics of learning, especially for those who rightly reject the excessively modular and non-holistic ways in which contemporary lesson plans, courses, and curricula are designed.

Whatever the reason for the interest, however, one consequence has been for philosophers and educators to take the stages of education seriously enough to ask how, if at all, they might be related to Whitehead's metaphysics. The aim of this essay is to provide a viable, and I think interesting, answer to that question.

2. Two False Starts

The usual answer is to say that the stages of education are homologous to the phases of concrescence. Romance is like the initial stage comprising a nascent occasion's physical and conceptual prehensions of its past, precision is akin to the subsequent stages by which these data are ordered so as to be coherently harmonizable, and generalization is similar to the culminating synthesis by which concrescence issues is a determinate satisfaction.

The structures are similar, the analogy obvious, and therefore the metaphorical possibilities attractive. But the stronger claim that the structures are homologues is, to say the least, controversial. Mapping the micro-grained character of an actual occasion's concrescence onto the macro-terrain of how enduring objects such as human beings develop and sustain their defining characteristics, those in particular that are cultural rather than biological, is a huge intellectual leap. The history of Whiteheadian scholarship is strewn with the bleached bones of scholars who have failed in trying to apply what is said of actual occasions that endure for nanoseconds to features of the everyday world in which school children must attend classes that seem to endure for ever.

A more prudent approach, I think, is to map Whitehead's stages of education onto his analysis of the modes of experience, as done in *Symbolism: Its Meaning and Effect* (1985). In this way, epistemology can serve as a transition between ontology and pedagogy. How we experience reality offers a bridge by which to link what that reality fundamentally is with who we humans are such that we can learn to interpret our experiences as telling us truths about its character.

Whitehead, in the *Symbolism* book, argues that we perceive reality directly in two distinguishable ways – in the mode of causal efficacy and in the mode of presentational immediacy. Both "introduce into human experience components which "'objectify' for us the actual things in our 'environment'" (1985, 17). These differing components are then "fused into one perception" by a "synthetic activity" called symbolic reference (1985, 18).

This tripartite characterization might seem at first blush to provide the likely epistemological homologues for romance, precision, and generalization. Causal efficacy is "the primitive element in our external experience," its content "vague, haunting, unmanageable" (1985, 43), "heavy with the contact of the things gone by, which lay their grip on our immediate selves" (1985, 44). Similarly, the stage of romance is "the stage of first apprehension" (1967, 17), in which we open ourselves appreciatively to the world around us, accepting it for what it is and reveling in its surprises and possibilities. Romance is in this sense naive: uncritical, uncalculating, unconstrained. Education begins by our discovery of this world, of the world simply as we find it.

In contrast, presentational immediacy involves "our immediate perception of the contemporary external world" as "a community of actual things" (1985, 21) related "by reason of their participation in an impartial system of spatial extension" (1985, 23). This systemic whole is "effected by the mediation of qualities" (1985, 21) called "sense-data," "generic abstractions" (1985, 22) that are "vivid, precise, barren," and largely "controllable at will" (1985, 23). Similarly, the stage of precision teaches "exactness of formulation" (1967, 18), achieved through the deployment of systems of order, whether grammatical, legal, or scientific.

Symbolic reference is then the synthesis of causal efficacy and presentational immediacy, the way by which "the various actualities disclosed respectively by the two modes are either identified, or at least correlated together as interrelated elements in our environment" (1985, 18). Similarly, the stage of generalization is synthetic; it is "the final success" whereby romance is transformed by the addition of "classified ideas and relevant technique" (1967, 19), whereby "concrete fact" is "studied as illustrating the scope of general ideas" (1967, 26).

These apparent similarities are at best superficial, however. There can be no homology because perceptive experience – experience involving the two perceptive modes and their symbolic reference – is primitive, whereas the stages of education involve sophisticated modes of experiencing. Perceptive experience is our spontaneous way as higher organisms for becoming aware of and dealing with our world. It is 'natural' in the sense that its basis is biological not cultural, intuitive not critical.

Our bodily feelings of the world and their correlation with sense data are instinctual, the way by which we construct a meaningful world from the double deliverance of direct perception, a way sufficiently adapted to the exigencies of circumstance to have allowed our species reproductive success over its various competitors. We are born with these capacities and we survive as well as we do because of them. Perceptive experience, therefore, is what education presupposes and where it therefore begins.

3. Romance and Perceptive Experience

The epistemological package composed of causal efficacy, presentational immediacy, and symbolic reference thus finds its educational homologue in the stage of romance. Both are initial moments in an increasingly sophisticated development. By linking romance to perceptive experience, hence making symbolic reference one of its important features, dimensions of romance that are far too often neglected will come into focus.

As I've already noted, Whitehead calls romance the stage of "first apprehension" (1967, 17). What we apprehend are the commonsense objects of immediate experience: initially our aching hunger, an offered breast, and warming arms; slowly expanding to include the noise of our own crying, flashes of movement, cold touches and warm textures, smiles and hugs; eventually encompassing the sticks and stones, chairs and tables, cats and dogs, fathers and mothers of the everyday world.

This openness to the world as we find it is only a partial characterization of what apprehension involves, however. For Whitehead's world is profoundly organistic, its individual objects internally related to each other. So if romance is an "awakening to the apprehension of objects," it is therefore also an awakening "to the appreciation of their connexions" (1967, 19). The objects of our experience, we come to realize, have an "import": they come redolent with "unexplored relationships" (1967, 18). What we apprehend "holds within itself unexplored connections with possibilities half-disclosed by glimpses and half-concealed by the wealth of material" (1967a, 17). Glimpsing an object, we reach out for it and bring it to our mouth, taste what it's like, and from the resulting sensation realize we are sucking our own finger. A stone unturned is a mystery we must set about solving, a constant banging noise draws us around the corner so we can see what's making it, each page of a new picture book is fraught with the unknown pages still to come. For everything we encounter, there is a "more" it conceals, a *terra incognita* still to be disclosed.

We cannot but appreciate that what we apprehend is seeped in an import that invites exploration. Hence "interest is the *sine qua non* for attention and apprehension" (1967, 31). Romantic experience is inquisitive because it involves us in a world vivid with novelties, a world of such unbounded plenitude that it cannot be noticed without its unexplored connections catching our attention and evoking our response. In adolescence, when our childish world has grown more complicated but therefore even more unbounded, when our everyday experiences are augmented by literary and artistic experiences, our interests grow accordingly more sophisticated. Adolescent romance, says Whitehead, is a time when "ideas, facts, relationships, stories, histories, possibilities, artistry in words, in sounds, in forms and in colour, crowd into the child's life, stir his feelings, excite his appreciation, and incite his impulses to kindred activities" (1967, 21).

Romantic experiences 'stir' us, 'excite' us, and 'incite' us to 'kindred activities'. We learn to delight in the multifarious gifts of the world, delighting in them for their own sake and responding to those gifts in all the ways they invite response. We hear stories and then imagine ourselves as participants in them, ourselves Arthur as he grasps the sword in the stone, Guinevere as she wrestles with her incommensurable loves. We entertain an idea and spin out its exhilarating implications. We set out down a path, and when it forks we imagine going both ways at once. The world proposes and we respond in kind, making ourselves kindred spirits with it, and through it with each other.

Robinson Crusoe, to take Whitehead's example, is just a character in a story, an imaginary man stranded on an imaginary island. We know about men and women, our parents and adult friends, we know about their busy comings and goings in the cities and towns where we live, we know about our own experiences in the home, at school, around the neighborhood. And we know about islands, about their beaches and about how walking on them leaves footprints in the sand. "But the sudden perception of the half-disclosed and half-hidden possibilities relating Crusoe and the sand and the footprint and the lonely island secluded from Europe constitutes romance" (1967, 18). What would it be like, we wonder, to be so far from civilization, to be forced to seek food and shelter on our own, to have the courage and craft it would take to survive. What might the dangers be? What carnivores might be lurking on such an island, wanting us for their evening meal? And then, amid these questions – that footprint in the sand, adding mystery to danger, the uncanny to the unknown. Even Excalibur might not be enough, nor Lancelot riding to our rescue. And yet if we were Crusoe we could surely manage, and, oh, look: it seems he does. He has the right stuff, that guy, and so would we.

The "natural mode" for stirring our imagination, for exciting our interest, for inciting us to explore the undiscovered import of our immediate experiences, is "enjoyment" (1967, 31). Whitehead doubts the efficacy of birch rods. We are more likely to eat our food because we enjoy eating a good meal than because we know that without food we will die or because we are dutiful to our parents' insistence that we eat everything on our plate. We are more likely to build a bridge across the river because we are curious about what lies on the other side than because we have been ordered to do so by a boss or commanding officer. The birch rods work, to be sure, but only as long as an authority figure is wielding it. "Undoubtedly pain is one subordinate means of arousing an organism to action. But it only supervenes on the failure of pleasure" (1967, 31). A person's education is best furthered "along a path of natural activity, in itself pleasurable" (1967, 31).

Whitehead calls this path of natural activity "discursive" because it is "a process of discovery, a process of becoming used to curious thoughts, of shaping questions, of seeking for answers, of devising new experiences, of noticing what happens as the result of new ventures" (1967, 32). Romance, in other words, has a trajectory. It involves not only apprehension, appreciation, and interest but also their iteration until they become habits of the heart and mind. Education in the romantic stage of a person's development should strive to turn momentary acts of curiosity into habitual practices. A particular experience might excite a curious thought, but a romantic's inclination should be to find something curious in every experience.

Some events thrust us willy-nilly into questioning their significance, even wondering about their intelligibility, but romantic education should teach us to ask questions of even what is apparently obvious or trivial. We should be interested not only in exploring the unexplored dimensions of our known world but also in poking around for other unnoticed or hitherto unknown dimensions, and wondering about what lies beyond even that known world and all its unexplored dimensions. The romance stage of education has done its work when "there has been plenty of independent browsing amid first-hand experiences, involving adventures of thought and of action" (1967, 33).

The wise pedagogue teaches romance best by not getting in the way of this habitual curiosity, but rather by providing as rich an environment as possible for its exercise. So the teacher intervenes: creating an appropriately stimulating environment, setting tasks and challenges, encouraging and suggesting, admonishing and redirecting. But these interventions have to be done in such a way that the students respond out of their own kindled interests and not because they feel compelled to do so, eventually responding because of their proclivity to do so, their habitual curiosity, their cultivated wonderment. "Education is not a process of packing articles in a trunk" where they can safely be kept "till you take them out again." It is more akin to "the assimilation of food by a living organism": it has to do with being sure the food is "palatable" and is provided "under suitable conditions" (1967, 33).

In Whitehead's striking example, a teacher may assign a student the task of looking at the stars through a telescope, but unless the student's experience is marked by the "transfiguration of imposed routine" that romance cultivates, unless for the student this is not an assignment to be carried out but rather "free access to the glory of the heavens" (1967, 33), no genuine educational growth will occur. "Without the adventure of romance, at the best you get inert knowledge without initiative, and at the worse you get contempt of ideas – without knowledge" (1967, 33).

By linking the stage of romance to Whitehead's epistemology of perceptive experience, we can better appreciate why romance is a stage of discovery. Romance is effected by encouraging the enlargement of perceptive experience through the enlargement of symbolic reference. Our sense of the "circumambient efficacious world of beings" (1985, 55) cries out for interpretations that are more adequate, that do not suffer unnecessarily from the loss imposed by the abstractions required in order to frame a structure of sense-data able to make sense of them. And, reciprocally, the colored shapes and spatial perspectives, the sound textures and temporal lines, of our sense-data need to be rigorously coherent as a way to rescue the meanings they harbor from the danger that the past from which those meanings were derived might not be applicable to the contemporary events, which are taken as "relevant to each other, and yet preserve a mutual independence" (1985, 16), upon which they are projected. So we are all the time spontaneously adjusting the fit between our feelings and our thoughts, between our dim intuitions of what is vital for us and our bright shining systems of interpretation.

We should not understand appreciative apprehension, therefore, as merely affective, as simply a matter of our feelings, our emotional responses. Romance is not a 'touchy-feely' way of learning. It involves the interplay of two modes of perceiving, the one vague, haunting, unmanageable, the other precise, vivid, barren. The romance encompasses both efficacious power and presentational pattern, and it involves integrating these contrasting features of experience by taking those at one pole of the contrast as referring to those at the other pole.

So 'growth in mentality' – growth in the scope and power of our appreciative apprehension of the world – occurs as we hone our capacity for symbolic reference, exploring new ways in which our sense-data are taken as signs of the impinging world. This exploration takes the exterior form of occupying ourselves in "the coordination of [our] perceptions with [our] bodily activities" (1967, 19). It takes the interior form of coordinating our perceptions with our feelings. The features that are bare but vivid abstractions are taken as referring to those that are vague but fraught with importance. The abstractions derived from presentational immediacy organize in new ways the feelings resulting from causal efficacy, creating novel frameworks of connection by which they can be understood and acted upon. These frameworks are linguistic and behavioral, words and deeds, myths and rituals, ways by which we apprehend appreciatively what our world is like and by which we engage it.

The romantic phase of education, therefore, involves more than passive appreciation. We are insufficiently romantic if all we do is revel in the forms and colors of our surroundings or in the flow of passion that fills our every moment. Aestheticism of either sort is anemic, a mere beholding of our direct and incorrigible experiences without seeking their import, or a mere reveling in our feelings without seeking their meaning. Romance delights in both features of our experience, but not so much for their own sake as for ours. We enjoy the play of our senses and our emotions for their relevance, for the way they fulfill our lives. Our apprehension is active not passive. It takes the form of curiosity: wondering about, ferreting out, poking into. We apprehend the world by engaging it; we appreciate it by appropriating it. We make a world by using our experiences to fashion from them something meaningful, something relevant to our needs. We apprehend the world as useful or dangerous, we appreciate it as rife with opportunities for enjoyment or as beset with threats to our present or possible enjoyment.

Our propensity to actively engage the surrounding environment is innate, a part of our biological inheritance. We are born to be world-makers, but how we make those worlds, how we interpret our experience, how we correlate by symbolic reference the data of presentational immediacy with the deliverances of causal efficacy, is by no means deterministic. There are many ways to interpret experience, to decide how best to construe what our sense-data signify. In construing them as we do, we therefore exhibit ourselves as free. Not arbitrarily free, for the organism has no choice over what impinges upon its senses, but free in that it construes what has impinged, making what it is given into the intelligible world it seeks to understand and shape. Romance, says Whitehead, is the "first period of freedom" (1967, 31). It is that stage of learning in which the focus is on encouraging the expansion of our freedom, broadening the range of facts experienced, deepening those experiences through exploration of their import – augmenting the opportunities for refurbishing and remaking the worlds with which we have become familiar.

So the appreciative character of romance is not solely nor even primarily aesthetic but also and more fundamentally pragmatic. We are aware that our experience is an artifact, that we have fashioned its specific unity from the raw materials gained through our twin modes of perceiving, and that how we have fashioned it is as relevant to our purposes. How we take our environment has consequences for our happiness and well-being. If we take the sudden motion as a dangerous sign, we may be able to avoid a falling object or an onrushing opponent. If we take the motion as a positive sign, we might manage to catch the ball or embrace a lover. If we interpret the kind words as a facade masking deep animosity, we can respond in ways that will not lead us into an embarrassing trap. If we take those words as meaning what they say, we might gain a new friend or improve a business opportunity.

Therefore, educational experiences that are romantic should be ones that have consequences. Not serious consequences, having to do with our students' very survival, but ones consequential enough to satisfy the interest that led them to those experiences in the first place.

The great virtue of playing a game is that it creates a world sheltered from the serious world, sets conditions that are interesting both with respect to goals sought and the means for their pursuit, and then offers rewards for success and punishments for failure that are modest and transient. The amateur football game is exciting and the victory worth celebrating, but those who were defeated will live to try again another day and both the winners and the losers will soon return from their play to the serious tasks of earning a living, raising a family, and contributing to the social good.

Imaginative literature also is a kind of game we are invited to play. The world in which a novel leads us may be one in which the heroes are lauded and villains punished, or it may lead us across a dark landscape into some dreadful valley of death, but when the story ends we are still very much alive, neither a hero nor a villain but the better for having pretended to be them both or to champion one or the other's cause. In a romantic classroom, teachers should widen and deepen their students' sense of the serious consequences of their choices, but in a manner that incites them to undertake new and bold adventures – to do so prudently and with eyes wide open, but to do so eager to rise to fresh challenges not shrink from them. In romance, all things should still seem possible, teaching us that the worlds in which we dwell are ones we have made and that they are therefore ours to engage as we see fit and through that engagement to find fulfillment.

To summarize. The stage of romance is that recurrent period in a person's education when appreciation should be dominant. I have argued that by noting the homology between romantic appreciation and perceptive experience we can appreciate appreciation as an active mode of learning. Romance is a process of imaginative engagement – playing with the patterns and content of those interpretations by which our world is taken to have meaning, exploring ways by which these interpretations locate us effectively in that world or might better do so, always being aware of the values they create or enhance or diminish.

No wonder, then, that Whitehead argues that "without the adventure of romance, at the best you get inert knowledge without initiative, and at the worst you get contempt of ideas – without knowledge" (1967, 33). For without an educational moment in which our capacity for imaginative appreciation is promoted, there will be little sense of the way what is taken as fact is haunted by what might have been and might yet be, and so there will be insufficient interest in how what is good can be used to transform it into what is better.

4. Precision and Conceptual Analysis

Whitehead says that the stage of romance in a person's educational development should in due time pass over into a stage of precision, a stage in which "width of relationship is subordinated to exactness of formulation" (1967, 18). The exactness is twofold: achieving greater clarity about a fact by analyzing it, and incorporating that fact into a system. Precision thus provides "both a disclosure and analysis of the general subject-matter of romance" (1967, 19). The vagueness is penetrated; boundaries and differences are specified; an ordered system of relationships is imposed. The grammars of language and science are Whitehead's prime examples of how precision works, deploying a unitary coherent structure upon a raucous multiplicity of particular experiences. Precision is "an instrument for classifying [our] contemplation of objects and for strengthening [our] apprehension of emotional relations with other beings" (1967, 19).

The right time for precision is when the freshness of romance has begun to wane, when our initial curiosity has been satisfied and we are growing dissatisfied with the limitations inherent in appreciative apprehension. If it appears in timely fashion, "precision will always illustrate subject-matter already apprehended and crying out for drastic treatment" (1967, 25). Otherwise, the analysis will be "an analysis of nothing," merely "a series of meaningless statements about bare facts, produced artificially and without any further relevance" (1967, 18). Students have a natural "aptitude for exact knowledge (1967, 22), so that, if cultivated properly, it should enhance rather than deny the inexact knowledge swept into experience by romance. Morever, new facts will be acquired through the analysis and systematizing of the vague facts, but they will be facts acquired "in a systematic order" (1967, 19) and ones that "fit into the analysis" (1967, 18).

Precision involves accepting discipline – in the sense not only of learning to think systematically and rigorously but also of learning what constitutes "the best practice" already accepted with regard to each area of knowledge (1967, 34). It means developing "the habit of cheerfully undertaking imposed tasks" (1967, 35), of becoming a practitioner of a specific established way of knowing, of thinking and acting. It is an "inescapable fact," claims Whitehead, "that there are right ways and wrong ways, and definite truths to be known," and so "knowing the subject exactly" means "getting to know the fundamental details and the main exact generalisations" of that subject, and "acquiring an easy mastery of [its] technique" (1967, 34).

If we take the stage of precision as akin to what Whitehead in *Symbolism* calls conceptual analysis, we can gain some fresh insight into why precision is the obvious and appropriate next educational step after romance. It has to do with the sense of limit inherent in romance, the way in which error is an inescapable feature of interpretation, and how this enlarges our understanding of the pragmatic dimension of symbolic reference.

Romance, understood as embracing the two modes of perception and their integration through symbolic reference, entails a sense of limit often overlooked by our romantic quest for new and fascinating experiences. Romance discloses, but its practitioners tend not to appreciate, that our interpretations and actions are necessarily partial. After all, we are taking the highly abstracted sense-data of presentational immediacy as characterizing the complexly felt concrete realities of causal efficacy, and so obviously that characterization must be inadequate.

Nonetheless, the correlation of presentational immediacy with causal efficacy is natural, something we do constantly, routinely, unthinkingly. We 'trust' it to continue being effective because it always has been. We cannot justify our assumption that the surrounding environment is the way our sense-data tell us it is – or rather, the way we interpret our sense-data as telling us it is. We experience vague impinging presences; we experience vivid colors, shapes, and sounds; we say that the presences are objects here in front of us with those particular visual and auditory features. Yet the presences are too vague to justify being so characterized, and these characterizations are too abstract and fleeting to justify assigning them to any particular region of our environment. The only possible justification is a "pragmatic appeal to the future" (1985, 31). These ways of taking the specifics of presentational immediacy as signs for the location and meaning of the deliverances of causal efficacy have worked. We rely on them and they pay off. The world these linkages effect is one in which we are able to live and to aspire to live better. They work, and that is truth enough.

Why they work is because the two modes of perceptive experience have "structural elements in common" (1985, 30). They are two ways of taking the same concrete reality, of interpreting the circumambient environment which we experience. What is given for experience is a "natural potentiality," the potentiality inherent in the limitations of its brute facticity to which our experience must conform. "All components which are *given* for experience are to be found in the analysis of natural potentiality. Thus the immediate present has to conform to what the past is for it" (1985, 36). The sense data we use as the symbols by which to disclose the meaning – the intelligibility and significance – of what we feel impinging are abstractions from the same reality as are those feelings. Our correlation of the two perceptive modes by which we experience things is not arbitrary because the two modes have the same source. They are versions of the same reality: pale and incomplete versions, to be sure, but versions.

Indeed, the two modes and their correlation arose through long aeons of biological evolution as features of certain organisms which enhanced their reproductive success. As Whitehead puts it: "The symbols do not create their meaning: the meaning, in the form of actual effective beings reacting upon us, exists for us in its own right. But the symbols discover this meaning for us. They discover it because, in the long course of adaptation of living organisms to their environment, nature taught their use" (1985, 57).

Symbolic reference works because in a Darwinian world where there are more organisms striving to secure their lives and those of their offspring than there are resources sufficient for those ends, the ones that have been successful are our own ancestors. We trust our habits of symbolic reference because we acquired those habits by inheriting them from progenitors whose use of them is why we now exist. These habits successfully provided our ancestors with "the determination of the positions of bodies controlling the course of nature" (1985, 56) and so they were able to avoid dangers, secure needed resources, and find suitable mates for creating and nurturing the progeny we are. If it was good enough for them, it's good enough for us.

These habits do not always work, however. We may hope that what our habits of symbolic reference ignore is unimportant, redundant, superfluous. But it may not be. Error occurs when the symbolic reference is inadequate to the needs of the moment, when it overlooks what should have been taken as important, hiding what we might have enjoyed or distracting us from what might secure our success, or when it mischaracterizes that to which it refers, leading us along false pathways away from the available pleasures and opportunities. Any organism that possesses sufficient consciousness to perceive things presentationally as well as causally, and so to require some modicum of symbolic reference in order to unify its experience, is vulnerable to error. Whitehead mentions "Aesop's fable of the dog who dropped a piece of meat to grasp at its reflection in the water" (1985, 19). It mistakenly took the presented image as evidence of a threatening canine challenger.

Organisms are more likely to survive if they, or at least a sufficient number of their kind, can learn from their mistakes. Such organisms, including human beings most obviously but not exclusively, have evolved the capacity to treat symbolic reference as a datum, not only to engage in it but to take it as an object of interest, as a fact relevant to how the correlation of sense data and felt environment will be differently effected. Conceptual analysis is what Whitehead calls this reflective stance toward symbolic reference. In conceptual analysis, the coherence and adequacy of the interpretive symbols are explicitly questioned, the meanings they express adjusted, certain of the data degraded as "delusive appearances" and other data treated as salient. In such ways, we "revise our conceptual scheme so as to preserve the general trust in the symbolic reference" (1985, 54).

The stage of precision thus has two specific functions. It is where we learn the skills needed to recognize both error and the potential for error. It is also where we learn how to frame alternative conceptual schemes, alternative systems of symbolic reference, by which to remedy those actual or possible mistakes. Romance provides our reason for wanting to do so: to prevent the loss of what we have found to be significant. Precision is where we equip ourselves with the tools by which actually to accomplish the ends for which romance hungers. Analysis ferrets out the problems our enthusiasm for an idea or course of action overlooks. System building sets our enthusiasms in their proper context, shows how what we know is related spatially and temporally, hierarchically and causally, to those things upon which it is dependent or which depend on it and to those things that are incompatible with it or can best thrive at its expense.

This disclosure of limitation, of the inadequacy of what we take to be the way things are, not only leads us to appreciate that we are vulnerable to making mistakes. It also leads us to appreciate constraint as good. We are limited in what we can do by previous fashionings, by the ways in which the physical universe, our planetary biosphere, our organismal lineage, and our cultural histories have developed. We cannot do certain things because we are not massive enough or long enough enduring, we cannot evade the boundary conditions set by our genetic destiny or our linguistic heritage. And yet, recognizing that these limitations are artifacts, we realize that what we take as possible is not all that could be possible, that by disciplined thought, by careful analysis of what has as yet not been analyzed and by novel but carefully systemized reformulations, we might find our way toward unimaginable possibilities, toward things even here amid our heaven and earth that are not found in any of our philosophies.

The discipline of precision comes from the recognition that without subjecting our thoughts and actions, and memories and expectations, to careful analysis and systematic organization, we will never learn from our failures. And if this is so, we will never develop intellectually and morally, and so in the long run will be unable to sustain our involvement with what romance has shown to be the most important things in life. If precision blooms as a fruit of romance, therefore, as its champion, then the discipline it requires can become self-discipline because we will recognize that although it may lack much in the way of its own intrinsic importance its instrumental importance is fundamental. Without a proper grounding in romance, however, precision is boring and students forced to learn it as a deadly parade of "inert knowledge" will suffer a "dulled mind" (1967, 31), the schools producing as they so often do "a plentiful array of dunces" (1967, 34), "a disheartened crowd of young folk, inoculated against any outbreak of intellectual zeal" (1967, 38).

The grammar of the natural sciences is where we usually turn for a paradigm of precise knowledge, but unfortunately science education far too often also offers itself as a paradigm of inert knowledge. Teaching the results of prior scientific inquiry as a self-contained system is to divorce those results from the romantic interests they were devised to clarify, protect, and further. Instead of plunking students down in lecture halls where they are taught theories and formulae along with the facts those ideas correctly predicted, science students should be in laboratories from the very first, engaged in inquiries that are initially romantic and that become precise only as it becomes apparent precision is called for.

In the beginning, apart from any measuring instruments and laws of nature, is the problem – into the presence of which teachers should lure but not lead their students. The problem then needs to be specified more clearly, analyzed into smaller seemingly solvable problems, distinguished from all sorts of pseudo-problems and irrelevancies, and some hypotheses suggested for how to set about resolving the problem. Only then, with the issues sized up and the likely lines of inquiry suggested, is it time to take measurements, to begin refining the problem by quantifying it, formulating the hypotheses in ways that are testable, setting up protocols and control groups and other useful assurances of objectivity. As these systematic methods are instituted, and again as preliminary results suggest refinements or even major reformulations, literature searches will be appropriate, and consideration of the relevant established theories and formulae. Science so taught, hands-on, problem-oriented, collaborative, is an example of how to keep precision married to romance, to have its resulting knowledge lively rather than inert.

Precision in the humanities should be similarly construed. There are other ways to be precise than by acts of quantification. The grammar of language has its appropriate precisions, and so humanities teachers should be always fashioning ways by which students can learn to speak a language competently, to express an idea within the framework of a particular genre's expectations, to think through a complex qualitative issue critically, to express oneself clearly and gracefully, to argue a case cogently, to reason systematically around a hermeneutical circle. Here too there is a right way and a wrong way, appropriate and inappropriate methods and styles and stances, and the only way to success is through discipline at first imposed but eventually become self-discipline.

Whitehead locates the humanistic and scientific stages of romance and precision at different places in his calendar of how the stages of education should cycle from pre-school through completion of a university degree. It needs to be underscored that precision belongs to both modes of learning. Whitehead rejects the common assertion made of his views, that romance is a humanistic enterprise, precision a scientific one. All knowledge must begin with curiosity and imaginative exploration, and then lead on to analysis and systematization. If learning is to be genuinely developmental, it must all begin with a stage of freedom that matures into a stage of discipline.

5. Generalization and The Art of Free Society

Both stages of education, however, ought then to find their completion in a new stage of freedom, which Whitehead calls generalization. This third stage of education is the "fruition" of the other two, "a return to romanticism with added advantage of classified ideas and relevant technique" (1967, 19). The abstractions of precision, the well-established theories and methods of systematic inquiry, now need to be cashed out. "The pupil now wants to use his new weapons. He is an effective individual, and it is effects that he wants to produce" (1967, 36-7). The freedom generalization offers a person is "the active freedom of application" (1967, 37).

We are back in the world of romance, a world redolent with important matters for our consideration, significant problems requiring our attention. But now we come furnished with the tools needed to address these issues effectively. Our mind is now "a disciplined regiment instead of a rabble" (1967, 37); it is time to send our forces into combat. We are clearer about the facts, to be sure, and that clarity has uncovered far more facts than we had previously appreciated, but what is important for generalization is not the facts as such but the systemic structures – the general ideas – by which they are organized.

In this new stage of learning, "concrete facts should be studied as illustrating the scope of general ideas" (1967, 26). The facts cease to be in the foreground of our interest, serving primarily as illustrations of interpretive theories. Likewise, theories cease to be uninterpreted abstractions, serving instead as instruments for guiding our understanding and hence our action, making it possible for us to identify ends worth pursuing and then effectively to achieve those ends. Putting general ideas into practice, however, takes practice. Generalization involves "comprehension of a few general principles with a thorough grounding in the way they apply to a variety of concrete details" (1967, 26).

With respect both to the comprehension of theory and to its grounding in fact, Whitehead wants us to be so thoroughly conversant with them that they both become habits. He defines a general principle as "rather a mental habit than a formal statement." It is "the way the mind reacts to the appropriate stimulus in the form of illustrative circumstances" (1967, 26). At the same time, he argues that the active application of principles so understood means "shedding details," fashioning interpretations with "the details retreating into subconscious habits" (1967, 37).

I don't think Whitehead means, however, that the principles are mental habits, which would suggest they are unthinkingly utilized. The habit crucial to generalization is the habit of using principles, and so any particular principle will be brought into play as part of our habitual use of a repertoire of workable ideas, but this application will be done critically, the principle's particular relevance constantly under scrutiny, its coherence and consistency constantly open to revision. Similarly, the retreat of details into subconscious habits is not a process by which the details become unimportant but one in which their importance lies not in their isolated features but their relevance to the applicability and adequacy of the principles they putatively illustrate and so constantly test.

Generalization, thus, is "the habit of active thought, with freshness." It is "active mastery" of knowledge, "knowledge so handled as to transform every phase of immediate experience" (1967, 32). In our experiencing, always to be attempting to frame freshly a suitable interpretation of facts that are always being brought forward to be tested freshly against that interpretation, is the apotheosis of "mental cultivation." It is "the satisfactory way in which the mind will function when it is poked up into activity" (1967, 27). The habit of generalization is a way of being in the world, a style of engagement. It has to do not with what we know but with how we put our knowledge to use, so that it both achieves our immediate ends and, by criticizing our way of doing so, improves our chance for achieving our subsequent ends.

Whitehead identifies university education as "the great period of generalisation" (1967, 26), chastising professors for constantly succumbing to the temptation to turn it into an extension of secondary school where romance and precision are predominate. For the task of a university is to give students the opportunity to practice generalization until it becomes habitual for them. "The ideal of a University," Whitehead argues, " is not so much knowledge, as power. Its business is to convert the knowledge of a boy [or girl, of course] into the power of a man [or woman]" (1967, 27).

We typically think of Whitehead's stage of generalization and its empowering results as having to do with the last stage of acquiring mastery of a field of study, in particular mastery of an academic discipline. We have in mind the story of how from a romance with our native language and a love of the poetry written in that language, through acquiring the precise know-how of grammar and rhetoric, meter and rhyme, textual analysis and hermeneutic interpretation, someone was able to win a Pulitzer Prize for poetry and tenure at a prestigious university. Or our story is about how from a romantic attraction to Jurassic dinosaurs, through a rigorous training in biology and paleontology, someone achieved world renown as a field anthropologist in eastern Africa. Certainly such forms of intellectual success, as well as the more modest successes of most professionals in their fields of endeavor, are evidence of having learned to generalize in Whitehead's sense.

Whitehead's focus is elsewhere, however – not toward the academy and job preparation but toward achieving the social good. The business of the university is to prepare men and women to become active, contributing citizens. Its business is to empower them not merely by broadening their interests in the natural and cultural world they inhabit, nor merely by training them in the socially useful technical skills needed to succeed in that world, nor merely by doing both. The business of the university, already presuming the educational stages of romance and precision, is "the guidance of the individual towards a comprehension of the art of life; and by the art of life," says Whitehead, "I mean the most complete achievement of varied activity expressing the potentialities of that living creature in the face of its actual environment" (1967, 39).

The full expression of a person's potentialities calls for "subordinating the lower to the higher possibilities of the indivisible personality" (1967, 39). It involves more than simply developing one's capacities. We engage in the art of life when we try to fashion from the varied activities in which we engage some unified whole – an indivisible personality, a moral character. The art of life is to make of our life a work of art, to craft for ourselves a whole self, a self with integrity. In discussing the art of life, Whitehead turns to science, religion, morality, the fine and practical arts. For they all "take their rise from this sense of values within the structure of being. Each individual embodies an adventure of existence. The art of life is the guidance of this adventure" (1967, 39).

So generalization so understood has a moral dimension, for we are responsible for what we make. We are moral agents in the sense that we give things value or detract from their value by what we understand them to be and by how we engage them. Their worth is in part what we make of them, and we are answerable to ourselves and others for those valuations. Disdaining the friendly gesture as insincere rather than genuine, preferring one possibility over another, encouraging a course of action while railing against its competitor, joining forces with these people but not the others – in such ways we create or destroy values, and validate or invalidate others' values. These are all moral actions, constructings and deconstructings of worth, realizations of utility or violations of right. Because our character is composed of the pattern of these choices and of how we go about making them, because it is a matter of our preferential habits, we thereby create ourselves and our worth as selves. As moral agents, we make the private world of our immediate experience, externalize that world through our engagement with our material environment, and interlace our world with others' worlds through our interactions with them, transforming personal goods into a common good, private utility into altruism, immediate satisfaction into a sense of duty toward ancestral practices and toward future generations.

As they were in the stage of romance also, games are an excellent pedagogical strategy, in this case as a way to introduce students to these moral dimensions of how they think and act as generalizers. Most obviously, competitive team games thrust players into a world where the team's success depends on teamwork. There is a common good to be sustained in the face of an opponent's challenge, and every member of the team has a role to play in meeting that challenge. Students need also to learn about a less obvious but more important moral dimension to their game playing, for the competing teams compete because they both subscribe to the rules of their game, rules they must both embrace as constraining them in their sharply divergent goals. We have to fashion a wider common good concerning the rules of engagement as the context for the narrower common good of our team's victory, just as our own personal success as a hero for the winning side or a valiant defender for what proved to be the losing side depends on our prior acceptance of the team's importance. Altruism and self-interest are interdependent goods. Generalization needs always to draw students from the narrower to the broader dimensions of their responsibilities, helping them glimpse the gyre of nested goods that comprise the moral import of any world they might enter.

Generalization, as Whitehead understands it, thus has to do with a relational sense of self-fulfillment, with the cultivation of those moral habits that express, indeed that comprise, who we at our best can be. We will be what we have made of ourselves and of the communities we share with other such selves. Taken in this way, generalization finds its epistemological homologue in *Symbolism*'s discussion of the art of a free society. The art of life does not involve merely the fulfillment of self-interest, because life has a fundamentally communal dimension. Our freedom arises because our environmental obligations are cultural as well as biological, just as much a matter of nurture as of nature. It is the family and neighborhood, the tribe and nation, that both nurture the emergence of individuality and permit it to spread and flourish. The selves we fashion are selves deeply interrelated with other selves, so the task of the art of life is to balance in some viable way both individual freedom and group solidarity.

Life is "a bid for freedom on the part of organisms, a bid for a certain independence of individuality with self-interests and activities not to be understood purely in terms of environmental obligations" (1985. 65). As organisms capable of symbolic reference, we live by symbols, by the instinctual ways in which we take the sense-data of presentational immediacy as signs for interpreting the impinging importances that we feel in the mode of causal efficacy. As we develop the skills of conceptual analysis, we gain a modicum of critical distance from our instincts and our unreflective proclivities. We learn to channel or divert or suppress them, to develop a style of responding to the world that individualizes us. We not only critique our interpretations of experience, we do so habitually, such that our actions are consistently conditioned by our critiques, guided systematically and not merely happenstantially by them.

Whitehead calls actions that depend on conceptual analysis of this sort symbolically conditioned actions. Symbolically conditioned action, he argues, "enables an organism to conform its actions to long-ranged analysis of the particular circumstances of its environment" (1985, 80). Our actions are disciplined by judgments we make about their likely relevance to our long-range ends. We attend not only to the immediate satisfactions an action offers, nor merely to the consequences we think are likely to flow from that action. We attend to their relevance as well, to their positive or negative contribution to the realization of our long-range purposes. We choose how we wish to live our lives, freeing ourselves from simple dependence on the biologically given proclivities we share with all other humans. We shape those proclivities, as best we can, to suit our purposes, and by doing so individuate them, express them as features not just of our biology but also of our chosen purposes. Symbolically conditioned action is the tool by which an organism's bid for freedom results in a unique self, a self with certain characteristic habits regarding the exercise of that freedom.

Symbols are how instinct is transformed into emotion. The feelings derived from causal efficacy are vague. We sense their importance but cannot quite identify their origin or nature or consequence. They are too diffuse to grasp; they lack meaning. When certain sense-data derived from presentational immediacy are taken as referring to those feelings, when these wonderfully definite and highly manipulatable sense-data function as symbols for our feelings, they interpret those feelings as having a specifiable meaning. A vaguely felt unease becomes my anger at a friend's slight. An ill-focused attraction becomes my appreciation for the grace of the dancer's movements.

The symbols enhance the feelings they interpret by lifting them into the meaningful world within which we dwell, but reciprocally the symbols are in turn enhanced by the feelings, which endow them with an importance they otherwise lack. 'Anger' and 'love' are just words, but when taken as words that signify my feelings those words are filled with the affective power of what they name. The words gain a connotation, and so in speaking them we bring our conduct into harmony with the emotive power they evince. We speak the words "I am angry." angrily, the words "I love you." lovingly. We believe, and rightly so, that there is something inappropriate about hostile words said lovingly or words of endearment said angrily. "The object of symbolism is the enhancement of the importance of what is symbolized," but it also charges the symbols with "emotional efficacy" (1985, 63).

Thus for Whitehead an important function of symbolic expression is that it "preserves society by adding emotion to instinct" (1985, 70). It does so because symbols that have taken on the intensity of the feelings they symbolize are powerful tools for social cohesion. They evoke an emotional response in a person who sees, hears, or enacts them, and if they are presented to a number of people they are likely to provoke similar responses in each of them. "The self-organization of society depends on commonly diffused symbols evoking commonly diffused ideas, and at the same time indicating commonly understood actions" (1985, 76). Furthermore, since symbols can be transported easily from place to place, adapted to varying contexts and purposes, they tend to outlast their initial purpose. So they begin to accumulate connotations that reach back generations. "A word gathers emotional signification from its entire history in the past; and this is transferred symbolically to its meaning in present use" (1985, 84).

Whatever the obscure origins of the word 'freedom' and its Indo-European cognates, it became vested with the aspirations of slaves and peasants, the conquered, the dispossessed, the marginalized – everyone whose choices about the sort of individual they would make of themselves were subjugated to another's will. Those aspirations took on a new significance during the mid-sixteenth century revolt of the Puritans against their Stewart masters, and, a century and a half later, during the American war of independence from its colonial oppressors and the French class war against an uncaring aristocracy. The aspiration to be free has continued to the present day serving as a battle cry uniting the oppressed against their oppressors in civil, class, ethic, religious, and regional wars. No one any more is against freedom, although many are content to define their privileged place in society as an expression of freedom while downplaying the plight of the under-privileged, blaming their condition on their unwise exercise of freedom.

Today, in telling others that we prize our freedom, our words thus do more than describe our wish to be left alone. Our words also conjure up flickering images of brave Athenians at Marathon or embattled GIs on Omaha Beach, pictures of a bare-breasted Liberty at the Parisian barricades or Frodo struggling with himself and Gollum in an attempt to cast the One Ring into Mount Doom, memories of suffragettes marching on Washington or Martin Luther King making his 'I have a dream' speech.

These images and countless more haunt our words, investing them with an intensity quite out of proportion to the realities of the situation in which they are uttered. We are, after all, only saying we can't be bothered to accept a particular obligation with which others might hope to saddle us. Yet anyone who wants to gainsay our wishes must do battle with all the heroes whose defense of freedom has made our trivial appeal to its value possible. Were we to say merely that we prize our selfishness, that resistence would vanish, for selfishness conjures narrow virtues and a host of important vices, whereas freedom is home to virtues that are among the widest, deepest, most profound of our culture's goods, and in thinking of it we rarely think of any associated vices at all. We define ourselves, and protect ourselves against how others might define us, by the symbols to which we pledge allegiance.

The power of historically freighted symbols like the word "freedom" lies both in their massive connotational significance and in their ability to bring people together whose understandings of that significance are not as congruent as they might think they are. "The symbol evokes loyalties to vaguely conceived notions, fundamental for our spiritual natures" (1985, 74). The notions are still vague enough that they can encompass a considerable range of actual difference, while yet being precise enough to be lifted from instinct to emotion, to become something consciously embraced by those who feel their importance. For one person, the predominant feature of freedom might be economic, for another religious, for a third sexual, yet they stand side by side at the barricades, their rifles aimed at the approaching enemies of freedom, believing in their mutual equality and finding comradeship in their common purpose. Their shout of 'freedom' is a portmanteau ample enough to hold them all.

The "efficacy of symbols," says Whitehead, is that they are "at once preservative of the commonweal and of the individual standpoint" (1985, 66). They both bind us together and, by individuating us, free us from that self-imposed bondage. Both the binding and the freeing are crucial. If the first function of symbols is to preserve society, their second is to afford "a foothold for reason by its delineation of the particular instance which it expresses" (1985, 70). Symbols afford that foothold by sustaining multiple interpretations within the binding unity they create. We express our individuality by taking "freedom" as an economic, a religious, or a sexual ideal; we express our commonality, our community, by thinking these differences are compatible versions of the same ideal. "Language binds a nation together by the common emotions which it elicits, and is yet the instrument whereby freedom of thought and of individual criticism finds its expression" (1985, 68).

We are now in a position to understand why, according to Whitehead, the educational stage of generalization is a return to the freedom that marked the stage of romance. The work of precision has been to hone the skills of conceptual analysis, so that we are adept at clarifying and systematizing our sense-data. With generalization, we take precision a step further by applying its skills to a critique of the established ways our sense-data have been interpreted. Conceptual analysis is not enough. It improves upon instinctual forms of symbolic reference by correcting mistaken interpretations and enhancing the emotional and pragmatic relevance of successful interpretations. But it needs to mature, to become symbolically coordinated action, if our lives are to have any chance of making the transition from mere living to living better or living well. For this improvement to occur, our critiques must be made in conscious awareness of the wider environment of meanings they inhabit, most importantly of the deeply rooted cultural meanings that are the basis for both our community and our individuality. Generalization occurs when reason is put to work in the criticism of our socially accepted symbols, and these critiques are carried out habitually.

It is through the creative application of what we know in order to address the inadequacies of the present situation that we become free and simultaneously enlarge the scope and relevance of the freedom present in our society. By means of generalization, the reform of our established symbols becomes our standard practice. The reform is an expression of individuality: it requires the freedom of interpretation made possible by selves who have developed their critical skills in individuating ways, and it results in a furthering of those skills and hence that individuality. But what are reformed are the symbols of societal solidarity, those we and our fellow citizens hold in common, our shared heritage. The reform strengthens those symbols and hence those common goods. It binds us closer together even as it sharpens our individuality.

As Whitehead puts it, "the symbolic expression of instinctive forces drags them out into the open; it differentiates them and delineates them. There is then opportunity for reason to effect, with comparative speed, what might otherwise be left to the slow operation of the centuries amid ruin and reconstruction" (1985, 69). The symbols in need of reform are matters of social ritual and command, acceptable practices and explicit rules, established conventions and legislative acts, systems of value and faith commitments. "Codes, rules of behavior, canons of art, are attempts to impose systematic action which on the whole will promote favourable symbolic interactions. As a community changes, all such rules and canons require revision in the light of reason" (1985, 87f).

Generalization is thus the practice of symbol revision, the way by which frays and tears in the social fabric are constantly repaired. It is the way by which the rules of our common life are kept attuned to "the ultimate purpose for which the society exists" (1985, 88), attuned to the system of meanings that constitutes the cultural worldview by which our social interactions are nurtured and therefore by which our lives, our distinctively individuated selves, are fulfilled. "Free men obey the rules which they themselves have made" (1985, 88). The practice of generalization make us free because by thinking and acting as generalists we make a social order that depends on the freedom of its citizens and by doing so enhances their freedom.

We are free only if we act freely. Unless we are habitually critiquing our established symbols in order to restore their effectiveness as sources of both solidarity and individuality, our freedom will be lost. Insofar as we accept the standard ways of thinking and acting uncritically, we slip into a new kind of instinctive way of living that Whitehead calls reflex action. We have transformed our instincts into emotions by giving them meaning, and then we have shaped those emotions to express our individuality, all by acts of conceptual analysis iterated sufficiently to become conditioned symbolic actions. If we don't sustain the critique of symbols central to this process, however, the important beliefs and values by which we live will become blind routines, the emotions they express will fall out of conscious awareness, and we will come to behave in ways no different than we did when our ideas and actions were governed primarily by our natural instincts. We will have reverted to a pre-romantic stage educationally, to a pre-civilizational stage culturally. "Reflex action is a relapse toward a more complex type of instinct on the part of organisms which enjoy, or have enjoyed, symbolically conditioned action" (1985, 79). The acts of jingoistic patriotism to which we so often succumb in times of war are reflex actions, as are our routine acts of conformity in which public opinion becomes our opinion and the current fads a substitute for our own preferences.

This rebarbarization process is our destiny unless we are endlessly laboring to prevent it. It is the default setting, as it were, for social order because that order is always a fragile achievement, always needing to be regained in order to be sustained. Our communal achievements, the fruit of critique, will rot in the absence of further critique. Just as education, in that vivid image of Whitehead's already mentioned, is not like "packing articles in a trunk" (1967, 33), as though what we know was a boot which once acquired can be kept safely in a closet until we have need for it, so also civilized order. Our educational development and the viability of our communal arrangements are like food, needing to be fresh and suitable if they are to nurture us. Symbolically conditioned action, the soul of generalization, is the source of the seed and manure, and also of the plow and hoe, by means of which fresh concepts and practices will sprout from established ones, and can eventually be harvested for the continued sustenance of the civilization they express.

And so Whitehead ends *Symbolism* thus:

> The art of free society consists first in the maintenance of the symbolic code; and secondly in fearlessness of revision, to secure that the code serves those purposes which satisfy an enlightened reason. Those societies which cannot combine reverence to their symbols with freedom of revision, must ultimately decay either from anarchy, or from the slow atrophy of a life stifled by useless shadows. (1985, 88)

Generalization is the art of life, the practice of which is the art required of a free society. It is a form of wisdom, an "active wisdom" relentlessly "battling with the immediate experiences of life," seeking to "qualify each immediate moment with relevant ideas and appropriate actions" (1967, 37). The "final mark" of such wisdom is adaptative power: "the successful adaptation of old symbols to changes of social structure" (1985, 61). It is transformational power: "that knowledge which adds greatness to character is knowledge so handled as to transform every phase of immediate experience" (1967, 32). Active involvement not passive withdraw, but for the sake of transformation not replacement, of adaptation not rejection. The art of life, the art of a free society, is wisely being able to avoid the atrophy resulting from a society that becomes mired in the blind loyalties kindled by reflex action, and instead to effect change by renovation rather than by the collapse into anarchy that is the inexorable result of revolution.

6. Concluding Expectorations

By interpreting Whitehead's stages of education in the light of his epistemology, we are led to thoughts about generalization that resonate with his philosophy of history and his philosophy of nature. The dialectic from romance through precision to generalization, the threefold art crucial for a free society, is echoed in Part I of *Adventures of Ideas* where Whitehead focuses on how the vague notion that humans have souls becomes a transformative symbol nurturing the gradual development in the Western world of ideals of individual liberty and democracy, culminating in their actualization historically. This dialectic is also echoed in *The Function of Reason* where nature is interpreted as a clash between the blind force of entropy and the transformative power of an originative element, the self-disciplining of which is the work of reason, a work that can succeed only if practical reason and speculative reason can be harmonized through the development of a method for their dynamic coordination.

So our exploration of the homology between Whitehead's philosophy of education and his epistemology suggests further homologies. One of these moves us onto the stage of world history and the other embraces the whole of our cosmic epoch. Perhaps after exploring these homologies, becoming as familiar with them as we must become with the practices of conditioned symbolic action if we are to function adequately as free citizens, we might be ready to see if there is an homology after all between Whitehead's model for the rhythm of education and his metaphysical model for the concrescence of an actual occasion.

Such considerations, of course, lie well beyond the horizons of this essay.

Bibliography
Whitehead, A. N. (1967/1929): *The Aims of Education and Other Essays.* New York: Free Press.
Whitehead, A. N. (1985/1927): *Symbolism: Its Meaning and Effect.* New York: Fordham University Press.

Whitehead's Cyclic Theory of Learning and Contemporary Empirical Educational Research

Franz Riffert

Abstract

Whitehead has outlined a theory of mental development, learning and teaching in several of his articles. This approach, contrary to traditional theories of learning and education, is essentially cyclic and rhythmic. This concept of *cycles of rhythm* is one of Whitehead's basic intuitions. It plays a central role also in his philosophical approach. A basic learning act is a cycle which consists of three phases: romance, precision and generalization. These basic learning cycles in turn are nested in bigger cycles which again are part of yet wider cycles. The biggest cycle, the life-cycle, can in turn be divided into three major cycles: the cycle of infancy, the language cycle and the science cycle.

Kurt Fischer's Neo-Piagetian skill theory and its methodological equivalent, the micro-developmental approach, illustrated by Nira Granott's empirical research on learning processes are presented and parallels to Whitehead's speculative account of mental development and learning are outlined. It is shown that the two approaches show far-reaching parallels in their basic conceptions. This on the one hand implies an empirical confirmation of Whitehead's speculative approach; on the other hand it opens new developmental possibilities for Fischer's and Granott's theories of mental development and learning which may profit in certain respects from Whitehead's broader philosophical theory.

1. Whitehead's Cyclic Concept of Learning

One topic to which Whitehead repeatedly comes back to in his papers on education is 'learning'. Although Whitehead touches this topic again and again in his educational writings the most intense treatment takes place in the two articles 'The Rhythm of Education' (1967a, 15-28) and 'The Rhythmic Claims of Freedom and Discipline' (1967a, 29-41). If we accept it to be one of the major aims of education to improve the learning process in students (of all ages) then of course we first have to know what learning is and how it functions; only then we are in a position to arrange our teaching according to the needs of effective learning.

Whitehead accuses traditional concepts of education (among other things) of being based on a false linear concept of learning: bits of independent, disconnected information are added to already existing items of knowledge in mechanic way; like bricks on a pile. His own theory of learning on the contrary is essentially rhythmic. This idea of periodic rhythm according to Whitehead is not only important in the field of education but in all domains of reality. It certainly is central to human life. Whitehead held this position since his first writings in mathematics: "Our bodily life is essentially periodic. It is dominated by the beatings of the heart, and the recurrence of breathing. The presupposition of periodicity is indeed fundamental to our very concept of life." (Whitehead 1982, 11) But it not only pervades all of life but all of reality: "There are minor eddies, each in itself a threefold cycle, running its course in each day, in each week, and in each term" (1967a, 38) and in each year and longer time periods (seasons, years, epochs). In Whitehead's metaphysics actual entities account for this pulsating, cyclic rhythm. Actual entities, the fundamental constituent of the universe, grow out of preceding actual entities and when reaching their satisfaction they vanish by taking over the role of a preceding actual entity for further concrescences of actual entities – a new cyclic pulsation starts. This phased process of an actual entity starts from mere passive and vague reception of what is there, passing on into an (more or less) actively approached definiteness which again dissolves into newly emerging actual occasions. Such pulsating micro-processes stretch throughout the whole universe and become especially obvious in living organisms. And therefore it is not astonishing that this cyclic and rhythmic feature re-occurs at the level of human learning processes.

1.1 The Three Phases of a Full Cycle of Learning: Romance, Precision, Generalization

A single unit of a learning process according to Whitehead consists of three phases which he termed 'romance', 'precision', and 'generalization' (1967a, 31).[1]

At the *stage of romance* the student is in a process of discovery; s/he for the first time is confronted with new stimuli. "The stage of romance is the stage of first apprehension." (1967a, 17) As long as the new stimuli are at least faintly conceived as relevant by the student it will evoke interest and some sort of emotional arousal in the learner. Relevant is a new situation to student if s/he can relate him/herself to the new situation i.e. the situation should not be completely new, different or foreign to him/her but that it should be possible for the student to discern possible connections to his/her earlier experiences. "Education must essentially be a setting in order of a ferment already stirring in the mind: you cannot educate mind in *vacuo*." (1967a, 18) However, at this stage the relations and connections of the new stimuli among themselves and to the student still remain vague, only half disclosed; hardly grasped visions. Such a vision "holds within itself unexplored connexions with possibilities half-disclosed by glimpses and half concealed by the wealth of material." (1967a, 17) These half-disclosed relevant connections of novel situations are emotion laden "Romantic emotion is essentially the excitement consequent on the transition from bare facts to the first realization of the import of their unexplored relationships." (1967a, 18)

This first phase of a learning process is not to be underestimated. It provides the learner with excitement and emotional arousal towards the possibilities which flash up in the learner: curiosity is triggered in the student. Without this intrinsic arousal hardly any further interest for and curiosity in exploring the situation in any depth would be shown on the side of the student. This *descriptive* aspect of *learning* has implications for a *prescriptive* theory of *teaching*: no intrinsic motivation without giving enough room and time for the stage of romance. Traditional education has violated this central postulate of a process theory of teaching because of its linear piecemeal account of learning.

---

[1] Whitehead sometimes also terms these stages a „threefold cycle of freedom, discipline, and freedom" (1967a, 31).

The second phase is termed the *stage of precision* by Whitehead. At this stage the student investigates and elaborates in detail the exact relationships of the new stimuli among themselves, in relation to well known stimuli and to her/himself. "In this stage, width of relationship is subordinated to exactness of formulation. It is the stage of grammar, the grammar of language and the grammar of science." (1967a, 18) Again and again Whitehead draws our attention to the fact that "a stage of precision is barren without a previous stage of romance: unless there are facts which have already been vaguely apprehended in their broad generality, the previous analysis is an analysis of nothing. It is simply a series of meaningless statements about bare facts, produced artificially and without any further relevance." (1967a, 18). It is of utmost importance that the phase of precision always *follows* and never precedes a phase of free roaming romance; if this rule is violated – as in fact it is the case in traditional linear piecemeal education – inert knowledge is the very likely result. "Thus precision will always illustrate subject matter already apprehended and crying out for drastic treatment." (1967a, 25) Whitehead accuses traditional education with its lack of emphasis on the romantic phase of producing such inert ideas "that are merely received into the mind without being utilized, or tested, or thrown into fresh combinations." (1967a, 1)

The stage of precision adds precision to the contents grasped at the stage of romance. It consists "of analyzing the facts, bit by bit." (1967a, 18) The broad but vaguely apprehended and only half disclosed contents of the romantic phase are specified in detail and systematized. Such elaborations require discipline. In its ideal form such discipline is *self*-discipline motivated by the lures introduced at the stage of romance.

There are many different sources according to Whitehead why traditional teaching failed (see for instance the *Introduction* to this book). One, as we have already seen, is that the teaching process tacitly was modeled after a linear concept of development – of step by step packing one unrelated item after the other into a trunk. Another one, not less disastrous mistake of traditional education, consists in the production of inert knowledge because the phase of precision or discipline is over-emphasized and the stage of romance is neglected. "Without the adventure of romance, at the best you get inert knowledge without initiative, and at worst you get contempt of ideas – without knowledge." (1967a, 33)

But, of course, there are ditches on both sides of the road. And so Whitehead argued not to over-emphasize the stage of romance either. He repeatedly stresses the fact that romance has to be complemented by what he called the stage of 'precision' or 'discipline'. And in this line of argumentation Whitehead draws our attention to the fact that there "are right ways and wrong ways, and definite truths to be known." (1967a, 34)[2] Therefore the stage of disciplined precision is important as well. There cannot be any doubt that "a certain pointing out of important facts, and of simplifying ideas, and of usual names really strengthens the natural impetus of the pupil." (1967a, 33) Whitehead's criticism of Maria Montessori's approach to education illustrates this point: While he concedes that the success of Montessori's system is due to the fact that she had recognized the importance of the stage of romance he never the less points out that its unbalanced emphasize on the romantic phase of learning also marks its major deficit: "it lacks the restraint which is necessary for the great stages of precision." (1967a, 22)

The third and final phase of each learning cycle is the *stage of generalization*. It is at the same time the culmination of the learning cycle in question and the start of a new cycle. So Whitehead can say that here the "return to romanticism" (1967a, 19) takes place. The newly acquired detailed and interrelated definitive knowledge is applied to new, wider situations i.e. to new challenging stimuli; in doing this, again new exciting perspectives and fascinating half-disclosed insights are gained: a new cycle of learning is about to start.

Whitehead sums up the general character of a full learning cycle in the following words: "There is the general apprehension of some topic in its vague possibilities, the mastery of the relevant details, and finally the putting of the whole subject together in the light of the relevant knowledge." (1967a, 38)

Before we advance any further in the discussion of Whitehead's theory of learning we must keep in mind that we are speaking here about a highly developed form of learning i.e. a form of learning which today usually is referred to as a *processes of problem solving*. Such

---

[2] Here Whitehead obviously departs from radical constructivist views of learning and teaching. (see also: Riffert 1999, 75)

processes require the higher mental functions of human beings, even consciousness.

But of course we must not forget that there are more forms, more *primitive* forms of learning as well. But if so, the question arises immediately of how these lower forms of learning, which can occur without conscious analysis and elaborations – one may think of classical conditioning (Pawlow, Watson) and instrumental conditioning (Thorndike, Skinner) – are linked to these higher forms of problem solving.[3]

Here Whitehead's "doctrine of symbolism" (1985, 78) comes into play. This theory of symbolism "enables [Whitehead] to distinguish between [1] pure instinctive action, [2] reflex action, and [3] symbolically conditioned action" (1985, 78). In what follows I shall briefly present this theory of symbolism which is relevant for our topic because it will enable us to show how lower forms of learning are connected in Whitehead's philosophy to the higher forms of learning and problem solving.

First it is interesting to notice that Whitehead distinguishes *three* types of learning activities which underlie the process of acquiring these forms of action; and Whitehead's theory of perception also consists of *three* different types, the so-called three modes of perception. And since action and perception are intimately connected in Whitehead's approach it is not astonishing that these three perceptive modes correspond to the three modes of action presented theory of symbolism and action.

Let us first turn to what Whitehead had called 'pure instinct actions' (1). Pure instinct actions are defined as those actions of an organism which are "wholly analyzable of those conditions laid upon its development by the settled facts of its external environment." (1985, 78) If the actions of organisms are purely analyzable into its external conditions then this means that in pure instinct actions are passive and no genuine self-activity what so ever from the side of the organism plays a(n important) role. These kinds of activities are almost completely determined by external factors. Of course this reminds us of the mode of causal efficacy in perception; here also the content of a perceptive act is determined by external (i.e. antecedent) conditions. And

---

[3] Olson and Fazio (2001) found strong experimental support for their thesis that "attitudes can be [classically] conditioned in the absence of of contingency awareness." (2001, 416). (See also: De Houwer, Hendrickx & Baeyens 1997)

so Whitehead can write: "This pure instinct is the response of an organism to pure causal efficacy." (1985, 78) Pure instinct is the most primitive type of reaction to external stimuli; mere accommodation to environmental forces. In its pure form this type of action can only be detected in very primitive forms of living organisms; most obvious according to Whitehead it is, however, at the *inorganic* level as for instance in the movements of electrons, atoms and molecules for instance. (1985, 82)[4] However there are certain forms of pathologies which show similar characteristics. For instance pathologies in the frontal lobes lead to what is termed 'stimulus boundedness': the stimuli perceived seem to automatically trigger a specific form of behavior. "The perception of food, for example, cannot be easily separated from eating. ... Some patients with frontal damage exhibit social disinhibition, much to the embarrassment of their families. For instance, a young patient with bilateral frontal damage we saw in the clinic reacted daily to every wastebasket in the office by spitting into it, despite being asked repeatedly to stop this behavior." (Schweiger 2003, 111f)

The second type of action is reflex action (2). It is defined by Whitehead as "that organic functioning which is wholly dependent on sense-presentation" (1985, 81). So this type of action is based alone on the perceptive mode of presentational immediacy; no symbolic reference and therefore no consciousness is involved in this type of action. In humans the reflex type of action occurs only when it is "unaccompanied by any analysis of causal efficacy *via* symbolic reference." (1985, 81) It arises when "the organism has acquired the *habit* of action in response to immediate sense-perception" (1985, 81 italics added). When humans for instance act without conscious attention their activities are automatically triggered reflex actions in Whitehead's sense. To put it in behavioristic terms: reflex action takes place when an automatism – Whitehead speaks of habits – has been established between two stimuli (perceived in the mode of presentational immediacy); If I see correctly, Whitehead's concept of reflex action accounts for the well-known learning processes of classical and instrumental conditioning.[5] This means that he can include empirically well

---

[4] But even at this level occasional flare-ups of self-initiative may occur. According to Whitehead these flare-ups break the iron grip of environmental forces and are responsible for the statistical character of the laws of nature.

[5] Here the term 'conditioning' is used in its technical meaning within behavioristic learning theories while in all other statements of this chapter the term

established behavioristic learning theories into his own approach on learning and give them a new interpretation by connecting them to higher theories of learning and problem solving: reflex actions are more primitive forms of learning which only presuppose presentational immediacy but not symbolic reference. When symbolic reference comes into play the highest form of learning, which can be termed conscious problem solving, is reached.

Symbolically conditioned action (3) is a form of action which is "conditioned by analysis of the perceptive mode of causal efficacy effected by symbolic transference from the perceptive mode of presentational immediacy. " (1985, 80) While neither pure instinct action nor reflex action can be wrong – but never the less (very) harmful[6] – symbolically conditioned actions can be wrong or right since they are based on the fallible perceptive mode of symbolic reference. "[S]ymbolically conditioned action can be wrong, in the sense that it may arise from a false symbolic analysis of causal efficacy." (1985, 81) And: "This analysis may be right or wrong, according as it does, or does not, conform to the actual distribution of efficacious bodies." (1985, 80) Whether the undertaken symbolic analysis of the contents presented in the perceptive mode of causal efficacy is correct or not, usually cannot be tested "apart from the indirect check of pragmatic consequences – in other words, either survival-value or self-satisfaction" (1985, 80). Although the introduction of the possibility of error may seem to be unfortunate, in fact is a highly valuable advance: error becomes possible because the organism by use of symbols is able to disconnect itself from the iron grip of immediately preceding environment. The use of symbols opens the possibility of thinking and so allows exploring different *possible* routes of *future* action. "Thus mankind by means of its elaborate system of symbolic transference can achieve miracles of sensitiveness to a distant environment, and to a problematic future." (1985, 87) So symbolism opens the way for thinking and problem solving, the highest form of learning. Thinking is based on "a chain of

---

'condition' is used in Whitehead's broader and weaker, non-behavioristic sense of 'bringing about' or 'influencing'.

[6] What is classically conditioned is conditioned - for good or for bad; if the conditioned response is right or wrong (in the sense of adequacy or inadequacy to the environment) is not in question. The conditioned 'habit' response was acquired and is present now – full stop. The phobic patient fears cats; be this fear adequate or not.

derivations of symbol from symbol whereby finally the local relations, between the final symbol and the ultimate meaning, are entirely lost. Thus these derivative symbols, obtained as it were by arbitrary association, are really the results of reflex action suppressing the intermediate portions of the chain." (1985, 83) Language is such a system of symbols. It is an important tool for thinking. Symbol systems such as "[c]odes, rules of behavior, canons of art" aim at the promotion of favorable life conditions. But as life and its demands change "all such rules and canons require revision" (1985, 88). Such revisions "wreck the society in which they occur" (1985, 88) but are never the less necessary if the society is to be saved form "slow atrophy of a life stiffed by useless shadows." (1985, 88)

Now, when symbolically mediated activities are repeated again and again they become habits which can be and finally are performed automatically. Such routines can be conducted without any conscious awareness of the activities themselves: they have become blind habits. Driving a car is such a routine: rarely we pay attention and are aware that we shift a gear and even less so about the movements we have to make in order to achieve the gear shift. The same is true of using the breaks when we approach a familiar crossing near our home. In such cases symbolical activities relapse to the level of reflex actions. The familiar sight of the crossing automatically (i.e. implicitly or unconsciously) triggers the movement of pressing at the break; and one movement of the driver automatically brings about the next move when we drive the car. It cannot be doubted that such automatization of behavior holds great advantages. We can (and must) focus our attention on the traffic instead of the break and the gear. Only in exceptional moments, for instance in dangerous situations, our conscious attention is focused on the ongoing automatic processes again. The relapse to the execution of such routines also is possible in mathematics and symbolic logic. A simple proof can often be performed automatically by professionals. And so their limited mental capacities are free to focus on different aspects. It is this capacity which distinguishes chess champions from average chess players. And vice versa (and also of great importance for education!) "reflex action is hindered by thought, which inevitably promotes the prominence of symbolic reference." (1985, 81) A pianist who has to consciously reflect on the next move of one of his fingers will hardly play at a high level.

So usually we live our lives by use of (classically and instrumentally conditioned) reflex actions or reflex actions which are the result of a relapse from once symbolically and thereby consciously entertained activities. Only temporarily we consciously think and approach problems with full awareness. And even when we were successful in solving a problem and coping with a new challenging situation our activities sooner or later either will be forgotten (if we do not practice the newly acquired skill) or will – the faster the more it is practiced – sink back on a sub-conscious automatic reflexive level of acting. As Whitehead has put it: "When routine is perfect, [conscious] understanding can be eliminated, except such minor flashes of intelligence as are required to deal with familiar accidents, such as a flooded mine, a prolonged drought, or an epidemic of influenza. A system will be the product of intelligence. But when the adequate routine is established, intelligence vanishes, and the system is maintained by coordination of conditioned reflexes." (1967b, 90) Since social life presupposes stability and since routines produce stability and maintain it, societies rest on routine. (1967b, 90-91) Research has even shown that sub-conscious routines in certain types of complex tasks outdo conscious problem solving activities. (see for instance: Reber 1989, Berry & Dienes 1993)

Now, when turning back to the topic of (higher forms of) learning it is important to keep in mind that Whitehead's symbolic theory allows for accounting of primitive forms of learning such as classical and instrumental conditioning processes. This implies that Whitehead's learning approach can account for behaviorist learning theories. This certainly is one of its major advantages. However, we will now have a closer look at the higher forms of learning which involve consciousness: symbolically or cognitively conditioned actions. A prototypic case of this kind of learning is *problem solving* which aims at understanding why the problem has evolved and why a certain strategic activity leads to a solution; it does not consist of blind trial and error processes, although they may also reach the goal set. In his educational essays Whitehead primarily is concerned with such higher type learning. Such problem solving activities presuppose at least the dawning of conscious thought since the new situation or problem is actively explored for relevant elements.

1.2 Of Cycles and Cycles of Cycles (Stages)

Single higher cyclic learning processes, according to Whitehead, form the basis of larger cycles of mental development; the former therefore are the organic units of mental growth. "Such a cycle is a unit cell [...]." (1967a, 31) According to Whitehead "the development of mentality exhibits itself as a rhythm involving an interweaving of cycles, the whole process being dominated by a greater cycle of the same general character as its minor eddies." (1967a, 27) The full life-span of man can be conceived as the biggest such cycle: "The whole period of growth from infancy to manhood forms one grand cycle. Its stage of romance stretches across the first dozen years of life, its stage of precision comprises the whole school period of secondary education and its stage of generalization is the period of entrance into manhood." (1967a, 25)

Within this great *life*-cycle there are minor cycles (eddies) which we will term 'stages' in order to omit confusion which easily would occur if we would use the term 'cycle' at different levels. The stages show the same basic characteristics as the minor cycles it consists of. Whitehead distinguishes the following stages (cycles of cycles): the first stage is that of infancy ranging from about the age of one to eight years (although Whitehead does not give any definite year for the start of this first cycle, whereas he explicitly mentions the age of eight years when he talks about the start of the next cycle of adolescence (see: 1967a, 21)). The cycle of infancy starts with the romantic phase of "awaking to the apprehension of objects and to the apprehension of their connexions" (1967a, 19) and turns into the phase of precision by "mastering spoken language as an instrument for classifying its contemplation of objects and for strengthening its apprehension of emotional relations with other things." (1967a, 19) And by applying language to new settings the stage of generalization is reached. So Whitehead's stage of infancy is roughly identical with Jean Piaget's two stages of pre-operations and concrete operations (Piaget 1968, 17-38) which often are referred to as only one such stage or with Kurt W. Fischer's tire of representation (Fischer & Rose 1998, 58; Fischer & Bidell 1998, 102f) who also integrates Piaget's pre-operations and concrete stages into one single stage. This stage according to Whitehead is "the only cycle of progress which we can observe in its pure natural state." (1967a, 19) And there is one important thing about this stage toward which Whitehead draws our attention: in almost all cases it produces "complete success." (1967a, 20) So Whitehead suggests that educational scientists should study especially this period of development in order to be able to detect why it is so successful compared to the later periods of learning. This stage therefore "does offer food for reflection" (1967a, 20) for the psychological and educational scientists. Knowing why this stage is so successful should enable us to design the later stages according to this first stage of infancy. Whitehead offers a few hints why this stage leads to full success despite the fact that "the new-borne baby looks a most unpromising subject for intellectual progress when we remember the difficulty of the task before it." (1967a, 20) First he generally claims that "nature, in the form of the surrounding circumstances, sets it [the child] a task for which the normal development of its brain is exactly fitted." (1967a, 20) And the environment 'fits' the natural development of the brain because it shows three major characteristics: first (1) it offers cycles of learning,[7] second (2) these repeated but varied cycles continuously open the possibility of success and third (3) it offers a massive concentration of verbal stimuli. So according to Whitehead it is *rhythm, opportunity for success* and *concentration*, instead of "an unrhythmic collection of distracting scraps" (1967a, 21) of distinct subjects, which bring about the success of this first stage. Form this *descriptive* analysis Whitehead draws his *prescriptive* conclusions[8]. There are three characteristics

---

[7] It is interesting to notice that there does exist such a concept of ,learning cycles'. It was developed by the physicist Robert Karplus (Karplus 1977, Karplus & Karplus 1970, see also: Lawson 1995) on the basis of Jean Piaget's genetic structuralism. Its major application was to science teaching. Like Whitehead's cyclic concept Karplus' concept also consists of three phases which he termed 'Exploration', 'Concept Introduction'/'Explanation' and finally 'Expansion'/'Application'. These phases correspond to Whitehead's three stages of a learning cycle.

[8] Of course, I order to correctly obtain a prescriptive statement from premises, the premises must at least include one *prescriptive statement (norm or value judgement)*. In Whitehead's case it is obvious, although he does not mention this explicitly, that the prescriptive premise can be formulated in the following way: 'If a certain stage of learning and development with its specific characteristics is successful, one should apply the characteristics of this stage to other stages (in order to be just as successful in these stages).'

The full argument has the form of a *modus ponens* and therefore runs as follows:

which teaching processes have to show (according to Whitehead): (a) he demands not to teach too many subjects (1967a, 2), (b) pleads for concentration within each subject on central core concepts (1967a, 2) and c) points at the necessity that learning situation must offer continuous possibilities of reaching success.

The second stage that can be distinguished within the whole life-cycle is the "stage of adolescence" (1967a, 21); its phase of romance roughly falls "between the ages of eight and twelve or thirteen." (1967a, 21) from thirteen to fifteen the child goes through the stage of adolescent precision; from about fifteen to seventeen, eighteen years the child dwells in the phase of generalization of the adolescent stage. However, this is a very raw description; the years being only orientation marks and not indicating definitive limits. Whitehead further distinguishes two sub-stages within the wider adolescent stage: the 'language stage' and the 'science sage'. Both stages overlap but their starting points and subsequent cyclic unfolding is staggered: While the language stage can be roughly equated with the adolescent phase described above, the science stage overlaps with the language stage: when the child is in the precision phase of the language stage the science stage is about to start with its phase of romance or freedom; and when the language cycle turns into its phase of generalization the science cycle passes over into the phase of precision which finally is followed again by a phase of generalization (from about eighteen years onward).

Whitehead does not concentrate on the further cyclic development. Instead he generally comments that "at this period the problem is too individual, or at least breaks up into too many cases, to be susceptible of broad general treatment." (1967a, 25)

It is interesting to note here that Whitehead speaks of 'too many cases' into which the ongoing cyclic processes (stages) split. And since Whitehead has shown in his analysis of the adolescent stage that there

---

1) If a certain stage of learning and development with its characteristics is successful, one should apply the characteristics of this successful stage to other stages (in order to be just as successful in these stages).

2) The stage of infancy which is characterized by rhythmic learning cycles which continually offer possibilities for experiences of success is successful.

.: Therefore one should generate rhythmic learning cycles at other stages as well.

may well be overlapping cycles each starting at different times one can speculate that this process may increase as the process becomes more differentiated. So Whitehead does not hold a uniform linear stage theory of development – like many of the followers of Jean Piaget – which maintains that a child reaching one stage automatically acts in all domains according to the features (competences) of this stage. On the contrary, he explicitly expresses his conviction that "[t]he interior spiritual life of man is a *web of many strands. They do not all grow together by uniform extension.*" (1967a, 27 italics added) So Whitehead's conception does not only allow to account for inter-individual differences but also for intra-individual situation or domain specific differences in behavior and thought (information processing). It will be shown (2.2) that this position comes very close to Kurt W. Fischer's dynamic skill theory.

Finally we have to turn our attention to the fact that Whitehead was well aware that he only provided the 'broad speculative sketch', illustrated only by a few examples. Given his conception of a mutual heuristic as well as mutual critical interaction between the general scheme of philosophy (mainly metaphysics) and the more special schemes of the sciences (see for detailed presentations of this mutual relevance Riffert & Cobb 2003; Riffert 2004) it goes without saying that Whitehead advocated that, for detailed analyses, the singe sciences relevant to the problems in question play the crucial role. So for instance when discussing the concepts of space, time, causality and permanent substance from a physical as well as psychological point of view he declared after giving the general outline: "Here the experimental psychologist steps in. We cannot get away from him." (1967a, 161)

That he held the same position concerning his sketch about the cyclic nature of learning and developmental stages becomes clear when he self-critically remarks near the end of his article 'The Rhythm of Education': „Perhaps I have misconstrued the usual phenomena. It is very likely that I have so failed, for the evidence is complex and difficult." (1967a, 27) But after admitting possible errors *in detail* he continues by claiming to be right concerning the fundamental idea that learning and development do not advance in a linear way but are essentially rhythmic (cyclic): "But do not let any failure in this respect prejudice the main point which I am here to enforce. It is that the development of mentality exhibits itself as a rhythm involving an interweaving of cy cles, the whole process being dominated by a greater cycle of the same general character as its minor eddies." (1967a, 27)

All this opens the possibility for a fruitful dialogue between Whiteheads general position and non-linear or cyclical developmental scientific research positions. In the next section such a heuristic-critical comparison between Whitehead's cyclic theory of learning and development and the micro-genetic and dynamic skill approach will be undertaken.

2. Dynamic Skills Theory and the Microgenetic Approach

Before going into detailed comparison a broader presentation of the basic assumptions underlying dynamic skill theory and micro-genetic approach is in place. This broad sketch is necessary to show that the results of the more detailed comparison are not arbitrary and superficial but rests on a congruence of the basic assumptions.

During the first half of the twentieth century behaviorist and psychodynamic (psychoanalysis, analytical psychology, individual psychology) theories dominated psychology and education, especially since the decline of Gestalt psychology. Jean Piaget's genetic structuralism was an exception but made its break through not long before the sixties of the twentieth century. His revolutionary work certainly was one of the most important agents to bring about the so-called 'cognitive turn'. During the last two, three decades Piaget's work has been elaborated and critically evaluated. Especially his claim that development proceeds in a linear and universal stage-like way (Piaget 1970a) has come under severe attack. One important consequences of these attacks was the development a Neo-Piagetian approach; one of the most promising developments within these new developments is Kurt Fischer's dynamic skill theory and – congenial to it – the elaboration of the micro-genetic methodology (Granot, Fischer & Parziale 2002).

Kurt Fischer considers his *dynamic developmental skill theory* as "part of a *wider movement in contemporary science*: away from the traditional static, abstract models of reality toward viewpoints that capture the deep complexity, relationship, and dynamism inherent in behavioral, mental, and social phenomena." (Fischer & Bidell 1998, 471 italics added) So Fischer, in contrast to traditional conceptions, defines 'psychological structures' as "the organizational property of dynamic systems of activity" (Fischer & Bidell 1998, 471). So living systems are defined in a radical functional way: "All living systems – whether biological, psychological or sociological – must be organized as function. A living organism that becomes sufficiently disorganized dies." (Fischer & Bidell 1998, 472) Very interesting from a White-headian point of view is how Fischer and Bidell conceive these 'functions': functional relationships are seen to be "*intrinsic* relation-ships" (Fischer & Bidell 1998, 472 italics added). But functional systems (skills, cells, organs, …) not only are interdependent but are "*interparticipatory*" (Fischer & Bidell 1998, 479 italics added); they "participate in one another" (Fischer & Bidell 1998, 479). Such inter-participatory functions are "central parts of living systems, especially complex systems such as human beings." (Firscher & Bidell 1998, 479) It makes no sense to consider systems as 'functioning outside the context' of surrounding systems: "Living systems die when they are cut off from the other systems with which they *interparticipate*." (Fischer & Bidell 1998, 479 italics added) And Fischer and Bidell go on by pointing out that, due to this interparticipative relationship, any "system […] is composed of multiple subsystems whose *boundaries defy definition*." (Fischer & Bidell 1998, 479 italics added)

Interparticipation of systems further implies the necessity for hier-archical structure. "Thus, the very process of creating new systems through self-organizing coordination leads to a multileveled hierarchi-cal structuring of living systems. Note also that if systems were not integrative – that is, if they were not intrinsic related and interpartici-patory – they would not need to be hierarchically arranged." (Fischer & Bidell 1998, 480)

Interparticipation also has consequences for traditional psychome-trics since the assumptions underlying these measurement tools (for instance: the isolation and discreteness of variables) contradict the basic assumptions of the developmental skill theory: "The linear mod-els of psychometrics, experimental psychology, and of behavior genet-ics treat all behaviors as arising from linear combinations of inputs, tasks, prior conditions, or heredity and environment […] Person and environment are partitioned into separate groups of factors instead of being treated as dynamic collaborators in producing activities." (Fisch-er & Bidell 1998, 476)

Now, these traditional assumptions of traditional psychometrics are not only wrong but, according to Fischer and Bidell, lead straight to reductionism – or better: they are reductionist in their essence. Fischer and Bidell reject reductionism because of its "extracting component processes or properties from the context of their actual relationships in real natural or social systems and examining them in isolation." (Fischer Bidell 1998, 475) New (non-reductionist) measurement tools which are context-sensitive and do justice to the idiosyncratical organization of the 'research objects' (i.e. single persons and groups of persons) of measurement must be developed (see for instance: van Geert 2002). A first important step in that direction is to do away with reductionist metaphors in research. Development traditionally was described by the ladder metaphor (which many developmental psychologists used and favored; Piaget is but one, albeit important proponent here). This metaphor triggers the false impression of a linear process of continuing 'step by step' growth. According to Fischer and Bidell this is a static and determinist metaphor which makes it difficult to explain "the role of constructive activity or differential contextual support because there appears to be no choice of where to go from each step." (Fischer & Bidell 1998, 473) This misleading metaphor has to be substituted by the '*web*' metaphor: many interwoven strands develop in an interparticipatory way at different speeds.

Since according to Fischer and Bidell every system is actively functioning, the mind too cannot be conceived as a passive "container for knowledge" (Fischer & Bidell 1998, 474). It is not the case that the contents which we "know are discrete objects." (Fischer & Bidell 1998, 474) Such conceptions lead to wrong, yet even disastrous consequences: "They treat communication as the transfer of objects from one person to another, as if static objects are being sent through a conduit such as pipe or telephone line. In both communication and education, this metaphor often leads people to believe that telling someone an item of information (giving them an object) is sufficient to communicate it and even to teach it." (Fischer & Bidell 1998, 474) Learning is one of the fundamental mental functions. As such it does not consist of passive registration of static objects that were externally put forward to a perceiver. Learning in the contrary is an active, constructive act on the side of the learner. Static notions such as 'passive mind' or 'static and other abstract notions structure' are reifications which cannot do justice to the dynamic that goes on throughout reality. Instructional designs which are based on such passive conceptions of learning are doomed to failure from the start.

Micro-developmental analysis is a promising tool for describing such processes of constructing solutions in problem solving tasks. Micro-development is defined by its proponents as the "process of change in abilities, knowledge, and understanding during short time spans." (Granott & Parziale 2002, 1) Micro time spans range from months to minutes or even seconds. The shortness of the duration allows for detailed observation of the dynamic *change* taking place and not only of the static *outcome*. Contrary to traditional pre-post-test designs and even contrary to longitudinal studies which only provide isolated snapshots, by micro-developmental analysis, so it is argued, the *evolving process* of change itself, i.e. "the 'how' of development and learning" (Granott & Parziale 2002, 1) comes into focus and can be made explicit. Innovative technologies (like videotaping (see: Granott 1991) or the use of notebooks (see: Gelman, Romo & Francis 2002)) play an important role in this new approach.

2.1 Grantott's Study on 'Weired Creatures'

Nira Granott, one of the proponents of the dynamic skill theory and micro-developmental approach, has undertaken an interesting study on spontaneous knowledge construction (problem solving). The major results will be presented here and compared with Whitehead's position outlined above. By showing parallels between the two accounts some empirical support for Whitehead's philosophical-speculative position is hoped to be obtained.

Thirty five adults, divided into three groups, were confronted with "ill-defined problems in an environment with materials unknown to them. Thus they had to define the problem as well as the procedures they could use." (Granott 1991, 3, section: method). Each group met twice in two consecutive days. The meetings lasted about one and a half hour each. The first half of each meeting was dedicated to explorational activities while in the second half the participants discussed their experiences and hypotheses in the group. The participants further were asked to write notes about their experiences and findings during the exploration phase. They also were videotaped during the full duration of both meetings. It was the participants' task to find out the way six "weird creatures" (Granott 1991, 3 section: materials) functioned. These so-called 'weird creatures' were built of a special kind of Lego bricks, so-called "Braitenberg bricks" (Braitenberg 1984). These Braitenberg bricks were developed by Valentino Braitenberg at the Lego-Logo-Laboratory of the Epistemology and Learning group at the MIT. The small creatures which were built of these bricks were able to exert quite complex 'behavior': they "moved, changed directions, made noise, stopped from time to time and started moving again [...] However the causes of these patterns of 'behavior' were not obvious." (Grannott 1991, 3, section: materials). The six different 'weird creatures' were put in an environment with different stimuli to which their sensors were sensitive (sounds, light, shadow, tactile stimuli, ...). The participants could take up, manipulate and observe these creatures. In one corner of the room, extra parts of which the weird creatures were built of, divided into small drawers with labelled categories, were available for further 'investigations'.

Granott in her study found three phases concerning the way the participants dealt with the weird creatures. "The different phases of exploration were expressed in the way the participants interacted with the Weird Creatures." (Granott 1991, section: results) Granott termed them (1) the 'Behavioral Phase', the 'Close up Investigation Phase' and the 'Piecemeal In-Depth Investigation Phase'. (Granott 1991, section: A. Different Phases of Exploration) These phases also correspond to different levels of explanation.

Concerning the first phase of exploration and level of explanation she writes: "In the first phase, which corresponded to the 'behavioral' exploration, the participants' discourse was related to the global behavior of the Weird Creatures, and was of a descriptive quality. In this phase the participants were mainly describing the 'behavior' of the Weird Creature: – 'It's following the light on the wall.' 'The reflection?' (I.1.4) – 'At first it seemed pretty random, and then it became clear it wasn't random at all. It would go forward, hit a wall, and go backward, somebody would make a sound , it would change direction. One pattern we found was that first it seemed to go back a certain distance ...' (I.1.5) – 'It circles until it finds the light' (II.1.5)" (Grannott 1991, section: B. Corresponding Levels of Explanation)

At the next level of explanation, the 'functioning level' which corresponds to the close-up investigation phase "the participants' discourse was pointing to more specific functions in the Weird Creatures'

responses. (Granott 1991, section: B. Corresponding Levels of Explanation) A few examples must suffice to illustrate this phase: "'It wasn't
as sensitive to light ... Light controls direction but not movement' ... 'It
seems to escape the light.' (III.1.7-8) 'Something relating to light is
controlling that machine, that's very clear. It has some mood, or mode,
or ... that is happy feeling or blue feeling that after some 5 or 4 or 5
seconds that hits the wall it goes backwards, and another rule, in that
time the machine behaves another way, after it hits the wall. So he's
afraid of something so he'll go out (away) of the wall ...' (III.1.7)"
(Granott 1991, section: B. Corresponding Levels of Explanation).

At the third level of explanation the participants' discourse was
increasingly focused on the relations between the single 'behavior
units' of the weird creatures "seeing the Weird Creature as a system
combined of these parts" (Granott 1991, section: B. Corresponding
Levels of Explanation): "'It seems like words in a sentence, they only
make sense together ... It seems like there's a couple of things I have to
think about. One is what is each brick and what it's supposed to do, and
two is the sequence they're hooked in ...' (I.3.1) – 'The next brick I
want to work on is the flip-flop, to see what it does. And I'm worried
that it might have to be in connection to something else, but we'll see.'
(I.3.4) – 'I know it has to be a complete circuit.' (I. 3.2)" (Granott
1991, section: B. Corresponding Levels of Explanation).

Granott sums up the results of the experiment conducted with these
weird [Lego-]creatures in the following way: "In the first phase
subjects' understanding was global and *implicit*. They considered the
weird creatures as a whole, and explored its behavior. Their explanations were *fuzzy* and had a psychological character. In the second
phase, subjects' knowledge evolved through *progressive differentiation*
and *more explicit understanding*. They noticed *more subtle details* and
were able to *distinguish phenomena unnoticed before*. They also
started focusing on *specific components* (bricks) and their respective
functions. In the third phase, subjects started to *integrate* the components and to *synthesize* them into a single unit. They started to see
relations and connections among the bricks and to understand the
weird creatures as a composition. [...] Their knowledge about the
Weird Creatures seemed to *evolve from fuzzy, diffuse and implicit, to
differentiated, analytic and more explicit*." (Granott 1991, section:
Discussion, italics added) Whitehead put it in a very similar way when
he wrote: "The first procedure of the mind in a new environment is a

somewhat discursive activity amid a welter of ideas and experience. It is a process of discovery, a process of becoming used to curious thoughts, of shaping questions, of seeking for answers, of devising new experiences of noticing what happens as the result of new ventures." (1967a, 32) Or: "There is the general apprehension of some topic in its vague possibilities, the mastery of the relevant details, and finally the putting of the whole subject together in the light of the relevant knowledge." (1967a, 38) This correspondence between Whitehead's and Granott's characterization of genuine learning processes substantiates, I think, that Whitehead's philosophic speculations about the cyclic nature of learning processes is correct.

In what follows I shall present an example on how research can build on this quite general characterization of a genuine learning process. Concerning the context of this paper this means: I will show how creative elaborations of Whitehead's concept of learning can add to our understanding of the learning process.

Nira Granott, Kurt Fischer and Jim Parziale have undertaken a closer look at such genuine learning processes. Their aim was to investigate in more detail "how new abilities [are] created out of existing, less advanced abilities" (Granott, Fischer & Parziale 2002, 131). They have tried to do so by using Fischer's concept of 'bridging' (1998, 518-520). 'Bridging' is a concept which aims at explaining *how* new advanced knowledge is built from less advanced knowledge. The underlying concept accounts for the "process of leaping into the unknown" (Granott, Fischer & Parziale 2002, 131). The term 'bridging' is used as a metaphor referring to the fact that people can act at different levels of knowledge; more particularly it points to an activity which, starting from a low level, establishes "a target level of skill or understanding which lies unconstructed beyond their current level of functioning" (Fischer 1998, 519). They do so by inserting marker shells which indicate the target. These shells, of course, are mainly ill defined, vague place holders "that people use to direct their own learning and development toward achieving these targets." (Granott, Fischer & Parziale 2002, 131) It guides the search for new information and the construction of knowledge which gradually 'fills' the place holder (marker shell); "The shells do not contain the relevant knowledge yet, but they outline it." (Granott, Fischer & Parziale 2002, 131) It functions more like an attractor towards a vaguely defined aim.

An example taken from Granott, Fischer, and Parziale (2002, 140-

148) may illustrate this concept (using the formal language developed by Kurt Fischer in his dynamic skill theory (1980)): Kevin and Marvin, two students, are confronted with a weird creature which was sensitive to light stimuli; the setting is the same as in Granott's study described above. At their first encounter with the creature they observed it and took it in their hands. When Marvin put his hands around the weird creature "Kevin commented: 'Looks like we got a reaction there.'" (Granott, Fischer & Parziale 2002, 141) Now what happened is that Kevin created a marker shell of the form $[(X_a)$ reaction $(Y_b)]$. The whole expression (= everything between the two cornered brackets) denotes the marker shell. This shell is very vague. It only contains *one* explicit element, the expression 'reaction', which indicates that there should be some yet unknown cause(s) and effect(s) – presented in the shell by the components (X_a) and (Y_b). Although the components X_a and Y_b are still empty, a vague target level is already established by this shell. Our attention is directed at searching for causes and effects and a gradual process of filling the shell is triggered. However, Granott's, Fischer's and Parziale's use of the term 'empty' is misleading: it evokes an impression as if there is nothing there. But this is not the case. It is more the other way round: there are great numbers of possible elements in the environment which at this point of investigation all fit equally well for playing the roles of causes and effects. But neither the concrete cause nor the concrete effect is specified yet. To term this state (although not completely unjustified) 'empty' is not very fortunate. The terms 'unspecified' or 'vague' seem to better describe the situation. This becomes obvious when the authors compare the bridging process to drafting: "Like a bridging shell, the document's outline is still missing its content, which is not spelled out yet." But it is not 'spelled out yet', we may add, because it is only vaguely, maybe even implicitly (i.e. sub-consciously) present at the start of the drafting process – the sheets may be empty but the writer usually is not; he fights with fleeting thoughts and escaping ideas present in one moment, gone in the next.[9]

Out of the vaguely apprehended possibilities a single specific instance is 'sculptured out'. The shell may now gradually be filled:

---

[9] At the end of their paper one can observe that the authors increase to replace the term 'empty' by the term 'vague' (2002, 150, 151).

$$[X_a \text{ \underline{reaction} } \text{Creature}_{\text{change motor reaction (stop)}}].$$

The learner now may specify if his or her guess is correct or whether different or additional changes have occurred. In a next step s/he may search for the cause. This may lead to the following shell:

$$[\text{Shadow}_{\text{on top of the creature}} \text{ \underline{reaction} } \text{Creature}_{\text{change of motor reaction}}].$$

So the learner finally has established a full – or better: fully specified – shell.

By elaborating the phases of genuine learning processes as proposed by Granott's original research, with the help of the bridging concept the authors take a big step towards making the results applicable. They mention the school as one field of such an application: "At school as well, teachers utilize bridging as learning tool. Using bridging terms, the teachers introduce key words that guide the children's activity and discussion. Using bridging questions, they formulate questions that lead students to make statements they have not made before. Using bridging formats, they begin a statement or an activity and ask students to complete it. Using bridging intentions, they indicate intentions that operate as goals for the students' activity. Using bridging recasts, they reformulate students' answers, providing more advanced knowledge. Teachers making comments that suggest problems or hint at solutions in ways that *require students to* formulate the problems or find solutions. Through such bridging shells, they lead students to construct new knowledge." (Granott, Fischer & Parziale 2002, 150)[10]

So it seems that elaborating and creatively differentiating the dynamic skill theory will lead to fertile results. But let us finally turn from the single learning cycles to the cycles of cycles i.e. the stages of mental development.

---

[10] Whitehead terms this process of leading the students towards newconcept construction 'luring'. For more details on this process see John Cobb's paper in this book.

2. 2. Kurt W. Fischer on Stages of Mental Development

So far we have seen that according to Whitehead the basic cycles of learning are on the one hand interwoven with each other – there are many different strands of learning processes – and on the other hand these strands are nested in larger cycles. "It is that the development of mentality exhibits itself as a rhythm involving an interweaving of cycles, the whole process being dominated by a greater cycle of the same general character as its minor eddies." (1967a, 27)

Kurt Fischer has come to the same conclusion on the basis of empirical research: "This reorganization and simplification [which takes place at each newly developed level] is nested in a longer-term cycle, moving through four different forms of action and thought called tiers." (Fischer & Rose 1998, 59) These four tires (see Figure 1), however, are only present under *optimal* learning conditions when the student for instance gets support in the form of modeling or scaffolding. (see for instance: Fischer & Rose 2001) If a student does not get support and therefore is not in the situation to perform on an optimal level s/he may show set backs in his/her performance (as Vygotsky (1978) had expected). "Development has strong stage-like properties under conditions of high support, but not under conditions of low support." (Fischer & Immordino-Yang 2002, 14) So under everyday conditions the picture of mental development is very complex allowing for no simple stage-like explanations. This may be the reason why Whitehead wrote concerning his attempt to identify cycles in metal development: „Perhaps I have misconstrued the usual phenomena. It is very likely that I have so failed, for the evidence is complex and difficult." (1967a, 27) Humans develop along different strands which are interwoven to form webs so that under normal conditions set backs may easily occur which over shadows the stage-form which would be visible under optimal conditions.

Never the less it is interesting to compare Whitehead's speculations about the big cycles of mental development with Fischer four tires (see Figure 1).

In doing so it is interesting to see that Whitehead's first cycle – the cycle of infancy – corresponds to Fischer's first three cycles 'Rflexes', 'Action', and 'Representation' while his cycle of adolescence corresponds to Fischer's tire of 'Abstraction'.

So Fischer's (as well as Piaget's) stage theory is more differentiated than Whitehead's as far as the start of mental development is concerned. And in addition Whitehead does not give any explicit information when his first cycle starts: at birth, at the age of one or two?

Comparison between Fischer's Four Tires of Mental Development and Whitehead's Three Major Cycles of Learning

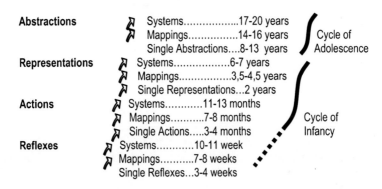

Fig. 1: The four tiers of (learning-)development (adapted form Fischer and Rose (1998)). The tiers are: reflexes, actions, representations and abstractions. At the right three curved lines are added, indicating the three major learning cycles which Whitehead explicitly discussed: the cycles of infancy, of language and of science.

On the other hand, Fischer's tire of 'Abstraction' corresponds very closely to Whitehead's cycle of adolescence. However, we have seen that Whitehead introduces a further distinction to this cycle: the language and the science cycle. Here I cannot deal with this problem in detail but I would suggest to follow Fischer's empirically corroborated theory as far as details of developmental sequences are concerned. This suggestion is supported by Whitehead's remark that he may "have misconstrued the usual phenomena" and that it is "very likely" that he has "failed, for the evidence is complex and difficult." (quotations: 1967a, 27) The differences may have their source in the fact that Whitehead's position seems to be derived from observations of everyday observations while Fischer's concept of tires refers to the development under optimal (supporting) conditions.[11]

In Fischer's account within the major cycles of development (tires) there are minor cycles (eddies) embedded. Each tier (major cycle) itself consists of minor cycles, which are termed "levels" by Fischer (Fischer & Bidell 1998, 102f). For instance the 'action' or 'sensori-motor' tier consists of sensori-motor units (=lowest sensori-motor level), of mappings of sensori-motor (=middle sensori-motor level), of sensori-motor systems (=more advanced sensory-motor level) and finally of sensori-motor systems of systems. These last 'systems of systems' at the sensori-motor level on the next tier, the representative tier, functions as the basic unit i.e. a simple representative units which in other minor cycles are elaborated into representative mappings which in turn are developed into representative systems and representative systems of systems. Now these representative systems of systems on the next tier again function as the basic starting unit.

Further, within each level of each tier there are single concrete learning cycles such as those which are characterized by Granott (see above 2.1). But also each developmental level above concrete learning cycles can be described by Granott's characterization of a learning cycle. For example at the reflex level the learner first only has vague of the whole mainly grasping only single elements. Then these elements are explored and partially integrated into what Fischer terms 'mappings'. Finally by the full grasp of their interconnections these mappings are integrated into a whole, Fischer's reflex systems which form the starting point of a new learning cycle.

This view that each bigger cycle consists of minor learning cycles is in full correspondence with Whitehead.

---

[11] It may well be that Whitehead was misled by his observations as far as the language cycle is concerned. His language cycle may well start at the age of about two years and end at the age of eight. If so, it would correspond to Fischer's tire of representation. Since language his one of the most important tools for creating representations this may well be the case.

3. Conclusion

In this paper I tried to provide some evidence that there are far reaching parallels between Whitehead's philosophically inspired reflections about mental development and learning and the empirically grounded dynamic skill theory.

Now, even if one may concede that this attempt succeeded one still may ask what the use of such a comparison may be.

In answering this question it is helpful to draw our attention to the fact that according to Whitehead there is a mutual interplay between the broader schemes of philosophy and the more narrow schemes of science (1958, 77). This interplay consists of mutual criticisms and of mutual enhancement.

If the broader and more narrow schemes do not fit together there is need of reversion of at least one of the two schemes – either the (broad) philosophical, or the (narrow) scientific or the both of them. This is essentially important for a philosophy since a philosophical system, due to its general and abstract character, hardly is empirically testable without its connection to the empirically confirmed single sciences. But with the 'interposition' of the scientific schemes an indirect empirical confirmation of the philosophic schemes becomes possible. (for details see: Riffert 2004)

On the other hand the sciences also profit from such an interconnection with a more general philosophic scheme: If the two schemes fit together, philosophy provides a) a broad general outlook for the connected science and b) the basis for rational handling of values and norms. Both aspects are essential for education.

First, education is no pure descriptive science; it also is an applied science – a *social technology* if you like – which intentionally aims at changing the (social) world (including the behaviors and the dispositions of students) towards some *positive* goal. The critical discussion and rational foundation of such positive goals is an essentially ethical/moral task. Therefore education, more than many other sciences, is in need of a justifiable treatment of values and norms (see: Frankena 1965). Despite the fact that Whitehead did not explicitly develop an comprehensive ethical theory, it never the less is possible to do so on the basis of his metaphysics and his frequent comments on its implications for ethics; and important steps in that direction have already been taken (see for instance: Birch & Cobb 1981, Riffert 2000, Sayer 2000).

Second, education cannot be content with producing specialists. On the contrary education always has to aim at helping the students (may they be children or grown ups) to become *wise*. And since according to Whitehead "[w]isdom is the way in which knowledge is held" (1967a 30) this implies a general outlook which transcends the narrow specialism and offers a wide perspective necessary for regulating specialism. Such a general outlook can only be provided by philosophy.[12]

Further the integration of a scientific theory into a philosophical approach such as Whitehead's opens possibilities for enhanced interdisciplinary research. In the first place, for instance, the mutual understanding will be facilitated between those different disciplines which are integrated into the same philosophical scheme because the philosophical scheme offers a uniform terminology. Further there is a basic outlook including basic principles which are shared by those scientific disciplines integrated into a certain philosophical scheme. This will enhance mutual understanding between proponents of different disciplines.

Another advantage, especially concerning modern constructivist learning theories, is the possibility to connect them to more traditional, behaviorist approaches of learning such as classical and instrumental conditioning. In a Whiteheadian framework these theories do not simply isolated theories which contradict each other but can be integrated into a more comprehensive approach and thereby are implicitly redefined. Such an integration of behaviorist and constructivist approaches is not only theoretically important: in the concrete everyday work of teachers the use of both, behaviorist and constructivist instruments, often is necessary to achieve an optimal result. So George Bear (1998) when discussing instruments which teachers have to deal with the problem of discipline calls for integration of both fundamental approaches because otherwise teachers might no be willing to accept those instruments which do not stem from the one approach they are trained in: "Unless integrated with a more comprehensive program with components more consistent with their constructivist beliefs about

---

[12] During the last two decades wisdom as one of the most important educational aims has come into focus of developmental and educational scientists again after being neglected for decades. The two major proponents who also try to investigate this topic empirically are Yale Psychologist Robert Sternberg (1990, 2003) and Paul Baltes, director of the Max Planck Institute for Educational Research, Berlin (1990, 2000).

the active and responsible role of the learner, today's teachers are likely to continue to reject operant behavioral strategies, especially as the primary or singular approach to school discipline." (1998, 732) Whitehead's philosophically based learning theory offers such an integrative frame.

In short it can be summarized that Whitehead's approach opens rich and promising possibilities for further educational research.

Bibliography
Baltes, P. B. & Smith, J. (1990): Towards a Psychology of Wisdom and Its Ontogenesis. In: R. J. Sternberg (Ed.): *Wisdom – Its Nature, Origins, and Development.* Cambridge: Cambridge University Press, 87-120.

Baltes, P. B. & Staudinger, U. M. (2000): Wisdom: A Metaheusristic (Pragmatic) to Orchestrate Mind and Virtue Toward Excellence. *American Psychologist*, 55/1, 122-136.

Bear, G. G. (1998): School discipline in the United States: Prevention, correction, and long-term social development. *School Psychology Review* 27/1, 724-742.

Berry, D. C. & Dienes Z. (1993): *Implicit Learning. Theoretical and Empirical Issues.* Hillsdale: Erlbaum.

Birch, Ch. & Cobb J. B. (1982): *The Liberation of Life.* Cambridge: Cambridge University Press.

Braitenberg, V. (1984): *Vehicles: Experiments in Synthetic Psychology.* Cambridge, MA: MIT Press.

De Houwer, J., Hendrickx, H. & Baeyens, F. (1997): Evaluative learning with 'subliminally' presented stimuli. *Consciousness and Cognition* 6, 87-107.

Fischer, K. W: (1980): A theory of cognitive development: The control and construction of hierarchies of skills. *Psychological Review* 87, 477-531.

Fischer, K. W. & Bidell, T. R. (1998): Dynamic development of psychological structures in action and thought. In: W. Damon & R. M. Lerner (Eds.): *Handbook of Child Psychology.* New York: Wiley, Chp. 9, 468-561.

Fischer, K. W. & Immordino-Yang, M. H. (2002): Cognitive development and education: From dynamic general structure to specific learning and teaching. In: E. Lagemann (Ed.): *Traditions of Scholarship in Education.* Chicago: Spencer Foundation.

Fischer, K. W. & Rose, S. P. (1998): Grow cycles of brain and mind. *Educational Leadership* 56, 3, 56-60.

Fischer, K. W., Shaver, P. R. & Carnochan, P. (1990): How emotions develop and how they organize development. *Cognition and Emotion* 4, 2, 81-127.

Fischer, K. W. & Rose, L. T. (2001): Webs of skills: How students learn. *Educational Leadership* 59/3, 6-12.

Frankena, W. K. (1965): *Philosophy of Education.* New York: Macmillan.

Geert, P. van (2002): Developmental dynamics, intentional action, and fuzzy sets. In: N. Granott & J. Parziale (Eds.): *Microdevelopment – Transitionprocesses in Development and Learning.* Cambridge: Cambridge University Press, 319-343.

Gelman, R., Rom, L. & Francis, W. S. (2002): Notebooks as windows on learning: The case of a science-into-ESL program. In: N. Granott & J. Parziale (Eds.): *Microdevelopment – Transitionprocesses in Development and Learning.* Cambridge: Cambridge University Press, 269-293.

Granott, N. (1991): Puzzeled minds and weired creatures: Phases in the spontaneous process of knowledge construction. Available at: URL: http://lcs.www.media.mit.edu/groups/el/elmemo/14-90memo/ (access: 26.08.2004); the paper also published in: Harel, I. & Papert S. (Eds.) (1991): *Constructionism.* Norwood, NJ: Ablex.

Granott, N., Fischer, K. W. & Parziale, J. (2002): Bridging to the unknown: A transition mechanism in learning and development. In: N. Granott & J. Parziale (Eds.): *Microdevelopment: Transition Processes in Development and Learning.* Cambridge, UK: Cambridge University Press, 131-156.

Granott, N. & Parziale, J. (2002): Microdevelopment: A process-oriented perspective for studying development and learning. In: N. Granott & J. Parziale (Eds.): *Microdevelopment: Transition Processes in Development and Learning.* Cambridge, UK: Cambridge University Press, 1-28.

Karplus, R. (1977): Science teaching and the development of reasoning. *Journal of Research in Science Teaching* 14, 169.

Karplus, E. & Karplus, R. (1970): Intellectual development beyond elementary school. *School Science and Mathematics* 70, 398-406.

Kesselring, T. (1981): *Entwicklung und Widerspruch – Ein Vergleich zwischen Piagets genetischer Erkenntnistheorie und Hegels Dialektik.* Frankfurt a. M.: Suhrkamp.

Lawson, A. (1995): *Science Teaching and the Development of Reasoning.* Belmont, CA: Wadsworth.

Miller, G. A,. Galanter, E. & Pribram, K. H. (1960): *Plans and the Structure of Behavior.* New York: Holt-Rinehart-Winston.

Olson, M. A. & Fazio, R. H. (2001): Implicit Attitude formation through classical conditioning. *Psychological Science* 12, 5, 413-417.

Piaget, J. (1968): *Six Psychological Studies.* New York: Random House.

Piaget, J. (1970a): *Structuralism.* New York: Basic Books.

Piaget, J. (1970b): Piaget's theory. In: P. H. Mussen (Ed.): *Carmichael's Manual of Child Psychology.* New York: Wiley, 103-128.

Reber, A. S. (1989): Implicit learning and tacit knowledge. *Journal of Experimental Psychology: General,* 118, 219-235.

Riffert, F. (1999): Process-philosophy and constructivist education – Some basic similarities. *Salzburger Beiträge zur Erziehungswissenschaft* 3, 2, 68-77.

Riffert, F. (2000): Whiteheads Prozessethik. *Freiburger Zeitschrift für Philosophie und Theologie* 50/1-2, 171-187.

Riffert, F. (2002): On non-substantialism in psychology. *International Journal of Field Being* online journal: www.ijfb.org (retrieved: 03.02.2005); special issue 'Whitehead and the Sciences'

Riffert, F. (2004): Whitehead's process philosophy as scientific metaphysics. In: T. Eastman & H. Keeton (Eds.): *Physics and Whitehead – Quantum, Process, and Experience*. New York: SUNY, 199-222.

Riffert, F. (2005): Whitehead's theory of perception and the concept of microgenesis. *Concrescence – Australasian Journal of Process Thought* online journal, URL: http://concrescence.org/ (access: 31.01.2005).

Riffert, F. & Cobb, J. B. (2003): Introduction. Reconnecting sciene and metaphysics: General considerations and pioneer works on process-psychology. In: F. Riffert & M. Weber (Eds.): *Searching for New Contrasts. Whiteheadian Contributions to Contemporary Challenges in Neurophysiology, Psychology, Psychotherapy and the Philosophy of Mind*. New York: Lang, 19-35.

Sayer, R. (2000): *Wert und Wirklichkeit*. Würzburg: Ergon.

Schweiger A. (2003): The common origin of perception and action. In: F. Riffert & M. Weber (Eds.): *Searching for New Contrasts. Whiteheadian Contributions to Contemporary Challenges in Neurophysiology, Psychology, Psychotherapy and the Philosophy of Mind*. New York: Lang, 103-112.

Sternberg, R. J. (Ed.) (1990): *Wisdom – Its Nature, Origins, and Development*. Cambridge: Cambridge University Press.

Sternberg, R. J. (2003): *Wisdom, Intelligence, and Creativity Synthesized*. Cambridge: Cambridge University Press.

Vygotsky, L. S. (1978): *Mind and Society: The Development of Higher Psychological Processes*. Cambridge: Harvard University Press.

Werner, H. (1957): The concept of development from a comparative and organismic point of view. In: D. B. Harris (Ed.): *The Concept of Development: An Issue in the Study of Human Behavior*. Minneapolis: University of Minneapolis Press, 125-148.

Whitehead, A. N. (1958/1929): *The Function of Reason*. Boston: Beacon.

Whitehead, A. N. (1967a/1929)): *The Aims of Education*. New York: Macmillan.

Whitehead, A. N. (1967b/1933): *Adventures of Ideas*. New York: Macmillan.

Whitehead, A. N. (1985/1927): *Symbolism. Its Meaning and Effect*. New York: Fordham University Press.

Whitehead, A. N. (1982): *An Introduction to Mathematics*. London: Oxford University Press.

Part I.2

PREHESIONS, CREATIVITY, PROCESS AND TEACHING

Prehensive Selectivity
and the Learning Process

Adam C. Scarfe

Abstract
This paper comprises a detailed study of the theme of selectivity in Whitehead's theory of prehensions and philosophy of education. Having previously argued that the theory of prehensions is inclusive of, and conducive to a critical, process philosophy of education (Scarfe 2003, 1), here, I fully set forth the analogy between the creative process outlined in Whitehead's theory of prehensions and learning processes. The analogy between the theory of prehensions and the learning process is made possible through a non-exclusive interpretation of the term, 'prehending subject' as 'learner'. With clues from *The Aims of Education* (1967a), the article provides a systematic analysis of the theory of prehensions, as depicting learning processes. I demonstrate how selectivity, via the fluctuating interplay of positive and negative prehensions, is the efficient causal element at work in the learning process. Consequently, as one side of a logical contrast, Whitehead's theory of prehensions can be said to be conducive to a critical, process pedagogy, focusing on the development of consciousness, including the cognitive awareness and judgment of states-of-affairs in the world.

1. Toward a Systematic Examination of the Role of Negative Prehensions in the Learning Process

This paper provides a systematic reading of the theory of prehensions with a focus on the role(s) of 'negative prehensions', with the aim of setting forth the analogy between the creative process outlined in Whitehead's theory of prehensions as contained in *Process and Reality* and learning processes. The analogy between the theory of prehensions and learning processes is made possible through a non-exclusive interpretation of the process of concresence as a learning process, and subsequently, the notion of 'prehending subject' as 'learner' or 'student'. Armed with clues from Whitehead's *The Aims of Education* (1967a), by examining each stage of the process of concrescence, I demonstrate how negative prehensions, which, in their fluctuating interplay with positive prehensions form the basis of a process of selection, are the efficient causal element at work in the learning process. By 'efficient causal element', I mean to suggest that the operations of negative prehensions, that eliminate data from experience in virtue of a process of selection, *bring about* a critical consciousness in regard to the subject-matters being learned. In other words, negative prehensions are what 'moves' or 'drives' learning processes. Consequently, as one side of a logical contrast, Whitehead's theory of prehensions can be said to be conducive to a 'critical' learning process, focusing on the development of consciousness, including a conscious awareness and judgment of concrete states-of-affairs in the world.

In carrying out this analysis of prehensive selectivity in learning, it will first be necessary to define how Whitehead's notions of a 'prehension' and a 'prehending subject' are pertinent to learning processes and to learners. Second, it will be imperative to set out the analogy between the stages Whitehead elucidates as the 'Rhythms of Education' and the process of concrescence depicted in the theory of prehensions. Third, I shall analyze the functioning of negative prehensions in relation to the initial, appropriative phases of concrescence which lead to consciousness, including: 1.) simple physical feelings, 2.) conceptual feelings, 3.) transmuted feelings, as well as 4.) propositional feelings. Together these phases can be said to constitute the educational stage of Romance. Fourth, the roles of negative prehensions will be elucidated in terms of the stage of Precision, namely, in terms of the phases in which a consciousness awareness of the subject-matter learned is attained, as in 'conscious perceptions' and 'intuitive judgments', comprising Whitehead's class of 'intellectual feelings'. Fifth, I shall examine the function of negative prehensions in the stage of Generalization, involving the application of the subject-matter learned to actuality and the awareness of the logical contrasts.

2. 'Prehensive Appropriation' and Learning

There is an evident connection between Whitehead's philosophy of education and the creative processes described in the theory of prehensions. As defined by Whitehead, learning is a process whose "nearest analogue is the assimilation of food by a living organism" (1967a, 33). This statement implicates the Whiteheadian concept of a 'prehension' in the definition of 'learning'. In explanation of the notion of a 'prehension', one of the main problems his speculative philosophy attempts to overcome is that of the presupposition of consciousness embedded in the epistemology of previous modern philosophers, such as Descartes, Locke, Hume, and Kant. In Whitehead's account, these figures did not take into account non-conscious experience in their epistemologies. In his analysis, they assumed that the notions of 'perception' and 'sense-perception' entailed cognition. However, Whitehead's view is that "consciousness presupposes experience, and not experience consciousness" (1978, 53), a standpoint that paves the way for his claim that most of our experience is not cognitive. He suggests that most of our experience is emotional, and is comprised by physical, bodily, and conceptual feelings of the 'blooming, buzzing confusion' that surrounds us. Through subsequent integrations, eliminations, and re-enactments of experienced data, as represented through Whitehead's elucidation of the phases of concrescence, a conscious perception of 'objects' within our environment, is developed. For Whitehead, "consciousness is the crown of experience, only occasionally attained, not its necessary base" (1978, 267). That is to say, while one major task of learning is the development of a conscious awareness of various subject-matters and states-of-affairs in the world, consciousness is only the 'tip of the iceberg' in terms of our modes of experiencing the world. As distinct from traditional philosophical notions of 'perception' or 'sense-perception' which are "shot through and through with the notion of cognitive apprehension" (Whitehead 1967b, 69), the term, 'prehension' refers to the apprehension of data at the root of experience, an activity which may or may not be cognitive. Hence, the word 'prehension' in Whitehead's system denotes the "uncognitive apprehension" (1967b, 69) of experienced data. But, the term, 'prehending', has many other connotations as well. It also means 'feeling', 'grasping', 'taking-account of', or "seizing" (Kraus 1998, 16). These terms refer directly to the Latin root of 'prehension': *prehendere*, and

do not necessarily imply cognitive activities. As in biological processes, such as the ingestion of food, a prehension designates an
organism's "appropriat(ion) for the foundation of its own existence, the
various elements of the universe out of which it arises" (Whitehead
1978, 219). That is to say, a subject appropriates data from outside of
itself for its own process of self-development, growth, and self-realization. Correspondingly, from a Whiteheadian perspective, the 'prehensive appropriation' of data is very much analogous to learning. In
the learning process, students are the 'prehending subjects' appropriating data for the sake of their own self-development. For instance, in
the classroom setting, students learn by seizing the data presented by
the teacher, making them their own, transforming them, and applying
them to the actualities of life, toward their educational self-realization
and satisfaction.

By associating the terms, 'student' or 'learner' with 'prehending
subject', I by no means wish to suggest that students are the only
prehending subjects. For Whitehead, all organisms or 'actual entities',
whatsoever, are prehending subjects. Teachers are also prehending
subjects, and hence, they are also learners. Therefore, I am not here
employing Whitehead's notion of 'prehending subject' exclusively in
its association with the terms 'student' or 'learner'. But, for the sake of
analyzing the theory of prehensions in terms of learning and in terms
of concrete situations in higher education, students are emphatically
the 'prehending subjects', engaged in appropriating data for the sake of
their own educational self-development, self-realization, fulfillment, or
satisfaction. In part, for Whitehead, the self consists in what is appropriated from the outside environment. But, by associating the term
'prehension' with 'learning', I also do not intend to suggest that
learning is the mere reception of the 'deposits' a teacher makes, as in
the 'banking model' of education that Paulo Freire is critical of. To be
sure, for Whitehead, every act of prehending involves a process of
selection in which data are positively accepted and appropriated in
virtue of data that are excluded or eliminated. Specifically, he depicts
the activities of 'positive' and 'negative prehending' which operate in
conjunction with one another in virtue of a process of selection. As
Whitehead defines, while the activity of positive prehending "is the
definite inclusion of (an) item into positive contribution to the subject's
own real internal constitution" (1978, 41), the activity of negative
prehending "is the definite exclusion of (an) item from positive con-

tribution to the subject's own real internal constitution" (1978, 41). In other words, while a positive prehension involves a student's seizure, inclusion, and retention of data (as a potentiality for future actualization), a negative prehension consists in the elimination and rejection of data from experience. In Whitehead's scheme, all positive prehensions are accompanied by negative prehensions, and it is only in virtue of the elimination of irrelevant data that relevant data are accepted. Prehending subjects, in this case, learners or students, "eliminate, by negative prehension, the irrelevant accidents in (their) environment" (Whitehead 1978, 317) in virtue of eliciting attention to data that leave an impression on them, seem important, or are relevant to their aims. Through alternating prehensive integrations and prehensive eliminations, selected data are assimilated by the learner. For instance, note-taking, as a main activity involved in higher learning, is an interpretive process of selectively appropriating relevant articulations made by the teacher or read in a text, and rejecting others which either lack in causal force or are not of interest to the student. Note-taking is not necessarily a conscious activity. The data, the knowledge-contents, or the propositions that are taken down are largely pre-consciously selected by the student, in virtue of a number of possible criteria; sometimes even in virtue of the intonation of phrases, the linguistic style of the articulation, or the student's emotional enjoyment of it. Similarly, notes, taken down by students are largely transformed from the way in which they were originally articulated. Consequently, they may lose their original emotional impact in the process. In any case, as one of the main activities of students in higher learning, the activity of note-taking exemplifies what a 'negative prehension' is; a largely uncognitive operation of elimination or exclusion in virtue of a process of *selective appropriation* at the root of experience.

Negative prehensions can be said to account for a student's exclusion of uninteresting, imposed, inert, dead, valueless and useless data, namely, data that is immediately irrelevant to their lives, as well as to the development and realization of their own purposes or 'subjective aims'. As defined in Whitehead's philosophy of education, 'inert ideas' are "ideas merely received into the mind without being utilized, or tested, or thrown into fresh combinations" (1967a, 1). Inert data include bits of 'stale' and useless information, which are felt by students to be uninteresting. For the most part, in the learning process, uninteresting ideas are negatively prehended or eliminated from experience, while novel, exciting, and interesting ideas are positively entertained by the student. For Whitehead, "there can be no mental development without interest. Interest is the *sine qua non* for attention and apprehension" (1967a, 31). As the main 'filtration' vehicle involved in selective appropriation, the operation of negative prehending is the basis of the student's agency, enabling them to entertain data that are of interest and of importance to them, and to not engaging those that are not of interest or of importance. Therefore, a definition of 'learning' stemming out of the notion of a 'prehension' must include a reference to the negative prehensions and to the processes of selection which lead to the learner's development of a conscious awareness of the subject-matter in question. As such, learning does not consists in the pupil's passive intellectual reception of knowledge presented by the teacher, but rather, it consists in an activity of selective appropriation on the part of the student. Furthermore, the fact of selection in learning is representative of the student's voluntary capacity for "free choice" (Whitehead 1967a, 30), in respect to their own process of self-formation, including their desires, their purposes, and their aims. As a result, by describing learning processes in terms of Whitehead's theory of prehensions, there is no risk of depicting them as analogous to Freire's 'banking model' of education.

While the agency of the learner stems from processes of selection within the learning process, the basic fact of selectivity results from the limits of the student's capacity for assimilating knowledge. From a Whiteheadian perspective, the learner, like all finite, living beings, is engaged in creative processes of self-realization. A learner would not be a self-realizing creature, if he or she enjoyed a static, intellectual infinitude. As a finite organism, like all other beings, a learner does not have the capacity to appropriate knowledge infinitely. Rather, Whitehead writes that "there are more topics desirable for knowledge than any one person can possibly acquire" (1967,a 29). In other words, it is due to the limitations of the finite human organism that "the development of learning and the success of education, require selection. The human mind can only deal with limited topics, which exclude the vague immensity of nature" (Whitehead 1948, 159).

3. The 'Rhythms of Education' as Representative of the Stages of Concrescence

Whitehead's three 'Rhythms of Education', namely, Romance, Precision, and Generalization, can be said to parallel the various phases of the concrescence or the 'growing together' of actual occasions as depicted in the theory of prehensions. Whitehead's outline of the 'Rhythms of Education' loosely coincides with the pattern pertaining to the process of concrescence, each stage cumulatively being the condition for the possibility of the next. In the process of concrescence, the bare feeling of data develops into a conscious awareness of the subject-matter, and may be followed by the awareness of the logical contrasts inherent to it. The stage of Romance can be considered to comprise the 'affective' phases of the process of concrescence, characterized by the well-spring of feelings and emotions stemming from the educational environment and the data to be learned. It also involves the development of concepts relating to actualities in the world. In Whiteheadian philosophy of education, the stage of Romance, comprising the 'initial' stages of the prehensive appropriation of data, constitutes the underlying foundation of learning processes. Second, the educational stage of Precision is comprised by the attainment of a conscious awareness of the subject-matter learned and/ or the development of a critical consciousness, involving the judgment of propositions stemming from it. While for Whitehead, the attainment of consciousness is a rare event, as one side of a logical contrast, it is the 'summit' of learning and self-realization, as it is for cognitivist theories in educational psychology. Third, the stage of Generalization may be considered the stage of the utilization of the knowledge-content learned in terms of *praxis*, by applying it to life and to the actual world. The stage of Generalization is also characterized by further reflection and action respecting the subject-matter learned, and/or an awareness of the logical contrasts therein, constituting the ultimate realization in learning. For Whitehead, Generalization leads to a new stage of Romance and a new cycle of learning. Here, I provide a systematic reading of the theory of prehensions in respect to the learning process, with a thematic focus on the cumulative functioning of negative prehensions and processes of selectivity. To reiterate, by way of this analysis, I intend to demonstrate that negative prehensions, in their fluctuating interplay with posi tive prehensions, are the efficient causal element involved in learning, bringing about a critical consciousness of the subject-matter in question.

4. Negative Prehensions and Selectivity in the Stage of Romance

In *Process and Reality*, the process of concrescence runs through various phases, beginning with the most primitive, namely, that of feelings. This original, affective stage, comprised by feeling in contrast to consciousness, can be termed the stage of Romance. However, it must here be mentioned that the phases or stages of concrescence, including the process ontology of feelings that Whitehead advances, are abstract divisions within the continuum of experience made solely for the purpose of his analysis. These help him describe the processes by which objective data, in this case, the knowledge-contents to be learned, are absorbed by the prehending subject into their internal constitution. In fully defining the activity of prehending or, alternatively, of feeling, Whitehead lists the five determinate, yet inter-linked factors involved. Every prehension includes: 1.) the 'subject' which feels, (i.e. the actual entity, the prehending subject, the body of the actual entity or, in this case, the learner; the student in the process of self-development); 2.) the 'initial data' which are to be felt (i.e. what the feeling feels); 3.) the 'elimination' in virtue of negative prehensions; 4.) the 'objective datum' which is felt; and, 5). the 'subjective form' which is *how* that subject (namely, the learner or the student) feels that objective datum (Whitehead 1978, 221).

While each of the five factors operate in conjunction with all of the others in the process of prehending, it is to be emphasized that negative prehensions accompany every positive prehension in terms of 3.) the elimination. As such, negative prehensions can be said to play a role in every stage of learning. In prehending data, there is a transition from the many 'initial data' experienced into one 'objective datum'. This transition is effected through negative prehensions in virtue of a process of selection, which is informed by the subjective form of the feeling. For the most part, data are eliminated or excluded from feeling in virtue of their lack of causal impact on the learner, in contrast to other data felt which are dominant in the learner's environment, claiming his or her attention. Data are also eliminated due to the fact that they are not relevant or of interest to the learner. As Whitehead describes, while negatively prehended data are felt and do procure a subjective form, they are left 'inoperative' from further contribution to the particular process of concrescence. In other words, while experienced by the learner, the multiplicity of negatively prehended data are left as 'background' in virtue of the data that are selected, which go to form the objective datum.

In the learning process, prehended data or knowledge-contents are selected, become owned, transformed, and later applied to actuality by the student. The learning process 'begins' with the prehending subject feeling its environment, selecting data by way of the fluctuation of positive and negative prehensions, integrating the selected data into their own internal constitution, and utilizing them in terms of their own self-formation. It is by way of the cumulative role of negative prehensions that, "in the passage from our lower type animal experience to our higher type human (conscious) experience, we (acquire) a selective emphasis whereby the finite occasions of experience receive clear definition" (Whitehead 1968, 77). For Whitehead, consciousness occurs in the higher phases of experience, and is not the necessary base of experience or of learning. Hence, his cosmology, interpreted as a theory of learning, attempts to describe learning processes from the bottom-up, starting with 'simple physical feelings'.

4.1 Simple Physical Feelings

In outlining the initial phases of concrescence, as distinct from conceptual experience, Whitehead defines that "a feeling will be called 'physical' when its datum involves objectifications of other actual entities" (1978, 245). As his philosophy of organism is 'provisionally-realistic', holding to the notion that all learning commences with experience of the actual world in the 'present moment', simple physical feelings are among the most primitive type of non-cognitive feelings that Whitehead analyzes in his theory of prehensions. In its emphasis on physical feelings, Whitehead's doctrine of simple physical feelings "generalizes (Hume's) notion of 'impressions of sensation'" (1978, 242), but stands in opposition to the sensationalist presupposition that sense-perception entails conscious experience. As one commentator has suggested, for Whitehead, simple physical feelings constitute the "bedrock of experience and learning" (Fidyk 1997, 74), in contrast to consciousness, which is a 'high-level' mode belonging only to the higher organisms, but born of abstraction from our basic physical experience.

As in simple physical feelings, learners feel the 'raw data' of experience with their senses. Simple physical feelings can be said to involve the learner's absorption of data in the environment by way of their sensory organs, as in touch, smell, sight, hearing, and taste. Feelings that contain no apparent reference to external objects may also fall under Whitehead's category of simple physical feelings. For example, the case of an itch whose origin is not known, in the body's feeling of itself, or with respect to autonomous bodily functions, internal bodily feelings felt by other bodily organs, are also instances of simple physical feelings. Even bodily existence is something that is physically felt, even though throughout most of our experience we do not maintain a conscious awareness of this fact. However, Whitehead's analysis focuses on how simple physical feelings involve the registration of the causal "inflow of the actual world" (1978, 245), which is partially responsible for procuring emotions. In particular, simple physical feelings involve the bodily reactions of the prehending subject, such as: blinking from a flash, shivering from the cold, or even shuddering due to fear of the possibility of a predatory animal lurking nearby, prior to conscious awareness of the 'causes' of these reactions. As such, to a large extent, simple physical feelings involve bodily feelings and emotions (as their subjective form), which are, at once, caused by and seized from other entities (not yet fully objectified) in the environment.

It is by way of the fluctuation of positive and negative prehensions, cumulatively transforming the initial data into objective datum, that entities become objectified at the level of consciousness. That is to say, in Whitehead's theory, data that are felt go through processes of negative prehension and objectification in order to 'become' the particular physical objects that they are for us in consciousness: desks, tables, podiums, pencils, pens, chalk-boards, the teacher's body, and the bodies of other students. But, at the primitive stage of simple physical feelings, such objects are not yet realized as, or determined to be 'objects' or as 'the cause of our feelings or our emotions'. Rather, at this stage, the data felt in physical prehensions are only potentially 'objects' or 'the causes of our feelings or emotions', as indicated through language and in conscious experience. In describing simple physical feelings in language here, we are doing so from the level of consciousness. Recognizing the abstract character of these descriptions and the violence I am doing to the nebulous character of real 'here and now' experience, I offer these descriptions here only for the sake of explanation.

Since learning has long been viewed as the development of a comprehension of concepts or mental events, in abstraction from the physical feelings and experience, many educational theorists either avoid or omit any reference to the body or to emotions. In contrast, Whitehead's philosophy of organism emphasizes the fundamental fact of organic embodiment and of the importance of physical feelings in respect to educational states-of-affairs. His philosophy of education points to the fact that all learning contents that are to be appropriated by a student must originally be heard, seen, smelled, touched, or tasted. That is to say, concepts cannot be communicated or transmitted by a teacher to a learner save through the fact that they are felt in some way through the senses. For Whitehead, "the body is the organism whose states regulate our cognizance of the world" (1967b, 91). Similarly, he writes,

> I lay it down as an educational axiom that in teaching you will come to grief as soon as you forget that your pupils have bodies. [...] The connections between intellectual activity and the body though diffused in every bodily feeling, are focused in the eyes, the ears, the voice, and the hands. There is a co-ordination of senses and thought, and also a reciprocal influence between brain activity and material creative activity. In this reaction the hands are peculiarly important. It is a moot point whether the human hand created the human brain, or the brain created the hand. Certainly, the connection is intimate and reciprocal (1967a, 50).

As such, for Whitehead, the learning process is fundamentally constituted by bodily feelings in reciprocal relationship with the mind. In the classroom setting, simple physical feelings account for the student's physical experience of their educational environment, as well as for the basic visual, auditory, and tactile experience of the pedagogical materials presented by the teacher. For the most part, if what is experienced is clearly felt and registered by way of the sight, the nose, the ears, the taste-buds, or the touch, the data in question are more apt to be positively prehended. Conversely, if what is experienced is not clearly felt or registered by way of the eyes, the nose, the ears, the taste-buds, or the touch, then the data in question are more apt to be negatively prehended or eliminated from the student's experience. For the most part, in the process of physical feeling, students are more likely to select data that are more impacting to the senses than those that are not, or those which are physically enjoyable over those which are boring or painful. For example, unconsciously, we tend to enjoy food that is tasty, sounds which are pleasant, and tactile feelings provoking pleasure, and to avoid food that is bitter, sounds which are unpleasant, and feelings of bodily pain. Similarly, physical data that produce feelings of physical enjoyment are also more apt to procure 'positive' emotions, than 'negative' ones.

In connection with simple physical feelings, Whitehead's cosmological notion of 'perspective' is fundamental to educational states of affairs. For Whitehead, perspective is arrived at through the process of prehending. With respect to simple physical feelings, it is largely through the elimination in virtue of negative prehensions that a learner acquires their physical perspective with respect to the initial data, which is the resulting objective datum. Whitehead's notion of perspective does not simply denote the location of a single body in space and time. It always involves a multiplicity of physical feelings, emotions, as well as the functional inter-relationships between the body of prehending subject and the physical make-up of other entities, not necessarily realized in consciousness. Due to the fact that perspective depends on other entities, no two prehending subjects will have the exact same physical experience in the classroom setting. Since, for Whitehead, the event of learning is 'relational' and is not atomic, physical perspective, derived from previous prehensions, is crucial in terms of what a student is able to further prehend, select, and pay attention to in the classroom setting. For instance, we may ask: is this particular student's body poised in relation to the teacher such that they are able to take in curriculum materials presented? Can the student hear the teacher when there is background chatter or noise? Can the student see the writing on the blackboard from the back of the class? Is the writing on the projector screen legible? Is the teacher smiling or frowning and how do the students feel in respect to the learning-contents prehended? Is the position of the professor's body, in relation to a student's, provoking emotions of intimidation in them? These types of questions pertaining to physical feelings and to perspective in learning may be said to underscore any consideration of the 'concepts' or contents to be learned. And, some of them underlie the reasons why classroom discipline is so important. In any event, physical or bodily perspective is the condition for the possibility of a student's ability and freedom in prehending learning contents. Visually legible or illegible writing on the black-board; a teacher's inaudible tone, unintelligibility, vocal clarity, or intonation when speaking; the gestures a teacher makes with his or her arms; the teacher's facial expression, hunger-pangs or groans originating from a student's stomach; or even the odor emanating from a nearby chemistry lab, are all examples of factors that are involved in a student's attention and in their prehensive selection of data. In other words, for Whitehead, all contents to be learned must undoubtedly be felt in some way through the senses. As a result, physical and bodily factors affect the possibility that certain know-ledge-contents will be relevant or will not be relevant to students, or that they will have or will not have a causal impact on students. Phy-sical impediments to the possibility of seeing and hearing learning contents may subsequently influence a student to exclude or to elimi-nate particular knowledge-contents, particular teachers, or even classes and educational programs from their learning experience. Hence, physical experience is of vital importance to whether or not a student positively or negatively prehends knowledge-contents. As a result, the extent to which a teacher seeks to accommodate or enhance students' physical experience, may be an issue in respect to these selections. Moreover, as regards the physical aspect of the classroom setting, learning necessitates an attunement to, or selective focus on the bodies of the participants, and the physical activity of, and expressions emana-ting from those bodies, in exclusion from other data. If one is to learn effectively, for the most part, the objects outside the window, the door, the ceiling, or the tables at the front of the classroom, another student's knapsack or t-shirt, the bodies of other students', etc... cannot claim more attention than a teacher's body.

While all stages of learning imply some reference to physical feelings, physical feelings are part of the educational stage of Ro-mance, which exemplifies a "first apprehension" (Whitehead 1967b, 17) of wonder and curiosity. For example, a first day of class is, to a large extent, constituted by becoming physically attuned to an educational environment, to the teacher's bodily appearance, and to other students' bodily appearance. Particularly, a student becomes accustomed to those physical factors which underlie the possibility of developing a conscious awareness of the subject-matters in question, in abstraction from the conceptual content. However, as isolated to physical feelings, learning is largely constituted by an immediate perception of flashes, smells, tactile feelings, and squeaks, with reference to nothing further.

4.2. Conceptual Feelings

In maintaining the 'provisional realism' of his cosmology, Whitehead emphasizes the importance of physical feelings and defends the Humean notion that "we can never conceptually entertain what we have never antecedently experienced through impressions of sensation" (1978, 242) or more accurately, through physical feelings. For Whitehead, we cannot imagine anything except what has not previously been prehended physically, nor can we think of anything except what is comprised by webs of such prehensions, synthesized together in conceptual experience. Thus, in his analysis, simple physical feelings are the 'starting-point' from which all experience and learning begins, characterizing the immediate, unconscious experience of the present moment, namely, that of the here and now, and nothing more. But, Whitehead also claims that both physical and conceptual poles of experience jointly originate the learning process. Physical and conceptual feelings, in their reciprocal relationship, are considered to be the primary feelings from which all other forms of feelings are originated. For Whitehead, it is through conceptual experience that ideas are developed and are felt. But, in his view, conceptual feelings do not involve consciousness, and thus, must be classified within the scope of the learning stage of Romance.

Whitehead's elucidation of conceptual prehensions can be said to illuminate the transmission and appropriation of learning contents, simultaneous with their presentation to the physical senses. In outlining the factors constituting conceptual feelings, Whitehead defends the notion that in immediate experience, the prehending subject or learner brings with them not only the feelings of the past, but anticipations of, and projections into the future, as well as references to other places and perspectives. The reference, in immediate experience, to what is not present, preserves the continuity of the learner's experience. In this sense, for Whitehead, "a prehension is [also] a process of unifying" (1967b, 72). The notion that the prehending subject 'grasps together' the present in virtue of representations of the past, anticipations of the future, as well as other perspectives and places in the immediate experience of the present, points to the reality of conceptual experience. Such prehensive unification stands in contrast to the unmitigated Hume's standpoint of empirical realism, which views induction to be problematic and holds that what is actual is only what is present to the senses in immediate experience. For Hume, no experience, other than direct sense-perception in the present moment, is representative of what is actual, although, as Whitehead points out, this experience is falsely presupposed by Hume to be cognitive. Whitehead claims that Humean scepticism, which does not admit any form of conceptual experience, leads inevitably to what George Santayana calls the 'solipsism of the present moment', namely, the confinement of experience to the present moment (i.e. to 'presentational immediacy'), with no appeal to anything beyond. In this situation, all conceptual experience would be rejected, reason would not exist, and nothing could ever be 'learned'. In this case, we could not arrive at any knowledge about the world, nor could we articulate any meaning in regards to it. Without conceptual experience, logically identifiable 'objects' could not be affirmed to exist and the student would be left with the conceptual void that characterizes physical feelings in themselves, being unable to access anything beyond them. Furthermore, without any representational reference to the future, the student could not embark at all on a stage of Romance characterized by the type of anticipatory feelings that characterize 'curiosity' and 'wonder' about any subject-matters in general. In elucidating the Humean lacuna, Whitehead writes that it is a

> very baffling task of applying reason to elicit the general
> characteristic of the immediate occasion, as set before us in
> direct [perception, but it] is a necessary preliminary, if we are
> to justify induction; unless indeed we are content to base it
> upon our vague instinct that of course is right. Either there is
> something about the immediate occasion which affords knowledge of the past and the future, or we are reduced to utter
> scepticism as to memory and induction (1967b, 44).

However, in attempting to overcome this lacuna, Whitehead points to the internal contradiction within Hume's position in respect to his emphasis on presentational immediacy, maintained at the same time as presupposing consciousness. He also points to the fact that the 'with-ness' of the body is always both an empirical and a conceptual datum in our own experience, but that it is curiously omitted in the Humean account. And, pointing to Santayana's ascription of the intuitive belief in such conceptual reference to 'animal faith', Whitehead reasonably concludes that in experience, we do carry an appeal to a reference to other times and places with us in the present moment. Whitehead shows how this reference to other times and places implies a more primordial mode of perception, what he calls, 'causal efficacy'. Similarly, Whitehead accepts induction on the limited basis of the ability to draw upon the past to make sense of the present, thus preserving the uniformity of experience. To be sure, he maintains that "the objective content of the initial phases of reception is the real antecedent world, as given for that occasion (which) [...] is the 'reality' from which the creative advance starts" (1968, 210). Hence, his standpoint of provisional realism holds that conceptual experience is primarily derived from direct physical experience, pointing undeniably to the importance of education and learning in the lives of human beings. It is on this footing that Whitehead elucidates the nature of conceptual experience.

In pointing to the feeling of the past in the present moment, according to Whitehead, conceptual experience is largely characterized by the reproduction and re-enaction of an objective datum positively prehended in the physical sense. The objective datum of a physical feeling, which is selected via negative prehensions, enters into the learner's internal constitution, thus effecting conceptual experience. The process by which the datum 'enters into the student's internal constitution as a possibility for future actualization', becoming 'assimilated' and 'owned by the learner' in the process, consists in operations of reproduction. For example, in note-taking, there is a conceptual reproduction of a past occurrence, event, or statement, enabling the learner to re-enact the experience, or alternatively-stated, to remember or recollect it in the future. As alluded to previously, the selectivity in recollecting the past is, in part, based in the finitude of the human mind, namely, in its inability to absorb and to carry with it every element of its experience.

According to Whitehead, together, the mental operations of reproduction and re-enaction, which issue in conceptual experience, are fundamental to what it means to 'learn'. Through the process of prehending, conceptual data are integrated into the prehending subject's constitution. But, for Whitehead, a conceptual re-enaction is not perfect because it subjects the datum to abstractions not found in the original immediate, physical experience of it. In re-enacting or 'imitating' the original experience, to a large extent, the original feelings felt in direct perception by the prehending subject cumulatively 'lose' their force and vivacity, which is the meaning of the Heraclitean phrase that 'one can never step in the same river twice'.

Even though Whitehead holds conceptual data are largely derived from mental reproductions and re-enactments of physical feelings, he describes that conceptual experience contrasts with physical experience. A conceptual feeling is the feeling of an eternal object in contrast to feeling the physical experience of actual world. As he defines, a conceptual feeling *qua* 'conceptual' is constituted by "the feeling of an unqualified negation; that is to say, it is the feeling of a definite eternal object with the definite extrusion of any particular realization" (1978, 243) or, alternatively, without reference to actuality. Loosely, for our purposes here, 'eternal objects' can be said to designate 'ideas', 'representations', 'learning contents', or definite 'potentialities for future actualization', in the sense of being 'objects' for thought, namely, they are what is felt by way of conceptual feelings. Against Hume's defense that the only reality is that which appears in immediate perception, eternal objects are the condition for the possibility of preserving the continuity of experience and making sense of our world, enabling us to represent and make reference to other times and places. Exemplifying the provisional realism of his scheme, eternal objects are, in part, the result of conceptual re-enactions of data that have been positively prehended physically. In this sense, the initial, 'appropriative' phases of concrescence chart the "development of an idea" (Whitehead 1978, 167).

Positive and negative conceptual prehensions are perhaps the most fundamental mental operations involved in learning. As described by Whitehead, conceptual prehensions involve mental processes of selection. An eternal object "may be included positively by means of a conceptual feeling; but it may be excluded by a negative prehension" (Whitehead 1978, 239). By way of the fluctuation of positive and negative conceptual prehensions, some reproductions and re-enactions are selected and kept as eternal objects, namely, as ideas introducing creative purpose in the sense of being a novel potential for future actualization. Others are creatively modified or enhanced by their synthesis with component elements derived from other occasions or ideas, as in what Whitehead calls, 'conceptual reversion'. In conceptual reversion, the learner may synthesize conceptual data with other conceptual elements recollected and derived from other experiences, thereby creatively adding 'value' to them and increasing both their relevance and intensity. They may then be selected as potentialities for future actualization, namely as eternal objects or ideas forming the basis of self-development. Still other re-enactions and eternal objects are excluded, eliminated, rejected, and utterly dismissed from the learning process, as in the case of the negative prehension of 'inert ideas'. Therefore, while admittedly actualities are 'given' and have to be felt physically in some way, largely imposing themselves on the prehending subject through experience and forcing accomodation, to a large extent, eternal objects, to some extent can be freely dismissed by the learner through negative conceptual prehensions.

In conceptual experience, negative prehensions are the chief operation involved in a student's process of selectively 'valuating' eternal objects and deciding which are to be integrated into their constitution in virtue of those which are not. Through the fluctuating interplay of positive conceptual prehensions and negative conceptual prehensions, the student "values up, or down, so as to determine the intensive importance accorded to the eternal object" (Whitehead 1978, 241). In valuating eternal objects as to their intensive relevance, students select which contents are important to them in their process of self-formation, particularly, those which are to be 'owned', thus remaining potentialities for future actualization, in virtue of those which are not. Whitehead asserts that

> any item of the universe, however preposterous as an abstract thought, or however remote as an actual entity has its own gradation of relevance, as prehended, in the constitution of any one actual entity: it might have had more relevance; and it might have had less relevance, including the zero of relevance involved in the negative prehension (1978, 148).

Hence, in the learning process, determinations of intensive relevance of ideas chiefly involve negative conceptual prehensions. By way of the valuation of eternal objects through negative prehensions, the learner selects and determines how the conceptual data are to be utilized in their learning process. In ideal learning conditions, these valuations of learning contents are made freely and independently by students themselves, in respect to their own individuality, their interests, their perspectives, their specializations, their subjective aims and purposes. While valuation is central to self-formation and educational self-realization, imposed valuation by a teacher may be said to constitute the essence of dogmatism.

By reading Whitehead's description of conceptual feeling as part of the learning process, an imminent critique is brought to light of the common 'banking-model' of education, as articulated by Freire. The 'banking-model' is represented by those pedagogies which insist that students reproduce and memorize curriculum materials pre-selected by the teacher. In the 'banking-model' of education, an imposition of curriculum materials is made, for example, by way of evaluation practices that emphasize mere reproduction, recall, and regurgitation of pre-selected data. These methods of evaluation only test whether a content has been successfully 'deposited' in the student, but do not take into account a student's own volition to select or to reject particular data. Since Whitehead claims that "conceptual feelings do not necessarily involve consciousness" (1978, 239), by merely developing a student's capacity for re-enacting and remembering learning contents, learning does not rise to the level of the development of a critical consciousness. In other words, without independent selection, rigorous analysis, and/or application of knowledge-contents to actuality on the part of the student, a critical consciousness of the subject-matter is not attained. Therefore, while conceptual reproduction, re-enaction, imitation, representation, and memorization are representative of chief mental operations involved in conceptual experience, from a Whiteheadian point of view, they remain at the initial educational stage of Romance.

4.3 Transmutation and Transmuted Feelings

As Whitehead describes, physical and conceptual experience jointly originate the process of concrescence. Precisely, 1.) through their reproduction and re-enaction, physical feelings originate mental experience, and 2.) conceptual feelings refer back to physical experience. Whitehead's notions of 'transmutation' and of 'transmuted feelings' partially explain this second movement whereby conceptual experience re-acquires its reference to actuality, thus integrating conceptual data with physical experience. The operation of transmutation is central in learning new concepts and terminology, and in being aware of what they apply to. Transmutation is a first step in 'making-sense' of the world by objectifying and making reference to the actualities physically felt with the concepts derived from the original stages of conceptual experience. To be sure, for Whitehead, "there is no character belonging to the actual apart from its exclusive determination by selected eternal objects" (1978, 240). Through the mental operation of transmutation, the learner "transmutes the datum of (a) conceptual feeling into a contrast with the nexus of those prehended actual entities" (Whitehead 1978, 251). In other words, the learner ascribes an eternal object to actualities physically felt, thus qualifying those actualities and enabling them to be felt as 'one'. The eternal object is felt as encompassing the actualities composing the nexus of actualities in question, without regard for the multiplicity in their detail or the discordance of the individual members within that nexus. As Whitehead explains,

> transmutation is the way in which the actual world is felt as a community, and is so felt in virtue of its prevalent order. For it arises by reason of the analogies between the various members of the prehended nexus, and eliminates their differences. Apart from transmutation our feeble intellectual operations would fail to penetrate into the dominant characteristics of things. We can only understand by discarding. (1978, 251).

For example, through transmutation, the learner may apply a concept of 'tree' (not yet conceived consciously or linguistically, but, derived from past experience), to a multitude of entities in the world, regardless of the individual differences of particular trees. In transmutation, the function of negative prehensions is to eliminate the differences between the members within a class of entities, or of the differences between the microscopic functionally interrelated entities that together, comprise a macrocosmic entity. In other words, the discordances of the individual actual entities within the nexus are massively eliminated by negative prehensions, so that the objectified nexus, with reference to an eternal object, may be felt as 'one'. In this way, "the irrelevant multiplicity of detail is eliminated, and emphasis is laid on the elements of systematic order in the actual world" (Whitehead 1978, 254). Transmutation, with its massive eliminations of such discordances, is one of the main operations by which human beings have arrived at language and symbolism, our scientific taxonomies, and our ontologies. In transmutation, the student determines what actualities a particular concept learned pertains to. The mediation of actualities and sets of actualities through selected concepts, is a crucial activity in the process by which their conscious awareness of the subject-matter in question is developed.

With the ascription of an eternal object to a set of entities through transmutation, 'transmuted feelings' are the feeling of the contrast between the ascribed concept and the actuality physically felt, namely, they are the feeling of *this* concept in conjunction with *these* actualities. As the actualities in question is felt together with an eternal object, the feelings of the eternal object are also ascribed to the actualities in question. Precisely, the set of actualities in question are felt in conjunction with the feelings of a valuated eternal object conceptually felt. On the one hand, if the actualities are associated with an eternal object which in its conceptual feeling was valued upward in terms of its intensive importance to their own process of self-realization, then, for the most part, the learner will react favourably, namely, with adversion to those actualities. On the other hand, if the actualities are associated with an eternal object that was valued downward in terms of its intensive importance to their own process of self-realization, then the learner, for the most part, will react negatively, namely, with aversion to the actualities in question. Adversion and aversion are exemplified by emotional responses towards the actualities felt through the mediation of eternal objects. As Whitehead writes, "anger, hatred, fear, terror, attraction, love, hunger, eagerness, massive enjoyment, are feelings and emotions closely entwined with the primitive functioning of 'retreat from' and 'expansion towards'" (1985, 45). While we can conceive of a neutral, or unemotional response in terms of transmuted feelings, it is because of either the positive or negative valuation of the eternal object that is transmuted onto the set of actualities in question that a student will have adversion or aversion towards them. Through transmuted feelings, actualities are themselves valuated and selected through the mediation of eternal objects, themselves valuated and selected. Again, the chief operation in transmuted feelings is negative prehension. Aversion, for instance, to a thing, a person, or a learning content, involves the negative prehension not only of the concepts indicating them, but of the actualities in question, as well.

From this analysis, it is evident that through transmutation, actualities in the world are felt under great abstraction, omitting (by negative prehension) the multiplicity of detail truly found in the world. The eliminations in virtue of negative prehensions are responsible for the notion that "in respect to membership of (a) class, one member is as good as another" (Whitehead 1948, 228). Furthermore, in transmuted feelings, learners may react with adversion or aversion towards actualities on the basis of their valuation and selection of eternal objects, apart from the world. As a result, Whitehead's category of transmutation and his notion of transmuted feelings, as applied to learning processes, demonstrates that "intellectuality consists [largely] in the gain of a power of abstraction" (1978, 254). While transmutation does not involve judgment, there is the possibility for the negative prehensions involved in transmuted feelings to exclude actualities on the sole basis of conceptual valuation, which, according to Whitehead, is a main source of 'error'. As applied to some more unfortunate learning contexts, for example, those in which indoctrination are prevalent, transmutation could be said be the operation responsible for a student developing an attitude of discrimination, or reacting with aversion to members of particular realities or groups on the basis of mere conceptual valuation. In any case, while the operations involved in transmutation and in transmuted feelings constitute "the first step towards intellectual mentality (and Precision), [...] they do not amount to consciousness" (1978, 254, my addition).

4.4 Propositions and Propositional Feelings

Transmutation and transmuted feelings are largely the basis for the formation of propositions and propositional feelings. As described by Whitehead, the ascription of an eternal object to a set of actualities, as in transmutation, and the feeling of the contrast between those actualities and their ascribed eternal objects, as in transmuted feelings, are the chief operations leading to the development of propositions. Symbolic reference, consisting in the emergence of meaning and in the endeavour to give reasons for this or that, is acquired largely through transmutation. Propositions are a further integration of physical and conceptual feelings, involving "the potentiality of the objectification of certain presupposed actual entities via certain qualities and relations" (Whitehead 1978, 196). Precisely, according to Whitehead, both propositions and eternal objects are "definite potentialities for actuality with undetermined realization in actuality [...] but they differ in that an eternal object refers to actuality with absolute generality, whereas a proposition refers to indicated logical subjects" (1978, 258).

In forming propositions, a learner links the indicated logical subjects (the actualities in question) indicated by way of an eternal object, with another set of eternal objects, which are the predicates. In other words, in a proposition, the predicates are attributed to the logical subjects (i.e. the referent actualities) in question. The meaning of any given proposition is a formal contrast between a definite set of actualities, in particular, the logical subjects indicated by a set of eternal objects, namely, the predicates, as represented by another definite set of eternal objects. For Whitehead, a proposition is initially a potential; it "is the possibility of *that* predicate applying in *that* assigned way to *those* logical subjects" (1978, 258). In virtue of a process of selection, by excluding all other actualities and other types or classes of actualities, and eliminating differences within the class in question, negative prehensions play a chief role in acquiring the logical subjects, restricting them only to those indicated. For instance, in the proposition, 'All penguins are black and white', the class of entities: 'penguins' are the indicated logical subjects to the exclusion of all others. Similarly, negative prehensions limit, by elimination, the range of predicates attributable to those logical subjects. Specifically, we are just attributing 'blackness' and 'whiteness' to the logical subjects, to the exclusion of other colors and qualities. Also, in the process by which a proposition is formed, negative prehensions limit the ways in which the logical subjects and the predicates are connected, determining how are related through a selection of a copula or linking verb. In this case, the subject and predicates are linked through the possibility of the particular logical subjects 'being' or 'having' these specific predicates.

Propositional feelings are the feelings of a proposition, particularly, in terms of either element: the logical subjects (as in an 'indicative' feeling) or the predicates (as in a 'predicative' feeling), or of the synthesis of the two. With respect to propositional feelings, negative pre-hensions may serve to eliminate those propositions in which the predicate is immediately inapplicable to the logical subjects and vice-versa. Or, they may eliminate irrelevant, erroneous, or uninteresting propositions, especially those not issuing from the learner's own experience. In the classroom setting, it may be completely irrelevant or uninteresting to students to have to entertain propositions that do not apply to their lived experience. Thus, here we are reminded again that learning-contents must be relevant to the lives of students, and must not be constituted by 'inert ideas', nor webs of 'inert ideas', as consti-tuted by propositions. On the contrary, if a proposition is to be enter-tained by the learner, then it will be analyzed and determined whether it is 'true' or 'false'. Or, the learner will use the propositions as build-ing blocks for syllogisms, deductive and inductive arguments, experi-mentation, and the testing of theories. These intellectual operations are part and parcel of the stage of Precision. In this regard, negative prehensions will be the main intellectual operation in determining the truth or falsity of the propositions, the validity and soundness of argu-ments, and/or the probability of hypotheses. For Whitehead, determina-tions as to the truth or falsity of propositions or theories, the validity and soundness of arguments, and/or the probability of hypotheses all involve intellectual feelings, and the capacity to criticize and to judge. From a Whiteheadian perspective, such criticism and judgement comes only at the level of Precision, where the workings of consciousness may be exhibited.

It is further to be noted here that the development of propositions involves the use of language, as in thought, speech, writing, and other forms of symbolism and signification. For Whitehead, language is the vehicle of expression, of articulation of meaning, and of emancipation from the shackles of our environment. Language constitutes 'the store-house of knowledge' which preserves the past through the ever-peri-shing present, but it is the result of a high level of abstraction from immediate experience. Consequently, Whitehead writes that for the most part, language is "hopeless(ly) ambiguous" (1978, 196). As a central feature of human experience and learning, the very use of lan-guage assumes a lot about the world. The use of language presupposes particular manners of 'division' and 'decision' of the extensive conti-nuum, as for example, the manners assumed in 'substance' ontology, which verge on 'doing violence' to the entities in our environment.

Negative prehensions and processes of selection are the chief operations by which human beings to conceptually 'carve up' the world, and are thereby responsible for any such 'violence' to it. Whitehead's whole cosmology of organism is an attempt to overcome some of these manners of division and decision which are presupposed in contemporary language and consciousness.

5. Negative Prehensions and Selectivity in the Stage of Precision

From a Whiteheadian point of view, the stage of Precision in the learning process may be characterized by the higher phases of experience, as described in the last chapter of Part III of *Process and Reality* (1978), 'The Theory of Prehensions'. These higher phases of learning and experience, in part, highlight a learning process conducive to a critical, process philosophy of education. At the same time, his scheme maintains that experience is primarily 'feeling-based', thus doing justice to feelings and emotions in the learning process. The higher phases of learning are chiefly comprised by critical inquiry and the attainment of a conscious awareness of the subject-matters in question. While consciousness is a rare event, it is only through consciousness that the student overcomes the naïve experience as characterized by the stage of Romance and acquires the capacity for critical thought. As characterized by Freire, it is by way of critical thought and reflection that the learner "increasingly organizes their thinking and thus leads them to move from a purely naïve knowledge of reality to a higher level, one which enables them to perceive the *causes* of reality" (2002, 131). As learners become fully aware of the causes underlying their experience, they are no longer at the mercy of external factors acting on them. They become able to independently select from, and to act on that environment of their own volition. Similarly, they develop their ability to be sceptical, to reflect, to deliberate, to judge, and to criticize propositions, arguments, hypotheses, and ideologies pertaining to the subject-matter, deciding which are valid, sound, just, reasonable, and lead to emancipation, in contrast to those which are invalid, unsound, unjust, unreasonable, oppressive, or subversive. As such, a common activity in higher education that exemplifies the level of Precision in the Arts and Humanities is essay writing, in which a student must construct and coordinate a multitude of propositions. In essay writing, an attempt is made to provide valid and sound arguments in which various perspectives and actualities are critically evaluated, making intellectual decisions in the process. Negation and selectivity via negative prehensions underlie consciousness and are the key elements in cognitive development and in intellectual progress. According to Whitehead, not only is "consciousness [...] the feeling of negation" (1978, 161), but "criticism is the motive power for the advance of thought" (1948, 87). In the higher stages of learning, criticism and sceptical negativity exemplify the operations of negative prehension and selectivity. For example, it is through criticism that learners logically determine what can and should be selected, adhered to, defended, and supported in virtue of what cannot and should not be selected, adhered to, defended, and supported. In a similar spirit, Dewey writes,

> Criticism [...] is judgment engaged in discriminating among values. It is taking thought as to what is better and worse in any field at any time, with some consciousness of why the better is better and why the worse is worse. Critical judgment is [...] not the enemy of creative production but its friend and ally (1930, 12).

As alluded to previously, the operations of transmutation, transmuted feelings, as well as the development of propositions and propositional feelings are processes in which eternal objects are selectively ascribed to actualities. These 'prior' phases of concrescence provide the underlying conditions for the possibility of consciousness. To be sure, Whitehead states that "consciousness follows, and does not precede, the entry of the conceptual prehensions of the relevant universals" (1978, 273) into our experience of the actual, and subsequently, that "there is no consciousness apart from propositions as one element in the objective datum" (1978, 243). By experiencing actualities with the mediation of concepts and propositions, in consciousness, the world is perceived as divided into the fully objectified entities that we conventionally entertain: 'grey tables', 'high chairs', 'black cats', and 'big dogs'. Alternatively-stated, at the level of consciousness, the world is fully objectified or "named" (Freire 2002, 88-89) in the Freirean sense, opening up the possibility for problem-posing, dialogue, and communication. Such division and decision of the extensive continuum is primarily effected by the operations of negative prehending, demonstrating that they are the primary operation in conscious experience. In the higher phases of learning, negative prehensions, as exemplified in the mental operations of scepticism, criticism, decision, division, and judgment are at their most intense. For Whitehead, critical consciousness does not fully sever itself from its basis in feeling, although it may equally be conjectured that feeling does not sever itself from its basis in prior conscious intentionality.

5.1 Intellectual Feelings and Consciousness

Consciousness of learning-contents is attained in a class of feelings which Whitehead calls 'intellectual feelings', comprising a subdivision of 'comparative feelings' in his ontology. There are two types of intellectual feelings: 'intuitive judgments', and 'conscious perceptions.' Essentially, both types of intellectual feelings involve the comparative feeling of the contrast between the nexus of actualities, namely, the logical subject(s) and the proposition in question, which is hypothesized. In both conscious perceptions and intuitive judgments, negation and selectivity are in full force. But, the main difference between them is the fact that conscious perceptions comprise a selective focus on the original objectified actualities that were physically felt or perceived by the learner in immediate experience. In other words, in conscious perceptions, the learner is consciously aware of what was felt, namely, what *caused* the particular feeling felt in the appropriative phases of experience. In intuitive judgments, the reference to actualities is perhaps more generalized, including those not directly perceived by the prehending subject. As Whitehead states,

> what differentiates an intuitive judgment from a conscious perception is that a conscious perception is the outcome of an originative process which has its closest possible restriction to the fact, thus consciously perceived. But the distinction between the two species is not absolute (1978, 272).

By way of the comparative feeling of the actual in its contrast with the potential, as in intellectual feelings, not only is the truth or falsity of the proposition is determined by the learner, but the actual and the potential are themselves either affirmed or negatively prehended. As Whitehead describes, intellectual feelings are comprised by the feeling of the "contrast between a nexus of actual entities and a proposition with its logical subjects members of the nexus" (1978, 266). Precisely, they constitute the feeling of the "contrast between the affirmation of objectified fact in the physical feeling, and the mere potentiality, which is the contrast between '*in fact*' and '*might be*', in respect to particular instances in *this* world" (Whitehead 1978, 267). In Whitehead's synopsis, consciousness is the subjective form of intellectual feelings and is defined as how the learner feels this 'affirmation-negation' contrast, regarding the judgment of what is actual (i.e. what is) and what is potential (i.e. what might be). He elucidates the meaning of consciousness as follows:

> in awareness actuality, as a process in fact, is integrated with the potentialities which illustrate *either* what it is and might not be, *or* what it is not and might be. In other words, there is no consciousness without reference to definiteness, affirmation, and negation. Also affirmation involves its contrast with negation, and negation involves its contrast with affirmation. Further, affirmation and negation are alike meaningless apart from reference to the definiteness of particular actualities. Consciousness is how we feel the affirmation-negation contrast. (Whereas) conceptual feeling is the feeling of unqualified negation; that is to say, it is the feeling of a definite eternal object with the definite extrusion of any particular realization, [...] consciousness requires that the objective datum should involve (as one side of a contrast) a qualified negative determined to some definite situation (1978, 243, my addition).

Therefore, for Whitehead, consciousness implies the judgment of the contrast between actuality and potentiality, with respect to their logical affirmation by positive prehensions or their logical negation through negative prehensions. In the stage of Precision, negative prehensions may be exhibited as scepticism and/or criticism, which, according to Whitehead, are largely based in selective feeling. There are four basic, yet interrelated possibilities with respect to the comparative feelings of actuality and potentiality in the higher levels of learning.

First, there is the case in which actuality is affirmed while the proposition is negatively prehended. The learner critically judges a proposition to be 'false' or 'unsound' since there is incompatible diversity with respect to the proposition and the objectified nexus. It is the judgment that in the face of the empirical or the actual, the proposition is merely imaginative, or even delusional. It is the judgement and criticism of a proposition as 'false', namely, the claims made do not correspond with what is factual, nor with what should be the case. Either it is judged that: 1.) the proposition does not correspond to the actualities or the logical subjects indicated, 2.) the predicate of the proposition is judged to not exemplify the logical subjects in question, or 3.) the predicate of the proposition is not attributable to the logical subjects in the manner signified in the proposition. The judgment that the proposition is false in light of what is actual, exemplifies both the scepticism inherent to the various philosophical forms of realism, as well as in the 'scientific attitude'. In respect to this first possibility, actuality is held to stand higher than what is conceptually entertained, which is negatively judged as 'untrue', doing so with certainty and finality. The negative prehensions here exemplify the analytic meaning of 'being critical' of untrue and dogmatic statements, theories, and beliefs.

Second, there is the case in which the learner affirms a proposition that is incompatible with actual states of affairs, or is 'false', with an "indifference to truth" (Whitehead 1978, 275). The student negatively prehends the actual, while positively embracing the proposition, per-haps as *what should be the case*. The learner is here refusing to eliminate what is being entertained conceptually even in the face of the actual. Or, alternatively, the student is enjoying the imaginative quality of the proposition in question, to the negative prehension or exclusion of what is actual. Or, the student is affirming their own imaginative freedom in virtue of the negative prehension of actuality, thereby entertaining interesting concepts and propositions. Or, quite possibly, the learner may be anticipating that the proposition will be true in the future, or they are perhaps affirming its validity with respect to dif-ferent times and places. This second possibility can be said to char-acterize: 1.) the scepticism inherent to the various philosophical forms of idealism, 2.) ethical conscience, which, for example underlies social activism, in the sense of upholding a certain principle and/ or in the conviction that oppressive states-of-affairs in the world need to be transformed from their present course, 3.) certain aesthetic sensibilities, as well as 4.) religious belief and faith, whereby conceptual experience is held to stand intrinsically higher than actuality. This second case represents a 'negative intuitive judgment'. For Whitehead,

> The triumph of consciousness comes with the negative intuitive judgment. In this case there is a conscious feeling of what might be, and is not. The feeling directly concerns the definite negative prehensions enjoyed by its subject. It is the feeling of absence, and it feels this absence as produced by the definite exclusiveness of what is really present. Thus, the explicitness of negation, which is the peculiar characteristic of consciousness, is here at its maximum (1978, 274).

As such, in a negative intuitive judgment, while actual states-of-affairs are judged negatively, an ideal possibility, realized as itself 'not actual', is affirmed. Negative intuitive judgments, in which negative prehensions are at there most intense, are the hallmark of the attainment of a critical consciousness of concrete states-of-affairs in the world.

There is a third possible situation in which the learner suspends judgment, negating both the potential and the actualities in question. Here, the proposition is positively entertained, but is neither judged to be true nor false. As Whitehead points out, the suspension of judgement is common in the scientific disciplines, as for example, in prolonged hypothesizing or theorizing, without necessarily testing the propositions in question for their truth or falsity. In his descriptions, suspended judgments are "weapons essential to scientific progress" (1978, 275). In many disciplines, such as astronomical physics, there is no contemporary experiment that can prove certain theories or hypotheses to be true or false. According to Whitehead, the suspension of judgment ensures the possibility of progress. Alternatively, in the history of philosophy, the suspension of judgment (*epochē*) was the main doctrine of the original schools of scepticism in Ancient Greece. The ancient Sceptics were masters of the dialectic and used their 'tropes' (*tropoi*) or strategies of argumentation in order to neither give assent, nor dissent to any proposition whatsoever. The negative prehensions involved in the suspension of judgment can be characterized in these ways.

Fourth, there is the possibility that the learner will judge a proposition to be 'true' in which case the proposition corresponds to actuality, which what Whitehead calls an 'affirmative intuitive judgement'. In this case, both the proposition and actuality are affirmed and neither are negated. The proposition is judged to represent or conform empirically to the 'facts' with respect to the actualities indicated. For White-head, "'truth' is the absence of incompatibility [...] in the patterns of the nexus and of the proposition in their generic contrast" (1978, 271). In particular, there is identity with respect to the proposition and the objectified nexus. To this extent, an affirmative intuitive judgment represents the satisfaction of a correspondence theory of truth. As Whitehead describes,

> The theory of judgment in the philosophy of organism can [...] be described as a 'correspondence' theory [...]. It is a correspondence theory, because it describes judgment as the subjective form of the integral prehension of the conformity, or of the non-conformity, of a proposition and an objectified nexus (1978, 190).

Here, truth is 'the absence of incompatibility' between, or of 'the conformity of' the proposition and the actualities in question. The subsequent affirmation of the compatibility between the proposition and what is actual, exemplifies the satisfaction of the scepticisms inherent to the various philosophical forms of realism and idealism. However, for Whitehead, 'truth' does not necessarily imply an affirmation of the correspondence between the proposition and the actual on the part of the prehending subject. For 'true' propositions can conform to facts that are painful, horrible, or otherwise negative to the feeling subject.

The operations of negative prehensions are at their most intense in respect to these four interrelated possibilities. But, as Whitehead observes, at this higher level of learning, there is a double problem. Not only does the learner judge the truth and falsity of propositions in terms of what is in practice, but either affirms or negatively prehends what is actual or what is conceptual, both, or neither. In the stage of Precision, propositions are not only judged to be true or false by way of the operations of negative prehensions, but their truth or falsity is not the only criteria by which the learner either affirms or negatively prehends them. Therefore, judgments as to the truth and falsity of propositions in relation to what is actual require not only logical negation and objectivity, but are part and parcel of selective interest, based in the learner's subjective feeling. In this regard, Whitehead suggests that "in the real world it is more important that a proposition be interesting than that it be true. The importance of truth is, that it adds to interest" (1978, 259).

As exemplifying the thesis that negative prehensions are the efficient causal element involved in the learning process, the preceding characterization of the stage of Precision has emphasized that their operation is at their fullest force. Negative prehensions are intrinsic to the attainment and to the constitution of a critical consciousness of the subject-matter in question. In the same vein, Dewey proclaims, "creative activity is our great need; but criticism, self-criticism, is the road to its release" (1930, 25).

6. Negative Prehension and Selectivity in the Stage of Generalization

Whitehead's stage of Generalization is the stage of educational 'self-realization', of the 'satisfaction' of the student's 'subjective aims', and of synthesis, in which the negative prehensions involved in the comparative feeling of actuality and potentiality are fully worked out in virtue of a correspondence theory of truth. In the stage of Generalization, the 'rift' between actuality and potentiality, as exemplified by the inherent scepticisms and critical antagonisms exemplified by philosophical forms of realism and idealism, is bridged. As such, Generalization is the moment of speculative endeavour and inquiry.

In the stage of Generalization, the learner: 1.) selectively applies the knowledge gained to life and experience; 2.) continues to think independently, critically, and creatively about the subject-matters considered, possibly even criticizing judgments made in the stage of Precision; 3.) acts concretely on what has been learned in terms of *praxis*; and 4.) is or becomes aware of the logical contrasts inherent in the knowledge or subject-matters learned. The student develops their ability to "convert [...] exclusions into contrasts" (Whitehead 1978, 223), thus "correcting the initial excess of subjectivity" (1978, 15) developed in the stage of Precision, and "recover(ing) the totality obscured" (1978, 15) by the selective character of the critical consciousness developed therein. That is to say, in the stage of Generalization, the student overcomes the 'misplaced concreteness' stemming from the divisions, decisions, eliminations, exclusions, and bifurcations of the stage of Precision, by an awareness of logical contrasts.

According to Whitehead, a logical contrast signifies the notion that "opposed elements stand to each other in their mutual requirement"

(1978, 348). In Whiteheadian terminology, a logical contrast runs counter to an incompatibility of extremes. The awareness of logical contrasts does not merely signify 'neutrality', 'liberalism', 'relativism', or a 'suspension of judgment'. Rather, it involves the comparative feeling of, and a prehensive selection from more complex perspectives, standpoints, and realities. It also may involve the negating of the negation that divides opposed perspectives and the further honing of the student's capacities to judge. Particularly, it is the awareness that two or more concepts, propositions, or positions mutually condition one another, and can be critiqued in their interrelation. Thus, negative prehensions play an overriding role in developing an awareness of logical contrasts. Precisely, the logical interrelation of two or more concepts, propositions, or positions becomes evident when two or more opposing sides are negated, and in some cases, when they are mediated by a third term. In this sense, in logically dissolving oppositions into contrasts, negative prehensions have a two-way eliminatory role, as distinct from their largely one-way eliminatory roles as exemplified in the stage of Precision. Similarly, it is by being aware of logical contrasts that we know the limitations of one-sided positions, and can determine, select, or create novel standpoints that are more reasonable and effective. For example, ideally, having completed an Environmental Ethics class, a student develops their own critical perspective and adopts some of the values of an ecological perspective, acting so as to defend ecological justice. Through action at the level of *praxis*, the student applies what they have learned, bringing the potentialities of the ecological perspective into actuality. Through social action, the learner insists that local power plants measure the emission of fossil fuels, to ensure that they fall within ecological standards. However, the student also knows that her perspective stands in contrast to the type of militant standpoint of radical environmentalists who use violence to promote their views. While the student holds an anti-anthropocentric view against the prioritization of human life over nature, she also feels that radical groups which one-sidedly value nature over human life are not justified in their actions when they place traps in forests in order to hurt or kill loggers. In the student's deliberation of the contrast at issue, human life does not stand condescendingly higher than nature, nor does nature stand infinitely higher than human life. Therefore, as distinct from the stage of Precision, in Generalization, the development of the awareness of logical contrasts may involve the two-way negation of interrelated factors, an awareness of their causal inter-connection, and the overcoming of one-sided positions and one-sidedness in judgment. Generalization, as pertaining to the stage of 'satisfaction' in Whitehead's theory of prehensions, also constitutes a return to Romance, to feeling-based experience, and to a new cycle of learning. Having completed a particular cycle of learning, the student moves on to anticipate and learn new subject-matters, or perhaps to teach the ones previously learned.

From a Whiteheadian perspective, the awareness of logical contrasts and of contrasts of contrasts, implying the capacity to synthesize antagonistic perspectives, as in the stage of Generalization, is of the essence of wisdom, and constitutes the ultimate realization in learning. But, it must also be reiterated that each of the three Whiteheadian stages of Romance, Precision, and Generalization, or 'feeling', 'consciousness', and 'contrast' as alternatively characterized in terms of the theory of prehensions, have their respective places in higher education. None of these moments should be overstated at the expense of the others. Rather, the three moments constitute a rhythmic process, each complementing and providing relief for the overemphasis of the previous one, as in a conceptual whole. The theory of prehensions is perhaps an articulation of the cycles Whitehead describes as the 'Rhythms of Education' in their widest possible trajectory.

7. From Selectivity in Learning to Selectivity in Teaching

The preceding analysis has linked Whitehead's outline of the stages of learning, namely, the 'Rhythms of Education' with some of the general contours of the theory of prehensions. It has endeavoured to show that Whitehead's theory of prehensions provides us with a comprehensive framework within which we may understand learning processes. In this paper, I have pointed to the theme of selectivity in learning, which occurs primarily by means of the operations of negative prehensions in their fluctuating interplay with positive prehensions. I have shown that negative prehensions function in every phase of concrescence and, at each stage, can be said to 'move' or to 'drive' the process by which the student selects, appropriates, owned, modifies, transforms, utilizes, and acts on learning contents. Negative prehensions 'guide' the entire creative process by which both contrasts logically emerge and the awareness of contrasts is developed. In short, negative prehensions may be described as the 'lure' for contrasts. However, with respect to its application to pedagogy in higher education, the implications of this thesis demand further reflection, qualifycation, questioning, and contrast. This is the case since, in direct relation to learning processes, Whitehead writes that while "the right coordination of negative prehensions is one secret of mental progress, [...] unless some systematic scheme of relatedness characterizes the environment, there will be nothing left whereby to constitute vivid prehension of the world" (1978, 254). Hence, by defending the thesis that negative prehension is the efficient causal element involved in learning, it is not my intention to here endorse an instrumental use of negation and selectivity as a pedagogical strategy. Instead, my intent is precisely to question the current instrumental over-emphasis on, and demand for radical critique, sceptical negativity, selectivity in higher education. Especially, I take issue with those pedagogies in which teachers dogmatically impose curriculum contents onto students as well as neglect any questioning of the abstractions of consciousness.

In subsequent papers, I shall emphasize the alternate side of the 'growing together' of student and teacher, focusing on the theme of selectivity in teaching. Since the teacher's own process of self-realization is based in the process of self-realization of students, I will outline the role of selectivity in nurturing and directing learners in their processes of self-development, from a Whiteheadian point of view. There, I shall demonstrate the affinity between the notion of teacher and Whitehead's notion of 'subject-superject'. Later, I will deal with the question as to what the limits, ethical or otherwise, should be placed on the role of negative prehension and selectivity in education. Arguing against those instrumental pedagogies of excessive negativity, objectification, and ontological division of reality, I will evaluate the extent to which professors in higher education should foster attitudes of negation and selectivity in their students.

Bibliography
Dewey, J. (1930): *Construction and Criticism*. New York: Columbia University Press.
Flynn, M. (2001): Learning in the Process of Teaching, *What is a Teacher-Scholar? Symposium Proceedings*, Gwenna Moss Teaching and Learning Centre, University of Saskatchewan, 1-9.

Fidyk, S. L. (1997): *Experience and Learning in the Educational Thought of Alfred North Whitehead: A Teacher's Perspective*, M.Ed Thesis dissertation, University of Saskatchewan, Howard Woodhouse, Robert Regnier, and Mark Flynn, 1997.

Freire, P. (2002/1970): *Pedagogy of the Oppressed*. New York: Continuum International Publishing Group.

Kraus, E. M. (1998): *The Metaphysics of Experience: A Companion to Whitehead's Process and Reality*. New York: Fordham University Press.

McMurtry, J. (1988): The History of Inquiry and Social Reproduction: Educating for Critical Thought, *Interchange* 19, 1, 31-45.

Mellert, R. B. (1998): Searching for the Foundations of Whitehead's Philosophy of Education, *Paideia*, Twentieth World Congress of Philosophy, Boston, Massachusetts, 1998, URL: www.bu.edu/wep/Papers/Educ/EducMell.htm.

Santayana, G. (1955/1923): *Scepticism and Animal Faith*. New York: Dover Publications.

Scarfe, A. (2003): Whitehead's Theory of Prehensions as Inclusive of, and Conducive to a Philosophy of Education. *Process Studies Supplements* Issue 4, URL: http://www.ctr4process.org/publications/PSS/.

Schilpp, P. A. (Ed.) (1951): *The Library of Living Philosophers, Vol.3: The Philosophy of Alfred North Whitehead*. New York: Tudor Publishing.

Sherburne, D. W. (Ed.) (1966): *A Key to Whitehead's Process and Reality*. Chicago: University of Chicago Press.

Smith, J. E. (1983): *The Spirit of American Philosophy*. Albany: SUNY.

Whitehead, A. N. (1948): *Essays in Science and Philosophy*. New York: Philosophical Library.

Whitehead, A. N. (1967a/1929): *The Aims of Education*. New York: The Free Press.

Whitehead, A. N. (1967b1925): *Science and the Modern World*. New York: The Free Press.

Whitehead, A. N. (1967c/1933): *Adventures of Ideas*. New York: The Free Press.

Whitehead, A. N. (1968/1938): *Modes of Thought*. New York: The Free Press.

Whitehead, A. N. (1978/1929): *Process and Reality*. (Corrected Edition) New York: Free Press.

Whitehead, A. N. (1985/1927): *Symbolism: Its Meaning and Effect*. New York: Fordham University Press.

A Whiteheadian Theory of Creative, Synthetic Learning and Its Relevance to Educational Reform in China

Ronald P. Phipps

Abstract

The theory of creative synthetic education holds that curiosity should function as the driving force in educational systems. Education must concurrently transfer the knowledge resultant from antecedent processes of discovery and enhance the lure felt by students for future discoveries and innovations.

Educational systems must lead students on journeys of curiosity and develop a passion in students for discovery. To do so, synthetic and relational modes of thought are essential to achieve the generalizations of insights that are the foundation for wisdom. Research processes appropriate to local conditions, interests and abilities must pervade educational processes from primary to secondary to advanced stages of learning.Analytic and synthetic modes of thinking must be integrated and harmonized.

The reform of education systems is vital to China and, moreover, constitutes a task of increasing global importance. Education, as Whitehead stressed, must move beyond passive absorption of inert ideas and facts.

Progressive educational systems must develop forms and modalities to stimulate and nurture the innovative, imaginative and creative capacities and passion of students. These methods and modalities requisite to stimulating creativity and synthetic modes of thought must transcend the limitations inherent in over reliance upon standardized examinations. Only if and when educational systems do so, can education contribute to the vibrant and vigorous advance of human civilization from lower to higher levels. Synthetic creative education guides students and teachers as co-participants on journeys of curiosity amid communities of related problems and related phenomena,

which journeys are resolved through adventures of disovery
and generalization of insight. Such processes form the foundation of wisdom and provoke the experience and emoion in
students of exhilaration for the intrinsic value of learning and
discovery.

1. Introduction

The interaction among Process thinkers from the East and West holds
great promise to help liberate the creative potentials of our cultures to
cooperatively contribute to the advancement of human civilization. The
most general expression of this potential resides within the realm of
education, which embraces all forms of human inquiry and human
curiosity.

My own academic work centers on the philosophy of theoretical
physics and the creation of an alternative theory to the reigning dogmas
of 20th century physics, namely relativity theory, quantum mechaics,
string theory and the big bang theory. Specifically I have developed,
under the influence of process philosophy, a vision of an infinite and
open universe, infinite and eternal in its spatial and temporal magnitudes, and manifesting a dynamic, integrating orderliness among fields
of events from which is derivative infinite qualitative variety at the
core of Being.

In this metaphysics, the quest for causal orderliness amid qualitaive
variety is primary and reductionism's quest to suppress and reduce
apparent qualitative variety to: 1) qualitative sameness of constituents
and 2) immense geometric variety is secondary and limited, though
often of considerable philosophic and scientific value. The philosohical
hypothesis that both qualitative variety and orderliness are omnipresent
and fundamental to the core of Being in an infinite and eternal universe
is relevant to the philosophic perspective underlying the theory of
creative, synthetic learning.

I would like to discuss the creative application of process philosophy to educational reform.

2. The Goals of Educational Reform

Among western Process thinkers, Alfred North Whitehead holds a unique place for the depth of his creative originality and the broad scope of his contributions to intellectual history, which range from:

1) mathematical logic expressed in Whitehead and Russell's monumental *Principia Mathematica* which, in the judgment of the great German mathematician David Hilbert, was potentially "history's crowning achievement of axiomatization of systems," (Hilbert 1918, 412)

2) theoretical physics, where Sir Arthur Eddington, the great British astro-physicist, judged Whitehead to have produced insights more profound than Einstein's,[1] to

3) metaphysics, where at Harvard, Whitehead developed the most coherent, consistent, creative, comprehensive and challenging philosophic system in human history.

Whitehead, having creatively bridged intellectual disciplines and the continents, attained a position which should warrant our thoughtful attention to his theory of education. Moreover, we should seek to develop and apply Whitehead's theory to reform and transform current

---

[1] Eddington, who was so instrumental in persuading physicists of the importance of Einstein's work, was also intrigued by Whitehead's approach to theoretical physics and increasingly came to perceive its profundity. He wrote, "We agree that at the end of the synthesis there must be a linkage to the familiar world of consciousness, and we are not necessarily opposed to attempts to reach the physical world from that end. From the point of view of philosophy it is desirable that this entrance should be explored, and it is conceivable that it may be fruitful scientifically, if I have rightly understood Dr. Whitehead's philosophy – his method of 'extensive bstraction' is intended to overcome some of the difficulties of such a procedure. I am not qualified to form a critical judgment of this work, but in principle it appears highly interesting – I think it ould be true to regard him as an ally who from the opposite side of the mountain is tunneling to meet his less philosophically minded colleagues." (Eddington 1927, 249f) Victor Lowe draws our attention to a similar remark made by Eddington: "Eddington who had done much to get Einstein's work accepted, remarked in 1933 that he could see that in some respects the philosopher's insight had been superior, but that it had come out of season for the physicist." (1990, 127)

systems wherever such systems restrain the advance of wisdom and understanding.

Whitehead criticizes the uselessness of reforming educational systems without a clear conception of the attributes which you wish to evoke in the living minds of students. (see: Whitehead 1967, 7-8) The characteristics which must be the aim of meaningful educational reform include:

- Integrity and independence of thought;
- Deep and relentless curiosity;
- Coherency of thought;
- Respect for the collective genius that is the legacy that the past bestows upon the present;
- An abiding sense of romance, adventure and delight in discovery;
- Compassion;
- Integrative thinking;
- A bold, courageous and challenging spirit willing to question entrenched intellectual and cultural presuppositions;
- Ability at problem-solving;
- Creativity;
- Students who are readers and, moreover, thinkers;
- Imagination capable of envisioning novel phenomena, relationships and modes of orderliness.[2]

A copy of Rodin's great statue The Thinker stands before the library at Stanford University. The Thinker's hands are not occupied holding books, but it is upon his hands that his head rests, lost in deep contemplation. Reading must be subservient to thinking, for without independent, reflective and contemplative thinking, reading, for Whitehead, degenerates into effete bookishness. Whitehead's personal assistant at Harvard, the former President of the American Philosophy Association, Professor Henry S. Leonard, challengingly observed "the trouble

---

[2] "A scientific education is primarily a training in the art of observing natural phenomena and in the knowledge and deduction of laws concerning the sequence of such phenomena." (Whitehead 1967, 49)

with American intellectuals is that they read too much and think too little."[3]

In this talk I want to begin the development of a Whiteheadian Theory of Creative Synthetic Learning. I define this theory as *the guidance and nurturing of students upon journeys of curiosity amid communities of problems, journeys which are resolved in adventures of discovery and generalization of insight.*

The key concepts are:

1) Journeys of curiosity;
2) Communities of problems;
3) Adventures of discovery;
4) Generalization of insight.

Education has two concurrent functions. The first is to transfer into the present the trillions upon trillions of individual and collective acts of discovery throughout the globe and history which form the intellectual legacy which history bestows upon the present. "After all the child is heir to long ages of civilization, and it is absurd to let him wander in the intellectual maze of men in the Glacial Epoch." (Whitehead 1967, 33) The second function is to instill the lure and the romance felt in the present by living, active students for discoveries and generalization of insight in the future.

If educational systems address only the first function and neglect the second, students are rendered passive and education becomes, in Whitehead's metaphor, 'like a trunk, passively stuffed with articles' or like a passive, caged and force fed Beijing duck – delicious, but without a future. It is the second function that makes education alive, as students become active explorers of future possibilities. Curiosity becomes the engine driving creativity.

It is only under conditions where the roots of curiosity are nurtured and those roots spread widely and penetrate deeply that societies become vigorous, vibrant, creative and innovative.

---

[3] Leonard, Henry S. (personal conversation with Ronald Phipps). Whitehead similarly commented: "Great readers, who exclude other activities (including reflective and independent thinking) are not distinguished by subtlety of brain. They tend to be timid conventional thinkers." (1967, 51)

A Whiteheadian theory of creative and synthetic learning is consistent with Whitehead's broader philosophic perspectives. Whitehead's philosophy of process and organism emphasizes that the constituents of the world are processes which exist in interdependent relationality with other events which together constitute still broader, enveloping and interacting communities. Events arise from multiplicities of antecedent events and their characters are developed from multiplicities of variables. Inherent within events are rich and multiple potentialities to influence the character of those succeeding events which will constitute a given event's causal future. The universe is rich in qualitative variety, orderliness, causal potentiality and openness. Within communities of events there is the perpetual perishing and the perpetual emergence of events, the perpetual frustration and the perpetual realization of potentials for causal efficacy that are compatible for co-existence within, but incompatible for co-realization by, the events constituent of the universe. It is precisely because of the structure and relationality of our universe of communities of dynamically interacting events and communities of ideas and forms that synthetic learning is necessary for the advance of knowledge and wisdom.

3. China, Creativity and Educational Reform

China's history is one of immense and glorious contributions to world civilization. Whitehead notes with profound appreciation the creative and innovative role which the people of China have played. The encyclopedic work of Professor Joseph Needham of Cambridge University regarding the history of science and civilization in China describes the breadth and depth of scientific innovation and intellectual creativity which occurred in Chinese history.[4] For a long period of time, however, that creativity has been largely stifled and stagnant. Whitehead, in *Science and the Modern World*, like other observers of

---

[4] Needham and colleagues (1994) demonstrated in their monumental work the historic breadth of the Chinese peoples' creativity and the immensity of their contributions to world civilization. It is now important to comprehend both the causes and the cures for the comparative inhibition during many centuries of the creative capacities in science of Eastern civilizations. The cure, in this author's view, resides in the development and universalization, within all levels of learning, of creative, synthetic modes of learning.

intellectual history, notes and ponders this comparative stagnation: "[T]he more we know of Chinese art, of Chinese literature, and of the Chinese philosophy of life the more we admire the heights to which that civilization attained. For thousands of years, there have been in China acute and learned men patiently devoting their lives to study. Having regard to span of time, and to the population, China forms the largest volume of civilization the world has seen. There is no reason to doubt the intrinsic capacity of individual Chinese for the pursuit of science. And yet Chinese science is practically negligible...the same may be said of India." (Whitehead 1953 6) The fact remains that for many reasons the gap between the great potential for scientific and engineering genius and innovation and the actual results is, as Whitehead notes, a large gap.

The causes of this phenomenon are both external and internal. China, for several centuries, was the victim of predatory European imperialism and Japanese fascism, and Japan's and Europe's talons penetrated deeply into the soul of the Chinese nation. Preceding the time of China's victimization by external empires, China's culture also exhibited a national chauvinism which led Chinese scholarship to fixate geographically upon China, conceived as the Middle or Central Kingdom, and temporally upon China's accomplished past not its creative potentials for the future. The failure to look beyond either its spatial borders, or its temporal past, were underlying factors in creating the weakness which allowed the victimization of China, a victimization which brought to its people such immense and heart breaking suffering, poverty and stagnation during the 17th through the 20th centuries.

Following Golden Centuries of discovery, innovation and invention, the comparative stagnation suffered by Chinese society was also a consequence of an entrenched, underlying philosophy and morality based upon hierarchies. Officials were subservient to the Emperor, the people subservient to officialdom, the young to the authority of the old, the female to the male, the student to the teacher, the future to the past and innovative discovery to the feudal and highly formalistic Confucian examination system.[5]

---

[5] "The best procedure will depend on several factors [...] the genius of the teacher, the intellectual type of the pupils, their prospects in life, the opportunities offered by the immediate surroundings of the school [...]. It is for this

Progressive and vibrant social development reduces such extenuated and retrogressive hierarchies. Government is subservient to the people's interests and democratic dialogue, discussion and decision making processes supercedes the authoritarianism of officialdom, the old exists in service to the positive potentials of the young, the female and male are co-equal, the teacher's function is to elicit the creativity of the student, the past guides and enriches the future and examination systems are secondary to processes of discovery, curiosity, creativity, innovation, invention and profound and fresh insights.

The transformation of China, beginning in the middle of the 20th Century, is widely acknowledged as an astounding feat in world history. No one talks today of China as 'the sick man of Asia.' Despite the impressive achievements of the Chinese people, China's contributions to path-breaking discoveries and its articulation of new theoretical vistas, are largely underdeveloped or merely nascent. This gap between China's potential and its achievements, in respect to original research and path-breaking innovation, persists in the present. This gap harms both China and the larger world to which China may contribute.

The great Chinese writer and social critic Lu Xun (1881-1936) noted how the Chinese people came to vascillate between the extremes of condescension towards the external 'barbarians' and blind, uncritical worship of all things foreign. Lu Xun noted the errors which inevitably follow when, and if, a nation exaggerates the virtues or vices, strengths or weaknesses, of either itself or other nations and cultures. Cool eyed, objective and balanced appraisal and understanding of both oneself and others, are essential to all successful and progressive reforms.

China today stands at the crossroads between: i) remaining a largely imitative but powerful global economic force, and (ii) restoring its historic position as a world center of creativity, innovation and invention. Whether or not China can integrate systems of creative synthetic learning within its educational processes and, thereby, infuse and inspire students with a deep sense of the intrinsic value and romance of learning will determine if China takes the path of imitativeness or the path of innovation.

This choice is relevant to China but not peculiar to China. Developing meaningful methods to evaluate talent is, of course, relevant to

---

reason that the uniform external examination is so deadly." (Whitehead 1967, 5) all nations. However, the deeper imperative concerns not the evaluation of talent but the development and cultivation of creative talent, synthetic thinking and relational understanding. When creative synthetic learning is absent from the ethos and spirit of societies, and their educational systems, those societies either decay or stagnate into mediocrity. In contrast, when creative synthetic learning characterizes and impels a society's educational system, that society will more fully liberate its positive potentials and contribute to the creative advance of human civilization.

4. Curiosity and Living Organisms

The role of curiosity is fundamental. The great Harvard scientist E. O. Wilson cites "boundless curiosity" as a precondition of the scientific revolution and calls it "the greatest of all human virtues." (Wilson 1998, 52 & 61) Curiosity is indeed intrinsic to, and thus, inherent within, all complex forms of zoological life. Whitehead consistently reminds us that the student is "a living organism which grows, by its own impulse toward self-development. This impulse can be stimulated and guided from outside the organism, and it can also be killed. But for all your stimulation and guidance the creative impulse towards growth comes from within, and is intensely characteristic of the individual." (Whitehead 1967, 39) The intensity of curiosity differs both among and within species, but the active presence of curiosity is essential to both the survival and advancement of all complex life forms.

In 1867, the German mathematician of the infinite, George Cantor, centered his doctoral dissertation upon the theme that 'in mathematics the art of asking questions is more valuable than solving problems'. (see: Cantor 1867) The German mathematician David Hilbert challenged the world of mathematics in the beginning of the 20th century with "23 fundamental unanswered mathematical problems." (Hilbert 1900) E. O. Wilson has observed, "[…a scientist] searches his imagination for subjects [of inquiry] as much as for conclusions, for questions as much as for answers." (Willson 1998, 62)

Whitehead, throughout his writings on education, speaks of the evocation of curiosity: "The evocation of curiosity, of judgment, of the power of mastering a complicated tangle of circumstances, the use of theory in giving foresight in special cases – all of these powers are to be imparted by a set rule embodied in the schedule of examination subjects." (1967, 5) He speaks of curiosity as the engine to discovery. Countless discoveries have arisen in human intellectual history because someone asked a question not asked before, someone challenged an entrenched presupposition of thought, someone altered a set of variables, someone synthesized concepts or observations, which previously were detached, fragmented and, thereby, in Whitehead's view, inert. (see: Whitehead 1967, 1) Whitehead also recognizes that, "We subdue the forces of nature because we have been lured to discover by an insatiable curiosity." (1967, 31)

Whitehead points out that "The basis of the growth of modern invention is science, and science is almost wholly the outgrowth of pleasurable intellectual curiousity." (1967, 45) The centrality and pervasiveness of curiosity in the behavior of complex life forms is not fully appreciated. Curiosity is indeed at the core of purposeful, teleological processes. When a book is read, a movie looked at, a sport competition observed, a symphony or folk song heard, a card or board game played, or a problem's solution pursued, curiosity is present as the driving, impelling force. What will happen next, how, when and why it will happen, are questions that intensely engage humans.

Curiosity, furthermore, plays an enormous and largely unrecognized role in aesthetic appreciation. A flat surface or a straight line in contrast to a bending surface and curving line, will exhibit the same direction manifest between its parts A and B and its parts B and C. Whereas, in a curving and bending surface or line, the direction between parts A and B and parts B and C exhibit continuous change. Change in direction among their parts is definitive of intrigue for curved entities. For irregularly curved and bending entities, the degree of change in direction among their parts varies at different transition points. When there is balanced, harmonious and concentrated change and contrast within the nexus of events perceived, aesthetic experience emerges and high levels of aesthetic satisfaction are attainable. Change and the potential for change, in contrasts to sameness, provokes curiosity which itself is integral to aesthetic experience.

Consider viewing the vast Pacific Ocean from the mountains and cliffs of central California. The coastline is scalloped. The bays and the coves manifest the curvature of the coastline itself. The sacred mountains and cliffs rise and bend with countless undulations. The ocean's waves rise, fall and crash. In a plethora of curves, the waves advance towards the sea's shore. The waves advance, retreat and reach moments of equilibrium in which, for a period, the waves neither advance nor retreat. Within this 4 dimensional spatial and temporal environment, the perceiving individual is confronted with countless experiences of curiosity regarding the manifold changes with their varying magnitudes of intensities that are manifest within the spatio-temporal domain of mountains, cliffs, sea and sky. It is like the straight, flat-planed rectangle, which when twisted and transformed into a mobius strip, becomes an object of fascination, intrigue and beauty. Curiosity about change and contrast is implicated in the aesthetic experiences of complex living organisms.

The soaring curves of a hawk in the azure sky, the movement of and billowing of clouds and the transition of color from bright crimsons, turquoise, greens, rich purples, pure whites, brilliant oranges and dazzling yellows of the sunset as the sun descends below the horizon, are also manifestations of the provocation of curiosity during heightened aesthetic experience.

Curiosity is essential and intrinsic to all purposeful and teleological phenomena. Curiosity is fundamental to the general experience of adversion. The character of the past is perceived in the present and options regarding the character of future events are envisioned, wondered about, anticipated and pursued or avoided under what Whitehead calls the 'subjective forms' of adversion or aversion which impels and propels teleological behavior.

Appetition always involves the anticipation of and lure towards future possibilities. The anticipation of such possibilities (propositions) is interwoven with curiosity regarding the consequences of their transition from the realm of the possible to that of the actual. This tapestry of appetition and curiosity woven together propels the adventures and creative urges of civilized existence.

Curiosity functions at the very core of all purposeful, teleological and aesthetic experience. Rigid authoritarianism resulting in the passive absorption of facts and data too often dulls curiosity. In contrast, curiosity should and must freely roam as the most active, most alive, most dynamic and most cherished force of meaningful and enriching mental activity. Curiosity is analogous to the force of gravity, which is to say that it must be respected if educational systems are to do their job well. Curiosity must be fundamental to all forms and all stages of the educational process. Without the active presence of curiosity, education is like stuffing inert ideas into a trunk destined to go nowhere. This general philosophic understanding of the centrality of living, breathing and pulsating curiosity must better guide the methods and modalities of educational systems if those systems are to accomplish and further their progressive mandate.

Curiosity is not only one of the greatest of virtues but it is a pervasive element present from the inception to the cessation of complex organisms. The cessation and diminution of curiosity is indeed concomitant with the cessation and diminution of life itself.

5. Journeys of Curiosity

Educational systems must welcome and nurture curiosity, not stifle nor thwart it. This is true of preschools, elementary schools, middle schools, high schools, universities and graduate schools. All levels of schools must be nurseries cultivating curiosity which is transplanted into the broader life and purposes of social being. Only when, and to the extent to which, curiosity is nurtured is it possible to not only transfer existent knowledge but to advance knowledge.

Education, if it is to infuse students and teachers with the lure of future discoveries, must inspire and guide students upon journeys of curiosity. There are 3 types of journeys: One is the solitary, contemplative and reflective journey illustrated in the famous walks of Louis De Broglio, the Nobel Laureate, who developed quantum wave theory. The second type of journey is typified by the collaboration of a team, such as Whitehead and Russell's collaboration in creating the magnus opus, *Principia Mathematica*, or that of the young Einstein and his wife Mileva Maric-Einstein, in pondering the questions of light that led to relativity theory. The third type of journey is the extensive, broader and often international collaborative effort that is expressed when, for example: 1) hundreds of scientists examine data from particle accelerators; 2) cosmologists cooperatively examine and collect data from astronomical observatories located throughout the globe; 3) data is gathered on global weather patterns and global environmental conditions; or 4) data on the economic trends both within and among the world's nations is compared. Educational systems can and should expose students to each of these fundamental forms of journeys of curiosity and their ultimate interplay one with another.

While group journeys of curiosity of type 2) and 3) are invaluable, we cannot underestimate the vital role of contemplation, of mulling problems over, of pondering and lingering over data and concepts. Einstein once remarked, "It is not that I am so smart, it's just that I stay with problems longer." (Singh 2005) Creativity, synthesis of ideas, cogency of thought and discovery necessitate that concepts, axioms, data and theorems deeply enter both conscious and unconscious mental processes. That is the valuable lesson to be learned from the contemplative sage. The consequences of premises are never fully perceived. (see: Whitehead 1967, 109) It is only through processes of conscious and unconscious contemplation of concepts and axioms that we can discern the fuller implications of ideas and propositions.

The acquisition of knowledge must be active, not passive. Conscious and unconscious processes must be free to mull over the rich meaning of concepts and axioms. Whitehead, speaking of the transforming capacity of knowledge, writes: "This atmosphere of excitement, arising from imaginative consideration, transforms knowledge. A fact is no longer a bare fact: it is invested with all its possibilities. It is no longer a burden on the memory: it is energising as the poet of our dreams, and as the architect of our purposes." (1967, 93) How beautifully expressed! Facts are invested with all their possibilities as students and teachers alike perceive facts within that broader community constituted by the implications and relationality of a given set of facts and ideas with other facts, concepts and possibilities. It is the contemplative entertainment of ideas that invest ideas with 'all their possibilities.'

Understanding is not instantaneous nor can it be rushed; nor is it ever complete; understanding simmers into richness as a wine ages into higher levels of quality and smoothness. This is why Einstein speaks of 'staying with problems longer.' Understanding deepens as the relations among propositions are integrated through deductive and imaginative processes of conscious and unconscious thought.

It should be noted that teachers can and should be co-participants with their students on these journeys of curiosity and adventures of discovery. The teacher may be a guide and stimulus but need not be a figure of dominance, hierarchy or authoritarianism. Indeed, the student must have the freedom to point out new vistas of beauty and intrigue not previously noted and new problems not previously raised. We should always remember there are no bad questions. What is bad is the suppression of questioning. Even questions that may seem on the surface to be simple may require profound and powerful concepts for their fuller understanding. For example the question why 1 plus 1 equals 2 was elucidated by the mathematical logic of *Principia Mathematica*. The simple question of why an apple falls from a tree to the ground was central to Newton's creation of classical mechanics. The type of phenomena raised by Newton's question has historically generated different theories of gravitational attraction, such as Newton's theory of classic mechanics, Einstein's Theory of General Relativity and Whitehead's Process Metaphysics.

The discernment and the cultivation of these creative abilities for discovery are essential. And yet the discernment and cultivation of creative abilities, it must be noted, does not enjoy a direct and consistent correlation with skillfulness at "test taking." The impulse, the initiative, the ability, the curiosity, the creativity, and what Whitehead stresses as the "passion" for discovery, need to be nurtured and evaluated through multiple modalities not confined to, nor constricted by, skill at taking standardized examinations. This is an important matter for China's educational system, but also for Western educational systems. American educational systems have too often become stifled by simplistic and compulsive obsessions with state and national examinations to the sacrifice of the cultivation of curiosity and discovery skills which are integral to progressive and effective educational systems. Teachers are reduced to teaching to the test, not teaching about an exciting subject. The integration of intellectual skills and active curiosity is absent from many educational systems that emphasize a narrow form of pragmatism as their guiding educational philosophy.

In America there is growing criticism from student, teachers and educators regarding the over emphasis upon standardized testing. This critique is very intense in Texas, which in recent years has aggressively promulgated reliance on state examination conducted under the slogan "Leave no Child Behind". One very bright student, Macario Guajardo, commented about Texas' testing program, "[...it] keeps kids from expressing their imagination." (Blumenthal 2005)

Theorists of education policies have postulated that there is an inverse relationship between the emphasis upon "teaching to the tests" and "educating students." The critique has been succinctly expressed with the observation that for every efforts to add to the student's scores, there is a corresponding diminution of the students' creativity and curiosity.

It is vital for all cultures, including Chinese culture which has revered the "aged" and the "sage," to recognize that wisdom, insight, profundity and creativity are not confined to the aged. The capacity for creative synthetic insights is what we must consider in assessing genius, not age.

Chinese culture, under the weight of Confucianism, revered the learned sage with the '100 li white beard.' Yet Sir Isaac Newton, educated at Cambridge University, invented both calculus and classic physics by the time he was 25. Einstein invented the Theory of Special Relativity by the time he was 26. Though I disagree with both the logic and narrowness of this theory, Einstein asked questions about the prevailing presuppositions concerning Time, Space and Light that were not asked before. In the asking and challenging of those previously prevailing presuppositions, Einstein opened new vistas on fundamental physical phenomena and provided humanity with profound insights regarding processes of transformation among diverse forms of energy that are present in the structure of the Universe.

Lord Byron composed great poems before he died in his twenties. Jesus was crucified at 33 but had already created a body of moral teaching and theology urging our world to greater compassion, reverence and humility. Countless examples of youthful genius exist that range across cultures, religions, historic periods and ethnicities.

Whitehead left mathematics and Cambridge University to teach theoretical physics at the University of London. Some years later, Harvard waived its mandatory retirement policy for the first time, and there Whitehead culminated his career as a speculative philosopher. There are two things worth noting. In the midst of creating his great philosophic works integrating mathematical logic, theoretical physics and philosophy, students observed that whenever they met Whitehead, he would ask "What are you working on, what are you thinking about?" And secondly, it was said, "Though he was the oldest person at Harvard, he was the youngest." (Price 1956) His spirit and mind were the most active, the most vibrant, the most profound, and the most embracing of new inquiries, whether his own or others.

It is the intellectual spirit of challenging prevailing presuppositions, asking questions not asked before, synthesizing and integrating phenomena and concepts that were separate, and creating new and fresh solutions, which educational institutions must value and stimulate in students, and in our broader human family. We must do so irrespective of age, gender, race or the moment of time during which curiosity is alive, active and irrepressible. It is important that many of history's greatest innovators and creative geniuses came from neither professional family backgrounds nor urban environments. The scope of educational services, therefore, must be broad and without borders among social stratas.

Reverend Martin Luther (Address at Lincoln Memorial 1963) proclaimed, "It is by the content of one's character, not the color of one's skin that humans should judge each another." The success of education similarly must be assessed by deeper and more revealing criteria. Experience is of great value but so too are independence of thought and freshness of insight. Curiosity must be irrepressible and borderless for civilizations to be innovative and creative. The function of education systems and creative synthetic learning is to ensure that educational systems neither stifle nor diminish, but instead intensify, deepen and broaden that curiosity inherent in life.

Journeys of curiosity must take place within an intellectual domain which is borderless.

6. Generalizations of Insight

Intellectual genius throughout human history, and especially during intense periods of intellectual ferment, innovation and discovery, challenged, questioned and overcame prevailing dogmas and prevailing presuppositions of thought. Genius always widens, broadens and deepens the range of phenomena to which new theories apply. By passing from the stage of journeys of curiosity to the stage of adventures of discovery, genius envisions and discerns previously unobserved and unimagined patterns manifested within an increasingly diverse set of phenomena. For example Newton's classic laws of motion cover all speeds, all distances and all accelerations or decelerations of speed for all entities with mass, irrespective of the spatial and temporal locations in which motion occurs. Adventures of discovery lead to higher generalization of insights, as do those embodied in Newton's laws of motion.

While the main emphasis of the theory of creative synthetic education concerns the achievement of generalization of insight, creative
synthetic education also concerns insight into and illumination of particular phenomena. By enhancing human discernment of general patterns we can illuminate the particular. Whitehead's philosophy conceives all concrete phenomena as emerging from antecedent fields of
events. Within such causative and generative fields are expressed a
multiplicity of variables that collectively, but with diverse relative
significance, causally influence the characters of the concrete in its full
particularity, qualitative definitiveness and individuality. It is only by
grasping general patterns of causal orderliness that we can understand
and influence the variables that influence the character of emerging
events.

It is inadequately appreciated that these journeys of curiosity must
be taken within the environment of communities of related problems
and related phenomena. Whitehead criticizes "teaching small parts of a
large number of subjects" and sees such an approach to learning as
constituting the passive reception of disconnected ideas not illumined
with any spark of vitality.

He correctly admonishes that "the main ideas introduced into a
child's education should be few and important, and let them be thrown
into every combination possible." (Whitehead 1967, 2) Whitehead's
student at Harvard, Professor Victor Lowe from Johns Hopkins University, observed that Whitehead believed "the teacher ought to concentrate on the basic general ideas behind the formulas. He should present only the minimum number of ideas, with their interrelations [...
t]he power of these ideas could be shown by throwing them into fresh
combinations." (Lowe 1990, 3)

In current educational theory there is growing and proper attention
to the possibilities and value of interdisciplinary studies. However,
what is lacking is a deeper appreciation and implementation of the
need for study of communities of problems within an *intradisciplinary*
context. When Whitehead speaks of throwing ideas into 'every possible combination' he is talking of changing variables, tweaking variables, altering environments within which similar phenomena occurs.
This is the natural process of active curiosity and inquiring minds. It is,
furthermore, the exploratory phenomenon that allows discovery and
generalization of insight. It is the antithesis of detached, isolated, fragmented facts passively absorbed by students. Neither facts, atoms nor

elementary particles, exist in isolation and independence from other facts, atoms, elementary particles or atomic occasions.

Whitehead speaks of "the process of discovery as the process of becoming used to curious thoughts, of shaping questions, of seeking for answers, of devising new experiences, of what happens as the result of new ventures." (Whitehead 1967, 32) The new ventures are constituted through the alteration of variables. The shaping of questions concerns the consequences of changing variables and changing the environments within which phenomena develop. This is what constitutes journeys of curiosity amid communities of problems. Whitehead's metaphysics in all its manifold dimensions, including education, stresses the centrality of community to all concrete and real entities. No entity dwells devoid of community nor in pure, exclusive privacy. The reality of community pertains to both (i) concrete events in the contingencies of their relations and (ii) abstract entities, like eternal objects, characteristics and numbers, in their necessary, logical and mathematical relations. Community and contrast of character are integral to all existence, both concrete and abstract.

Therefore, generalization of insight expresses awareness of general patterns exhibited among a plethora of phenomena within which diversity and variability are universally found. Generalization represents abstraction from multiplicities, i.e., abstraction from communities of related phenomena.

7. Modes of Perception

It is of cardinal significance in the education of children to understand how education and culture influence modes of thought, modes of perception and creative impulses. Intriguing experiments conducted by T. Masuda and R. E. Nisbett which compare the contrasting modes of perception in children raised in eastern and western cultures are revealing. (Masuda & Nisbett 2000, 12): For example, Japanese and American students were asked to describe the same community tank of tropical fish. Those from an Eastern cultural heritage described the variety of fish, the plants, the sand and the rocks, making observations of a 'gestalt' nature. In contrast the Western children described the dominant or focal fish within the community. It may be that such perceptual emphasis upon relationality, community and encompassing environment demonstrated by the Eastern children's responses validates Whitehead's perception that the modes of thought in his philosophy of process and organism share a kinship and bond with Eastern modes of thought. But the main point is that the modes of thought, perception and creative response begin to be shaped early in the development and education of children, the stage when curiosity is acute, relentless and bright.

Eastern observers perceive the particular within the broader community, the organic among the inorganic, the animate among the inanimate, all in relationality and interdependence. Students from both Eastern and Western (American) cultures perceived and described the dominant fish with comparable detail but those from Eastern cultures described the broader environment both with detail and as the initial subject of their description. In a similar manner rich with philosophic symbolism, a Chinese postal address will begin with the nation, and is followed by the province, city, street and then the individual's family name followed by his or her given name. The concrete and particular cannot be comprehended apart from the broader realities from which they arise, within which they exist and interact, and to which they causally contribute.

Traditional Chinese landscape painting, in a similar manner, depicts the finite while evoking the infinite and the beyond which are immersed within qualitative contrasts, continuities and causal interdependencies of the one amid the many. (Fan & Phipps 2003)

8. The Abstract and the Concrete

Whitehead recognized that abstractions and generalizations are essential to intellectual understanding. In *Process and Reality* he writes, "intellectuality [...] consists in the gain of a power of abstraction. The irrelevant multiplicity of detail is eliminated and emphasis is laid on the elements of systematic order in the actual world." (Whitehead 1978, 254) Generalizations of insight illuminate particularity by discerning the general patterns, the general functions and functions of function, which describe how the qualities and relationships characterizing and present within and among present events causally influence the qualities and relationships of subsequent events. But to attain generalization, "irrelevant multiplicity of detail" must be discarded.

That is possible only when, and if, there are journeys of curiosity amid communities of related problems (phenomena). General patterns are discerned when effective patterns of orderliness are abstracted from the full character and relationality exhibited within the concrete. The discernment of those abstractions and generalizations is the burden of human genius, both individual and collective, and the fruit of discovery.

Mathematics, which Whitehead's and Russell's *Principia Mathematica* demonstrated is largely deducible from logic, deals with generalizations of generalizations among abstract qualities, relationships and classes. The concepts and propositions of mathematics are infinitely rich in their implications. Indeed, from any proposition there are logically deducible an infinity of other propositions. Mathematical logic and mathematics deal with an infinity of general propositions and the infinite number of consequences that follow. The human mind confronts an infinity of infinities when it enters the realm of mathematics. Kurt Gödel (1931) demonstrated in his Incompleteness Theory that for any axiomatic system, there are still other propositions whose truth or falsity is not deducible by that axiomatic system. Since we cannot fully understand any premise without understanding and perceiving its infinite consequences, and, furthermore, since from no axiom system, however powerful, can all true propositions be derived, our understanding is always partial and progressive in its nature. This is as true of the realm of mathematical logic as it is true of the realm of empirical science and the modes of orderliness science investigates.

The deductive interplay of the generalizations of empirical sciences, which investigate the contingencies constituting the variety and the order exhibited in the actual world, with the generalization of logic and mathematics, which concern abstract qualities, relationships and classes, illuminates the world of events. It is precisely by means of this interplay between abstractions and the concrete between necessary and contingent propositions that human understanding of the actual world advances from lower to higher levels.

The advance of knowledge requires a continuous discourse between the abstract and the concrete. The discourse with the concrete must be with increasingly open systems within which greater variability is exhibited, allowing modification and refinement of the initial abstractions and the initial generalizations. The creative advance of human knowledge requires this continuous discourse as knowledge always retains an aspect of tenuousness and incompleteness. Whitehead insists that we understand the relation between abstract concepts and the concrete world from which those abstractions are derived and do not identify the abstract with the concrete. But, if more general truths are to be discovered, those abstractions can only be derived from continuous journeys of curiosity amid wider and more open systems of problems, phenomena and variables. It is through processes of widening the community of phenomena investigated that the role of variables previously not observed becomes transparent and generalization both more accurate and powerful.

9. The Romance of Research

Whitehead cites the danger present in many systems of education as follows: "I do not think that it is possible to take a whole class very far along the road of precision without some dulling of the interest. It is the unfortunate dilemma that initiative and training are both necessary, and the training is apt to kill initiative." (Whitehead 1967, 35) It is the thesis of the theory of creative, synthetic education that the solution to this dilemma resides in developing forms and structures so that research becomes an integral and necessary part of the continuum of the entire educational process. Research, despite its own challenges, becomes that breath of fresh spring air that relieves the tedium of training. Whitehead counsels us that "From the very beginning of his education, the child should experience the joy of discovery." (1967, 2) The integration of research and training, of novelty of thought and the absorption of accumulated knowledge, is essential to the joy of education.

Without this rhythmic integration of training and research, the vitality of education is diminished and the soul and enthusiasm of students are drained. Adventures of discovery and generalization of insight drive research and sustain and nurture the intellectual interest and enthusiasm which Whitehead correctly understood as essential to mental development.

One of the key imperatives of creative synthetic education involves exposing students to the profound distinction between processes of discovery of what is not known versus the learning of that which has already been discovered. Whitehead, in stressing that 'from the very beginning of his education, the child should experience the joy of discovery,' explains that "the discovery which he has to make, is that general ideas give an understanding [...] of that stream of events which pours through his life." (1967, 2)

This integrative theory helps to explicate Whitehead's more general persuasion that there must be a rhythm to educational processes. He sees this rhythm as vaguely analogous to Hegel's theory of development through the stages of thesis, antithesis and synthesis. Whitehead calls these stages:

- The Stage of Romance
- The Stage of Precision
- The Stage of Generalization

From the perspective of the theory of creative, synthetic learning, the stage of Romance is constituted by journeys of curiosity amid related problems. The stage of Precision is the stage of learning of techniques and engaging in processes of synthesis of concrete data and the variables manifested within that data. The stage of Generalization is when the gathering and synthesis of data culminates in discovery and generalization of insight, provoking a symbiotic relation between the investigation of the abstract and that of the concrete. If education does not thrust students at all stages of the education experience into the process of discovery, education will deny the student the essential romance of learning.

If educational systems are to contribute to the creation of independent, profound, enthusiastic and innovative discoverers who advance human knowledge, education processes must begin with research, end with research and be permeated by research much as a farmer, who seeks to harvest the ripe fruits and vegetables in autumn must first sow the seeds in the spring and tend and nurture the growing plants in summer. It is counterproductive to think that enthusiastic and innovative researchers are to be harvested only in graduate schools. Whitehead refers to this fallacy when he writes, "[...] during the last thirty years the schools of England have been sending up to the universities a disheartened crowd of young folk inoculated against any outbreak of intellectual zeal." (1967, 38)

It is, we stress, only within a context of creative synthetic education that learning becomes an intrinsic, not an extrinsic factor in a student's life. Whitehead speaks of the love of a subject in and for itself. Innovative and creative societies depend upon the internalization of the motivation of learning. That internalization depends upon the free reign of curiosity and the romance and adventure of discovery. Whitehead summarizes the social significance to historic development of these ideas in the general proposition, "we subdue the forces of nature because we have been lured to discovery by an insatiable curiosity." (1967, 31)

The creative advance of our global community depends upon the internalization of the love of learning and the free, vigorous and relentless pursuit of knowledge and wisdom gained at the successful culminations of journeys of curiosity.

One of the most profound experiences of my education was a class in the Calculus, taught to very gifted mathematical students by a Professor who coached the leading university math team in North America. He thrust upon his students a fundamental question of calculus, which had vexed mathematicians and eluded discovery for 2 millennia. For one week, students dwelt in a state of ignorance, of trial and error, of advance, retreat and advance again, until, we were able to discern some fundamental techniques of the calculus discovered by Newton and Leibniz in the 17th century. Perhaps this group of students could have learned the relevant techniques in an hour. Instead, we spent a week struggling and searching in our ignorance and incomplete insights. This was at once frustrating, exciting and ultimately exhilarating. We tasted the difference between the processes of learning what was discovered and the exhilarating process of discovery itself. Awareness of this distinction is a priceless contribution to the education process. It engenders both respect for the cumulative nature of knowledge and thirst for new and more advanced knowledge.

Part of the educational process itself involves deepening students' awareness that education is a process proceeding stage by stage from lower to higher levels of truth, understanding, wisdom and generality of understanding. The educational experience should instill in students the awareness that the active exploration of communities of problems is the path to generalization and discovery.

Whitehead metaphorically describes these journeys of curiosity amid communities of problems that are resolved in adventures of discovery as the continuous discourse between the abstract and the concrete, the data and the generalization, "like angels ascending and descending Jacob's ladder to heaven." (1967, 52)

Process philosophy and traditional Eastern modes of perception and thought point to the significance for discovery and insight of synthetic, relational thinking. The sense of romance of research and discovery is tied to the exploration of relationality and the quest for generalization. Whitehead expresses this in the statement "Romantic emotion is essentially the excitement consequent on the transition from the bare facts to the first realizations of the import of their unexplored relationships." (1967, 18) Synthetic and relational thinking is relevant to all realms of human inquiry from physics, biology, psychology, history, literature, cosmology, mathematics, aesthetics, economics, civil engineering to environmental studies et al.

As Whitehead stressed that education should begin and end in research (1967, 23), he also wrote that "[p]hilosophy begins in wonder. And, at the end, when philosophic thought has done its best, the wonder remains. There have been added, however, some grasp of the immensity of things, some purification of emotion by understanding." (Whitehead 1966, 168f) This sense of wonder should range over the totality of existence.

The theory of creative, synthetic learning modifies Whitehead's dictum so that education not only begins and ends in research, but research should be omnipresent constituting a continuum throughout the entire educational process. The arena within which journeys of curiosity occur is life itself, including but not exclusive to schools. The communities of problems differ among subjects and disciplines. They also naturally differ relative to the student's stage of learning, interests and level of knowledge. Yet the principle remains the same.

10. Developing Communities of Problems

The implementation of the theory of creative synthetic learning requires the continuous creation of communities of problems among which students' curiosity may roam. Schools and teachers must guide the formation of appropriate and compelling communities. The initiative and interest of the students themselves must be welcomed and elicited as an essential part of the creation of those communities which: 1) excite the enthusiasm; 2) express the interests; and 3) rouse the initiative of the individual student, the small team of students, or the broader community of students taking those journeys of curiosity aiming at adventures of discovery and generalization of insight. Students and teachers as co-participants can both chart and modify the path of the journey as it proceeds. There should be no Great Wall separating teacher as authority and student as passive receptor, the teacher as leader and the student as the guided. The journeys must be dynamic and collegial in their conduct.

With colleagues in North America, China and Europe, we are developing illustrative examples of communities of problems appropriate for students of various ages in such fields as mathematics, physics, biology, chemistry, botany, literature, history, archeology, environmental studies, metallurgy, civil engineering and aesthetics. The creation of these communities of problems is an area where, Whitehead would insist, local autonomy must be exercised by local schools and teachers developing curriculum under specific local conditions. The methods, forms, structures, topics and systems to generate appropriate communities of problems and ways to guide students on these journeys both allow and require diverse ways to pursue the general goal in the context of specific local conditions, needs and interests. (see: Whitehead 1967, 13-14)

The development of communities of problems can be aided by, but cannot be confined to textbooks. More spontaneity is required. Gifted student programs, advanced research classes, research projects, within ordinary classes, research contests, and/ or special schools oriented towards developing creative synthetic learning and research are among the many forms and methods that need to be systematically and vigorously integrated in national and local educational systems. It is not the case that these forms are entirely absent, but neither are they present in substantive, systematic and adequate forms within prevailing educational structures in either the West or the East.

Effective class curricula that achieve the aims of education described earlier cannot be constituted by a mere succession of exercises and facts. Class curricula must be formulated with the awareness that students are living, dynamic, exploring humans opening to the wonders of the universe. Each class must continuously receive the life enhancing breath of curiosity and with regularity experience challenging research processes.

Great teachers have always intuited and applied these general principles and, thereby, inspired a passionate and enduring love of learning among their students. But educational systems need these principles more integrated into, and continuously present within, the educational process from its inception through its maturation.

Creative synthetic education provides the philosophic perspective and points to the systematic methodologies and modalities needed to fully liberate the potentials for discovery, and, therewith, the advance of human civilization from lower to higher stages of knowledge and wisdom. As our world becomes increasingly integrated and modes of communication leap over provincial, national and continental divisions, the opportunity for regional and even international cooperative research increases. This not only broadens cooperation but it also creates opportunities to examine far broader ranges of variables by synthesizing data that is peculiar to different local environments, whether those environments are rural, urban or suburban, national or international. Exposing students to journeys of curiosity with a broadening geographic scope is becoming possible and practical at all levels of learning, not just universities. Such broad cooperative and integrative research efforts are very important in the era of globalization. Such opportunities bind our world together in more cooperative relations and mutual understanding.

Educational institutions can conduct specific cooperative research projects both laterally and vertically. Students from different institutes or schools on the same level can cooperate in research projects and students from lower levels can cooperate in research projects with institutions on a higher level. In America, there are many excellent examples of research projects that involve senior high school students working with university professors and graduate students. This vertical integration is powerful and inspiring in the students educational transition from lower to higher levels of research and understanding.

The examples of journeys of curiosity we can offer will represent merely a suggestive and infinitesimal set of communities of problems among the broad and infinite domains of communities of problems available for intellectual inquiry. The broader set is limited only by human imagination and the contemporary stage of human understanding and insight.

The American philosopher John Dewey established experimental schools associated with the University of Chicago; so too the theory of

creative synthetic learning can be associated with teaching and research universities in China, Europe, North America, South America,
Africa, etc. Such schools and programs can serve as living laboratories
for creative educational reforms.

Teaching universities and affiliated secondary and primary schools
can individually or cooperatively develop a variety of forms, structures
and systems, and a plethora of communities of problems, in diverse
academic fields which can guide and stimulate local academic systems
and schools to guide their students upon intellectual journeys that
nurture the curiosity inherent to life and, thereby, allow curious minds
to experience both the elation of discovery and the power of generalized insight.

11. Pragmatism and Process Philosophy

There is an important distinction to be drawn between Whitehead's
philosophy of the open and infinite, and pragmatic philosophy which
has influenced much of American educational theory. Pragmatism, as it
is often interpreted and applied, ultimately condemns itself, not by its
emphasis upon consequences, which emphasis is consistent with
Whitehead's philosophy, but through its emphasis in evaluating consequences based upon closed rather than more open systems of events.
The formulation of policies by reference to closed and narrow systems
of events often leads to disjunctive economic, social and educational
development, which realizes negative and discordant potentials among
events.

There is a relevant parallel between the environmental crisis confronting the globe and contemporary educational systems which may
be adept at generating groups of great 'test takers' but ineffective in
developing and advancing the collective genius of society. It concerns
differences between tactical and often neglected strategic goals for
economic, social and educational processes.

A century ago, 90% of Americans were farmers, whose lives were
conducted within small radii of local communities. The development
and popularization of the car utilizing fossil fuels led to the development of a social infrastructure characterized by an increasing and unprecedented dispersion of home, work, recreation, and shopping. The
geographic arena within which individual life occurred was immensely

expanded relative to historic norms and the dynamic pulsation of travel within those circles became more frequent and intense.

Within the closed system of events constituted by the first few decades of this fundamental infrastructural transformation, a sense of individual freedom and power emerged. But now, a large percentage of American working adults spend an enormous amount of their daily time driving personal cars in stressful commutes between home, work, school, shopping and/or recreation. These commutes lead to high annual death rates of about 50,000 people per year and even more numerous serious and permanent injuries. With respect to family life, the amount of time fathers spend with children and husbands with wives has been profoundly reduced, leading to great stresses and strains on family stability and interpersonal relationships. Furthermore, since carbon dioxide is a heat trapping gas, and this unprecedented infrastructure causes enormous expenditures of fossil based energy needed to move mass, people and cars, the global atmosphere is inexorably becoming saturated with enormous quantities of heat-trapping gases. Turbulent weather patterns become more frequent and destructive as a consequence of global warming.

Leading British environmental scientists have concluded that global warming is currently proceeding at the rate predicted under the worst-case scenario. Interestingly, global warming has been characterized by scientists as a real, not a hypothetical, 'Weapon of Mass Destruction' which, furthermore, is a 'terrorist weapon' that strikes with total unpredictability as to the place, time and form of attack: a drought, a flood, a hurricane, a fire, a scorching heat wave or a protracted freeze. Glaciers melt, sea levels rise and temperature differentials between land, sea and atmosphere become larger resulting in less stable and more chaotic global weather patterns, patterns that threaten the planet's long term capacity to feed humanity and provide a reasonable degree of stability and comfort. This is a serious issue for all humans in-cluding the Chinese and Indian people whose percapita arable land is expecially limited.

When viewed from a pragmatic, narrow and closed system of events, the fossil fuel car and the unique and historically dispersed social infrastructure it fostered, represented freedom and mobility. From a broader and more open set of events, this change in society's infrastructure constitutes a strategic danger to the viability of the global environment. The failure to view matters from an open and dynamic perspective rooted in a philosophy of process and relationality leads to disjunctive and discordant development rather than integrative and harmonious development. From the perspective of open systems, what appears in its initial stages of development as integrative and harmonious may degenerate into disjunctive and discordant development, viewed over broader fields of events.

In respect to educational systems that emphasize standardized test taking, we may observe several parallels with the stress resultant upon the changes in society's infrastructure. Enormous stress is exerted upon the individual students confronting standardized tests determinate of their futures and careers. Similarly great strain often develops in the relation between parent and child as the parent's expectation for their child's future is concentrated in the quality of their performance during a few hours and a few days of examinations in the student's life. There is also too often a correlative 'polluting' of the educational environment in which the values of prestige, money, fame and position (ranking) become the extrinsic motivation of learning concurrently overwhelming the purity of the love of learning, the free exercise of curiosity, the delight in discovery and the reverence for learning. There are numerous and poignant stories of how Japanese students focus incredible energy to pass tests to gain university admission which, once gained, ironically often leads to insipid efforts and dismal achievements during the university experience. The extrinsic value has replaced the intrinsic value of learning and, therewith, the death knell of creativity is sounded.

The lack of adequate and stimulating research and creative synthetic learning within the continuum of educational processes underlies the reason that many 'prodigies' become intellectually sterile adults and why far too much graduate research sadly constitutes empty, obscure and superficial exercises in pedantry, rather than intelectual achievements illuminating significant topics. The misuse of intellectual talent is an unspoken sad truth.

Educational systems must 'reform the reforms' and new reforms must weave the bright strands of creative, synthetic learning throughout the educational process from its inception to its conclusion. Education will then better perform its dual functions of: (1) transmitting, with appreciation and respect, the knowledge and wisdom of the past, gained by antecedent adventures of discovery; and (2) allowing the students of the present to feel the lure of future discovery. Educational experiences within which are found the brilliant strands of such learning foster and sustain the enthusiasm for learning and, concurrently, there is a deepening and purifying among students of the passion for discovery and the internal sense of significance and importance to knowledge and understanding.

The lure, which the future exerts in the present upon students and teachers, is a lure for understanding, discovery and wisdom, that should neither become dull nor diminish but rather intensify with time and with increased knowledge. Neither intellectual arrogance nor smugness has any positive role to play given the complexity and immensity of reality. A five-year-old child recently asked his father, "Dad, what is infinity minus 100?" The infinite minus any finite number is, of course, infinite. Humanity's collective genius and knowledge, however dazzling, remains finite and our ignorance remains infinite. Increased knowledge should increase humility, reverence and awe.

12. Creative Learning and World Civilization

To the extent that methods and modalities of creative synthetic learning intensifies that lure to future exercises of curiosity and discovery, societies are able to contribute to the creative advance of human civilization. There is an ancient Chinese saying 'In the heavens above are many stars. On the earth below, there is but one people.' It is increasingly clear that it is to that one integrated, interacting and interdependent global community that the creative advance of human civilization must contribute. With neither our environmental policies nor our educational policies and practices do we want merely narrow, "pragmatic" and short term bursts of success. We want and need strategic and integrative modes of development. In education, that means we must liberate humanity's collective genius.

It is interesting and relevant to note, as Viktor Lowe points out, that Whitehead's understanding of genius is more universal and less elitist than are more prevalent concepts of 'genius'. Lowe notes that genius was the topic of Whitehead's next to last lecture at Harvard. Whitehead wrote, "All education is the development of genius," and "genius is the divine instinct for creation, and that education for genius is the best education for eliciting common sense." (Lowe 1990, 60 & 61) It is this more universal understanding of creative genius which underlies the theory of creative synthetic learning.

China is the world's oldest continuous civilization and China made enormous contributions to human knowledge, discovery and innovation, as did ancient Greek civilizations, ancient Egyptian civilization, Europe during the Renaissance, India, Persian and Muslim civilization during other historic periods.

The world needs renewal on many fronts, including in the arena of education. The world needs rekindling of the spirit of innovation, boldness and creativity of thought. The world needs synthesis of ideas, fresh generalization of insight and more profound discoveries if the world is to creatively advance. The education reforms of China, India and other ancient cultures must contribute to this liberation and rebirth of curiosity, freshness of discovery and increase in wisdom. Just as Whitehead in his maturity was youthful, the ancient cultures of China and India must renew their youthfulness. Humanity as a whole needs that spirit of freshness, vitality and insatiability of curiosity in the young minds preparing for the future in a global civilization.

13. Synthetic and Analytic Thinking

Analytic thinking underlies reductionism and atomism. It considers complex entities in their rich variety in respect to their constituent parts with the underlying presumption that the parts will manifest less qualitative variety than that exhibited by the characteristics of the complex subject of analysis. As such, analytic thinking provides a powerful, illuminating approach to understanding phenomena. But it is, nonetheless, a limiting approach from the perspective of Whitehead's process philosophy.

Synthetic thinking views concrete entities (and the abstract entities of mathematics) in respect to the broader realities and broader environments which envelop those entities. It seeks to illuminate the character of the particular and the concrete with reference to the characteristics and relationships determining the qualitative definiteness of those realities beyond the entities that are subject to our endeavors at understanding.

Synthetic thinking, we must note, is not antagonistic to analytic thinking. Whitehead and Russell's *Principia Mathematica* is indeed one of history's most vigorous and monumental works in analytic thinking and Whitehead's *Process and Reality*, on the other hand, is a monumental example of synthetic thinking.

But analytic thinking without synthetic thinking is form without substance. In contrast, synthetic thinking untempered and unsculpted by analytic thinking is substance without form, clarity, coherency and cogency. At best synthetic thinking devoid of analytic thinking is evoaive, but not illuminating of truth. Educational systems need to enourage the integration of analytic and synthetic thinking, the harmony of form and substance.

During the 20th century, analytic thinking dominated much of western philosophic and political thinking. Philosophers, with the exception of Alfred North Whitehead, became immersed in analytic modes of thought and abandoned the synthetic and speculative modes of thought that had historically characterized the philosophic tradition. Philosophy increasingly assumed an acquiescent and passive position towards science. Philosophy became more concerned with the methodologies of science and less with the substance of scientific concepts, premises and the underlying view of reality. Philosophy's major conern became to interpret and justify science and its methodologies rather than to challenge and offer creative constructive alternatives to the concepts, axioms, theorems and presuppositions underlying contemporary science. By seeking: a) coherency where incoherency prevails, b) illumination and consistency where the bizarre reigns and c) breadth of vision where narrowness of perspective prevails, synthetic, creative philosophic insights can help advance science as philosophy has traditionally done.

When synthetic and creative thinking are active and vital, visions of new phenomena, new relations and new modes of orderliness emerge. While new and more coherent concepts and axioms may help interpret known phenomena and data, their central and creative function is to envision new phenomena, new relations and new laws of nature and order. Creative synthetic thinking aims to move beyond brilliance and to enter the realm of creative genius. Creative synthetic learning provokes and nurtures creative genius and the opening of fresh vistas of inquiring and understanding. It is crucial to instill the intellectual instinct to see beyond prevailing principles and known phenomena and to perceive with clarity and coherency of thought beyond prevailing presuppositions.

14. The Unconscious, Intuition and Discovery

One of the major detriments of 'bookishness' is that it puts priority on conscious mental processes over non-conscious perception and thought which, in fact, far exceed in their breadth and depth our conscious mental activity. When non-conscious mental processes are inhibited or suffer interference, intuition is correspondingly inhibited and depleted of its richness.

The power of unconscious mental processes is illustrated in the famous story of the great and prolific French mathematician Henri Poincaré who, as he stepped on to a Parisian trolley car, his conscious mind entertaining the sensations provoked by his busy and immediate environment, suddenly perceived the solution to a mathematical problem that had long absorbed his attention but eluded solution. Poincaré made many mathematical discoveries in pure mathematics, theoretical physics, applied mechanics, experimental physics and celestial mechanics. Poincaré advocated recognition of the importance of subconscious mental activity to processes of discovery and inventtion.

Protracted subconscious probing of problems is the prelude to intellectual creativity. The over-emphasis upon 'bookishness' and "performance in examinations" deprives developing minds of the vital cultivation of intuition and contemplativeness. It is precisely because of the need to evoke curiosity and wonder, to nurture the passion for discovery and to cultivate intuition that Whitehead warns educators that, "we rise above the exclusive association of learning with book-learning." (1967, 51)

Both boldness and originality of thought require the reign of protracted subconscious processes spurred by intrinsic interest. It is from such mental processes in their purity and authenticity that great intuitive insights burst into adventures of discovery. The development of the insights of intellectual genius, the instincts of great athleticism, the creations of the artist, all depend upon the development of inuition. And the development of intuition is hindered by the 'static' of excessive formalism, rigid structuralism and externally imposed prescriptualism, all of which are antagonistic to 1) free, spontaneous and imaginative entertainment of ideas, 2) the conscious and unconscious exploration and integration of ideas, observation and propositions (axioms and theorems) and 3) the spontaneity and determination of curiosity. Creativity, contemplativeness and curiosity are essential and interdependent components in adventures of discovery.

Whitehead's theory of prehensions (feelings) recognized the predominant role played by unconscious mental processes in respect to our perceptions of the world and our calibrated, subtle, evaluative, complex and imaginative responses to the concrete environments with which living organism react. In his discussions of 'The Higher Phases of Experience'. (see: Whitehead 1929, 266) Whitehead divides intellectual feelings into both conscious perceptions and intuitive judgements. Whitehead further holds that consciousness 'flickers' within a broader penumbra of experiences of dimmer and unconscious perceptions and intuitive judgment. (1929, 267)[6].

It is within the broader penumbra of unconscious mental processes that synthesis of ideas, observations, axioms and theorems ferment and occur leading to the creative, intuitive judgments and flashes of discovery which emerge from the subconscious to the conscious. Adventures of discovery frequently have their genesis in such unconscious synthesis of concepts and axioms.

Anxiety and fear, excessive competitiveness, extrinsic rather than intrinsic motivation, often function as static and interference to the subconscious mental processes necessary to attain illumination. Such interference is comparable to and probably derivative from the interference that occurs among certain types of transmissions of electromagnetic waves. Intuition requires freedom to roam without the mental interference of the extraneous; it requires the fusion of concentration, focus and relaxation. This is as true of great intellectual achievements as it is of great artistic and athletic achievements. Educational systems must recognize and foster such fusions within the environments in which education, research and discovery take place.

Educational systems need to ensure that research is omnipresent throughout the educational process. Active, vivid and probing curiosity, present in infancy and the inception of learning, must be con-

---

[6] Whitehead notes "This account agrees with the plain facts of our conscious experience. Consciousness flickers, and even at its brightest, there is a small focal region of clear illumination and a large penumbral region of experience which tells of intense experience of dim apprehension. The simplicity of clear consciousness is no measure of the complexity of complete experience. Also this character of our experience suggests that consciousness is the crown of experience, only occasionally attained, not its necessary base."

tinuously present into maturity and, indeed remain vital even if one, as Whitehead did, attains the status of a sage. Reality itself, in its breadth, depth and variety provides the foundation for the omnipresence of research and curiosity throughout the entire life of the individual and the entire creative advance of human civilization.

Educational systems must provide educational environments and communities of problems that foster the development of creative subconscious mental processes and intuition. Journeys of curiosity amid communities of problems are the antidote to excessive formalism, rigid structuralism and narrow prescriptionalism. Such journeys fertilize the emergence of intuition and creativity.

It is by means of intuition that creative and innovative insights emerge. If the conscious mind is merely stuffed with facts and inert ideas, non-conscious mental processes are divested of their richness and vitality. Educators must understand that intuition is a by-product of non-conscious mental processes. Insight, creativity and discovery are in turn causally a by-product of intuition. The emphasis on standardized tests and bookish learning leads to the failure to understand how intuition arises and to properly value the profound role intuition plays in discovery and creativity. Creativity is the result of both work and playfulness and for this reason Whitehead can properly speak of the essential playfulness of discovery. Whitehead writes "Science is almost wholly the outcome of pleasurable intellectual curiosity." (1967, 45) E. O. Wilson similarly notes, "And any discovery at all is thrilling. There is no feeling more pleasant, more addictive, than setting foot on virgin soil." (1998, 61)

It is important for educational systems to be imbued with a sense of and respect for the relevance and importance of theory to all fields of intellectual inquiry. The narrow emphasis upon practice and pragmatism misconceives and distorts the relationship between practice and theory.

When concepts, axioms, theorems and presuppositions are critically and constructively examined and transformed to achieve greater coherency, consistency and cogency, and when generalizations of generalizations (theories) are developed that attain greater comprehensiveness, such quantum leaps in theoretical understanding inevitably lead to new practical results, new technical innovations, new engieering applications and the perception and creation of new kinds of phenomena. Theory begets practice just as intuition begets insight.

Students should be made keenly aware of the role that theoretical understanding plays in transforming practical reality. There are innumerable examples throughout humanity's intellectual history of the power of good theories to transform practice. But refinement in theoretical understanding necessitate the continuous discourse between practice and theory; that discourse in turn requires the pro-active engagement of educators and their students with both the realm of practice and the realm of theory. From the throne of powerful theories, whether scientific, cultural, economic, social or moral, constructive transformations of practical reality invariably follow.

15. Creativity and the Global Community

The capacity of China and India to contribute to theoretical innovation should be neither neglected nor underestimated. The 21st century will witness the replacement of Great Walls separating theoretical creativity among the nations with the erection of Great Bridges allowing the 2-way flow of ideas, data and theories among nations and cultures. This global interaction necessitates the appreciation and the arousal of the potential for creative genius in the realm of theory by the East. The harmonious transformation of the world community requires that the world experiences the further integration and revival of European and Eastern genius. The world must not suffer either a brain drain or a concentration of intellectual talents within narrow geographic or cultural boundaries. India, China and even Europe, all of which felt concern for the brain drain of their indigenous intellectual and scientific talents during the 20th Century, are experiencing a brain gain inspired externally by political and economic issues and internally by the development and revitalization of their indigenous economies and institutes of advanced learning and research.

Several European Nobel Laureates in Theoretical Physics, when interviewed by the eminent mathematician and theoretical physicist Professor M. von Kryzwoblocki, indicated that they looked to India and China for a burst of imagination and creativity during the 21st Century.[7]

---

[7] Personal discussions between Kryzwoblocki and Ronald P. Phipps.

Whitehead was keenly sensitive to the need and potential for new creative genius to emanate from the East. The metaphysics Whitehead developed based upon process and organism, community and relationality, polar contrasts not strict dichotomies, openness not closeness, variety not sameness, is, as pointed out earlier, a philosophy very akin to traditional Eastern modes of thought. From a Whiteheadian perspective we anticipate during the Third Millennium enormous theoretical contributions from the East.[8]

The 20th century witnessed disjunctiveness and discordance in economic and social development, with two world conflagrations, the Great Depression, the Holocausts of both Europe and the East, enironental degradation, and accelerated cultural decay, comparable to the decays that have historically accompanied the decline of powerful empires.

In the realm of theory, the heretical became the new orthodoxy and new dogmas, like older dogmas, became unassailable. The bizarre and the incoherent were often taken to the nth degree and the results were often mistaken for illumination.

The fuller development of the creative potentials for discovery in China, the European Union, South America, the Middle East and Africa, along with the continued development of creative potentials in North America, will benefit humanity in many obvious and direct ways. One of the modes of benefit, that is not as clearly recognized, concerns the strategic fact that the security, peace and harmony of our planet will be enhanced to the degree to which there emerges greater equilibrium in the distribution of global intellectual and economic power among the major regions of the world. Non-equilibrium, as history reveals, breeds divisiveness and domination of the many by the few. Our increasingly globally interdependent world, in contrast, requires increased integration, cooperation and mutuality of benefit. (Phipps 2004, 4-6) History must move forward in such a manner that older forms of imperial domination become archaic and recessive while new forms of cooperation and mutual benefit become ascendant.

The world, in respect to issues of international relations, economic integration, environmental protection and development of fundamental

---

[8] It is worthy to note that five *Centers for Process Studies* have been established in China since the Conference 'Whitehead and China in the Third Millennium' held at Beijing Normal University in June, 2001.

theoretical understanding in many fields of intellectual inquiry, requires new harmonies and greater coherency. The theory of creative synthetic learning aims to contribute to the arousal of humanity to create new harmonies of harmonies in our world's cultural, intellectual and practical life.

16. Conclusion

The fundamental social mandate of educational institutions is to cultivate the capacity in students to 1) creatively apply and develop existent knowledge; and 2) contribute to the discovery of new knowledge and innovation. The capacity and skill at test taking should be secondary and subservient to the task of developing the capacity for creative discovery. The theory of creative, synthetic learning seeks to develop, methodologies and modalities that help the development of students' creative capacities and therewith fulfill the fundamental mandate of learning.

Journeys of curiosity, resolved in adventures of discovery, represent experiences that are both intellectual and emotional. It is the depth and purity of curiosity that: 1) impels the lure to discovery and 2) generates and sustains the determination and perseverance needed to overcome obstacles and traverse the twists and turns, rises and falls, dead ends, retreats and advances inevitably encountered in the process of discovery. Communities of problems also provoke a sense of wonder and humility in the conscious presence of the plethora of phenomena constituted by such communities. Adventures of discovery spark exhilaration. The attainment of generalizations of insight evokes that quietude of wisdom that arises when we discern patterns of orderliness among phenomena, which previously were perceived merely in their apparent randomness and differentiation. Generalizations of insights display the bonding, synthesis and connectedness of phenomenon where mere separateness was first presumed to dwell. This awareness of bonding and relationality evokes reverence for the diversity expressed in creation. Creative, synthetic learning leads students and teachers alike to experience the emotions of wonder, humility, lure, joy, determination, exhilaration and reverence. It is these emotions and cultivated instincts that synthetic creative learning aims to develop and which sustain self-motivation and inspire learning and discovery for their intrinsic, rather than extrinsic, value to the human mind, heart and soul.

Bibliography

Blumenthal, R. (February 25, 2005): Texas boy, 11, protests state tests. Edinburg, Texas: NY Times News Service

Cantor, G. (1867): *De aequationibus secundi gradus indeterminatis.* (Doctoral Thesis

Eddington, A. (1927): *The Nature of the Physical World.* New York: Macmillan.

Fan M. & Phipps, R. (2003): Process thought in chinese traditional arts. *Values and Culture* 3, 680-702.

Goedel, K. (1931): Über formal unentscheidbare Sätze in der Principia Mathematica. *Monatshefte für Mathematik and Physik*, 38, 173-198.

Hilbert, D. (1900): *Address to International Congress of Mathematicians.* Paris. Online document:
    URL: www.andrews.edu/~calkins/math/webtexts/tophilpr.htm (access: 26.03.2005).

Hilbert, D. (1918): Axiomatisches Denken. *Mathematische Annalen* 78, 405-415

Needham, J. & Yates, R. D. S. (1994): *Science and Civilisation in China.* Cambridge: Cambridge University Press.

Phipps, R. (2004): Whiteheadian Axioms of Progressive Internationalism. *Process Perspectives*, 27, 4-6.

Phipps, R. (2004): Whiteheadian Axioms of Progressive Internationalism. *Seeking Truth* 6, 18-19.

Price, L. (1956): *Dialogues of Alfred North Whitehead.* New York: New American Library.

Lowe, V (1985): *Alfred N. Whitehead, the man and his work*, Vol. I. Baltimore: The John Hopkins University Press.

Lowe, V. (1990): *Alfred North Whitehead, The Man and His Work, Vol. II.* Baltimore: The John Hopkins University Press.

Masuda, T., & Nisbett, R. E. (2000): *Culture and Attention to Object vs. Field.* Ann Arbor: University of Michigan.

Needham, J. & Yates, R. D. S. (1994): *Science and Civilisation in China.* Cambridge: Cambridge University Press.

Singh, S. (2005): Even Einstein Had His Off Days. *New York Times* (January 2).

Whitehead, A. N. (1967/1929): *The Aims of Education.* New York: Free Press.

Whitehead, A. N. (1978/1928): *Process and Relaity.* (Corrected Edition) New York: Free Press.

Whitehead, A. N. (1953/1925): *Science and the Modern World.* New York: Macmillan.
Whitehead, A. N. (1966/1938): *Modes of Thought.* NY: Macmillan Free Press
Wilson, E. O. (1998): *Consilience, The Unity of Knowledge.* New York: Vintage Books, Random House.

Learning In the Process of Teaching

Mark Flynn

Abstract:
If we regard truth as something handed down from authorities on high, the classroom will look like a dictatorship. If we regard truth as a fiction determined by personal whim, the classroom will look like anarchy. If we regard truth as emerging from a complex process of mutual inquiry, the classroom will look like a resourceful and interdependent community. Our assumptions about knowing can open up, or shut down, the capacity for connectedness on which good teaching depends (Palmer 1998, 51).

1. Introduction

In this presentation, I will speak of the on-going struggle I encounter in altering my own teaching methodology. This struggle embodies my thoughts and efforts to develop a more transformative teaching practice, that is, a practice of teaching that changes the lives of students rather than engorging their rote memories. As such, it also describes a humble attempt to create a constructive alternative to the University of Saskatchewan Teacher-Scholar Model (1998, 6). I believe this model distorts the true intentions of Ernest Boyer (1990) and his conception of the "scholarship of teaching" (1990, 23). This is important because the University claims Boyer's conception serves as the theoretical basis for their model of teaching scholarship. I opened this paper with a quote from Parker Palmer because his pedagogical ideas had a profound influence on Boyer (1990) and his conception of teaching (1990, 24). This influence is apparent in Boyer's description of university teaching as a "dynamic endeavour involving all the analogues, metaphors, and images that build bridges between the teacher's understanding and the student's learning" (1990, 23). Howard Woodhouse has shown, in a paper that appears in this volume, that the University of Saskatchewan's Teacher-Scholar Model emphasizes the transmission of research 'facts' while de-emphasizing the transformative aspects of the teaching and learning process. The transformative aspects of teaching are essential, according to Boyer, because they change the live-the bodily feelings and meanings of experience-for teachers and students alike. In his conception of teaching scholarship, "(t)heory surely leads to practice [...] (b)ut practice also leads to theory" (1990, 23). As Woodhouse notes, the University's model of teaching scholarship holds that it is primarily research which creates knowledge (i.e., theory leads to practice) while virtually ignoring the important role of teaching and learning in the creation of knowledge (i.e., practice also leads to theory). The Teacher-Scholar Model proposed by the University of Saskatchewan, therefore, distorts the essence of Boyer's conception of the scholarship of teaching by ignoring the integral relationship of research, teaching, and learning. Boyer makes it quite clear that these three aspects exist in an inextricable union.

My role in this symposium is to offer an example of my own teaching of Whitehead's (1932) theory of mental growth as an illustration of Boyer's (1990) conception of teaching scholarship. In this example, I attempt to build bridges between my own understanding of theory and that of the students. Moreover, it describes my struggle to move from a conception of teaching as the transmission of research 'facts', as proposed by the University's Teacher-Scholar Model, to a renewed conception of teaching as a process of learning that is mutually illuminating for both the students and myself. It is interesting that the attempt to change my teaching was inspired by students in my Learning and Learners course when they politely informed me that my teaching was almost exclusively of the transmission of 'facts' variety. They pointed out to me how this kind of teaching contradicted the very theories of learning I was lecturing about such as those of Jerome Bruner, Jean Piaget, Lev Vygotsky, and Alfred North Whitehead. These theorists argue that teachers and learners are engaged in the creation of new knowledge together. The dialogue between students and I, with regard to my teaching, exemplifies how my experience and knowledge of teaching was transformed through practice. In other words, practice informs my theory or scholarly understanding of the teaching and learning process. Truth be known, it is students and colleagues who should be thanked for any significant insight I may have into this process.

In this presentation, I propose a constructive alternative to the University of Saskatchewan (1998) Teacher-Scholar Model. To illustrate this alternative I incorporate the narratives of several students who use their personal learning experiences as examples of Whitehead's (1932) theory of the rhythmic cycles of mental growth, that is, the cycles of romance and freedom, precision and discipline, generalization and the return to romance and freedom. In using this type of teaching methodology, the students themselves provide concrete examples of the theoretical premises of Whitehead under consideration. These concrete examples help them understand the theoretical premises, and at the same time, they serve to challenge and broaden my own understanding as the teacher. Including the narratives or stories of students in a dialogue of learning and creating knowledge is not a new idea. It is, however, an idea consistent with Boyer's (1990) conception of the scholarship of teaching and inconsistent with the monologue that so often characterizes teaching focused on transmitting 'facts'. Boyer holds that "teaching at its best means not only transmitting knowledge, but 'transforming' and 'extending' it as well" (1990, 24).

I claim, in this presentation, that the narratives of students transform my knowledge, research, and scholarly work in human learning and enrich and extend my practice of teaching. I also claim that the blending of student narratives with my own, in the process of teaching, is a powerful form of scholarship not given due consideration in the University's conception of the Teacher-Scholar Model. Teaching scholarship is not merely the transmission of research 'facts', nor does the value of scholarship lie primarily in the marketability of knowledge created. I challenge the validity of the simplistic statement made recently by Dr. Branko Peterman (2002), President and CEO of U of S Technologies, in this regard. He stated that:When a scientist comes across a discovery, he can actually publish it, but when he does so, its commercial value is destroyed because anyone can use his information (2002, E3).

It is my claim that knowledge created by students and I in the process of teaching scholarship while having little 'market value' in the new reality of the University of Saskatchewan, is a form of scholarship that has real value for the common good and should be freely shared. Such knowledge creation, in my view, is valuable in making a substantial contribution to the development of more enlightened students and teachers. This development bodes well for the people of Saskatchewan, Canada, and the world at large.

2. Research Informing Students Informing Research

Along with research and other duties, it is my assignment at the University of Saskatchewan to teach theories of learning to prospective teachers in the College of Education in a class entitled 'Learners and Learning'. As I mentioned earlier, my students had observed the incongruity between my teaching practice and the theories of learning that were the content of my teaching. This new knowledge transformed both my thinking about learning and my teaching practice. Boyer (1990) might say that theory was not informing my practice at this point, rather, practice was informing my theory. The students were creating new knowledge with me and for me. Moreover, I think they were asking if their own personal understandings or narratives of the learning process were admissible. This, after all, was consistent with the research findings I was lecturing about.

Jerome Bruner (1996), for example, argues that university classrooms, and classrooms generally, should embody a process of learning that is "narrative" consisting of "spinning hypotheses about nature, testing them, correcting hypotheses, and getting one's head straight" (1996, 126). Bruner claims that evoking personal narratives in the classroom transforms the knowledge and experience of both teachers and students. I prefer to think of this form of teaching as consistent with a more natural process of human learning, that is, learning as a dialogue between teachers and students. This natural process of learning predates the highly rationalized institutional form of learning where teaching is reduced to the transmission of 'facts' (Callahan 1962, Tyack 1974, Tyack & Hansot 1982, Wise 1977, Wise 1979). Such dialogue - a mingling of teacher and student narratives - evokes a real learning that transcends the lifeless rote memory of class notes and highlighted textbook passages. For Bruner, university teaching is the "art of raising challenging questions" that are just as important as the "art of giving clear answers". The "art of cultivating such questions, of keeping good questions alive, is as important as either of those" (1996, 127). Good questions, according to Bruner, emerge from the observations of students as well as teachers and "pose dilemmas, subvert obvious or canonical 'truths', and draw incongruities to our attention" (1996 127). University teaching of this kind is comprehensive in that it connects our research with our teaching as well as connecting the learning of both students and ourselves. As Boyer (1990) states, theory leads to practice and practice also leads to theory.

I would like to share with you some brief examples of student narratives from the course Learners and Learning illustrating the point I am trying to make. To initiate the narrative process in this course, I ask students to describe for me in writing the most significant learning experience of their lives (Soini, 1999). To encourage them I share some brief stories of the seminal learning experiences in my life, including those situations where students influenced my thinking. We then attempt to locate our experiences in the context of the theory of learning we are studying. The narratives presented are examples of student attempts to locate their experiences in the context of Alfred North Whitehead's theory of the rhythmic cycles of mental growth. Whitehead's rhythmic cycles of mental growth include the cycles of romance and freedom, precision and discipline, generalization and freedom (Whitehead 1932, 27-30). I will define each of these cycles for you in the abstract and then use student narratives to provide more concrete illustrations of them. These illustrations, in turn, provide the substance for a brief description of what students and I learn from each other under these circumstances.

Whitehead states that the cycle of romance and freedom in mental growth or learning is characterized by the "vividness of novelty". Romance, in this cycle, is a feeling of curiosity and joy when first apprehending "unexplored connections" in the subject matter. Freedom is the free reign of curiosity in our initial contemplations of that subject (1932, 28). In their narratives, students refer to this cycle as an experience involving a "person's whole life" where playful exploration predominates and "whatever interests me" about the subject prevails. Such unencumbered exploration was beautifully put by one student in describing his romance with the piano:

A child loves to listen to his father play the piano. He is enchanted by the texture of the sound, the sight of the keys moving rapidly, the hammers hitting the strings. This is romance – open-ended wonder, innate curiosity, and an experience of pure delight at the sound.

In this passage, the young pianist describes the romance of 'listening to his father play'. That feeling we have when we are in the presence of such performances is something concrete that students and I can both understand. It is a bodily feeling that leads to the concrescence of the vague notion of romance, the 'humanization' of an abstract theoretical concept. In thinking about the narrative of the student pianist, my own understanding of Whitehead's cycle of romance and freedom was transformed into something more concrete and meaningful. His abstract conception of romance as the 'vividness of novelty' in mental growth becomes the more concrete experience of listening to someone play the piano beautifully. The abstract notion of freedom becomes more concrete and meaningful when the young listener makes his own choice to play the instrument.

The transformation of my understanding of Whitehead's (1932) cycle of romance and freedom is extended in the renewal of my teaching practice. Teachers who evoke romance and freedom in the experience of learners are described by students as those who demonstrate their own "love of learning" and a "respect" for the students' personal ideas. In other words, students were empathic with the learning experience of the teacher and sought empathy from teachers vis-a-vis their learning experiences. Students wanted to "feel (the teacher's) excitement and they wanted to know why (the teacher) felt that way". In his description of teaching scholarship, Boyer spoke of building "bridges between the teacher's understanding and the student's learning" (1990, 23). From student narratives I was beginning to understand that these bridges were rooted in the bodily feeling of empathy - a shared passion and freedom in exploring the subject. I learned from my students that good teaching was not merely transmitting the 'facts' and theories comprising the course content, rather, good teaching was exuding and sharing a passion for the ideas being taught. I needed to explain the value and relevance of these ideas for me in order to connect with the experience of students. In transforming my teaching from the transmission of research 'facts' to sharing my own narrative on the subject, and including the narratives of students, my understanding of theory was being renewed and, in turn, so was my practice of teaching. Moreover, I began to realize that defining teaching as the mere transmission of 'facts' garnered from research, as suggested by the University of Saskatchewan Teacher-Scholar Model, leads to what Whitehead calls "inert ideas" and "dead knowledge" (1932, v). This type of knowledge is transmitted in order to 'cover the content' and committed to rote memory by students primarily for the purpose of passing exams. It often fails to resonate with the personal experiences of students and, consequently, fails to enter their long-term memory and really change the meaning of their lives. In too many cases, this 'knowledge' is soon forgotten. It is a type of knowledge that virtually ignores the thinking and insights of students and their potential to revitalize the understanding and practice of teachers. As such, it has little to do with Boyer's (1990) conception of scholarly teaching.

Whitehead (1932) characterizes the cycle of precision and discipline in learning as a growing awareness, during one's free exploration of the subject in the cycle of romance and freedom, that the ideas present in the subject need a "setting in order" to be comprehended. It is a feeling that 'unexplored connections' first apprehended in the cycle of romance and freedom require some logic to be understood. This cycle of mental growth is characterized by a self-imposed discipline. A discipline which Whitehead describes as the aspect of experience when the "freshness of inexperience has worn off" and a "craving grows" for more precise thinking (1932, 53). Students in my Learning and Learners class describe this cycle of mental growth as the emerging awareness of "patterns or facts within" the newly intriguing subject and, in a wonderful metaphor from the Canadian prairies, a "harnessing of the inclinations of romance". My student pianist spoke of his emerging awareness of the limitations of free exploration in this way: "The child likes to bang away on the keys of the piano, again, taking pleasure in the sound, but, realizing he cannot make it sound the way his father does." As he put it, the young pianist realizes that to make the piano sound as it does when his father plays he must know the nuances of musical "interpretation" and develop the "technical skills" of keyboarding in order to perform more competently. It is also important to point out that he realizes his limitations intuitively. His feeling of inadequacy focuses his desire to learn and play music more fully. As was mentioned earlier, this romance or desire is the basis for self-discipline as opposed to working for mere reward.

From student narratives describing Whitehead's (1932) cycle of precision and discipline in the learning process, I began to understand more concretely how the need for a precise knowing of some subject emerges from a personal awareness of the limitations of free exploration in the cycle of romance and freedom. In this passage the young pianist, while banging away on the keyboard of the piano, realizes that he 'cannot make it sound the way his father does'. This is a description of the feeling of inadequacy we all experience at one time or another. It is a concrete bodily feeling telling us we need to improve our knowledge or ability in some area and sets in motion a mental quest for answers or solutions to the dilemma we are experiencing. Students spoke of this personal quest as needing to identify the 'pattern of facts' within the subject and a time of 'harnessing' our inclination toward further free exploration. It is a time of subjecting ourselves to a more disciplined inquiry. Our budding pianist, in this cycle of mental growth, realizes that to play beautifully, as his father does, he must learn the nuances of musical 'interpretation' and sophisticated keyboarding 'techniques'. In studying the narratives of students like this one, my own theoretical understanding of Whitehead's cycle of precision and discipline is transformed into something more concrete and meaningful. His abstract conception of precision as the 'setting in order' of 'unexplored connections' in the subject becomes the more concrete experience of realizing that pounding on the keyboard of a piano is different than playing it beautifully. The abstract idea of discipline as a 'craving' becomes the concrete attempts of the pianist to interpret a piece of music as its composer intended and learning the finger dexterity necessary for correct piano keyboarding to accomplish this end.

Once again, my own concrete understanding of the cycle of precision and discipline, described theoretically by Whitehead (1932), is enriched and transformed by the insights of my students and, in turn, my teaching practice evolves. I came to realize that a self-disciplined inquiry emerges when students feel a deep personal involvement or romance with the subject they are studying. This is why Whitehead claims that precision is "barren" or bereft of personal meaning without romance (1932, 29). It is the students' passion for knowing, conjoined with my passion for knowing, that feeds the self-discipline required for a more precise knowledge of human learning. With this in mind, I encourage students to use their most profound learning experiences to illustrate Whitehead's abstract theory of the rhythmic cycles of mental growth. In this process, I am attempting to evoke the passion and romance inherent in their personal experiences to nourish the self-discipline necessary for a more precise knowing of the subject. Using their own experiences as examples also helps the students' to formulate a more concrete understanding of Whitehead's theory, that is, they come to understand his cycles of mental growth on their own terms. This is not to say that my knowledge of the subject does not play a role in this process, it does. Students constantly turn to me for clarification of their understanding. Moreover, they turn to me because they 'want to know' not because they 'have to know' in order to pass an exam. I believe students and teachers sharing narratives as part of the learning process is consistent with Boyer's description of the scholarship of teaching, that is creating a "common ground of intellectual commitment" (1990, 24). A recognition of the 'common ground' necessary for the scholarship of teaching is essentially absent from the Teacher-Scholar Model proposed by the University of Saskatchewan (1998). Teaching is more than the transmission of research 'facts'.

The cycle of generalization and a return to romance and freedom in learning, according to Whitehead (1932), is characterized by the creative application of the knowledge and abilities gained in the cycle of precision and discipline. It is a cycle of transformation where abstract ideas from elsewhere are assimilated into a concrete personal knowledge and experience that can be utilized by individuals in their own unique ways (Flynn, 2000). As such, the cycle of generalization is also a return to the free expression of these ideas and abilities. Whitehead describes this as the "emergence from the comparative passivity of being trained into the active freedom of application" (1932, 59). In the words of the pianist, eventually I was able to "play concert repertoire". This ability grew from "cycles of romance, precision, and generalization repeated endless times in relation to different pieces, different styles, different composers, etc." This process led to the "man on the stage" and a return to romance "where once again the learner finds joy in making new connections and new applications".

As I contemplate the narratives of students who explain for me the cycle of generalization and a return to romance and freedom my understanding of this cycle, as before, is transformed and extended. From student narratives, I gain a more concrete understanding of Whitehead's (1932) abstract conception of moving from the 'passivity of being trained' to the 'active freedom of application' in one's mental growth. The young pianist has spent endless hours of practising in the cycle of precision and discipline and blossoms into a performer who plays 'concert repertoire' beautifully. His return to romance and freedom is complete when he 'finds joy' in his evolving talent for musical improvisation and composition. This joyful experience rejuvenates his desire to continue 'making new connections and new applications' in his musical journey. The student's narrative account of his experience in learning to play the piano transforms not only his understanding of Whitehead's cycle of generalization and return to romance and freedom, but mine. It provides me with concrete examples of this abstract cycle making it more meaningful. Once students gain a more concrete knowledge of Whitehead's theory by means of their own personal experiences of learning, I ask them to use this new knowledge to create their own learning environments in which his rhythmic cycles of mental growth are applied. These applications continue to interest me and challenge my way of thinking about teaching. Thus, the transformation of my understanding of Whitehead's theory of the rhythmic cycles of mental growth, through the shared narratives of students and myself, extends into my teaching practice. This process of mutual teaching and learning is consistent with Boyer's (1990) concept of teaching scholarship and is missing in the University of Saskatchewan (1998) Teacher-Scholar Model.

3. Conclusion

Boyer describes the scholarship of teaching as a "dynamic endeavour involving all the analogues, metaphors, and images that build bridges between the teacher's understanding and the student's learning" (1990, 23). By listening to, reading, and contemplating the narratives of students, I begin to understand, more concretely, the abstract theoretical ideas I am teaching – practice informs theory. A more concrete understanding of theory allows me to explain these ideas better in my teaching practice-theory informs practice. A more informed practice, in turn, evokes more substantial ideas in the narratives of my students in succeeding classes and these ideas continue to feed my growing knowledge of the subject - practice informs theory. This cyclical process transforms my knowledge, research, and scholarly work and, in turn, enriches and extends my practice of teaching. It is, therefore, consistent with Boyer's (1990) conception of teaching scholarship.

The process of 'transforming and extending' my own knowledge through teaching enriches my research. In contemplating the ideas and questions of students over the years, I have come to recognize the unexplored connections in my own understanding of Whitehead's (1932) theory of mental growth and the process of human learning in general. This knowledge revitalizes my own craving to know more about human learning and informs my research leading to renewed practice and so on. The 'common ground' of knowledge creation I am trying to describe for you, a grounding of teacher and student knowledge in the ebb and flow of being informed by research and informing research, is what I mean by learning in the process of teaching. Such a process of teaching scholarship is more complex and substantial than transmitting research 'facts' and this is why the University's (1998) conception of the Teacher-Scholar Model is wholly inadequate.

Finally, I believe the free sharing of knowledge in the ways that I have described is valuable in contributing to the common good. By encouraging students to participate in the process of scholarship and the creation of new knowledge, their lives are transformed. In the case of my young teachers, this transformation extends into the many class-rooms they will inhabit. While such knowledge may not be marketable or attract grant money, it lies at the very heart of our concept of civili-zation and the role of the university in the civilizing process.

The examples from this presentation substantiate my claims that the narratives of students transform and extend my own scholarly know-ledge, research, and practice of teaching. Moreover, such practice is more than a transmission of research 'facts' and has real value for the community. I would like to offer the teaching and learning experiences of students and myself as a modest example of a constructive alterna-tive to the University's (1998) Teacher-Scholar Model.

Acknowledgements

I would like to acknowledge and thank the students in my classes for their help in clarifying my ideas about human learning, among other things. In particular, Evan Rokeby-Thomas for sharing his experiences in learning to play the piano and my good friend Hannu Soini at the University of Oulu, Finland whose study of human learning continuously inspires me. As always, thank you to my colleagues in the University of Saskatchewan Process Philosophy Research Unit for their support over the years.

Bibliography

Boyer, E. L. (1990): *Scholarship Reconsidered: Priorities of the Professoriate.* Princeton, N.J.: The Carnegie Foundation for the Advancement of Teaching.

Bruner, J. (1996): *The Culture of Education.* London: Harvard University Press.

Callahan, R. E. (1962): *Education and the Cult of Efficiency: A Study of the Social Forces that have Shaped the Administration of the Public Schools.* Chicago: University of Chicago Press.

Flynn, M. (2000). Transforming what is there into what is here: the feel of knowledge in a university setting. Interchange, 31(2&3), pp. 243-257.

Office of the Vice-President Academic (1998). Framework for Planning for the University of Saskatchewan. Saskatoon: University of Saskatchewan.

Palmer, P. (1998) The courage to teach: Exploring the inner landscape of a teacher's life. San Francisco: Jossey-Bass.

Peterman, B. (2002). Saskatoon is science city. The Star Phoenix, June 13, 2002, p. E3.

Soini, H. (1999). Education student's experiences of learning and their conceptions about learning disabilities: Towards a comprehensive theory of learning. Acta Universitatiis Ouluensis: Scientiae Rerum Socialiym, E 40.

Tyack, D.B. (1974). The one best system: A history of American urban education. Cambridge, Mass.: Harvard University Press.

Tyack, D.B. & Hansot, E. (1982). Managers of virtue: Public school leadership in America, 1820-1980. New York: Basic.

Whitehead, A.N. (1932). The aims of education and other essays. London: Williams & Norgate LTD.

Wise, A.E. (1977). Why educational policies often fail: The hyper-rationalization hypothesis. Curriculum Studies, 9(1), 43-57.

Wise, A.E. (1979). Legislated learning: Bureaucratization of the American classroom. Berkeley: University of California Press.

Part II

APPLICATION

PART II.1

WHITEHEAD'S EDUCATIONAL THOUGHT IN THE FIELD OF MANAGEMENT

A Whiteheadian View of Management Education

Robert Chia

Education is the acquisition of the art of the utilisation of knowledge.
Alfred North Whitehead (*The Aims of Education*, 6)

Abstract
The field of professional management practice emerged as a consequence of the gradual separation of ownership from the operational control of production activities in the early part of the twentieth century. As the size and complexity of organizations became more of an issue in terms of effective control of the workforce, owners and shareholders began appointing managers to look after the daily running of their businesses. An elite class of managers was created. One major consequence of this emergence of a class of professionally trained managers is the tendency towards overspecialisation. Management education and training via the now universally-accept qualification, the Masters in Business Administration (MBA) has created a distinctive breed of bright, young, ambitious, and highly specialised individuals for the ever-burgeoning market for qualified managers. The MBA was initially offered by business schools in the United States (Harvard being the very first to offer this kind of management education in the early 1920s) but now has a world-wide appeal and is currently offered from Beirut to Bejing and St Pauls to St Petersburgh. In Britain alone there are some 120 institutions offering one kind of MBA or another. But despite the overwhelming popularity of this specialised training and preparation of managers the actual contribution of such professionalised training and education towards effective management practice remains contestable. Indeed, even within the United States itself, there has been a growing criticism of the adequacy of the MBA in preparing students for the real task of managing. According to one prominent source of criticism, MBA-type education pro-

duces 'silo-type' thinking. Each student comes in ostensibly as an 'empty-bucket' and is filled with knowledge about the functions of business – marketing, operations, finance and human resources – treated with a diet of artificially-simplified case studies and then let out onto the real world of work where they find themselves ill-equipped to deal with the cacophony of problems that confront them. What MBA training tends to do is to create what the philosopher Alfred North Whitehead calls "minds in a groove" (Whitehead, 1985: 245). For Whitehead, this kind of training inclines such individual professionals to live their lives contemplating a given set of abstractions and to actively encourage disconnection with the real world of managerial life. This tendency to produce and reinforce minds in a groove has wide-ranging ramifications for the practice of management. This chapter will explore this dominant trends in management education outline its consequences for the preparation of managers for the world of work and explore its implications for the effective and ethical management of enterprises in the twenty-first century.

1. Introduction

The field of professional management practice emerged in the early 20th century as a consequence of the gradual separation of ownership from the operational control of manufacturing activities. Since this important transformation in the history of modern business a new breed of professional managers dedicated towards improving the efficiency of business operations was brought into being. As the size and complexity of organizations became more of an issue in terms of effective control of the workforce, the resources and the financial aspects of business, owners and shareholders began appointing managers to look after the daily running of their businesses. An elite class of managers was created whose identity is now synonymous with the possession of an MBA (a Masters in Business Administration). Since the early 1960s, beginning with the United States and then more recently in Britain and Europe, business schools have sprouted up rapidly and the number of MBA graduates have risen exponentially within the last four decades. Today, the general perception within the United States and Britain in particular is that the MBA is an essential qualification that provides the key to a successful career in business management. Man-

agement education and training via this now universally-accept qualification, the MBA, has created a distinctive breed of bright, young,
ambitious, and highly specialised individuals for the ever-burgeoning
maret for qualified managers. The MBA has now a world-wide appeal
and is currently offered from Beirut to Bejing and St Pauls to St
Petersburgh. In Britain alone there are some 120 institutions offering
one kind of MBA or another and producing in excess of 15000 MBA
graduates each year.

One major consequence of the emergence this class of professionally traine/managers is that they are increasingly recruited not so much
for their experience of managing but for their formal accreditation.
Yet, despite the apparent success in producing qualified graduates,
there are real concerns about the method and curriculum employed in
MBA-type education and their consequences for the managerial quality
of the graduates produced. According to a number of prominent critics
MBA graduates have overly-inflated images of their own capabilities
and unrealistic expectations about their career progress. Instead of
being honed for the integrative practice of management, what the MBA
tends to produce are specialists in business functions. This is because
there is an overwhelming tendency to focus on subject-based business
specialisms rather than the actual practice of management in MBA-
type education. The typical MBA curriculum comprises eight to twelve
different functional specialisms that are taught generally independently
of each other. As a result MBA graduates acquire knowledge in the
various business sub-fields such as finance, marketing and human
resource management, but little is done to ensure that they possess an
integrative understanding of how these various functions operate collectively as a whole. In other words, what is taught in MBA programmes are business functions *not* the more general practice of management. This means that the MBA qualification is exactly what it
stands for a Masters in *Business Administration* not a Masters in Management. It is ill-equipped to prepare students for the task of management.

Despite the overwhelming popularity of the MBA, the actual contribution of such professionalised training and education towards effective management practice remains contestable (Locke 1996a, 1996b,
1998, Mintzberg 2004). In an extensive study of the impact of American management education on the growth and reputation of American
business, Locke found that America's prowess in management was

established way before the expansion and popularisation of MBA programmes in the US. Business schools and the popularity of management educaion blossomed and expanded exponentially in the 1960s
and 1970s quite some time after America had become a clear economic
superpower. In other words, business schools emerged as a *consequence* and not as the *cause* of the success of American business.

According to Locke, it was engineers and entrepreneurs who never
had the benefit of an MBA-type management education who actually
built up American business. Indeed, when the MBA programmes expanded in the 1970s, the reputation of American management went
into eclipse "as the German and Japanese economies surged ahead"
(Locke 1996b, 1). Both these then-progressive nations did not rely on
the MBA-type graduate to boost their economies. The question of
whether MBA-style education actually contributes towards the growth
of a nation's economy, therefore, remains a moot one. As Locke
concludes: "start-up entrepreneurs [...] could not have gained their
entrepreneurial insight in some MBA program. Consciousness about
the market possibility [...] depends on a thorough grasp (of the situation) acquired on the job" (Locke 1998, 9). Indeed, even within the
United States itself, there has been a growing criticism of the adequacy
of the MBA in preparing students for the real task of managing (Linder
& Smith 1992; Mitroff & Churchman 1992). Lataif (1992) contends
that the traditional narrow problem-solving approach taught in business
schools is woefully inadequate in preparing aspiring managers for the
complexities of a global business environment characterised by heterogeneity, nervousness and vastly different socio-political and economic
network confiurations. According to another prominent source of criticism, MBA-type eduation produces 'silo-type' thinking (Mintzberg
and Lampel 2001). Each student comes in ostensibly as an 'empty-
bucket' and is filled with specialised knowledge about the multiple
functions of business – marketing, operations, finance and human resources – treated with a diet of artificially-simplified case studies and
then let out onto the real world of work where they find themselves ill-
equipped to deal with the cacophony of problems that confront them.
Business schools because of their focus on a discipline-based educational curriculum that mirrors the research and teaching interests of
academics rather than the actual needs of the practitioner world, unwittingly propagate a mental attitude that pays far too much regard to
conventional academic priorities of analytical rigor at the expense of a

loss of imagination and resourcefulness in dealing with the affairs of the world. What tends to result is that an aspiring entrepreneurial manager is systematically transformed by an unimaginative MBA curriculum into a pedantic bureaucratic or administrator.

Yet, the MBA curriculum continues to attract would-be aspiring managers whose main concern is more the achievement of accreditation than the potential learning associated with a proper management education. This chapter will explore this dominant trend in management education to produce overly-specialised business functionalists that masquerade for the much more integrative practice of management. We begin by examining the root causes of this overemphasis on professionalised knowledge at the expense of practical experience in management education. We trace this tendency to privilege academic knowledge over experience to the analytical legacy found in the West that is inspired by the alphabetic system. This then leads us to examine the difference between knowledge created in the observer-domain and to show how significantly it differs from the knowledge possessed by actor-agents. We conclude that it is this latter form of understanding that is vital for the practice of management. We then propose a Whiteheadian approach to management education which emphasises education not so much as the acquisition of management knowledge itself but as the acquisition of the mode of thought required for effectively utilising what passes for management knowledge.

2. The Root Problem of Contemporary Management Education

The well-renowned management theorist Henry Mintzberg has very recently published a book entitled *Managers not MBAs* (2004) which provides a trenchant critique of the current dominant approach towards the education of managers in university business schools. Mintzberg's book is the latest in what might be perceived as a growing tide of disaffection amongst management academics and the practitioner world alike about the general direction in which management education particularly in North America and Europe has taken. The central thrust of Mintzberg's argument is that wrong people are selected and taught, wrong ways of teaching are employed and as a result there are wrong consequences and outcomes associated with an MBA-type education.

Conentional MBA programmes are targeted at young people with little or no experience of management. As a result students are unable to relate the theory learnt with their subsequent practice. The gap between theory and practice remains unbridged. Moreover, such MBA programmes overemphasise technique and analysis; what might be called the science of management at the expense of the *art* and *craft* of managing. The key focus is on analytical problem-solving. Problems are presented as already defined and 'ready-made' and students are expected to attend to these clearly delineated concerns. Decisional parameters are pre-specified and choices are thus rendered rationally unproblematic. This way the MBA student learns to develop strong analytical skills at the expense of a broader vision of the contexts within which problems emerge and also at the expense of the capacity for interpretation and sense-making.

As a result of the intellectual bias towards narrow discipline-bounded analysis, young MBA graduates develop a false impression of their own intellectual capacities and hence a related arrogance along with it, that they have been properly trained for the task of managing even though they have had little or no experience of it. One major consequence is that these young, ambitious graduates have overly unrealistic expectations about the tasks and rewards of managing, and are more concerned with short-term techniques for bloating share prices than with building strong sustainable and competitive business organizations that offer quality products or services to the public. Management is portrayed as exciting, fast-track and a disproportionately-rewarding activity.

Mintzberg's concerns and criticisms about education in general and management education in particular, welcome though it is at the present time with the scandals associated with Enron, WorldCom and Arthur Andersen, is not anything new. Very similar concerns were raised by the philosopher A. N. Whitehead more than seventy years ago. In *The Aims of Education* (1932) and in a chapter entitled 'Requisites for Social Progress' in *Science and the Modern World* (1985), Whitehead had already noted a worrying trend towards what he called "mental dryrot" in institutions of higher learning. Whitehead spoke out forcefully against the passive ingestion of "inert ideas" that passes for management education. "Education with inert ideas is not only useless: it is above all things, harmful – *Corruptio optimi, pessima*." (Whitehead 1932, 2) It produces "minds in a groove". (Whitehead 1985, 245)

Whitehead warned that the danger of being mentally in a groove is to "live in contemplation of a given set of abstractions. The groove prevents straying across country, and the abstraction abstracts something to which no further attention is paid." (Whitehead 1985, 245) The abstractions are subsequently mistaken for reality itself. There is a tendency to succumb to what Whitehead calls "the Fallacy of Misplaced Concreteness". (Whitehead 1985, 64)

The problem with such professionalised training which produces minds in a groove is that lived reality far exceeds and overflows our abstractions. Mistaking our abstractions for reality distorts our understanding of the latter, creates 'tunnel vision' and causes us to act on the basis of an insufficient appreciation of the underlying issues involved. There is much more to professional management practice than can be effectively taught in business school MBAs. Formal learning cannot be an adequate substitute for direct practical experience. "When you understand all about the sun and all about the atmosphere and all about the rotation of the earth" says Whitehead, "you may still miss the radiance of the sunset." (Whitehead 1985, 249) In other words "There is no substitute for the direct perception of the concrete achievement of a thing in its actuality." (Whitehead 1985, 248) Besides the narrow discipline-based training which produces minds in a groove, there is a need for developing a direct intuition of phenomena in all its completeness. Unfortunately, modern science, including the science of political economy and management has "riveted on men a certain set of abstractions which [...] de-humanises industry [...] fixes attention on a group of abstractions, neglects everything else, and elicits every scrap of information and theory which is relevant to what it has retained." (Whitehead 1985, 250) Even worse, it reverses our natural approach to learning. "In the Garden of Eden Adam saw the animals before he named them: in the traditional system, children named the animals before they saw them." (Whitehead 1985, 247) Likewise in the traditional MBA-type management education, students are taught about management concepts and ideas even before they have encountered the work of practice. What professionalised training such as the MBA does is to equip students with *a priori* categories and frameworks that are then uncritically brought to bear on phenomena that they subsequently apprehend. In this way phenomena are forced, often inappropriately, to fit into existing categories for the purpose of problem-solving. Such is the danger of creating and reinforcing 'minds in a groove'.

3. Language, Analysis and Representation

The gap between symbolic representations and living reality is an unbridgeable one and the tendency to mistake representations for reality pervasive and widespread particularly in the dominant Western culture which has acquired and refined an abstractive system of thought that goes back all the way to Aristotle and beyond. What defines this Western abstractive system of thought is an approach to the production of knowledge which Fenollosa (in: Pound 1969) succinctly captures in his illuminating comparison with the structure and logic of the Chinese language. Fenollosa writes:

> According to this European logic, thought is a kind of brick-yard. It is baked into little hard units or concepts. These are piled in rows according to size and then labelled with words for future use. This use consists in picking out a few bricks, each by its convenient label, and sticking them together into a sort of wall, called a sentence, by the use of either white mortar for the positive copula "is", or of black mortar for the negative copular 'is not'. In this way we produce such admirable propositions as "A ring-tailed baboon is not a constitutional assembly. (Fenollosa, in Pound 1969, 380)

Such an *analytical logic*, which deals with a phenomenon by breaking it down into part-elements and then reconstituting it, has been inspired by the spread of the alphabetic system in Western Europe. Indeed, Havelock (1982) has noted that it is the alphabetic system which defines what could be called the 'European mind'. "If today we are so often tempted to speak of the 'European mind' or the 'Western mind', vague as these determinations are, they have a factual basis in so far as we mean those cultures which have continued to employ the Greek invention." (1982, 346)

Introduced some 3000 years ago by the Phoenicians and appropriated and modified by the Greeks some three centuries later, alphabetic writing brought about a fundamental change in *sense-ratios* and hence attitudes of *observational discrimination* from the previously aural-oral cultures (Ong 1967; McLuhan 1967). The phonetic alphabet works by 'atomizing' linguistic sound, and in particular the syllable, into its acoustic components and then assigning a specific alphabetic shape to each of these sound elements. The letters A, B, C etc. represent sound elements that have been associated through convention rather than necessity. But they serve a vital role in converting sound elements into a visual form that can then be mentally reassembled into the words and sentences. Meaning, therefore, becomes possible at the operative level of words and not at the level of individual alphabets. In this way the alphabetic system facilitated a profound shift in human consciousness, bringing about the linear, abstract form of logic: an "ABCD mindedness" (Ong 1967) that we take so much as given today.

One major outcome of this alphabetization of the Western world was the popularizing of the method of 'atomization' – the breaking up of phenomena into part-elements and then the reassembling of these into meaningful wholes. It can be surmised that the development of the atomic theory of matter promoted by Democritus during the pre-Socratic era around 400 BC, was in many ways inspired by the adoption of the alphabetic system. This atomistic approach was revived during the Enlightenment and remains alive today in the method of *analysis* adopt within science in general and in the *methodological individualism* that underpins much of the social sciences in particular. In sum, the alphabet is, as McLuhan (1967) observed an "aggressive and militant absorber and transformer of cultures." (1967, 48) It promoted the abstraction, simple-location and objectification of phenomena for the purpose of analysis, and by reducing all our senses into visual enclosed spaces, it precipitated the rise of the Euclidean sensibility which has dominated Western thought processes for over 2000 years.

One major consequence of the introduction of alphabetic systems of knowledge is that the ideas of detachment, objectivity, clarity, linguistic adequacy and hence precision in the use of language are especially valued and emphasised in the method of analysis. Language is seen to be effectively literal and representational and hence meaning transparent. This leads to an instinctive confidence in breaking up phenomena into manageable parts, identifying and labelling each of these parts and then classifying them in a taxonomic scheme of things. We are good at it. "So good, we often forget to put the pieces back together again." (Toffler, in Foreword to Prigogine and Stengers' *Order out of Chaos*) The alphabetic system is the underlying inspiration for this ingrained analytical attitude. (McLuhan 1967; Ong 1967) Consistent with this method of analysis and representation, the production of knowledge has been intimately associated with the proliferation of systems of knowledge tabulated in the form of lists, tables, taxonomies, charts, lists, classifications etc. These systems of representation, including especially theories, concepts, certifications, reports, accountabilities, plans, etc., take on a life of their own independent of the actual activities they purport to represent. Indeed they frequently become more important than practice itself thanks to an Aristotelian legacy which consistently elevates knowledge over practice. For Aristotle, "it is not being practical that makes them wiser but their possession of an account and their grasp of the causes." (Aristotle *Metaphysics*, 5). Knowledge achieved through reason and representation is deemed more valuable and more important than practical experience. Such representational knowledge constitutes what is contained in the textbooks on management written by academic researchers who may never have had any experience of actual managing in the first place. Indeed, no less than 90% of those who teach on management education programmes in university business schools today have never had any actual practical experience of managing. There is little awareness that what is researched and taught in business schools are but pale and grossly inadequate representations of the actual world of practice. Not surprisingly both students and management teachers mistake theory for actual practice: they mistake the map for the territory or even better 'eat the menu instead of the dish'. It is this kind of abstracted theories and knowledge that is produced and disseminated in business schools.

4. Managerial Representations and Management Realities

In an applied field of study such as management, it is important to be clear about two different forms of knowledge and the functions they serve. On the one hand we have the forms of knowledge produced by academic researchers whose key task is to understand and explain to an essentially academic community the nature and essence of management practice. This scholarly form of knowledge is essentially generated in an 'observer-domain' (Maturana, in Maturana & Varela 1980). It is knowledge 'about' the practice of management. It is knowledge justified through the accepted conventions of a community of scholars. It has satisfied the demands of intellectual rigor and reliability imposed on all such knowledge claims. On the other hand there is knowledge

possessed by practitioners within an 'actor-domain' whose sole function is to aid effective action. It cannot justify itself on the terms expected in the academic community and hence may not be so easily
accessed by traditional academic research. These are tacit and embodied forms of understanding which resist articulation and symbolic
representation. It is this distinction between two vastly different forms
of knowledge which separates the world of academic ideas from the
world of practice. In a poem on death highlighting this distinction, the
biologist Humberto Maturana wrote:

> What is death for the beholder?/
> What is death for the dying?
> A weight beyond knowledge or understanding/
> A pain for the self-asserting
> ego, for the one;? for the other, silence, peace, and nothingness.
> Yet the one feels his pride in anger/
> And in his mind he does not accept/
> That beyond death nothing should arise,/
> And that beyond/there should only be death.
> The other, in his silence,/
> In his unknowing majesty feels,/
> He feels nothing,
> he knows nothing
> (Maturana, in Maturana & Varela 1980, xi).

In this poem Maturana gets at the heart of the distinction between the
knowledge of those who observe and those who experience. The observer of death in Maturana's poem experiences a 'pain for the self-
asserting ego' but for the dead it is just 'peace, silence, nothingness'.

But how does this distinction between knowledge derived from
observation and the knowledge of actors affect our understanding of
management practice and hence management education? The answer
lies in the academic world's propensity to take a detached observer
standpoint towards affairs of the world and to mistake that understanding for the knowledge actors themselves possess in carrying out
their managerial tasks. As academic researchers we instinctively adopt
a scholastic point of view in our attempt to understand the pattern of
observed consistency in behaviour exhibited by the management
practitioner. In so doing we impute to phenomena that which essentially belongs to ourselves. We collude in what the French sociologist
Pierre Bourdieu calls the "epistemocentric fallacy" (Bourdieu 1998,

130). This is the academic tendency to place the models that the researcher "must construct to account for practices into the consciousness of agents." (1998, 133) In this way the conceptual constructions that we must produce to understand and account for practices are assumed to be the "main determinants, the actual cause of practices" (Bourdieu 1998, 133) rather than our own inventions. The movement from detached observation to theory construction which is always done retrospectively by the researcher "lets slip everything that makes the temporal reality of practice in process." (Bourdieu 2002, 80) Moreover, even when "practitioners willingly provide quasi-theoretical accounts of their own practices, they are likely to conceal even from their own eyes, the true nature of their practical mastery." (Bourdieu 2002, 19) This is because 'practice has a logic which is not that of the logician' (Bourdieu 1990, 86). The logic of practice understands only in order to act and not to represent. As a consequence the logicism inherent in the traditional academic viewpoint "cannot grasp the principles of practical logic without forcibly changing their nature." (Bourdieu 1990, 90) In the context of this chapter, the theories developed and taught in business school MBAs are remote from the actual world of practice because they are based upon an analytical logic that is foreign to the logic of practice.

One major outcome of the typical MBA programme is that the inexperienced MBA student arrives at the practical scene with his/her head full of concepts and ideas about management even before he/she encounters the real world of business. Students are taught concepts and theories even before they have ever encountered live managerial situations. They are misled into believing that they 'know' about management despite lacking real-world experience. What is missing in MBA programmes including those like Harvard that pride themselves on using *the case-study approach*, is the need for students to take ownership of the naming, framing and sense-making processes involved in bringing a case to light. Critical to the skills of management is the ability to construct and make sense of the "blooming, buzzing confusion" (James 1996, 50) that is the real experience of managerial life. In the world of the practitioner, problems do not present themselves conveniently labelled, nor do they dutifully obey the disciplinary boundaries of business functions and specialisms. Indeed, in most real situations 'problems' may not be perceived to exist, actors may be 'blind' to them, so that there is little attention paid in the first place.

Problem-finding not problem-solving is the critical art of successful management. And, problem finding comes from the ability to sort out and define otherwise chaotic situations into meaningful and coherent scenarios. That requires a highly developed capacity for prospective sense-making. This is not something that the MBA case-study approach that is widespread in business schools can achieve.

Case studies are generally derived from research into specific corporations conducted by researchers, whose key task is to sift through a cacophony of organizational goings-on and data-bases and to extract some coherence from these inputs. The case study presented to students has therefore already undergone much selective filteration of data and information and subsequently rendered coherent in the form of a self-contained case study. As case-study writer, the researcher has already established and determined *a priori* what kinds of information are relevant and what are not. In so doing the case study deprives the student participant from making the more fundamental decision as to what is and is not relevant to the case in point and indeed of re-defining the case problem. The narrative of the case study provides selective focus and as such always already urges the student towards paths of analyses that conform to the interpretations rendered by the case-study writer. In short, what is silently removed in the presentation of a case study is the inherent contextual ambiguity surrounding any problematic situation and hence the need to exercise judgement and discretion in defining the situation in the first place. The key task of a practising manager is to exercise the capacity to carve out, label and take responsibility *for him/herself* the fluxing and evolving situation that is the real world he/she finds him/herself in. Case studies are of limited use and are only helpful for well-defined problem-solving but the more critical issue facing the practising manager is how to best frame and interpret the 'case' problem in the first place. By overemphasising the 'realistic' features of case-studies many business schools have deluded themselves into believing that such case-study exercises do in fact adequately prepare students for the task of management. The reality is that case studies are a pale shadow, a grossly inadequate representation of the messiness and multifaceted nature of managerial reality.

5. A Whiteheadian Approach to Management Education

It is clear that the forms of knowledge disseminated in MBA classrooms bear little resemblance from the actual cut and thrust of everyday management practice. Academic knowledge produced through rigorous scientific research approaches are bereft of the subtleties and nuances that practitioners must necessarily rely upon to keep their heads above water so to speak. Moreover, the typical MBA curriculum is taught through established business specialisms that discourage an integrative understanding of how businesses are actually run. The result as we have argued is that MBA graduates emerge with a distorted understanding of management practice and an inflated view of their own capabilities. But if this is the case and it is deemed to be unsatisfactory and even counterproductive, what are the alternatives to making management education more effective and relevant? Here is where we might begin to take a leaf from the Whiteheadian corpus.

In *The Aims of Education* Whitehead emphasised the importance of education as the productive welding of *imagination and natural experience*. The justification for a university education says Whitehead, is that it "preserves the connection between knowledge and the zest of life." (Whitehead 1932, 139) It is this imaginative acquisition of knowledge and the welding of it to life's experiences which defines the university. Apart from this importance of the imagination, "there is no reason why business men […] should not pick up their facts bit by bit as they want form particular occasions. A university is imaginative or it is nothing." (Whitehead 1932, 145) For this reason a number of contemporary management scholars including especially Mintzberg (2004) justifiably insists that it is the education of experienced managers and not young inexperienced students of management which should be the target priority of business schools. Unlike the typical profile of the MBA student who is young, inexperienced and essentially idealistic, it is mature, practising managers with real burdens of responsibility who should be the main target of management education. It is these existing managers who can significantly improve their practice in a thoughtful and intellectually challenging environment that a university business school can provide. Mintzberg's own International Masters in Practicing Management (IMPM) programme is designed as an alternative to the conventional MBA programme.

Unlike the MBA programme, the IMPM is targeted at senior practising managers. It is an attempt to provide a reflective space for practising managers to engage with the world of ideas and to consider their wider implications for practice. It uses the detached educational opportunity to leverage the learning of practising managers by deliberately creating a reflective space and context in which practical experience is re-examined and re-evaluated against a backdrop of new insights and understanding.

Unlike the traditional silo-styled teaching of business specialisms the IMPM programme emphasises the cultivation of five *managerial mindsets*: the reflective mindset, the worldly mindset, the analytical mindset, the collaborative mindset and the action mindset. Each of these mindsets emphasise a particular mode of engagement, a disposition towards the external world in the context of management practice. From the point of view of the world of practice, awareness of the variety of orientations that can be adopted in the face of emerging issues and concerns and confidence in their application is far more valuable than expert knowledge of business sub-functions. It is this emphasis on the shift away from the knowledge-content of business function to the cultivation of mentalities and modes of thought which resonates with Whithead's (1932) own emphasis on the cultivation of the business mind. The proper focus of management education should be on the 'art' of utilising knowledge.

Writing during the Great Depression in a chapter contribution to a book entitled *Business Adrift* (1931) by the then dean of Harvard Business School and subsequently reprinted in *The Adventures of Ideas* (1933), Whitehead noted the rise of a general type of mentality that was critical to the success of a commercial community. For him, the capacity for an "instinctive grasp of the relevant features of social currents is of supreme importance" (Whitehead 1933, 119) as is an "unspecialized aptitude for eliciting generalizations from particulars and for seeing the divergent illustration of generalities in diverse circumstances." (1933, 120) In other words, for Whitehead, it was more important in a management education process to cultivate appropriate modes of thought than it is to fill young MBA students with extensive amounts of specialised disciplinary knowledge. Like Mintzberg more recently, Whitehead saw the need to preserve the connection between knowledge and experience. This way a fact absorbed is not just a bare inert fact. Instead, "it is invested with all its possibilities. It is no longer a burden on the memory: it is energising as the poet of our dreams, and as the architect of our purposes." (Whitehead 1933, 139) Programmes like the IMPM do not focus so much on knowledge of business functions. Rather their objective is to develop an indepth understanding of the real dilemmas and predicaments of management practice and to cultivate the requisite local sensitivity to deal with these in a meaningful and productive manner. Deep understanding engenders conviction and commitment to a cause and steels the resolve in times of doubt and challenge. If anything, deep understanding consoles the practitioner of the rightness of a particular course of action and galvanises his/her will to stay the course in the face of mounting pressure to conform to popular opinion. It helps the practitioner resist the urge to act prematurely and to endure the open-endedness and ambiguity of an unfolding managerial situation. This is a capacity that the poet John Keats called "negative capability" (Chia & Morgan 1996). Yet this negative capability which fuels the *will* and resolve to achieve a desired outcome is not identified as a pedagogical objective in most MBAs. *Will* is what enables "managers to execute disciplined action, even when they are disinclined to do something [...] An insatiable need to produce results infects wilful managers. They overcome barriers, deal with setbacks, and persevere to the end. With willpower, giving up is not an option." (Bruch & Ghoshal 2004, 14) Will provides the energising force to see through a particular course of action.

A proper management education process not only informs but evoke and 'awaken' sensibilities and awareness to the tensions, inherent contradictions, dilemmas and predicaments of managerial situations. Knowledge is undoubtedly important but even more important is a heightened sensitivity to local situations. Management achieves outcomes *through* people. And people have hopes, aspirations, anxieties, preferences and fears that are not always expressed or articulated. They have to be patiently and sensitively elicited. A certain degree of naivete in dealing with sensitive situations can sometimes be helpful since a head-full of knowledge can often get in the way of understanding the human condition. For the Japanese industrialist Konosuke Matsushita, a vital quality for good management is the possession of a *sunao* mind. Sunao is a Japanese word that is used to denote meekness, tractability or an open-hearted innocence; an untrapped mind. "A person with this mind looks at things as they are at that moment and colours them with no special biases, emotionalism or preconception

[...] when a person looks at things with this sunao mind he is open to experience them as they are." (Matsushita 1978, 63-65) The art critic John Ruskin calls this the "innocence of the eye [...] a sort of childish perception [...] of colour, merely as such, without consciousness of what they signify." (Ruskin 1927, Vol. XV, 27) What is needed in management education besides the imparting of established knowledge is the cultivation of what Whitehead called the direct intuition of the "concrete achievement of a thing in its actuality." (Whitehead 1985, 248) Only then can the 'radiance of the sunset' be truly appreciated. In other words what is still much needed in management education is the cultivation of the capacity for directly grasping the totality of a phenomenon that we apprehend.

Because management is inherently an applied discipline, the problems of management can only be meaningfully discussed, analysed and pondered upon by managers who have already found themselves in a confusing variety of managerial predicaments. Only in relation to *their own* stock of experience can the practice of management be assessed, evaluated and learnt from. Managing is firstly and fundamentally the task of becoming aware, attending to, sorting out, and prioritising an inherently messy, fluxing and chaotic world of competing demands that are placed on a manager's attention. It is creating order out of chaos. It is an art, not a science. Active perceptual organization and the astute allocation of attention is a central feature of the managerial task.

6. Concluding Remarks: Requisites for University Management Education

In a retirement speech given at Stanford Business School in 1996, the eminent management theorist James March lamented the systematic erosion of scholastic ideals in American business schools especially in their research and teaching. March observed that because of the overwhelming dominance of an instrumentalist mentality, human action is frequently portrayed as calculative and consequential. "Action is seen as choice; and choice is seen as driven by anticipations, incentives, and desires." (March 1996, 1) Business schools teach this 'consequentalist theology' in MBAs as a sacred doctrine. For March, however, there is a second grand tradition for understanding, motivating and justifying human action that shouldbe emphasised in business schools. This is the tradition that is based, not on anticipation of consequences but on a mission to fulfil and realise ones identity, potential and sense of self. It is a tradition that "speaks of self-conceptions and proper behaviour, rather than expectations, incentives, and desires." (March 1996, 1) March cites Don Quixote as the quintessential character that exemplifies this uncompromising approach to life. When asked to explain his behaviour, Quixote does not bother to justify his behaviour in consequential terms. Rather his stock reply is; 'Yo se quien soy.' – 'I know who I am.' For March, Quixote's actions are driven not by the imperatives of external demands but by the imperative to realise himself. "He exhibits a sanity of identity more than a sanity of reality. He follows a logic of appropriateness more than a logic of consequence. He pursues self-respect more than self-interest." (March 1996, 2) Quixote misadventures, oftentimes verging on the comical, nevertheless celebrates an open-ended non-consequentialist and exploratory view of humanity. It warms us to an aspect of the human condition that is easily forgotten but that can better account for the achievements of our modern civilisation. March writes:

> Great enthusiasms, commitments, and actions are tied not to hopes for great outcomes but to a willingness to embrace the arbitrary and unconditional claims of a proper life. Quixote reminds us that if we trust only when trust is warranted, love only when love is returned, learn only when learning is valuable, we abandon an essential feature of our humanness – our willingness to act in the name of a conception of ourselves regardless of its consequences. (March 1996, 3)

For March, nowhere is this spirit of exploration and self-fulfilment more crucial for management education than it is today in a world where universities are more and more construed as markets and students 'customers'. This 'dumbing down' of academia has dire consequences. Quite ironically it leads, not to better business and management practice, but to a 'cheapening' of the value of university education. As Ruskin perceptively noted in his review of the production of great art which is eminently applicable to any human endeavour:

> The very primary motive which we set about business, makes that business impossible. The first and absolute condition of the thing's ever becoming saleable is, that we shall make it without

wanting to sell it; nay, rather with a determination not to sell it at any price, if once we get hold of it. Try make your Art popular, cheap–a fair article for your foreign trade; and the foreign market will always show something better. But make it only to please yourselves, and ever be resolved that you wont' let anybody else have any; and forthwith you will find everybody else wants it. [...] (Great) art has only been produced by nations who rejoice in it; fed themselves with it, as if it were bread; basked in it, as if it were sunshine; shouted at the sight of it; danced with the delight of it; quarrelled for it; fought for it; starved for it; did, in fact precisely the opposite with it of what we want to do with it. (Ruskin 1927, Vol. XVI, 184)

Paradoxically by attempt to popularise business schools and making the MBA curriculum more 'relevant' through focusing on the manifest aspects of business–the functional specialisms, case studies etc.,–business schools have actually trivialised their potential contribution to the education of managers. They have forgotten that their proper educational role as integral parts of the university tradition is the cultivation of deep understanding and the human imagination (Whitehead 1932, 139). This is the vital function it performs for society in its search for progress. This is what it is best able to do and what it should concentrate on; the imaginative cultivation of minds and the honing of mentalities to deal with affairs of the world. Thinking of universities and business schools as commercial enterprises 'cheapens' their vital role in society. As March puts it well:

A university is only incidentally a market. It is more essentially a temple – a temple dedicated to knowledge and a human spirit of inquiry. It is a place where learning and scholarship are revered, not primarily for what they contribute to personal or social well-being but for the vision of humanity that they symbolize, sustain, and pass on [....] Higher education is a vision, not a calculation. It is a commitment, not a choice. Students are not customers; they are acolytes. Teaching is not a job; it is a sacrament. Research is not an investment; it is a testament. (March 1996, 3)

Like Whitehead, March recognises that the real contribution of university business schools lie, not so much in attempting to be more apparently 'relevant' to the concerns of business but in being more true to its vocational commitment; the expansion of horizons of awareness and understanding. If I had my way, every management academic involved in teaching MBAs should be required to read Alfred North Whitehead's *The Aims of Education* and especially the chapter on 'Universities and their Function'. Only then will they begin to truly understand the real purpose and potential contribution of university business schools to societal progress.

Bibliography
Aristotle (1998): *Metaphysics.* London: Penguin.
Bourdieu, P (2002/1977): *Outline of a Theory of Practice.* Cambridge: Cambridge University Press.
Bourdieu, P. (1990): *The Logic of Practice.* Cambridge: Polity Press.
Bourdieu, P. (1998): *Practical Reason:* Cambridge: Polity Press.
Bruch, H. & Ghoshal, S. (2004): *A Bias for Action.* Harvard: Harvard Business School Press.
Chia, R. & Morgan, S. (1996): Educating the Philosopher Manager: De-Signing the Times. *Management Learning* 26, 1, 37-63.
Fenollosa, E. (1969): The Chinese Written Character as a Medium for Poetry. In: E. Pound (Ed.): *Instigations.* Freeport, NY: Books for Libraries Press.
Havelock, E. (1982): *The Literate Revolution in Greece and its Cultural Consequences.* Princeton: Princeton University Press.
James, W. (1996/1911): *Some Problems of Philosophy.* Lincoln and London: University of Nebraska Press.
Lataif, L. E. (1992): Deabate–MBA: Is the Traditional Model Doomed? *Harvard Business Review* 70, 128-40.
Linder, J. C. & Smith, H. J. (1992): The Complex Case of Management Education. *Harvard Business Review* 70, 16-33.
Locke, R. R. (1996a): *The Collapse of the American Management Mystique.* Oxford: Oxford University Press.
Locke, R. R. (1996b): The Introduction of Business Schools in the United Kingdom: Confusing Historical for Functional Events. Paper presented at the British Academy of Management Conference, Aston University, U. K., September 17th 1996.
Locke, R. R. (1998): Factoring American Business School Education into the Revolution in Interactive Information Technology. Paper delivered at Retrospective conference on "Educating French Management Professors in North America, 1969-1975" held at FNEGE (The French Management Foundation), Paris, November 1998, 1-14.
March, J. (1996): A Scholar's Quest. Stanford Graduate Business School Website.
Maturana, H. & Varela, F. (1980): *Autopoeisis and Cognition.* Dordrecht: D. Reidel Publishing.

Matsushita, K. (1986/1978): *My Management Philosophy*. Singapore National Productivity Board Publication.

McLuhan, M. (1967): *The Gutenberg Galaxy*. Toronto: The University of Toronto Press.

Mintzberg, H. & Lampel, J. (2001): Do MBAs Make Better CEOs? Sorry Dubya, It Ain't Necessarily So. *Fortune* 19, 244.

Mintzberg, H. (2004): *Managers Not MBAs*. London: Prentice Hall.

Mitroff, I. I. & Churchman, C. W. (1992): Debate–MBA: Is the Traditional Model Doomed?. *Harvard Business Review* 70, 128-40.

Ong, W. J. (1967): *The Presence of the Word*. New Haven and London: Yale University Press.

Prigogine, I. & Stengers, I. (1984): *Order out of Chaos*. London: Fontana.

Ruskin, J. (1927): *The Complete Works*. London: Nicholson and Weidenfeld.

Whitehead, A. N. (1985/1926): *Science and the Modern World*. London: Free Association Books.

Whitehead, A. N. (1932): *The Aims of Education*. London: Williams & Norgate.

Whitehead, A. N. (1933): *Adventures of Ideas*. Harmondsworth, Middlesex: Pelican.

Whitehead and Management: Learning from Management Practice

Paul W. D'Arcy & Mark R. Dibben

Abstract

This chapter offers a practitioner account of the influence of process-thinking on both the daily life of business management and the strategic planning of a global corporation. As such it is intended to complement contemporary work in the management literature that uses Whitehead and Bergson to articulate the changefulness of management to an academic audience. The chapter begins with a brief review of the uses of process philosophy in the organization studies, and in particular 'management learning' discourses and suggests these are largely conceptual in nature. This is in contrast to the writings of key process-thinkers on learning and education, which are characterized by their practical focus, offering well-found advice based upon experience. The chapter seeks to revisit this latter approach to the use of process-thinking in education by demonstrating how process-thinking informs the actions of management in business. In so doing, it relies heavily on the senior executive experience of the first author to consider such topics as the treatment of employees, product quality issues, management training and globalization. In the light of this discussion, the chapter revisits conceptual understandings of management learning and develops these further by incorporating certain core principles of process thought such as paraexperintialism and the actual occasion to provide a processual description of the management learning experience. The chapter argues that managerial actions such as those outlined are a key mechanism by which learning and knowledge transfer from the senior executive to other managers, and the wider organization in general, and proposes a processual articulation of this transfer in terms of Brackenian event fields. In this way the chapter presents the argument that a Whiteheadian-process-thinking approach to management learning ultimately involves the demonstration of – and thereby a more complete managerial reconnection with – natural human-life experiences of synthesis.

1. Introduction

Whiteheadian thought is used in most contemporary management writing to rework taken-for-granted understanding of the nature of professional knowledge and managerial discourse in terms of, for example, information, meaning and aesthetic logic. Such work has a tendency to constrain Whitehead's influence largely to the conceptual domain of academic writing. By comparison Whitehead's own thinking on education and learning (e.g. 1959; also Brumbaugh 1984, Lowe 1990, 43-68) was, along with other process thinkers such as Dewey (1938) and Oliver (1989), rather more practically oriented, offering well-found advice based upon experience, coupled with demonstrations of how such thought might be applied. Rather than follow a purely conceptual path in this chapter, therefore, we attempt to offer an alternative that is perhaps more in keeping with the earlier writings of process thinkers, while at the same time being complementary to the process-oriented work more commonly seen in the management discourse. To this end, we argue Whitehead's thought has a more immediate value to managers via a practical demonstration of the hands-on application of his philosophy in the day-to-day process of managing organizations. In this practical demonstration, we shall rely heavily upon the managerial experience of the first author, whose doctoral thesis on process theology under John Cobb provides a very different basis for his current work as a Senior Executive in a leading multinational than that commonly found among CEOs.

We shall begin by briefly examining certain contemporary process-oriented writings on management learning, so as to bring this to bear upon our discussion. We shall then summarise key aspects of Whitehead's thought that enable us to next unpack the daily practice of management, in terms of how we might more meaningfully engage in, for example, the treatment of employees, product quality, customer relations and, more broadly, strategic planning. We shall then engage in some comments on the nature of management training itself. As such we suggest that a Whiteheadian-process-thinking approach to management and management education involves much more than simply a conceptual re-orientation, however valuable this may be in articulating the changefulness of the managerial experience to the academic audience. We argue that such theoretical reconceptualisations do little in and of themselves to move the *practice* of management beyond its daily reliance on scientific regulation and the control of outputs – i.e. a contrived organizational experience of analysis. Rather a White-headian-process-thinking approach to management learning ultimately involves the demonstration of – and thereby a more complete managerial reconnection with – natural human-life experiences of synthesis.

2. Process-thinking in the Theorising of Management

The past decade has seen a growth in the use of process thought in the academic field of Management and Organisation Studies. While the genesis of such work can be traced back at least to the 1970s (e.g. Cooper 1976; Cooper & Law 1995) it is only in the past few years that the work of Whitehead and Bergson has come to be generally recognised as legitimate in the field. This is in no small part due to the scholarship of Robert Chia. A survey of subject areas within Management, such as managerial decision making (1994), entrepreneurship (1996a), organisation theory (1992, 1996b, 1997, 1998, 1999; Tsoukas & Chia 2002) and management learning itself (Chia & Morgan 1996; also Chia this volume) reveals that his use of process thought is invariably the benchmark for any subsequent analysis (Dibben & Munro 2003); a recent special focus of management writing in *Process Studies* (Dibben & Cobb 2003) relied heavily upon his thinking. Due to both the painstaking nature of its development and also its inherent conceptual richness, Chia's work is not only the first word on the subject, but often the final word also. Rarely has one person galvanised and reshaped the discourse of his discipline in such a manner, and in such a short space of time.

Chia's writing and that which has followed it (e.g. Wood 2002 & 2004; also Linstead 2002 & Styhre 2002) is characterised by what has been termed the 'selective application' of specific elements of the work of process philosophers (mainly Bergson and Whitehead) to unpack a particular aspect of the topic under study (Dibben & Munro 2003). As such, it rarely comes to grips with the technical details of process thinking, such as distinguishing between conscious discrimination, causal efficacy, presentational immediacy and symbolic reference, or acknowledging the significance of paraexperientialism. Rather, it uses process thought fundamentally to counter the Newtonian and Cartersian predelictions inherent in the social sciences (see for example Habermas 1972, 113-139) by turning passive static noun into active changeful verb, such that organisation becomes organising, management becomes managing, knowledge becomes knowing and so on. It then uses this reconceptualisation to derive insightful commentary on the nature of management. Thus, developing Whitehead's commentary regarding education and the business school (1959, 136-152), Chia argues for example that the philosopher-manager engages in an ongoing education of intellectual and emotional preparation. This allows him to be aware of the need to avoid the conceptual closure afforded us by the dominant cultural norms, actions and beliefs expressed through the professional language of managerial life (Chia & Morgan 1996). Such preparation consists of being open to Whitehead's 'creative advance into novelty', allowing a Whiteheadian 'awakening' of the senses to the myriad possibilities afforded by the imaginative recombining of new information into renewed understanding and, as a result, foresight. In this sense, Chia argues management learning consists of a continual intellectual process of knowledge making through the momentary stabilising and encoding of patterns of informational and human relations. Management knowledge is therefore "always about to become something other than itself" (Chia & Morgan, 1996, 58; also Chia 1996a).

Developing this understanding further, we can discern learning to be a subjective experience of 'transition' (Cobb & Griffin 1976, 14-15) from one moment of knowing to another. This knowing, as a momentary event, resides in one individual and to which the individual alone has direct access (Mead 1934). Since knowledge is understood to be the '"conscious discrimination of objects experienced [...] derived from, and verified by, direct intuitive observation" (Whitehead 1961, 176), learning also requires another individual or set of individuals as a stimulation for it (Dewey 1938, 35-37). As such the learning experience of the individual "does not go on simply inside the person, [...] but changes in some degree the objective conditions under which experiences are had" (Dewey 1938, 39). Educative growth (Dewey 1938, 35) through learning is thus not simply a subjective function of direct personal reflection by the individual as a separate experience of self-as-was a moment ago (Mead 1934) to which the self-as-now reacts. Rather, it has an objective character communicated in action towards others, the datum to which those others each respond. These responses, in their turn are objective reflections of new subjective experiences of learning. In this way, the philosopher-manager educates others through his actions, which are a result of his own learning.

Action informed by process-thinking is thus a key mechanism by which others learn in organisations, and through which the organisations grow. Beyond the purely conceptual understanding of the nature of management learning provided for by process scholars in management, therefore, a more complete understanding of management learning from a process perspective, in terms of its *effect* on managerial and organisational life, requires an examination of just exactly what actions a procesually informed manager might undertake in his daily life. This is because these actions are not only the result of processual learning, but are the mechanism by which that learning transfers itself onto the organisation and influences its intellectual (and thence economic) growth. Without such an examination, we argue, the conceptual reworkings of management and management learning discussed above remain oddly divorced from their practical application.

3. Process-thinking in the Practice of Management

In the light of the foregoing discussion, we therefore seek in the remainder of this chapter to provide some indication of how process-thinking can be applied to the business enterprise, and especially to business management, from a practitioner perspective. In so doing we hope to provide a practical basis for ongoing management learning that will be informed by managerial experience to complement contemporary process reconceptualisations of management theory. Our argument is first, that process-thinking has multifarious applications in the management of a business enterprise; these can occur in both the daily life of business management, (whether in short-term decision-making or medium-term-planning and leadership), and in longer-term strategic planning in a global corporation. And second, that the incorporation of process-thinking in the decision-making-process of management personnel in a business enterprise can have a profound effect on those personnel, the health of the enterprise itself, and the results or the consequences brought about by the activities undertaken by the enterprise.

In seeking to demonstrate these two theses, we will not deal with them sequentially, i.e., we will not set out first to establish the validity of the first thesis and then move on to establish the validity of the second thesis. On the contrary, what follows will show, within the context of discussing various 'applications' (thesis #1), how these applications 'make a difference and can have a profound effect' (thesis #2). To do this, we assume the following core principles of process-thinking, developed amongst others in Whitehead (1967, 1996, 1978, 1961 & 1968), Hartshorne (1975, 1976, 1962, 1970, 1972, 1983a, 1983b, & 1984), Cobb (1965, 1967, 1969, 1971, 1999; also Cobb & Griffin 1976 and Daly & Cobb 1994) and Griffin (1991, 1997, 1998a, 1998b, 2001, 2003) to be commonly understood by the reader:

1. The integration of moral, aesthetic, and religious intuitions with the most general doctrines of the sciences into a self-consistent worldview is one of the central tasks of philosophy;

2. Hard-core common sense notions are the ultimate test of the adequacy of a philosophical position;

3. Whitehead's non-sensationist doctrine of perception, according to which sensory perception is a secondary mode of perception, is derivative from a more fundamental, non-sensory 'prehension';

4. Paraexperientialism with organizational duality; all true individuals – as distinct from aggregational societies – have at least some iota of experience and spontaneity (self-determination);

5. All enduring individuals are serially ordered societies of momentary 'occasions of experience';

6. All actual entities have internal as well as external relations;

7. A Divine Actuality acts variably but never supernaturally in the world – the Whiteheadian version of naturalist theism;

8. Doubly Dipolar Theism;

9. The provision of cosmological support for the ideals needed by contemporary civilization is one of the chief purposes of philosophy in our time;

10. A distinction may be made between verbal statements (sentences) and propositions, and between both of these and propositional feelings.

Taking these for granted, we will not begin with a pre-established unpacking of these particular principles and then show how such principles are or can be applied to business management. Rather we shall rely heavily upon personal experience and then make reference to such principles of process-thinking as we can identify. We shall begin with some applications of process-thinking in the daily life of business management, and then consider some applications of process-thinking in the strategic planning of a global corporation.

3.1 Process-thinking in the Daily Life of Business Management

3.1.1 Treatment of Employees

During the course of managing a business enterprise, many situations arise where decisions must be made in respect to the treatment of employees – the front-line basic resource. These may have to do with elements such as work hours, compensation, policies, over-time, vacations, working conditions, insurance programs, performance, discipline, promotions, etc. Management in virtually all businesses must make decisions on an on-going-basis in all of these arenas and more. The question is not whether decisions will be made in these arenas; the question is *how* and *on what bases* these decisions will be made.

If, for example, a manager's basic philosophy holds that employees are *only* a means-to-an-end, that manager's treatment of employees and the various decisions regarding their welfare will likely be made on a purely pragmatic basis. If he is in the midst of a business-cycle where he really needs his employees (he can't afford to lose them), he may treat them positively and make decisions which are disposed toward their positive well-being. Or, if he has a special need for certain employees, he may treat them particularly well while simultaneously treating other employees disrespectfully.

Process-thinking incorporates certain insightful principles for application in this arena; we draw attention to three of them:

1)   All actual occasions (and all human beings) emerge out of particular contexts; understanding and appreciating this principle makes decisions regarding employees, their per-

formance and their development much richer than they would otherwise be. The bases for such decisions will likely be much more educated and broader, if based upon this process-principle, than they would otherwise be.

2) Each actual occasion (and each human being) is a value in and for itself. In the context of employee-relations, this principle means that, even though businesses may see employees as some means-to-an-end, i.e., that employees contribute something toward certain goals of the business, the life of an employee is also an end-in-itself, a value in itself. A keen awareness of this process-principle causes a manager, when considering human-resource issues, to think far beyond the simplistic pragmatic contributive role which an employee may provide to the business. Maintaining awareness of this process-principle provides the manager with a much larger perspective regarding the employee and his/her value than would otherwise be the case.

3) All actual occasions (and all human beings) are free and open-ended in their process of becoming. While each employee emerges out of a specific context which may set-the-stage-for or establish some of the parameters for behavior, each employee incorporates some elements which are free, free to change, free to introduce novelty, free to transcend past behavior patterns.

While a process thinker may manage Human Resource issues in a highly humanistic way by inviting and allowing employees to be involved dialogically in many issues related to human resources, the reality in many business-enterprises is that the overwhelming majority of the rank-and-file workers prefer not to be called upon to be the philosophical gurus regarding policy. They prefer, on the other hand, to have clear and simple policies issued so that they know (without question) what is expected of them. Furthermore, they prefer that enforcement of the policies be clear and decisive. As such, they want to know where they stand; they also are pleased to know that the company enforces its policies on a fair, regular, and consistent basis. In other words, it is important that the company be reliable and trustworthy; it may even be seen as a 'great place to work'. But, in this case, the 'humanitarian' may see the company as acting too harshly and disrespectful of its employees.

Decisions regarding human-resource-issues which are made by management personnel who are clearly aware of this process-principle will be based upon a much richer and a much broader range of characteristics and possibilities than those which are made without such awareness. Such a perspective encourages straight-forward and honest communication with an employee, not only regarding failures in performance but especially regarding potential alternatives or ways of improving performance. Overall, incorporating certain insightful-principles of process-thinking into the human resource issues of a business enterprise can make a profound difference in how employees are treated and can influence significantly the quality of life of the business enterprise itself.

3.1.2 Product Quality Issues

In the life of any business enterprise, the importance of product quality can be given more or less priority. Certain aspects of product-quality are regulated by one or more governmental agencies; such regulations are normally put in place for the protection of either human beings or the environment. The extent to which business enterprises comply with such regulations varies a great deal; beyond such base-line-regulations, the extent to which business enterprises place an emphasis on overall-product-quality also varies considerably.

The incorporation of certain process-principles into decisions regarding product-quality can make a considerable difference to how a company operates. Three of those principles are, 1) the law of implied-value or fairness; 2) the importance of compliance with law; 3) what goes around comes around, i.e., the Karma Samsara of Business. When a business enterprise delivers a product, it is important that such product provides the customer a fair-value; without the enterprise complying with this law of implied-value, one of the key ingredients essential for civilization, i..e., 'trust', is undercut. Furthermore, even although regulations may be in place regarding certain base-line product-quality requirements, a business enterprise may choose to comply or to not comply and run the risks associated with non-compliance. Here again, a deep respect for civilization and its related elements – a key principle of process-thinking – leads business management to make decisions in support of legal compliance, rather than to see if it can get-by or sneak-by with some more economical version of the product which may not fully comply with the relevant regulations. Lastly, making decisions regarding product quality within a business enterprise based upon this process-principle of 'what goes around comes around' is good for the enterprise, good for the customer, and good for the enhancement of civilization and its core virtue, fairness. Another way of stating the principle is to refer to it as compliance with 'The Golden Rule', namely, 'Do unto others as you would have others do unto you.'.

While these three principles may seem obvious (and they are certainly not unique to process-thinking), they represent key elements addressed by process-thinking. Furthermore, whether or not and/or the extent to which these principles are taken into account by business management when addressing issues related to product quality makes a big difference to the daily health of a business enterprise, its customers, and its impact upon the society, the environment, and the civilization within which it operates.

3.1.3 Fairness of Policies, Programs, Pricing, etc.

Every business enterprise is confronted on a regular and on-going basis with questions regarding how it will deal with the decision-making-process in respect to elements such as policies, programs, pricing, etc. Here again, the incorporation of certain process-principles into decisions regarding such elements make a fundamental difference in how a company operates. The three principles mentioned above in respect to product quality (the importance of fair treatment, compliance with laws, and the Karma-Samsara of business) apply equally well in respect to these elements.

Decisions made by business management, which are based upon the principle of fair treatment lead to a fair and equitable application of policies, programs, pricing, and so on. Regular utilization of this principle in decision-making by management provides a positive impression to all employees that this is an appropriate way for a business to operate and reinforces the importance of this principle. Depending upon the country or state in which a business enterprise finds itself operating, certain laws or regulations may be in effect which prohibit certain behavior of the enterprise in respect to its application of its policies, programs, pricing, etc. However, the agency responsible for enforcement of such regulations, e.g., prohibitions against price-fixing or price-discrimination, seldom have sufficient manpower to police the market-place thoroughly for violators. Therefore, the actual enforcement of such laws depends more upon the good-will of business management and the awareness of the market-place of the importance of compliance with such regulations. Business managers who are only looking for certain short-term success of specific 'positive' business-indicators may intentionally avoid compliance with certain laws. Such behavior by a business enterprise sets a bad example in respect to moral values for its employees, may be illegal in the eyes of the law and undermine the positive values of trust and confidence in the society upon which the business of the enterprise depends.

Business decisions in these arenas of policies, programs, pricing, etc., which are based upon a recognition and appreciation of the principle of Karma-Samsara tend, furthermore, to coincide with decisions based upon 'fairness' and 'compliance with laws.' Such decisions, however, bring to bear on the situation a very different angle, namely a pragmatic concern for how the business enterprise itself may be impacted (usually over the longer-haul) as a result of such behavior. Contrary to being altruistic, making decisions in the light of this principle can be seen, in certain ways, as selfish for the sake of the business enterprise. This arena of fairness in respect to policies, programs, pricing, and so on is only one example of a host of situations in which the enterprise, while making decisions which are truly good for the employees, good for customers, good for society and good for the expansion of civilized life is often making decisions which are, simultaneously, good for the business enterprise itself.

3.1.4 Honesty in Communication with Customers

Honesty in communicating with customers (or others) may be a characteristic or principle that has philosophic, theological, religious, or moral support from a broad range of alternative perspectives. Process-thinking, however, instills a very special character into this principle, namely the principle of essential-relatedness. Decisions of business management that are made in the light of this principle recognize that the 'other' (to whom one is communicating) is part of the 'one' (who is communicating) and vice-versa. Therefore, a lack of fidelity (or the introduction of dishonesty) in the communication-process infects the quality and reliability of that which is being communicated. The greater the lack of fidelity introduced into the communication from customers (e.g., with respect to projections, forecasts, or purchase orders), the greater the allowances are likely to be which need to be made by the supplier (e.g., with respect to parts acquisition, production-planning, inventory build-up, and margin fluctuation). In short, dishonesty in business-communications breeds inefficiency and a lack of productivity. On the contrary, honesty in business communication increases the efficiency and the productivity of the participating business enterprises.

This honesty-principle should not be misunderstood, nor should it be confused with sharing trade-secrets or information which is confidential to the Business Enterprise. In today's business environment, there is a great deal of information that is the preserve of the customer and which the supplier may have no right to know. Simultaneously, there is a great deal of information which is the preserve of the supplier which the customer may have no right to know. There is no reasonable need to 'tell the whole truth' about everything. This is because even though a process thinker in business will communicate honestly with customers, an excessive sharing of the companies' marketing strategy with customers may put certain of the company's competitive advantages in the hands of a competing company. In some cases, such an erroneous divulgence may impact the company's sales negatively, reduce its revenues substantially, and lead to the necessity of mass layoffs and even a closure of the business-enterprise. In short, the importance of honesty in business communications must never be simplistically understood to mean that one must always be excessively revealing.

It follows that practicing this principle of honesty in communication with customers on a regular basis in the life of business management is a more delicate challenge than these few sentences suggest. The challenge comes primarily in selecting what is necessary and/or appropriate to convey. Having a profound conviction of the principle of essential-relatedness along with a deep respect for the Golden Rule (mentioned above in our discussion of Product Quality) provides a foundation for decisions by management of the business enterprise which lead to better, more profound, and more trustworthy communications which tend toward results which are more reliable, more efficient and more productive for supplier and customer alike.

3.1.5 Qualities Developed in Management Training

In the process of training management personnel, the business enterprise has a whole host of qualities from which to choose for its focus. However, given some of the key principles of process-thinking, a business manager who takes his/her clue from process-principles will likely tend toward the development of certain Management Characteristics rather than others. Qualities a process-oriented enterprise will want to engender in its managers are those which coincide with the nature of reality and its processes of concrescence. By this we mean management training relies ultimately upon instilling the processual concept of inter-relatedness through interdependence.

From a philosophical perspective, some of the key process-principles that provide the foundation for the development of process-oriented-management include, The universality of creativity and freedom; the essential-relatedness of all actual occasions; the practical interdependence of actual occasions of experience. These are enriched by reference to the more theologically oriented process-principles of, The inexhaustability of wisdom and understanding; the Tenderness, Gracefulness, Forgiveness, and Omni-presence of the Universal One Who Calls Us Forward and the Eternal and Everlasting Lure towards greater variety, intensity, richness and harmony.

On the basis of these key process principles, some of the qualities that a process-oriented-enterprise will attempt to train into its managers include (but are not limited to) the following. First, leadership resembling those of a shepherd leading sheep or a bell-cow leading cows, as opposed to the more common bulldozer pushing over a building. Second, capabilities to influence resembling the power of water moving in a stream more than a sledge-hammer driving a spike. Third, good listening skills, rather than forcing one's own ideas on others. Fourth, collecting and taking into account the perspectives of persons at various levels of the organization. Fifth, separating desirable from undesirable behavior through thoughtfulness, communication, and the inspirational power of ideas, rather than the sword. Sixth, recognising the interdependence of actions and outcomes, including successes and failures. Seventh, emphasising the importance of teamwork-characteristics, rather than isolationistic or individualistic qualities. Eighth, considering the long-term impact or results of decisions as well as the short-term impact. Ninth, considering the multi-dimensional impact of decisions on all stake-holders, rather than focusing on only one impact or one result or one set of stake-holders. Tenth, appreciating the beauty and genuine power of consensus-decisions. Even though process-thinking does not seem to mix well with the notion of demands, requirements, or commandments, if we allow a good deal of flexibility in respect to nuance, the above-listed process qualities might provide a meaningful basis management practice.

3.1.6 Style of Managing Meetings

Although there are many ad-hock and exceptional meetings, and there are many exceptions to the general rule, awareness of and appreciation for the process-principles discussed above may lead the process-oriented manager to conduct or 'Manage' meetings with a unique style.

Recognizing that the actual style by which anyone responsible for conducting a meeting is partially dependent upon the 'personality of the conductor', a business-meeting which is led by a manager who has a keen sense of the principles of process-thinking would tend to incorporate in the meeting some (if not all) of the following style-elements or characteristics. The meeting would have a relatively clear established agenda, in which the basic issues would be stated as clearly and concisely as possible. This is so that all participants can have a relatively common ground for idea-exchange or consideration, and is especially important if the leader practices an open-forum approach to meetings. The manager would welcome and encourage input from participants, on the grounds that this is often more valuable than not and it is sometimes critical for success. There would be a thorough-going respect for opinions or perspectives which are unusual or abnormal, within which the aim is decisions developed by consensus rather than declaration by *fiat*.

3.1.7 Commitment to Interdependent Resolution among the Parties

In the daily business life of (especially) senior executives, the types of issues that tend to dominate the day are the exceptions, problems and conflicts. Conflicts may be of many different types and be be with a variety of stake-holders. The majority of conflicts experienced by the business enterprise, however, are between the enterprise and one or more of its stake-holders, e.g., Suppliers, Distributors, Dealers, Sales Representatives, Consumers, Employees, etc. Not all conflicts are equally the fault of the conflicting parties; many conflicts are the result of one party simply trying to 'bully' the other party, but such other party is not interested in being 'bullied.' Hence the conflict. In those cases where such bullying involves illegal behavior, any stake-holder may elect to use the legal system as a means to address the issue. On the other hand, the overwhelming majority of business conflicts are appropriately addressed by the business enterprise and its stakeholders, without the intervention of the courts.

How a manager goes about the process of resolving conflicts depends a great deal upon fundamental assumptions and basic philosophical principles. If he believes, for example, in a simplistic 'survival of the fittest' philosophy or one which emphasizes that 'only the strong survive', that manager's way of resolving conflict will tend to be quite different than that of the manager deeply committed to the principles of process-thinking. While the one manager may use demands, intimidation, and threats as tools, the manager incorporating process principles will tend toward the use of tools such as communication, cooperation, sharing of ideas for resolution, interdependence, and mutuality to resolve conflicts. While this latter method, the 'process-method', may take longer to arrive at the resolution, the probability of the resolution being a genuine resolution to the conflict is much higher than with the alternative method and simultaneously allows the conflicting parties to have some form of on-going-life thereafter.

3.2 Process-thinking in Strategic Planning of a Global Corporation

3.2.1 Maintaining Quality Levels and Consistency for Reliability

Similar process-thinking principles apply to the generic governance and long term development of the corporation. As a general rule, global corporations provide either products or services; for our discussions herein, we will envision the global corporation as a provider of products. At many junctures in the life of senior management personnel of the global corporation, decisions are required in respect to the degree to which maintaining-quality-requirements for the products is important.

In this decision-making-arena, there are many different elements involved, including (for example) cost-to-produce, expectations of the customers, competitor's offerings, contribution to Brand-Value, disposal impact on the environment, and so on. Certain perspectives of management would lead to decisions which produce product with just enough quality to "get by", cash-in the letter-of-credit, get paid and move on to someone else or something else. In the worst case, it may even have a consciously-built-in obsolescence-factor so that the product 'wears out' rather quickly and the end-user is required to replace the product with another identical one in a relatively short period of time.

On the other hand, as we indicated earlier when discussing product quality decisions in the daily life of business Management, the incorporation of certain process-principles into decisions regarding product quality make a huge difference in how a company operates. Decisions regarding product quality by senior management which are based upon the process-principles of the law of implied value or fairness, the importance of compliance with law, and the Karma Samsara of Business take into account a much larger panorama. Such decisions lead to product quality which not only comply with laws and reasonably meet the expectations of the customer, but also minimize the factor of built-in-obsolescence, especially in respect to the potential negative impacts of same upon the environment.

3.2.2 Issuing Accurate Specifications

The issuance of trustworthy and reliable specifications is an action the global corporation takes all the time. The philosophical/moral bases upon which such specifications are issued, however, makes a big difference in respect to the degree to which such Specifications are accurate, trustworthy, and reliable. In many cases, certain levels of Specifications provide a foundation for a certain perception of value and, hence, price. In aiming for maximum revenue, therefore, management persons may be prone to Issue a Specification claiming a 'higher' value than the product actually provides. This 'false' claim may work out more or less acceptably in the short-term, e.g., the building may not fall down, the product may not catch fire, the brakes may stop the car. Therefore, management persons whose primary-principles are to increase revenue, cash-flow, stock-value in the short-run will probably provide strategic direction to the corporation which results in an overstating of the specifications. In the long-run, however, such a practice will most likely impact the corporation negatively; the building may fall down, the product may catch fire, the brakes may fail to stop the care, the corporation may be found guilty of issuing false specifications, a broad product-recall may be required and the corporation may suffer irreparable damage as a result of same.

On the other hand, senior management personnel whose primary-principles are process-principles will direct their corporation to take great care to ensure that all specifications issued on its products are accurate and not over-stated. In complying with this direction, the corporation may be spending a little more than the 'falsifying' and 'cheap' competition, but will be complying with the law of implied value or fairness, complying with all relevant governmental regulations and laws as well as the Karma Samsara of business. As a result, such a corporation is doing the 'right' thing, It is operating in accordance with the Golden Rule, developing the quality of trust with its customers, strengthening its image as a reputable supplier of reliable products, and, in the process, enhances the likelihood that such a corporation will be healthy and successful over the long run.

3.2.3 Product Category Selection and Development

In the life of a Global Corporation producing products, one significant arena of decision-making which contributes considerably to the strategic direction and agenda of the corporation is the selection and development of product categories. If the primary value-principles of the senior management of the corporation surround the making of profits and doing so as quickly and aggressively as possible, then the selection of certain types of product categories for development, manufacturing and marketing quite understandably come to the forefront.

On the other hand, if process-principles provide the primary foundation for the values of senior management personnel, the selection of product categories for development will be quite different. They will tend to be products which provide a positive contribution to human beings, products that enhance the quality of life, and products which have a positive impact upon the environment (or at least reduce or minimize any negative impact on individuals, human society, civilization, and the environment).

3.2.4 Manufacture with Least Destructive Processes

As our economic world becomes increasingly globalized, one of the primary requirements for Corporations to be successful is to become 'low-cost-providers'. In searching to be such, corporations may naturally move toward the most economical materials and processes in the manufacturing of products. Recently, however, we have been learning rather clearly that certain materials and/or processes utilized in the manufacturing of productions is destructive to human beings, animals and/or the environment. Depending upon the degree of destructiveness of such materials or processes, certain governmental regulations and laws are more or less enacted and enforced. To whatever extent such regulations are enacted and enforced, all Corporations operating under such jurisdictions must comply.

In our actual Business environment today, however, regulations and laws regarding these materials and processes vary dramatically by country. This situation creates an uneven playing field and tends to encourage corporations to move their manufacturing to that location which has the least compliance-requirements in this arena. So, is this the end of such a story? The answer to this question can only be 'No'. All human beings of all nations and all faiths who have ever had an ounce of moral fiber within them recognize that the utilization of materials and processes which are destructive should be reduced, minimized and phased-out. On what bases shall such practices cease? Most who have given any thought to such a question recognize that further regulations by local and national governmental organizations are appropriate. Perhaps some international organizations, e.g. the United Nations, need to be given more responsibility and authority in this arena. Developing such international regulatory authority has proven to be difficult and time-consuming.

Until such time as appropriate international regulations are enacted and enforced in respect to these issues, the strategic direction put forth by senior management of global corporations can and will make a huge difference. To whatever extent the foundations of decision-making are based upon 'get rich quick' approaches, such corporations will continue to utilize the most 'economical' materials and processes (even though they are destructive to human beings and/or the environment) as long as the law allows same. On the other hand, to whatever extent process-principles (which we will not take time or space to reiterate here) provide the foundations of strategic direction of senior management, such corporations will proceed to reduce, minimize, and phase-out the utilization of destructive materials and processes.

Having said this, while strategic directives based upon process-thinking lead to the utilization of least destructive processes, for senior management of the corporation to simply and radically shift a manufacturing process to a 'clean' process which appears to be 'good' may not be good in the long run at all. This is because such radical change can at the same time radically increase the cost of the product, making it totally uncompetitive, putting the 'good' and creative company out of business completely. As a result, the wonderful experimentation of such a 'good' company with less destructive processes ceases. A 'better way' for such a company would be to gradually introduce less destructive processes which were not so radically costly that they killed the company. In this case, the company has the possibility of being a 'pioneer' in this area, challenge the industry of which it is a part, provide valuable information and assistance to government agencies which may be working to create incentives for the utilization of least destructive processes. By proceeding along these lines, the business enterprise may become both a good steward and a great leader toward a much larger Common Good.

3.2.5 Treatment of Workers in Third World or Developing Countries

In today's highly competitive business climate, there is a strong tendency for global corporations to simply move its manufacturing operations to whatever geographical labor market will provide the lowest cost in human resource related benefits or programs. Simultaneously, within any given manufacturing operation, when considering what salaries, benefits, or programs to offer employees, senior management of global corporations today will tend toward choosing lowest-cost-options. If the value-principles which provide the foundation for the senior management decisions and directions in these arena are based on any simplistic form of capitalism, such decisions may be easy; they will probably quite naturally proceed toward lowest cost options regardless of the quality of life resulting from same which is provided to the employees. This approach is only natural if one views employees primarily as tools to be utilized as means to an end.

On the other hand, strategic directives of senior management of a global corporation in respect to treatment of workers in a Third World or developing country which are based upon process-principles are likely to be quite different. As we indicated in an earlier section of this paper, when establishing strategic directives on the basis of process-principles, human beings, i.e., employees, must be understood as having value in and of themselves; they should never be treated simply as means to an end. The development and implementation of human resources policies and procedures will be fundamentally more humane than they would likely be otherwise, i.e., to whatever extent they are based upon process-principles. The positive impact of these are broad, and may include (amongst others) from hiring practices, salary-establishment, work-hours, working-conditions, disciplinary procedures, promotional advancements, benefits and program, termination policies.

Strategic directions based upon process-thinking which are put forth in a global corporation in respect to the treatment of its workers, will be humane, fair, and respectful. To jump to the conclusion, however, that what these qualities give rise to is identical (e.g. in respect to salaries, benefits, etc.) in all countries would be naïve, over-simplified and short-sighted. To implement policies based upon such over-simplification lead to the company's cost-structure becoming totally unreasonable and excessive compared with the competition; a likely result of such behavior would be the prompt or early death of that global corporation. In contrast, a thoughtful and gradual improvement of salaries and benefits based upon both process-thinking's vision of fairness, respect and humanity and the actual history and context of the worker's situation, could lead to the implementation of exemplary and humanistic policies.

3.2.6 Basic Stance Toward Environmental Issues

As we proceed further into this new Century, it is becoming apparent that some of the largest and most complicated challenges that lie before us are in the arena of Ecology and the Environment. Much has been written by process thinkers in this area and significant efforts are being put forth to make a positive difference; there is little point in revisiting these here. Our purpose is to point out that strategic corporate initiatives which are based upon value-principles which do not incorporate, at least, some of the key process-principles are likely to proceed with little or no reference to the impact of their implementation upon the environment.

Fortunately, here again, we can hope for significant legislation, regulation, and enforcement to help ensure the protection of the environment on which we and all creatures depend. Unfortunately, the early enactment of, or the global enforcement of, such legislation or regulation is not very likely. Until such time as broad regulation and sufficient enforcement is in place to make such regulations positively effective on a global scale, is there nothing that can and will be done in this arena?

A basic dual-conviction that all actual occasions of experience have value (including all forms of life and the environment) and that all aspects of life are interdependent, lead process-oriented senior management to provide strategic directives wherein the value of the environment is emphasized. Such a directive leads product development and engineering teams to design and develop products that are friendly to the environment. Such a directive leads managers respon-

sible for manufacturing operations to utilize materials and manufacturing processes that are safe, non-hazardous, and friendly to the
environment. All in all, strategic directives by senior management in
global corporations which are based upon process-principles could
make a huge impact upon the degree to which human life (and its
accoutrements) in the 21st Century is healthy for the environment.

3.2.7 Executive Salaries

In the business-world, perhaps since its inception, founders, origina-
tors, owners, and senior executives of business enterprises have been
known to generally receive a larger salary (or via some method, make
more money) than the rank-and-file workers of the enterprise do. Such
a practice may not only be factually true, it may also be *morally*
appropriate. Such 'owners' have often invested more of themselves in
the project than do rank-and-file workers; they have also often put a
great deal at risk in such ventures. So, the appropriateness of some
differentiation in pay-scales is not being questioned here.

However, as the development of global corporations have recently
given rise to radically new ways of doing business, radically new ways
to compensate senior management personnel in many global corporations has led to a radical disparity in compensation between selected
senior executives and the rank-and-file workers. The rationale for such
high compensation packages for a few persons is well-established. It
has to do, of course, with meeting certain business objectives, such as
sales volume, dollar profit and stock value. To this end, in some ways
the excesses we see in this arena are not so different from what we see
in the salary-ranges in the professional sports arena.

Nevertheless, the net result of this executive compensation practice
– which creates radical disparities between the compensation of certain
executives versus the rank-and-file workers (in the ranges from 20 to 1
to 100 to 1) – is that anger develops in varying degrees toward the
executives, the corporation, and the general business practices which
allow and perpetuate such inequities. While such inequities may be
considered by the thoughtful to be appropriate in any society or nation,
as global corporations become even more dominant in the lives of
people all over the world, such inequities become outrageous; they provide a reason serious conflict. Can process principles provide any

guidance to senior executives of a global corporation in this arena?

Strategic directives concerning directorial salaries which are based upon primarily capitalist value principles will likely be to continue the current method of piling up wealth with a few executives, as long as they don't have an up-rising against same by some other stake-holders, e.g., employees or shareholders. The key directive will be how to not up-set the apple cart, how to keep-a-lid on the information, and how to avoid some negative back-lash against such gross inequities.

In comparison, strategic directives based upon process-principles are very different. While they may recognize and appreciate some differentiation in compensation, they will incorporate fairness, respect and appreciation for all contributors (including rank-and-file workers), and recognize and appreciate the profound interdependence of all stake-holders. Based upon this process-perspective, profits from the global corporation will not be 'piled-up' with a few executives or 'sucked-off' into a few peoples' pockets. On the contrary, profits will be utilized wisely and spread reasonably among the various stake-holders, including stock-holders, management, non-managerial employees and research and development. In this way, corporations whose senior executives adopt process principles are more likely to contribute to the to the betterment of mankind in general and become a friend and supporter of the working-class, rather than maintain an unjust and damaging divide.

3.2.8 Globalisation

In various times and places during the historical evolution of human experience and thought, there have been periods during which the tendency to rush to 'black and white perspectives' on issues or trends seems to increase. Such a tendency is often associated with non-philosophical periods or non-Enlightenment-eras. After such periods, the philosophically minded tend to reflect upon such periods as being without merit, without value, or without advancement; in the worst case, such periods are seen as periods of decay, reversal, decline, or fall. The concept of 'globalization' is one of those trends which is being bolstered simplistically by its supporters and being battered simplistically by its enemies. Those of us who have the fortune of education, life experiences, rational awareness, and the thoughtful and enlightened philosophical perspective of process-thinking have the natural and challenging responsibility to avoid either simplistic approach in respect to globalization.

Globalization is dually potent; it has great potency for evil and it has great potency for good. The potency for evil which lies within globalization is relatively well-known. It has been emphasized or publicized by a relatively broad range of forces including labor unions, environmentalists, certain student-movements within academia and a good portion of religion. On the other hand, the potency for good which lies within globalization is not so well-known. However, to the process thinker living and working in business management within a global corporation, there are several powerfully good outcomes which become possible as a rather direct result of the potency for good which lies within Globalization. Finally, seven of these potentially positive direct results are:

1) a movement toward the spreading of the world's wealth through a gradual equalization of wages, benefits;.
2) a sharing (exportation/importation) of materials and technology across national boundaries around the world, placing all (or most) countries on a more and more even-playing-field;
3) a spreading of investment-capital through a broad range of geographical locations to develop businesses, markets, manufacturing;
4) a spreading of reasonable workers' rights to a broader and broader segment of the world's population;
5) a spreading of environmental regulations and best-practices around the world;
6) an increasing recognition that we are all interdependent upon each other, resulting in a higher respect for differentiation and appreciation of 'otherness';
7) a radically profound educational-understanding, informational-flowing, cultu-ral-exchange, and religious dialogue and transformation which may become the most significant and most positive direct result of the globalization-process.

4. Revisiting Management Theory, The Processual Nature of the Learning Experience

The purpose of the foregoing exposition has not to been to argue for or against management, or for or against globalization. It is to demonstrate by articulation of the basic principles of process-thinking as applicable to management practice, that process-thinking is a powerful tool in both the daily life of business management and the strategic planning process of a global corporation. In providing its critical-relational framework, process-thinking continues to drive us (or lure us) toward thoughtfulness. In so doing it prevents an overly-simplistic black and white perspective on the important issues of our time. In respect to Globalization, process-thinking is called upon to help keep our minds open, active, and inquiring; doing so in this arena may provide one of our greatest opportunities, greatest challenges, and greatest contributions to the unfolding and forward movement of human experience and Civilization in this current century, as we move toward providing appropriate foundations for the next (22nd) Century.

These foundations can legitimately be built upon by process-thinking since, as we have sought to show, the management experience, and thus management learning, consists of an expression of the synthesis of human qualities. In terms of the basic tenets of process philosophy, these are enjoyment, essential relatedness, incarnation, creative self-determination, creative self-expression, novelty and God-relatedness. These qualities of experience contribute towards an "emergent pattern of [corporate] governing" (Sun 2002, 206) consisting of the development of policies towards workers, directorial salaries, globalisation, environmental issues, product quality and so on. These in turn are "generated from complex and continuous social negotiations [...], selected out of multiple possibilities of contested meanings and interpretations" (Sun 2002, 207), and manifest in managerial acting *through* learning.

At the individual level, process-thinking enables an important distinction to be made in understanding the learning experience of management, similar to that concerning other complex human experiences (Dibben 2004, Whitehead 1933/ 1961, 183-4). That is, distinguishing between learning in the present from past knowing, and deriving learning from the present prehension of the informational datum of managerial action; the typical business interaction involves both. There is thus prehension of one's past experiences objectified in part by one's knowledge and largely conformed to. There is also prehension of novel information *now* with the subjective form of knowing. The two prehensions both belong to the first phase of the occasion, while their integration belongs to the second phase. This begins with the separation of the subjective form of knowing as an ingredient in the immediate prehension of the novel content of another's actions. This subjective form continues with reintegration into propositional feelings and intellectual feelings concerning that datum. The integration of these many feelings strengthens the experience of the learning occasion, which concresces ultimately as a new knowledge enitity to be enjoyed as a past datum in successive occasions of learning experience.

5. Conclusion, Business Organisations as Learning Event Fields?

During the course of this brief discussion, we have attempted to show that process-thinking is applicable to both daily life in business management and strategic planning in a global corporation. Additionally, we have attempted to show that the application of process-thinking in these arenas makes a difference, in terms of the actions of managers and the impact this has on the learning experience of management. Lastly, we have attempted to complement conceptual management writing and develop the process-oriented discussion therein, by bringing such topics as paraexperientialsim to bear more upon the subject of management learning than has been the case hitherto. Process-thinking lures us to a regular and continuous awareness of multi-dimensionality and how dialectical oppositions can help enhance the depth and breadth of awareness in decision-making in the daily life of business management, as well as in the establishment of strategic directives in a global corporation. If the business management experience is very brief or short-lived, process-thinking may have little opportunity to offer its perspective and contribution. In those cases where the business management experience is more extensive, some may argue that many of the insights and perspectives of process-thinking are no different than those which are brought forth by good common sense and/or good moral principles.

Fortunately, perspective and insight brought forth by process-thinking does coincide with good common sense and good moral principle. As such, the continuation, pervasiveness and importance of learning in and across managerial situations arises from the creative urge that transcends the actual occasion such that, upon concrescence, it is immediately part of the universe of entities which affect the concrescence of future managerial occasions. Thus, the dynamism that is the learning experience arises from the continuing creativity of new learning occasions. When viewed as the mechanism by which individual managers act in organisations, organisational growth and development – be this in terms of the daily practice of management or the establishment of longer term strategic policy – is a function of this learning process.

Yet how does such an individual learning experience precisely relate to the business corporation, or organisation? How can we reconcile the two very different levels of analysis of individual manager and organisation, and thereby unpack in process terms the mechanism by which managerial learning may transfer itself into the intellectual (and economic) growth of the business? As a final remark, we can only postulate that this transfer may be understood in as the inter-relation between occasions and the progressive layers of social order into which they are organised. Certainly an organisation in Whiteheadian terms is not a subject of experience as it is not able to make a "decision" (see also Chia 1994) with respect to its self-continuation. Nevertheless, it does possess "causal laws which dominate the social environment [...] and is only efficient through [the actions of] its individual members" (Whitehead 1978, 90f; in: Bracken 1989) – actions which, as we have sought to demonstrate throughout, are the result of process-thinking and learning.

Furthermore, the members of the organisation can only function as a part of it "by reason of the laws which dominate [it], and the laws only come into being by reason of the analogous characters of the members of the society" (Whitehead 1978, 91). These laws, or policies, procedures and recommendations – such as those discussed above – are in and of themselves a manifestation of managerial learning. In this sense, therefore, a business organisation may be thought of as an energy-field, perhaps analogous to a particular kind of extensive continuum, "progressively shaped and ordered by successive generations of [managerial learning] occasions, so that it effectively serves as the medium for the transmission both of physical feelings and of conceptual patterns from one generation [...] to another" (Bracken 1989, 155). This rendering certainly emphasises the process-thinking manager's connection with the human life experience of synthesis demonstrated in the foregoing discussion. Nevertheless, we are aware it subscribes also to a disputed argument that Whiteheadian societies are structured fields of activity that are both objectively real and progressively structured by the events taking place within them. Whether such a 'field-oriented approach' (Bracken 2002) to the interrelation between manager as learner and learning organisation is best left as a metaphor, or can be technically shown to be philosophically accurate in some degree is therefore a topic for further study.

Bibliography

Bracken, J. A. (1989): Energy Events and Fields. *Process Studies*, 18, 153-165.

Bracken, J. A. (2002): Continuity Amid Discontinuity – A Neo-Whiteheadian Understanding of the Self. *Process Studies*, 31, 115-124.

Brumbaugh, R. S. (Ed.) (1984): Alfred North Whitehead – Discussion Upon Fundamental Principles of Education. *Process Studies*, 14, 41-43.

Chia, R. (1992) *Organisational Analysis as Deconstructive Practice*. University of Lancaster: PhD Thesis to the Department of Behaviour in Organisations, August.

Chia, R. (1994): The Concept of Decision – A Deconstructive Analysis. *Journal of Management Studies*, 31, 781-806.

Chia, R. (1996a): Teaching Paradigm Shifting in Management Education – University Business Schools and the Entrepreneurial Imagination. *Journal of Management Studies*, 33, 409-428.

Chia, R. (1996b): *Organisational Analysis as Deconstructive Practice*. Berlin: de Gruyter.

Chia, R. (1997): Thirty Years On – From Organisational Structures to the Organisation of Thought. *Organisation Studies*, 18, 685-707.

Chia, R. (1998): From Complexity Science to Complex Thinking – Organisation as Simple Location. *Organisation*, 5, 341-369.

Chia, R. (1999): "A Rhizomic Model of Organisational Change and Transformation – Perspectives from a Metaphysics of Change. *British Journal of Management*, 10, 209-227.

Chia, R. & Morgan S. (1996): Educating the Philosopher-Manager – Designing the Times. *Management Learning*, 27, 37-64.

Cobb, J. B. Jr. (1965): *A Christian Natural Theology Based on the Thought of Alfred North Whitehead*. Philadelphia: Westminster Press.

Cobb, J. B. Jr. (1967): *The Structure of Christian Existence*. Lanham: University Press of America.

Cobb,J. B. Jr. (1969): *God and the World*. Philadelphia: Westminster Press

Cobb, J. B. Jr. (1995/1971): *Is It Too Late? A Theology of Ecology*. Denton: Environmental Ethics Books.

Cobb, J. B. Jr. (1999): *The Earthist Challenge to Economism – A Theological Critique of the World Bank*. London: Palgrave MacMillan.

Cobb, J. B. Jr. & Griffin, D. R. (1976): *Process Theology – An Introductory Exposition*. Philadelphia: The Westminster Press.

Cooper, R. (1976): The Open Field. *Human Relations*, 29, 999-1017.

Cooper, R. & Law, J. (1994): Organisation – Distal and Proximal Views. *Research in the Sociology of Organisations*, 13, 237-274.

Daly, H. E. & Cobb, J. B. Jr (1994): *For the Common Good, 2ⁿᵈ Edition*. Boston: Beacon Press.

Dewey, J. (1938): *Experience and Education*. New York: Collier Books.

Dibben, M. R. (2004): Exploring the Processual Nature of Trust and Cooperation in Organisations – A Whiteheadian Analysis. *Philosophy of Management* , 4, 25-42.

Dibben, M. R. & Cobb J. B. Jr. (2003): Focus Introduction – Process Thought and Organisation Studies. *Process Studies*, 32, 179-182.

Dibben, M.R. & Munro, I. (2003): Applying Process Thought in Organisation Studies. *Process Studies*, 32, 183-195.

Griffin, D. R. (1991/1976): *God, Power, and Evil – A Process Theodicy*. Lanham: University Press of America.

Griffin, D. R. (1997): *Parapsychology, Philosophy, and Spirituality – A Post-Modern Exploration*. Albany: SUNY.

Griffin, D. R. (1988a): *God and Religion in the Post-Modern World*. Albany: SUNY.

Griffin, D. R. (1998b): *Unsnarling the World Knot – Consciousness, Freedom, and the Mind-Body Problem*. University of California Press

Griffin, D. R. (2001): *Re-enchantment without Supernaturalism: A Process Philosophy of Religion*. Cornell University Press.

Griffin, D. R. (2003): *Beyond Anarchy and Plutocracy – The Need for Global Democracy*. Thousand Oaks: Sage.

Habermas, J. (1972/1968): *Knowledge and Human Interests*. London: Heinemann.

Hartshorne, C. (1962): *The Logic of Perfection and Other Essays in Neo-classical Metaphysics*. La Salle: Open Court.

Hartshorne, C. (1970): *Creative Synthesis and Philosophic Method*. Lanham: University Press of America.

Hartshorne, C. (1972): *Whitehead's Philosophy – Selected Essays, 1935-1970*. Lincoln: University of Nebrasca Press

Hartshorne, C. (1975/1937): *Beyond Humanism – Essays in the New Philosophy of Nature*. Gloucester: Peter Smith.

Hartshorne, C. (1976/1953): *Philosophers Speak of God* (with William L. Reese). Chicago: Midway Reprints

Hartshorne, C. (1983a): *Insights and Oversights of Great Thinkers – An Evaluation of Western Philosophy.* Albany: State University of New York Press.

Hartshorne, C. (1983b): *The Divine Relativity – A Social Conception of God.* New Haven: Yale University Press.

Hartshorne, C. (1984): *Omnipotence and Other Theological Mistakes.* Albany: SUNY.

Linstead, S. (2002): Organsiation as Reply – Henri Bergson and Casual Organisation Theory. *Organisation,* 9, 95-112.

Lowe, V. (1990): *Alfred North Whitehead – The Man and His Work, Vol. II.* Baltimore: The Johns Hopkins University Press.

Mead, G. H. (1934): *Mind, Self and Society.* Chicago: University of Chicago Press.

Oliver, D.W. (1989): *Education, Modernity, and Fractured Meaning – Toward a Process Theory of Teaching and Learning.* Albany, N.Y: State University of New York Press.

Styrhe, A. (2002): How Process Philosophy can Contribute to Strategic Management. *Systems Research and Behavioral Science,* 16, 577-587.

Sun, X. (2002): *Rethinking Corporate Governance – A Processual Approach.* Leeds Metropolitan University: PhD thesis submitted to the Management School, May.

Tsoukas, H. & Chia, R. (2002): On Organisational Becoming – Rethinking Organisational Change. *Organisation Science,* 13, 567-582.

Whitehead, A. N. (1959/1932): *The Aims of Education and Other Essays.* London: Ernest Benn Limited.

Whitehead, A. N. (1961/1933): *Adventures of Ideas.* New York: The Free Press.

Whitehead, A. N. (1967/1925): *Science and the Modern World.* New York: The Free Press.

Whitehead, A. N. (1968/1938) *Modes of Thought.* New York: The Free Press.

Whitehead, A. N. (1978/1929): *Process and Reality.* New York: The Free Press.

Whitehead, A. N. (1996/1926): *Religion in the Making.* New York: Fordham University Press

Wood, M. (2002): The Process of Organising Knowledge – Exploring the In-between. *Organisation,* 9, 151-171.

Wood, M. (2004): The Fallacy of Misplaced Leadership. *Journal of Management Studies,* forthcoming.

Process and Reality
in Leadership Research and Development

Martin Wood

Abstract
Recent years have seen considerable industry in the area of
leadership research and development. The leadership literature
typically talks about the discrete *individuality* of its subject and
particularly the personal qualities and capabilities of a few key
people occupying top positions in a hierarchy. Current leadership research has now begun to generate new knowledge about
leadership practice in relations of interpersonal exchange. Nevertheless, there is an urgent need for the implications of this
insight to be developed more fully. The current discussion explores how a perspective of process studies challenges the dominance of the field by both self-identical individualism and
discrete schemes of relations. Its aims are twofold. First, it will
show how both of these latter *epistemologies* are lacking and
suggest that current leadership research and development activities must rise to the *ontological* challenge of *processes* rather
than *things*. Second, it looks at some methodological implications of this way of thinking as a productive incitement to future leadership research and development.

1. Leadership Theories

What leadership is has been an enigma of social democracy since the
classical philosopher-kings of Plato. It also remains a perennial issue in
leadership research and development, with significant debate concerning the problem of understanding the nature, role and development of
leadership. Are leaders (extraordinarily) necessary? Do leaders pull
their followers or do those behind push them? Are our theories of
leadership too static and individualistic (see, for example, Gemmill and
Oakley 1992, Grint 1997, Hosking 1988)? What are the skills, compe-
tencies, personal attributes required to work within integrated environ-

ments? And, how can we get satisfactory answers to the question of leadership development in the long term? (Bolden, Wood & Gosling 2005).

Early leadership theories treated the individual personality traits of key people as critical – the so-called "great man" or "qualities" approach – (Stogdill 1950). However, Stogdill concluded leadership could not be pinned down through the isolation of a set of traits. This led to a twofold focus on styles and acquirable skills rather than inherited qualities. Contingency models allocate significance to the personality characteristics of the individual leader *and* the context of the environment, believing both determine the kind of leadership behaviour required (Fiedler 1967). Similarly, transactional models define a good leader as someone who integrates getting the job done with concern for those actually doing the work (Blake & Mouton 1964).

Modern leadership theories extend this focus on the transactions between leaders and followers. Situational analyses allow the individual leader a degree of flexibility in generating a repertoire of styles (Hersey & Blanchard 1977). Hersey and Blanchard's (1977) model centres on the contingency of follower maturity as an indicator of necessary style from directing to supporting and delegating. Unfortunately results are largely inconclusive and beg the following questions. First, are leaders able to alter their style to suit the situation? Second, are assumptions about the significance of maturity allocated to the individual follower objectively or subjectively measured? Third, if they are subjective, whose view is taken? Although Elgie (1995) suggests leadership style makes a difference this is exercised within a context of macro social and institutional structures, whose norms and rules govern individuals' behaviour. Heifetz (1994) anticipates this, arguing the critical issue is whether people have the ability, motivation and perhaps the freedom to intervene in those situations requiring 'adaptive' responses (i.e. leadership). Furthermore, the shift in emphasis over recent years, from planned goals to visions, from communication to trust, from traits to self awareness and from contingency to effective presentation, distinguishes between economically driven models of transactional-leadership and the transformational, and sometimes transcendent, appearance of leaders (Bass 1985). Such individuals "move followers to go beyond their self-interests to concerns for their group or organisation" (Bass and Avolio 1997, 202). Transformational leadership may simply mark a "sanitised" return to neo-traitism

(Rickards 1999), however, elevating those qualities filling followers with longing and desire and so ultimately represent a blatant retreat to the "discredited heroics" of stand alone leaders (Gronn 2002, 426).

A problem with such 'individualistic' approaches is the psychological origin of much of the theory and data. An assumption is that leaders have certain 'essential' qualities and capabilities that can be best developed through the provision of increased training opportunities for a few 'high flyers'. This literature presupposes only certain individuals can be leaders, only certain leaders are appropriate for certain contingencies, or only certain individuals have sufficient flexibility in their leadership styles to match the needs of a number of different situations. Furthermore, this viewpoint represents the dominant and "seductive game" (Calás & Smircich 1991) of leaders as meaning creating subjects (Hosking 1988, Smircich & Morgan 1982). It is leaders who impress others; inspire people; push through transformations; get the job done; have compelling, even gripping, visions; stir enthusiasm; and have personal magnetism (Maccoby 2000). Leaders are thus seen as Prime Movers rather than as emergent phenomena within leaderful situations.

Nevertheless, such identity-locating attributes turn out to be more prescriptive than descriptive. Managers may well need to do these things, but simply doing them does not privilege them as 'leader' nor as someone who can be the cause of 'leadership'. Such prescriptions simplify and may not be the most appropriate units of analysis within new and 'virtual' modes of organising, whose speed, simultaneity and interconnectivity are now forcing a new kind of encounter with the phenomenon of leadership.

Inspired by the process studies of the British mathematical physicist and philosopher Alfred North Whitehead (1967a, 1967b, 1978), as well as those of his contemporary, the French 'intuitionist' philosopher Henri Bergson (1921, 1983, 1991, 1999, 1974), the current discussion attempts to engage with our excessive preoccupation with the psychological approach to leadership research and development. It starts with the conjecture that leadership is best understood as a *process* rather than a property or *thing*. Extending from Bergson (1974, 137), our construal of leadership does not reveal an already given set of 'discrete elements' or components (for example, leaders and followers). Looked at from the perspective of process the elements can be seen to permeate and melt into one another without precise outlines. Whitehead (1967a) similarly points to the qualities of an enduring individual part already pervading the constitution of those parts succeeding it. In other words, the essential character of leadership is a continuity of flow rather than a solid state.

This claim is discussed before being used to mount a challenge to the hegemony of more omniscient leadership models and methodologies. At this stage the discussion is meant to be suggestive rather than conclusive. Its limited aim is to make a plausible case for process thought in current leadership research and development activities in the belief that this can help rigorously explain both the phenomenon of leadership and for the purpose of imaginatively explicating multi-dimensional leadership problems so that both research and development policy deliberations avoid the trap of seeking 'magic bullet' answers.

2. Process Studies

Process philosophising is a distinctive sector of philosophical tradition. Its basic doctrine opposes the commonplace Western metaphysic that the nature of reality is 'here, now, immediate, and discrete' (Whitehead 1967b, 180). By contrast, process studies are committed to the fundamentally processual nature of the real and the terms of reference in which this reality is to be explained and understood. It stresses inter-relatedness and sees "process as constituting an essential aspect of everything that exists" (Rescher 2002, 1). The guiding idea is that "process *is* the concrete reality of things" (Griffin 1986, 6, original emphasis). Process studies, in general, seek to emphasise emergence and *becoming* rather than sheer existence or *being*. They rest on the premise of openness in the progress of human experience and civilisation. Life and society are conceived as a process of creative advance in which many past events are integrated in the events of the present, and in turn are taken up by future events – just as people living in Europe are affected by particles released from Chernobyl, so too do business practices in Japan affect the global community.

The "interconnectedness" (Whitehead 1967b, 227) and the 'mutual penetration' (Bergson 1921, 101) of these physical, social and economic processes often seem ineffable and mysterious. Because of this our theories of movement and endurance unwittingly reconstruct experience into concrete 'things', each one of which touches "without pene-trating one another" (Bergson 1921, 101); in a word, we take a number of abstract states, which we set "side by side in such a way as to perceive them simultaneously, no longer in one another, but alongside one another" (Bergson 1921, 101). A key insight of process studies suggests the reality of something existing "concretely in itself without transition" (Whitehead 1967a, 49) is a matter of abstractive thinking and *not* a property of the underlying thing itself. Concrete things – for example, leaders, followers, and organisations – are surface effects. They are simple appearances we employ to give substantiality to our experience, but under whose supposed 'naturalness' the fundamentally processual nature of the real is neglected.

   This unwitting intellectual strategy continues to inform leadership research and development. We may be thinking of business gurus, policy makers, political leaders, spiritual teachers, fashion icons, pop idols, and sporting heroes, but in all these senses an individual subject is a prerequisite for 'leadership'. Our abstract habits distinguish an individual subject from everything it is not, as being one thing but not another – a self-identical *'It'*, both discrete and enduring. In doing so we tend to disregard the significance of the internal heterogeneity, or "milieu" (Deleuze 1994, 211) of the subject, even though no subject can be distinguished or isolated from it. When we establish the per-sonal identity of leaders, for example, we often do so in relation to a set of distinguishing qualities. Such normative qualities can fill follow-ers with longing, desire, and envy, which in turn require regulation, control, denial, exclusion, or, alternatively, sublimation and catharsis. By focusing on the figure of the leader as the omniscient character of those qualities, however, research and development methodologies might be colluding in extant power relations. For Whitehead (1967a, 51), this individualistic way of thinking is an example of the error of mistaking our abstract conceptualisations for the concrete things them-selves: *the fallacy of misplaced concreteness*. To overcome this it is necessary to question and problematise the conventional view that individual 'identity' can obtain in a secure and concrete sense, without any reference to past, present and future events. Whitehead attempts to do this by deliberately emphasising the individual figure as 'a mode of attention', one that only provides "the extreme of selective emphasis" (Whitehead 1967b, 270).

The critical issue in process studies, therefore, is not the actual qualities of a particular figure, but how such a figure "condenses within itself [...] a multitude of social dimensions and meanings" (Cooper 1983, 204). Looked at this way, leadership is not located in "the autonomous, self-determining individual with a secure unitary identity [at] the centre of the social universe" (Alvesson & Deetz 2000, 98). On the contrary, the emergence of leadership is more properly described as a "systematic complex of mutual relatedness" (Whitehead 1967a, 161), one in which our conceptual interpretations are always "an incompletion in the process of production" (Whitehead 1929, 327). Leadership is found neither *in* one person or another, nor can it be simply located *between* several people. Instead it is "the point of difference" (Cooper 1983, 204) at which each turns around the other. In this sense, leadership is already a 'complete' relation: each part necessarily referring to another, but without 'completion' in a straightforward way. Leadership cannot be reduced to a particular individual or to discrete relations among people. Rather, it is the unlocalisable 'in' of the 'between' of each, a freely interpenetrating process, whose 'identity' is consistently self-differing.

3. The Misplacing of Leadership

We have seen how the affirmation 'leaders make things happen' is an obvious and rarely questioned way of thinking. Indeed, it is inherent in leadership research and development to consider "the leader as consistent essence, a centred subject with a particular orientation" (Alvesson & Sveningsson 2003, 961). This individualistic way of thinking is now widespread. Consider the BBC'S recent searches for the 'Greatest Briton' (2002) and the 'Greatest American' (BBC 2003), or, more seriously, in the events following the September 11 attacks, the tendency of the West to look toward key figures to exercise 'leadership' and to entrust individual commanders-in-chief with the power to go to war. Consider also the false familiarity television establishes between the viewers and the well-known profiles of US presidential candidates. The electorate were urged to pick candidates as much on personality as on key issues, in the 2004 campaign. Candidates whose backgrounds and qualifications for office were not well known, for example, tended to use biographical advertisements to present the most favourable versions of their life stories – John Kerry volunteered to serve in Vietnam where his 'leadership, courage, and sacrifice earned him a Silver Star, a Bronze Star with Combat V, and three Purple Hearts' (Kerry-Edwards 2004) – or else the words, or image, of a candidate are used against them to show that the candidate cannot be believed, has broken a promise: 'There's what Kerry says and then there's what Kerry does.' (Bush-Cheney, 2004), or to show that the candidate is in touch with the concerns and feelings of 'real people' – or that the opponent is not: 'The America that George Bush has created is one with fewer jobs, increasing health costs and more obstacles to achieving the American dream. Kerry-Edwards (2004).

It is the same with charismatic-, effective-, visionary- and transformational-leadership. These beliefs in leadership often attribute power to individuals and therefore it is individuals who cause events (Gemmill & Oakley 1992). UK management consultants Goffee and Jones (2000, 64), for example, characterise an inspirational leader as needing 'vision, energy, authority, and strategic direction' so as to "engage people and rouse their commitment to company goals" (Goffee & Jones 2000, 63). Moreover, those who are led often find the responsibility a leader assumes for visioning and strategic direction to be important and comforting (Bolman & Deal, 1994). People often look to a leader to frame and concretise their reality (Smircich & Morgan 1982). What gets to count as real, however, is often a consequence of incipient power. For example, leaders may seek to extend managerial control in the name of practical autonomy through a project of strengthening or changing an organisation's culture. They might try to promote quality, flexibility and/or responsiveness improvement by ensuring subordinate commitment to an instrumental structure of feeling and thought (Willmott 1993).

The misleading conviction lying behind each of these projects is the existence of an order of 'completed' things through which the individual figures of our experience are apprehended (Whitehead 1967a, 27). But the leader "is always social first and only mistakenly claims the personal self as the origin of experience" (Alvesson & Deetz 2000, 97). We conceive certain qualities or characteristics of 'leaders'; there is something about them we note. We then find somebody who possesses these qualities or characteristics and it is through them we apprehend the individual person. In other words, the individual is the material of which we predicate the qualities and characteristics. As such, a number of interconnected issues and key questions can be introduced to debate our ascription of leadership to individual social actors (Pfeffer 1977). For example: How, precisely, are these individual leaders identified? What if their exemplary conduct and attitudes turn out to be important symbols representing the choice of a social collectivity? Might this lead to the selection and development of only those individuals who match the socially constructed image? Does this suggest the primacy of social relations above individual behaviour? If we want to determine whether a leader is charismatic, for example, we might ask in what sense is their charisma a personal quality? Apart from other people would the leader be charismatic? Logically a leader cannot be charismatic in a vacuum. In other words, charisma, effectiveness, vision, and transformation only appear as personal qualities because we have mistaken our abstraction of them for concrete reality. What is at stake, in all of these issues and questions, is our identification of/with 'the leader' but, as we have already pointed out, this abstraction is a purposive emanation from the "indeterminate ultimate reality" (Griffin 1986, 136) and not a property of the underlying thing itself.

Gilbert Simondon (1992) continues this line of thought in his essay *Genesis of the Individual*. For Simondon, what is required is a complete change in mental habit, one in which the process of individuation is considered instead of a misplaced focus on extant figures. As he puts it: "[...] to grasp firmly the nature of individuation, we must consider the being not as a substance, or matter, or form, but as a tautly extended and supersaturated system" (Simondon 1992, 301). Nevertheless, the problem of individuation continues to be formulated in either 'substantialist' terms of the completed individual or the 'hylomorphic' operation of completion.

The first view expresses a complete determinateness of the individual. In this it looks a lot like leadership research and development, which treats the substantial appearance of leaders as unproblematic and sees the process of their individuation "as something to be explained rather than as something in which the explanation is to be found" (Simondon 1992, 299). These normative strategies "aim toward achieving a presence of person qua the ideal of the classical subject" (Day 1998, 96). Each presumes "leadership is all about the person at the top of the hierarchy" (Barker 2001, 471), or else provides examples of a "first among equals" (Gronn 2002, 430), bypassing the constitutive processes through which such figures are created. The second view does not presuppose any absolutely distinct individuality, but does assume a teleological matter-form relation putting the principle into effect. Terms such as "charismatic leadership" (Conger & Kanungo 1998), "servant leadership" (Greenleaf 1977, Greenleaf & Spears 1998), "intelligent leadership" (Hooper & Potter 2000) and "transformational leadership" (Bass 1985), all call to mind the clear idea of a relation between things. Here, the finite circumstances in one term provide a model for the other to aspire to. In the above examples, 'charisma', 'service', 'intelligence', and 'transformation', are all preconceived conditions or functions anticipating development in a structured leadership programme.

The origin of individuality, therefore, is thought to be *either* an idealised figure exercising influence on external circumstances, *or* a discrete relation capable of reconciling singular terms. Either way, the process of individuation is *not* thought to be capable of supplying the principle itself. In both cases, Simondon (1992) argues, the tendency is to understand the problem of individuation retrospectively from the principle of things completed (the end of a process), rather than from the perspective of the process of individuation, in which their correlation is an already complete relation (process itself). It is this point leadership research and development often misses. It typically places the omniscient leadership figure at the centre of its activities and thereby forgets this figure is already a synthesis of differences, not linked through some principle of identity, but through irreducibly heterogeneous processes, which surround and suffuce it.

4. Process as Ontology and Epistemology

Current leadership research has now begun to pay attention to leadership as a process of individuation, rather than as a definite figure (see, for example, Barker 2001, Gemmill & Oakley 1992, Gronn 2002, Hosking 1988, Yukl 1999). Such approaches variously define leadership as 'a process of transformative change' (Barker 2001, 491), or a created socio-cultural 'myth' to ward off feelings of uncertainty, ambivalence, and instability (Gemmill & Oakley 1992). Hosking (1988) points to leadership as a skilful process of reality constructions and shifting influence and Yukl (1999, 292) emphasises how this process is shared, thereby 'enhancing the collective and individual capacity of people to accomplish their work roles effectively'. Gronn's (2002) dissatisfaction with individualism leads him to suggest distributed leadership as a technical solution to the idealised figure of the leader as a creating and influencing subject, set apart from social relations. He defines leadership as relations of 'reciprocal influence': A→B and B→A and sees distributed leadership as a 'concertive action' that extends the existing unit of analysis to include leadership as joint action, rather than simply aggregated or individual acts. He suggests a renewed interest in "distributed leadership [...] offers an exciting window of opportunity for qualitative longitudinal field studies" as "one of a number of structuring reactions to flows of environmental stimuli" (Gronn 2002, 445).

Pettigrew (2003), operating in the allied fields of strategy and organisational change, expresses a closely related point. He perceptively argues that process is "a sequence of individual and collective events, actions and activities unfolding over time in context" (2003, 309). On his view, process is *epistemology* we can put to work in explaining strategy and organisational change: to 'catch reality in flight', so to speak (Pettigrew 2003, 306). However, this outlook maintains an extant matter-form relation and importantly fails to recognise the fundamentally processual nature of the real (cf. Chia 1996, 195-204, Chia 1999; Tsoukas & Chia 2002). It also contrasts sharply with the thesis offered by Whitehead, for whom process is specifically of *ontological* concern. From a process-as-ontology perspective, Pettigrew's (2003) contribution does not in itself overturn the commonsense recognition of process as something to be completed, as a change in the positioning of individuals, events, actions and activities in space and time, but whose *sovereignties* are never touched by the change. In other words, rather than recognising reality 'in flight', his process-as-epistemology attends only to those aspects of concrete experience that lie within some discrete scheme of relations. Pettigrew sees process as *bounded* by human agency and *employed* as a mode of attention or critical factor in *understanding* individuals, events, actions and activities over time. As such, he does not provide a pervasive account of the processual *nature* of the real.

Each of these contributions has considerable merit in helping us to rethink our epistemological commitments. However, the full implications of their insights "will be drawn out only if their calls for a greater attention to process lead to a consistent reversal of the ontological priority" (Tsoukas & Chia 2002, 570). Two useful problematisations of the epistemological focus on process in management and leadership studies have been Hosking's work in a relational perspective (see, for example, Brown & Hosking 1986, Dachler & Hosking 1995, Hosking 1988, Hosking 2001, Hosking & Morley 1991) and Barker's (2001) definition of leadership as a process of transformative change. Hosking uses the terms 'processes' and 'relations' in order to point out the on-going connections that construct social realities. Here, her concern is with asking *how* relational processes are involved in understanding leadership. This relational perspective strongly resembles a 'moderate' social constructionist philosophy (Burningham & Cooper 1999) and expresses a closely related line of argument to Berger and Luckmann's (1966) original thesis of reality construction. However, Hosking does not start with the presumption of discrete relations between singular terms (for example, A→B and B→A) and, therefore, has to find some other way to speak of what is related to what. By refusing to reproduce certain taken-for-granteds about *what* can be known about processes and relations, Hosking leaves their nature open to conjecture, and so begins to explore ontology.

Barker (2001) also attempts to provide important metaphysical support for this endeavour. He too believes the problem of studying leadership as stabilised forms of various unpredictable social processes lies in the, perhaps inevitable, tendency to separate leaders from "the complex and continuous relationships of people and institutions" (Barker 2001, 483). He too argues the error is in assuming that an isolated, 'centred' leader can explain the complex and continuous nature of leadership. Leadership, he claims, "is precisely the complex and continuous relationships of people and institutions" and these "must be the foci of the explanation of leadership" (Barker 2001, 483). Barker proposes a new framework for leadership studies, one built upon a 'direct, phenomenological experience of leadership' (Barker 2001, 483) as a "dissipative system [...] continually renewing itself within a dynamic context (Barker 2001, 487). Whatever we experience as leadership, therefore, *is itself transforming* as a part of the system; the macro-system continually changes as a part of the transformation.

It is this ontological, rather than epistemological, character of transformation and relatedness we can invoke to appreciate leadership as process. Appropriating Cooper's (1998, 171) terminology, the process of leadership is "always momentary, tentative and transient [... it] occurs in that imperceptible moment between the known and the unknown". Instead of approaching leadership simply as the has/has not qualities and capabilities of individual leaders – whose conduct may be termed 'leaderful' by their conformation to the perfection of some hoped for ideal, or else by reason of some fortunate spontaneity within a situation – it is the relation itself, the both/and sharing or "vacillating interaction" (Cooper 1987) of subjective form and advantageous circumstance that should be our logical subject.

As we have already seen, the advantage of confining our attention to individual subjects is we confine our thoughts to clear-cut definite things with clear-cut definite relations. Nevertheless, nothing in our experience actually possesses the character of simple location. To so confine our experience is an example of the fallacy of misplaced concreteness, to which Whitehead (1967a) refers. Such a mechanistic view presupposes "the ultimate fact of a brute matter, or material, spread throughout space [...] following a fixed routine imposed by external relations which do not spring from the nature of its being" (Whitehead 1967a, 17). It does has the disadvantage, however, of neglecting events and functions important to our experience. The result is a "one-eyed reason, deficient in its vision of depth" (Whitehead 1967a, 59), and which, once again, does not re-establish the continuity of leadership as process.

So, whilst we may not be able to think without the selective pressures eliciting clear-cut definite things, we ought to be more critical of our basic distinctions and divisions. Our conception of leadership is only a fleeting glimpse of a qualitative movement of difference that has a certain 'internal resonance requiring permanent communication' (Simondon 1992, 305). If we want to trace this internal qualitative movement we must start to investigate the question of individuation itself. Here, our concern is with revaluing a leadership figure's constitutive milieu in all its variety. This will require us to rethink our ontological priorities.

5. An Emanation of the Excluded Middle

The principle of the excluded middle is an example of classical Aristotelian logic. It has a marked bias toward things and substances, which it conceives as either having or not having a certain *definiteness* of being, a natural existence that is subject to a law of all or nothing – i.e. A is either B or not B – (Andrews 1996). In the current discussion, this amounts to some positive quality or substantial character of a particular leadership figure in opposition to a lacking other. The principle of the excluded middle also suggests the concept of 'exclusion': to shut out; to hinder from entrance or admission; to debar from participation or enjoyment; to deprive of; to except, etc., which appears to rule out the possibility of a middle ground between is/is not and either/ or axioms, as a third state, or mediating position.

Hegel's dialectical synthesis offers a partial solution to this problem. For Hegel, once the substantial figure is no longer treated as a thing-in-itself, it ceases to have any positive quality or essence. Any subsequent quality is marked only in the process of negating its nothingness. To continue to be definite a figure must actively engage with (negate) what it is not. For example, A *is not* B and B *is not* A. This negative reciprocation enables Hegel to declare all differences can be mediated in an Identity of identity and opposition: there can be no identity prior to its relation to others – which is both negative and oppositional (Widder 2002). Without this opposition 'being will fade into nothingness' (Hardt 1993, 3-4). Logically, however, it also consolidates the place of the opposite and identifies it – the 'not B' is itself an identity. Thus Hegel continues to rest on the categorisation of identity, in which each empirical figure "through its own nature relates itself to the other" (Hegel, quoted in Houlgate 1999, 99). The dual nature of this relationship means that identity and difference are reconciled and so his displacement of quality or essence is only partial.

From a process-as-ontology perspective the reciprocal movement of *negation* is a misleading notion of difference. Hegel's "dialectic of negation [...] fails to grasp the concreteness and specificity of real being" (Hardt 1993, 4). The necessary quality of leadership we can outline here is *positive* difference, "a positive internal movement" (Hardt 1993, 14). This necessary quality is not definite individuality *per se,* but rather "an *undefined* number of potential individualities" (Bergson 1983, 261, original emphasis). According to Bergson (1983, 230) our mistake "is due to the fact that the 'vital' order, which is essentially creation, is manifested to us less in its essence than in some of its accidents [...] like it, they present to us repetitions that make generalization possible". However, as Bergson (1983, 230-231) continues: "There is no doubt that life as a whole is an evolution, that is an unceasing transformation." In other words, it is continuity that defines the composition of the real. Its 'accidents', by contrast, are simply a juxtaposition of points 'imitating' this vital order.

As such, we might consider the hitherto excluded middle as a kind of undefined order, one that exceeds the logic defining either the singular terms A (for example, the designated leader), or B (for example, the followers); or, for that matter, the dialectical synthesis reconciling one and the other. In other words, A is *neither* B *nor* not-B (Widder 2002). The ontological status of the excluded middle, its 'essence', is an open field of movement in which leadership is recognised as part and parcel of the vital process of continuity and not simply the juxtaposition of leaders and followers, "which are only arrests of our attention" (Bergson 1983, 343). Understanding leadership thus, we ought to take seriously the undefined middle sweeping singular terms away (Deleuze & Guattari 1987). This emanation of leadership is not directed toward distinguishing a state but rather toward the identification of an essential movement, in which what endures is undefined: the being-itself of difference, and not the definiteness of identity. The idea of simple, objective location has gone and the relation as a thing itself is brought to the fore.

If we are significantly to reframe our understanding of leadership we must go beyond both Aristotelian ideas of positive and pure identity and Hegel's identity of opposites. The nature of leadership must be seen as a creative process, one which exceeds the logic of identity and opposition and within which particular leadership figures are only syntactical conveniences; "technologies of representation convert[ing] the inaccessible, unknown and private into the accessible, known and public" (Cooper 1992, 267). Leadership is not located in A where it is apparent (i.e. the designated leader), nor is it simply at B from where it is being recognised (i.e. in the 'mind' of followers). Neither is it a series of discrete relationships *between* A and B (A→B and B→A). It is, rather, the undefined middle, the in of the between (A↔B), where both A and B are "inseparable moments" (Deleuze 1983), each necessarily referring back to the other.

Unfortunately, we are not used to this way of thinking. When we conceptualise leadership, we do so "only through a mist of affective states" (Bergson 1983, 231), which we then try to combine to produce our knowledge. Because indefiniteness is traditionally thought as an absence and because, as Bergson (1974, 141) observes, "we have an eye to practice", we always look for an immediate and complete soli-dification. Hence, for example, when *The Economist* (2003, 4) talks of a "gap between expectations and reality" and "a 'crisis of confidence' in corporate leadership", it means the perception of an *absence* of satisfaction and an apparent *lack* of certainty – we look for definiteness but find indefiniteness. We always express indefiniteness as a function of definiteness; an absence of definiteness, rather than as itself: 'it is indefinite'. This, Bergson (1983) reasons, is because indefiniteness is assumed to have no 'It'. The assumption is there is something – 'some things' – in definiteness, but indefiniteness is empty, it is an absence of things; it contains 'no things'. So, Bergson (1983, 334) concludes, the mind "swings too and fro, unable to rest" between two, irreducible kinds of order – definiteness/indefiniteness and presence/absence. We tend to affirm the first and shut our eyes to the second. It does not occur to us to detach ourselves from the partial expression and attend to the complete notion of in/definiteness in order to grasp this irre-ducibility – everything is double without being two (Deleuze 1994). It is rather like the frame of a painting, which, although separating itself not only from the body proper of the work, but also from the wall on which the painting is hung, simultaneously connects one to the other (Derrida 1987).

6. Processes of Becoming

The foregoing enables an awareness of the being of becoming, within whose internal relations a concretisation or occurrence appears and dis-appears before our eyes. What a pity leadership research and development has a tendency to assume concretisation within a particular leadership figure means "undifferentiated sameness" (Whitehead 1967a, 133) – a definite individuality, which is, however precariously, a natural thing-in-itself, enduring through time and across space. But what if endurance does indicate an indefinite pattern of inter-relatedness rather than a definite identity? A tune, as distinct from a succession of detached notes, is an example of such an indefinite pattern. The individual notes make only limited sense on their own, but can make a great deal of difference when referred beyond themselves to the particular tune – even middle 'C' is importantly relational in this respect. We do not hear the 'C' simply by segregating it from the endless complex of audible notes that are 'not C'. We hear it as a continuous flow from the 'E' played a moment before: the qualities of 'E' pervade the constitution of the 'C' that succeeds it. Thus, the notes do not exist in discrete juxtaposition; rather they intermingle and penetrate each other.

This displacement of individuality and simple location relates to leadership in the sense of those who are aware of themselves as centred 'inside' an insulated container – free from the contamination of the threatening 'other' which is located on the 'outside' – miss the subtle relations 'in' the 'between' of things. They are captured by an illusion generated by the mechanisms of "ego protection" (Battersby 1998, 52), safeguarding them from examination as reifications of individuating processes. These private predicates of experience no longer have to be thought as the definite individuality of strictly segregated things, however, but as a middle, as always in the middle, and always virtual and paradoxical. The middle is the non-individual as such, and being undefined cannot anchor the place of an individuality defined against it. Bergson's starting point, therefore, like Whitehead's, is ontological. He focuses on the emergence of enduring patterns having to be seized from the original flow of process. Patterns enjoy no individuality of content, being more properly conceived as "succession without distinction" (Bergson 1921, 100). Bergson describes a complex relationship involving a living interpenetration connecting all 'things' at all places and times and which "adopts the very life of things" (Bergson 1999, 53). Our experience of reality manifests itself as a continual change of form, where "form is only a snapshot view of transition" (Bergson 1983, 302).

Notwithstanding this, it would be a mistake to say there is no possibility of succession without distinction. Despite the linear word-space structure of phonetic writing, for example, there can hardly be a text written in which there is not some small trace of the time and labour of its writing (Derrida 1978), or else some personal mark left by its author. This time and labour and these personal marks put thoughts and words, as well as readers and authors like you and I, into an irreducible relation, one with the other, in a way that implies we are both immanent within a primary process. Moreover, there is an additional sense in which a text is also a difference in-itself. The moment a text is written there is evidence of a selection and, therefore, of organisation and this organisation already implicates some previous disorganisation. In other words, the definiteness of a text is always in dynamic relation with an indefiniteness preceding it. Furthermore, whilst Bergson (1983) himself admits representational writing is inescapable, we can choose to write in one of two ways: first, to represent states, or, second, to represent a concern for relations, processes, and differences. In general, Bergson argues, we too easily write to represent states rather than movement. Certainly, the tendency to abstract and represent has practical utility: breaking movement up into things allows us to act, but we can seek to do this from within the moving reality. Bergson advocates writing in verbs as this calls up the 'inner work' of movement rather than 'ready prepared' states (Bergson 1983, 11; cf. Bohm 1980). Derrida (1978, 219) similarly suggests writing 'theoretical fictions' within which there can be "no sovereign solitude of the author" (1978, 226). Both views chime with Whitehead (1978, 182), for whom 'imaginative writing' opens the world to our senses, precipitating endless feelings and thoughts and enabling us to bring our whole self to reading.

The important point is we can still gain considerable leverage by affirming the indefiniteness of leadership and not its definiteness as an object of nature, although the shortfalls of intellectual abstraction can never be wholly avoided. The former allows the possibility of supplementing the intellect with intuition (Bergson 1983). This is valuable because the intellectual perspective of definite being finds it impossible to conceive "properly human experience" (Bergson 1991, 184). The intellect will always settle on "the conceptual forms [...] it is accustomed to see" and, therefore, "will always neglect the part of novelty or of creation" (Bergson 1983, 270). By adopting the rhythm of its "relational essence" (Whitehead 1967a, 160) we find it difficult to divorce leadership from any reference to a social context or to some communistic processes. For example, the essence of leader 'A' is always undefined, fluxing, it always conjointly involves an ingression with and not simply recognition by another: 'B'. In this way the original *being* of leadership is properly described as a 'systematic complex of mutual relatedness' (Whitehead 1967a, 161). These processes *are* leadership. That is to say the becoming of leadership is affirmed as it's being. Leadership is a *becomingness* in which the fixity of ephemeral arrangements conversely comes and goes (Bergson 1974).

Accordingly, we can treat all appearances as transient abstractions as a mode of attention or symbolic fixing of this continuity of flow and not the apprehension of the distinct figures themselves. Furthermore, we might begin to ask how we might attend to the processes of creation laying behind the individual leadership figures we value so highly. Reaching an understanding of process and becoming not only requires a rethinking of ontological priorities, therefore, but also of our epistemological interests and methodological concerns.

7. Implications for Leadership Research and Development

Leadership research and development give us absolutely distinct leadership figures, but this is argued increasingly to be a misleading notion. The alternative analytical focus on the discrete relations of collective or distributed leadership, in which the relation remains external to the related things, is only a partial and relative solution. From the perspective of process-as-ontology, real endurance is inter-relatedness, or difference in-itself, and not individual identity or discrete relations of identity and difference. Process studies do not start from the position of leadership as an individual subject, existing in itself, pure and simple, or as negatively related, but as a becoming that escapes these categorical principles.

7.1 Epistemological Development

The epistemological problem is not to try and research or seek to develop the private world of passions, intentions and influence of individual figures, or the discrete operation of individuation, but rather to explore inductively the values associated with the internal movement of difference. Consider, for example, the appropriateness of the sentence "It is leadership" (Bohm 1980, 29). Adapting Bohm's (1980) enquiry into the subject-verb-object structure of language, we might ask: what is the 'It' doing the leading? Following Bohm once more, wouldn't it be more accurate to say 'Leadership is going on.'? Similarly, instead of saying 'Leaders act on followers.', we can more appropriately say, 'leadership is going on within a subtle synthesis of internal differences without mediation or relation to others'; an immanent relation making any bracketing of the abstractions customarily called 'leaders' and 'followers' difficult to sustain.

With this in mind, a particular leadership figure cannot be construed as a simple element, present at hand, getting caught up in life. The figure does not 'find itself' in relation to its 'environment', but rather the on-going 'relation' itself is an intrinsic feature of the figure's being. Moreover, the figure comes to be spoken in terms of a "non-localisable relation sweeping up [...] two distant or contiguous points, carrying one into the proximity of the other" (Deleuze & Guattari 1987, 293). The 'essence' of leadership is no longer the self-evident figure but the accelerating pace (and shrinking space) of relations of movement and rest, speed, slowness and simultaneity.

For example, new digital technologies like mobile phones, Internet software design and electronic positioning devices are transforming organizations from 'fixed entities' under one roof to networks of electronically connected individuals, commercial markets and interorganizational alliances. The much vaunted qualities and capabilities of individual leaders increasingly are being constructed, coordinated and consumed in 'without walls' organisation. One impact of these new and 'virtual' modes of organising has been to blur familiar representations and simple location. Leaders are 'ingested' into self-managing teams and groups, whose organisational working practices are constituted, renegotiated and extended by advanced information and communication technologies (Brigham & Corbett 1997). This concern implies a widening of the prevalent research and development emphasis from its conventional focus on the personal qualities and capabilities of a few key people occupying top positions in a hierarchy, and toward an understanding of their identification as *events*: only obtaining as an occurrence, incident, or accident under certain conditions. (Deleuze 1993, Whitehead 1967a, 1978; see also, Foucault 1972).

7.2 Methodological Considerations

A process approach to leadership research and development is consistent with Nietzsche's (1994) genealogical analysis as well as with ideas from critical management research, which emphasise leadership as a social field of activity (Alvesson 1996, Alvesson & Deetz 2000). A 'process methodology' applied to leadership brings three, interrelated factors to the fore. First, leadership is always enmeshed in social practice rather than in a clear-cut, definite figure. This focus brings the space of the stage or scene to the centre of analysis and *not* the immediate individuality of a leader who can be simply located, or the discrete relations, which obtain between familiar representations of 'leaders' and 'followers'. Second, because leadership is irreducible to simple location and subject to a myriad of "meanings, values, ideals and discourse processes" (Alvesson 1996, 472) we might conjecture leadership is fundamentally a process and a process is not an object, but a tending toward novelty, innovation, and emergence. In other words, a process methodology aims to study change and not things that change (Bergson 1946). Third, because the enduring figures we come to recognise in a specific social context are not the inherent qualities or substantial characteristics of leadership as it really *is*, but an ongoing creative advance, our methodological concern should be with the identification of an essential movement', a movement that has a certain temporal dimension, a process in time. A process methodology, accordingly, is something for which temporality, activity and change are basic propositions.

Now, it would be easy to assume an individual actor could possess leadership *if* it were reducible to such an underlying figure. But, as we have argued, the mistake is exactly this logic of leadership as if it were 'synonymous' with an immediate and individual figure. Leadership is not an *a priori* empirical figure entering into relations with others but whose own sovereignty is not dependent on those relations, or on something else other than itself. For a process methodology, leadership exceeds both locations. We can more appropriately call it a moving synthesis of differences; a process of individuation guided by difference and creation that gives an appearance of individuality.

Exploring leadership as an event implies a certain movement and a methodological focus on relations, connexions, dependences and reciprocities, over time: a set of advantageous circumstances becoming identical with the 'objective' subject of leadership. In other words, through such a focus, it is difficult to maintain the simple exteriority of leadership as a clear object of study from the whole domain of institutions, economic processes, and social relations, within which an individual leadership figure obtains. A process methodology offers a counterproposal to the neo-empiricist "treatment of theory and interpretation as separate from data" (Alvesson 1996, 456). Such approaches are "appropriate in order to get information about simple relatively fixed issues, where the meaning can be standardised and quantified", but not "more complex issues [... such as leadership, which] cannot be translated into abstract, standardised forms and language" (Alvesson 1996, 461). Instead, a process methodology expresses an historical sense that takes a particular period, encounter, issue, or situation, rather than familiar behaviour patterns, attitudes, or traits, as its focus.

Practically speaking this means attending to the withdrawn or background processes of individuation. This type of *mise en scène* implies the deployment of an inductive programme of qualitative, interpretive and ethnographic research and development, with a strong 'situational' focus (Alvesson 1996). Such an approach seeks to emphasise the "small details, minor shifts and subtle contours" (Dreyfuss & Rabinow 1982, 106) of leadership as a dynamic and energetic landscape of events, "less here than now [...] less in space than in time" (Virilio 2000, viii). What is interesting, within a process methodology, is to investigate how perpetual movement and divergent processes form a discrete body, or appear to obtain in a substantial set of individual qualities and capabilities, at the same time as preserving the uninterrupted continuity of our experience.

8. Conclusion: Leadership Research and Development as Process

Process studies provide a clear demonstration that 'successful leaders' are not simple, locatable figures, nor are they the completion of an operation of individuation. An apparent individuality is construed as a selective abstraction from the vast field of experience. This selective process is prevalent because leaders tend to immerse themselves in a misleading Western 'substance metaphysic'. They have done this by having certain ascendant characteristics ascribed: I am a visionary, I communicate well, I encourage participation, I build teams, I am clear what needs to be achieved, and so on. The view of the individual subject is epitomised by the prefix 'I' in these statements. We should not adduce any categorical distinction, however, between 'leaders' and their 'environments'. When viewed in process terms, absolutely distinct individuality becomes problematic. What is primary is leadership as process, an *internal* qualitative relation expressing difference in-itself, without mediation or relation to external others.

Deleuze and Guattari (1987) introduce the term 'involution' to express a relaxation of natural, obvious and reified forms and the cor-responding emergence of a complex field of heterogeneous combi-nations and novel alliances, which cut across and beneath seemingly individual subjects. Such aggregations are a non-localisable synthesis of differences recognising the continual participation of constituent parts *within* each other. The notion of leadership does not, therefore, refer specifically or exclusively to the transformational, charismatic or visionary figure of transcendent leaders, nor does it focus entirely on the behaviour of followers, or the discrete relations between one and the other, which leave the relations *external* to each. The emphasis on emergence and becoming rather than sheer existence or being connotes the excessive movement through which leadership frees itself from association with a 'thing' moving. Instead, leadership *is* movement, open and dynamic process, whose complete determination "does not follow from its possibility of becoming present. At best, it appears only in the most fleeting moments, when it does not even seem to have taken place" (Widder 2002, 59).

In conclusion, researchers and commissioners of development op-portunities, for the most part, have not drawn out the full implications of Bryman's (1986) call for engagement with ideas from different enquiry paradigms. If leadership research and development, as a way of understanding and as a practicable programme of development, is not to remain subjugated to the individualistic canon it must rise to the challenge of raising the status of and bringing to bear new and imagi-native ways of thinking about leadership. I have sought to extend current understanding of leadership as a creative process of becoming. The pressing strategic difficulty now is to provide developmental options that move away from the prescriptive definition of the form and substance of leaders *being-here-present,* to a possible inductive understanding of leadership *becoming-now-passing.*

Acknowledgements

This chapter is a revised version of an article published in *Journal of Manage-ment Studies* 42/6 (2005), 1101-1121; the author gratefully acknowledges copyright of that material (Blackwell, © 2005).

Bibliography

Andrews, F. E. (1996): The principle of the excluded middle then and now: Aristotle and *Principia Mathematica'*. *Animus* [online]. URL: http://www.swgc.mun.ca/animus>. (access: 23 September 2003).

Alvesson, M. (1996): Leadership studies: from procedure and abstraction to reflexivity and situation. *Leadership Quarterly*, 7/4, 455-485.

Alvesson, M. & Deetz, S. (2000): *Doing Critical Management Research*. London: Sage.

Alvesson, M. & Sveningsson, S. (2003): Good visions, bad micro-management and ugly ambiguity: contradictions of (non-)leadership in a knowledge intensive organization. *Organization Studies*, 24/6, 961-988.

Barker, R. (2001): The nature of leadership. *Human Relations*, 54/4, 469-494.

Bass, B. M (1985): *Leadership and Performance Beyond Expectations*. New York: Free Press.

Bass, B. M. & Avolio, B. J. (1997): Shatter the glass ceiling: women may make better managers. In: K. Grint (Ed.): *Leadership: Classical, contemporary, and critical approaches*. Oxford: Oxford University Press, 199-210.

Battersby, C. (1998): *The Phenomenal Woman: Feminist Metaphysics and the Patterns of Identity*. Cambridge: Polity.

BBC (2003): The Greatest American [online]. URL: http://news.bbc.co.uk/1/hi/programmes/wtwta/2997144.stm. (access: 6 September 2004).

Berger, P. L. & Luckmann, T. (1966): *The Social Construction of Reality: A Treatise in the Sociology of Knowledge*. London: Penguin.

Bergson, H. (1921/1889): *Time and Free Will: An Essay on the Immediate Data of Consciousness*. Trans. F.L. Pogson. London: Allen and Unwin.

Bergson, H. (1974/1946): *The Creative Mind: An Introduction to Metaphysics*. Trans M.L. Andison. New York: Citadel Press.

Bergson, H. (1983/1911): *Creative Evolution*. Lanham MD: University Press of America.

Bergson, H. (1991/1896): *Matter and Memory*. New York: Zone Books.

Bergson, H. (1999/1912): *An Introduction to Metaphysics*. Indianapolis: Hackett Publishing.

Blake, R. R. & Mouton, J. S. (1964): *The Managerial Grid*. Houston TX: Gulf.

Bohm, D. (1980): *Wholeness and the Implicate Order*. London: Routledge.

Bolden, R., Wood, M, & Gosling J. (2005): Is the NHS Leadership Qualities Framework Missing the Wood for the Trees? In: A. Casebeer (Ed.) *Innovations in Health Care: A Reality Check*. Palgrave Macmillan.

Bolman, G. L. & Deal, T. E. (1994): The organization as theater. In: H. Tsoukas (Ed) *New Thinking in Organizational Behaviour*, Oxford: Butterworth-Heinemann, 93-107.

Brigham, M. & Corbett, J. M. (1997): E-mail power and the constitution of organizational reality. *New Technology, Work and Employment*, 12/1, 25–35.

Brown, M. H. & Hosking, D. M. (1986): Distributed leadership and skilled performance as successful organization in social movements. *Human Relations*, 39/1, 65-79.

Bryman, A. (1986): *Leadership in Organisations*. London: RKP.

Burns, J.M. (1978) *Leadership*. New York: Harper and Row.

Bush-Cheney (2004): John Kerry: The Raw Deal [online].
    URL: http://www.georgewbush.com/KerryMediaCenter/ (2004). (access: 6 September 2004).

Calás, M. & Smircich, L. (1991): Voicing seduction to silence leadership. *Organization Studies*, 12/4, 567-602.

Chia, R. (1996): *Organizational Analysis as Deconstructive Process*. Berlin: Walter de Gruyter.

Chia R. (1998): Introduction. In: R. C. H. Chia (Ed.) *Organised Worlds: Explorations in Technology and Organizations with Robert Cooper*. London: Routledge, 1-19.

Conger, J. & Kanungo, K. N. (1998): *Charismatic Leadership in Organisations*. Thousand Oaks. Sage.

Cooper, R. (1983): The other: a model of human structuring. In: G. Morgan (Ed.) *Beyond Method: Strategies for Social Research*. Newbury Park: Sage, 202-218.

Cooper, R. (1987): Information, communication and organization: A poststructural revision. *Journal of Mind and Behaviour*, 8/3, 395-415.

Cooper, R. (1998): Assemblage Notes. In: R. C. H. Chia (Ed.) *Organized Worlds: Explorations in Technology and Organization with Robert Cooper*. Routledge, 108-129.

Dachler, H. P. & Hosking, D. M. (1995): The primacy of relations in socially constructing organizational realities. In: D. M. Hosking, H. P. Dachler, & K. J. Gergen (Eds.) *Management and Organization: Relational Perspectives*. Ashgate/Avebury.

Day, R. (1998): Diagrammatic bodies. In: R. C. H. Chia (Ed.) *Organized Worlds: Explorations in Technology and Organization with Robert Cooper*. London: Routledge, 95-107.

Deleuze, G. (1983): *Nietzsche and Philosophy*. London: Athlone.

Deleuze, G. (1993): *The Fold: Leibniz and the Baroque*. Minneapolis: University of Minnesota Press.

Deleuze, G. (1994): *Difference and Repetition*. London: Athlone Press.

Deleuze, G. & Guattari, F. (1987): *A Thousand Plateaus: Capitalism and Schizophrenia*. London: Athlone Press.

Derrida, J. (1978): *Writing and Difference*. London: Routledge.

Derrida, J. (1987): *The Truth in Painting*. Chicago: University of Chicago Press.

Dreyfus, H. L. & Rabinow P. (1982): *Michael Foucault: Beyond Structuralism and Hermeneutics*. Hemel Hempstead: Harvester Wheatsheaf.

Economist, The (2003): Tough at the top: a survey of corporate leadership. 25 October: 3-26.

Elgie, R. (1995): *Political Leadership in Liberal Democracies*. Basingstoke: Macmillan.

Fiedler, F. E. (1967): *A Theory of Leadership Effectiveness*. New York: McGraw-Hill.

Foucault, M. (1972): *The Archaeology of Knowledge*. London: Routledge.

Gemmill, G. & Oakley, J. (1992): Leadership: an alienating social myth. *Human Relations*, 45/2, 113-129.

Goffee, R. & Jones, G. (2000): Why should anyone be led by you? *Harvard Business Review,* 78, 5, 63-70.

Greanleaf, R. (1977): *Servant Leadership: A Journey Into the Nature of Legitimate Power and Greatness*. New York: Paulist Press.

Greanleaf, R. & Spears, L. (1998): *The Power of Servant Leadership*. Berrett-Koehler.

Greatest Briton (2002): TV. BBC 2. 24 November.

Griffin, D. R. (1986): *Bohm, Prigogyne and the Ultimate Significance of Time*. New York: SUNY.

Grint, K. (1997): *Leadership: Classical, Contemporary, and Critical Approaches*. Oxford: Oxford University Press.

Gronn, P. (2002): Distributed leadership as a unit of analysis. *The Leadership Quarterly*, 13, 423-451.

Hardt, M. (1993): *Gilles Deleuze: Apprenticeship in Philosophy*. London: UCL Press.

Heifetz, R. A. (1994): *Leadership Without Easy Answers*. Cambridge: Belknap Press.

Hersey, P. & Blanchard, K. H. (1977): *Management of Organizational Behaviour*. Englewood Cliffs NJ: Prentice Hall.

Hooper, A. & Potter, J. (2000): *Intelligent Leadership: Creating a Passion for Change*. London: Random House.

Hosking, D. M. (1988): Organizing, leadership and skilful process. *Journal of Management Studies*, 25/2, 147-166.

Hosking, D. M. (2001): Social construction as process: some new possibilities for research and development. *Concepts & Transformation*, 4/2, 117-132.

Hosking, D. M. & Morley, I. E. (1991): *A Social Psychology of Organizing: People, Contexts and Processes*. New York: Harvester/Wheatsheaf.

Houlgate, S. (1999): Hegel. In S. Critchley and W.R. Schroeder (Eds.): *A Companion to Continental Philosophy*. Oxford: Blackwell, 93-103.

Kerry-Edwards (2004): About John Kerry [online]. URL: http://www.johnkerry.com/index.html. (access: 6 September 2004).

Langmuir, E. (1994): *The National Gallery Companion Guide*. London: National Gallery Publications.

Margulis, L. & Sagan, D. (1986): *Microcosmos: Four Billion Years of Microbial Evolution*. Berkeley, CA: University of California Press.

Nietzsche, F. (1994/1887) :*On the Genealogy of Morality*. K. Ansell-Pearson (Ed.): Cambridge: Cambridge University Press.

Pettigrew, A (2003): Strategy as process, power and change. In: S. Cummings & D. Wilson (Eds.) *Images of Strategy*. Oxford: Blackwell, 301-330.

Pfeffer, J. (1977): The ambiguity of leadership. *Academy of Management Review*, 2/1, 104-112.

Rescher, N. (2002): Process Philosophy. *The Stanford Encyclopedia of Philosophy* Summer 2002, E. N. Zalta (Ed.) [online].
URL: http://plato.stanford.edu/archives/sum2002/entries/process-philosophy/ (access: 27 July 2004).

Rickards, T. (1999): *Creativity and the Management of Change*. Oxford: Blackwell.

Simondon, G. (1992): The genesis of the individual. In: J. Crary & S. Kwinter (Eds.) *Incorporations*. New York: Zone, 296-319.

Smircich, L. & Morgan, G. (1982): Leadership: the management of meaning. *The Journal of Applied Behavioural Science*, 18/3, 257-273.

Stogdill, R. M. (1950): Leadership, membership and organization. *Psychological Bulletin*, 47, 1-14.

Tsoukas, H. & Chia, R. (2002): On organizational becoming: rethinking organizational change. *Organization Science*, 13/5, 567-582.

Virilio, P. (2000): *A Landscape of Events*. Cambridge M.A.: The MIT Press.

Whitehead, A. N. (1967a/1925) *Science and Modern World*. Cambridge: Cambridge University Press.

Whitehead, A. N. (1967b/1933): Adventures *of Ideas*. New York: Free Press.

Whitehead, A. N. (1978/1929): *Process and Reality*. D.R. Griffin and D.W. Sherburne (Eds.). New York: Free Press.

Widder, N. (2002): *Genealogies of Difference*. Urbana and Chicago IL: University of Illinois Press.

Willmott, H. (1993): Strength is ignorance; slavery is freedom: managing culture in modern organizations. *Journal of Management Studies*, 30/4, 515-552.

Yukl, G. (1999): An evaluation of conceptual weaknesses in transformational and charismatic leadership theories. *Leadership Quarterly*, 10/2, 285-305.

Part II.2

WHITEHEAD'S EDUCATIONAL THOUGHT AND ITS APPLICATION TO COLLEGES

Alfred North Whitehead's Philosophy as a Conceptual Framework for Teacher Education

James Alexander & Bob Darrell

Abstract

This essay develops A.N. Whitehead's process philosophy to teacher education by 1) illuminating its relevance for teacher education; 2) applying his three stages of learning (*Aims of Education* (1967)) to a baccalaureate-granting, college teacher education program; 3) narrating how one college has implemented, developed, and evaluated this structure for more than a decade; 4) outlining a three-level approach to teacher education majors, from entering college through professional teaching careers. Finally, on the basis of benefits and relevance of Whitehead's philosophy and results of one institution's ten-year experience, the authors recommend further studies and implementations.

1. Introduction

1.1 Purpose and Background

This essay proposes two major ways Alfred North Whitehead's philosophy may provide a conceptual framework for instructing pre-service teachers.

To pursue this purpose, we frequently refer to a particular institution, to a specific conceptual framework, and to Whiteheadian concepts and terms, perhaps not in wide currency. Therefore, we begin our essay by identifying and explaining briefly these three topics.

1.1.1 The Institution

Kentucky Wesleyan College (KWC) in Owensboro, Kentucky has implemented, maintained, and monitored such a Whiteheadian conceptual framework for more than a decade. During this time, changes have occurred in our Education Department faculty, and we have rewritten our core documents. Our Department has negotiated successfully three state accreditation reviews. This achievement has elicited further reflection on the part of stakeholders-faculty, students, graduates, and others. Although we believe these developments improved the framework's developments, monitoring, and evaluations, in essence the basic principles remain as they existed when initially adopted. We also note that KWC supports a college-wide emphasis on leadership. Leadership skills training and the goal of developing ethical, compassionate, effective leaders pervade all course work and the significant extracurriculum.

1.1.2 The Framework Source

Whitehead's thought provided a natural, rational platform upon which to build such a framework (part of which we achieved at KWC). To educators unfamiliar with Whitehead's thought, attempts to understand Whitehead's thought beyond that published in *The Aims of Education* (1967) might cause many to throw up their hands in frustration. Many might give up when it becomes apparent that Whitehead's value to education is proportionate to attempts to understand his all-encompassing cosmology and metaphysic.

When we speak of applying Whitehead's philosophy to education – particularly as a conceptual framework for organizing and directing a department of teacher education, we must view carefully the whole sweep of his approach. Teacher education can benefit from examining how education fits into the broad strokes painting the Whiteheadian canvas.

1.1.3 Three Levels

Whitehead's philosophy suggests organizing and developing teacher education comprehensively in three levels: Programmatic Pre-professional, Personal Professional; and Leader Professional

1.1.4 Cycles

Within these levels occur three cycles: Romance, Precision, and Generalization, occurring in ever-deepening, ever-enriching stages. We will discuss these levels and cycles following an examination of key terms and concepts in Whitehead's philosophy, for they provide frameworks for teacher education, generally and specifically.

A review of literature relative to Whitehead and education reveals a tendency to build such cases solely from his *The Aims of Education.* This tendency likely results from its popular style, contemporary appeal, and the pragmatic nature characterizing this brief book's contents. Nevertheless, teacher educators will profit from ideas set forth in *Aims* in the context of the larger view afforded by a wider reading of Whitehead and will benefit from examining Whitehead's other works.

2. Whitehead's Philosophy for Educators: Overview

Breadth, Evolutionary, Interdependent, Beautiful, Process/Existence – these terms help us grasp essential Whitehead notions, both for his philosophy as a whole and for its application to education. We review each one briefly below.

2.1 Breadth

Lubbock correctly describes Whitehead's philosophy as 'all-embracing', with widespread applications in education, language, mathematics, political science, psychology, science, sociology, theology, and many other fields of knowledge. Certainly, moreover, Whitehead's thought complements other philosophical approaches and pedagogies.

For instance, it operates harmoniously with Husserl's phenomenology. Whitehead's ideas remain 'at home' in a post-modernist world and, yet, thrives compatibly with traditional ethics, morals, values. To cite a second example, constructivist psychology, widely influential in education, can benefit from Whitehead. One of the greatest appeals of Whitehead's thought resides in its continuous contemporariness. Inherently, this philosophy embraces *becoming*.

2.2 Evolutionary

Although, granted, Whitehead certainly considered philosophy as a rational attempt to systemize knowledge (Lubbock 1999), he did not deem static either its contents or its structures. Whitehead's philosophy envisions the universe, both material and non-material – including the world of thought – as constantly evolving. This evolution we might better describe in Lamarckian terms, based on *cooperation* and *community* and on an inherently purposeful *coming together*, contrasted to a 'cutthroat' Darwinism sense. This perspective remains true whether or not its evolutionary players are conscious of this purposefulness.

2.2.1 Breadth and Evolutionary: Example.

In a brief example embodying these characteristics, Whitehead analyzes the broad, evolutionary character of religion in *Religion in the Making* (Whitehead 1971). This religious perspective may well offer an illustrative beginning point for students of process. Although space precludes any substantial exploration of the formation and function of religion, three comments may clarify our notions. First, Whitehead does not advocate an institutionalized religion for education. Second, Whitehead suggests religion in human beings is part of process reality: Whitehead demonstrates that religion builds progressively from ritual and emotion to belief to, finally, rationalization. Yet, each stage contains all preceding stages and builds on those that precede. Third, the *coming together* of religion as a rational dogma exhibits that cooperative, evolutionary spirit pervading the universe (Whitehead 1971, 85). The actual world we relate to, "the world of experiencing, and of thinking, and of physical activity, is a community of many diverse entities" (Whitehead 1971, 86).

2.3 Interdependent

In speaking of the actual world as a 'community', Whitehead clarifies his notion of reality as interdependent. Yet, these "actual entities are, for themselves, their own value, individual and separable" (Whitehead 1971, 86). Whether organisms or God or final things or actual entities – all real things in the universe – are "drops of experience, complex and interdependent" (Whitehead 1978, 18). Accordingly, even though individuality inheres in that which is real, that precise individuality interdepends on other real things.

2.4 Beautiful

At its simplest, Whitehead's cosmology is not only a question of logic, but also of beauty – in short, aesthetics. The never-ending movement of all that *is* reflects this process of *becoming* that which is beauty, and the *becoming* itself *is* reflection of that beauty. Here is a philosophy full of hope.

2.5 Process; Existence

Whitehead declares, "One main doctrine [...] is the 'existence' in any of its senses cannot be abstracted from 'process.' The notions of process and existence presuppose each other"(Whitehead 1958, 131). Whitehead suggests that the "main doctrine" described above demonstrates the fallacy of thinking of "a point" in process." Process cannot be dealt with in atomistic fashion. Process cannot be broken down "into compositions of final realities, themselves devoid of process" (Whitehead 1958 131).

2.6 Two Metaphors Illustrating these Five Characteristics

Lubbock (1999) offers two metaphors to describe Whitehead's cosmology, metaphors so accurately illuminating that they embody visually many Whiteheadian concepts.

2.6.1 Free-Wheeling Jazz Festival

The first metaphor employs a 'free-wheeling jazz festival'. In this performance, many players perform, too many to count. Some are good; some, not so good; some, bad. But all of them are hard at work improvising, creating the composition as they play. Why do they play? Not for some 'external' motivation, such as God's glory or to celebrate the art or to earn money. They play for the sheer joy of playing – each adding one's part.

2.6.2 Jewel Net of Indra

A second metaphor involves The Jewel Net of Indra, central to Hua-Yen Buddhism. Here, the cosmos is like an 'infinite network of glittering jewels, all different'. Each jewel contains an image of all the others. Each reflection contains the reflection of all other images which contain the reflection of all others, and so on. Lubbock succinctly describes the controlling idea of this system: "There are no fundamental 'things' or 'objects' in the world of Whitehead. Whitehead's ontology, or parts list of the universe, contains only process." (Lubock 1999)

2.7 Terms and Concepts

Much of Whitehead's work included establishing vocabulary, definitions, and concepts, especially in *Process and Reality* (1978), a work usually considered foundational to understanding Whitehead. Thus, an introductory treatment of selected terms is useful (a treatment indebted to D.W. Sherburne's *A Key to Whitehead's Process and Reality* (1981)).

2.7.1 Actual Entities

Whitehead refers to actual entities as 'final real things of which the world is made up'. These entities "are drops of experience, complex and interdependent" (Whitehead 1978, 18). They are "the unity a-scribed to a particular instance of concrescence." These instances always perish; they do not endure. Thus, in process, the direction is always one of becoming. These entities are the final 'real things' in the world. Actual entities are units of process that join with other actual entities comprising a complex and interconnected 'society'. For example, such combinations form our individual souls. Distinct, yet inseparable, this collective reality is always perishing. As it passes away, each actual entity paves the way for a new becoming. Nothing is static: All is dynamic (Lubbock 1999)

This concept is embedded strongly, pervasively in educational theory but remains under-recognized and under-utilized. Often when recognized, educators refer it to as "the teachable moment" (Stewart 1993), the ever-changing conditions for learning as a microcosm of the universe. Such moments constantly present educators with opportunities and challenges. Brain research frequently refers to windows of opportunity when developmental conditions are just right. If environmental conditions are right as well, construction of new knowledge may occur.

This concept of change is central to constructivism. Reality confronts us. Constantly, the human task is to create and recreate meaning (see especially: Bruner 1990). Throughout much of Whitehead's thought, we encounter a system highly compatible with constructivism.

2.7.2 Creativity

In Whitehead, creativity belongs to the Category of the Ultimate, the general principle presupposed by all else. Creativity lies at the basis of process, identified as the principle that underlies 'ongoingness'. If we consider the universe a collection of diverse "manys", we may understand the constant move toward unity that always is creating a new "one" presupposing creativity (Whitehead 1929, 31-32).

Educators and cognitive psychologists have become increasingly aware of human beings as meaning-makers and pattern-constructors. Caine and Caine (1994), to cite one example, utilize this notion in describing how to render schooling 'brain-friendly'. If the view of the human psyche is correct, Whitehead's concept of creativity lies indeed at the core of being human beings and, therefore, can instruct us educators.

2.7.3 Metaphysics

One or another interpretation of experience underlies any metaphysics. Both interpretation and metaphysics must be idiosyncratic since either can include only, in the fullest sense, the recognition that we are conscious. Even this consciousness and metaphysics are always becoming. Nothing is carved in stone!

As an explanation, our metaphysic becomes a scheme (in the sense of cognition) that defines. Our metaphysic we might view as our script of reality, our representation of 'what is'. As we grow, mature, we can recognize the tendency for our scripts to become more entrenched, for example, in stereotypes or prejudices. We encounter the cognitive dissonance of a reality that does not fit our explanation as such. At that point, we proceed toward truth or retreat to the comfort of the familiar.

2.7.4 Nexus

Nexus refers to the coming together of entities of everyday experience. In the past, we often viewed knowledge as atomist, discrete, isolated, separate. Education advancements toward a holistic view, recognized most clearly in the triumph of 'social studies' over discrete social sciences (economics, history, etc.), evidences a relatively new view of knowledge (Ellis 2002). It has become increasingly important to view the study of human beings in economic, geographic, historical, sociological, and on and on and on contexts, often multi-layered or overlapping. Increasingly, we envision reality as a nexus of many entities: Indeed, current curriculum theory increasingly treats the human subject as such.

2.8 Appraisal and Summary thus Far

In the previous section, we offered terminological equivalences of a few Whitehead terms. These key terms indicate Whitehead's usefulness in education theory and practice. Much of what follows depends on acceptance of a congruity existing between Whitehead's thought and the modern science of cognition currently informing educational theory and practice. We contend that this congruity especially applies to constructivism. Likely, much of the usefulness of what we offer here may stand or fall on this congruity and corollary acceptance of a constructivist viewpoint.

This accepted, we suggest that Whitehead provides a starting point for constructing a model for teacher education: Administration, curriculum, personal development, career development, evaluation, a fundamental way of looking at all reality.

3. Three-Stage Cycles Throughout Three Levels

Whitehead's philosophy of education suggests dynamic levels of organization and development, each of which – like the cycle of romance, precision, and generalization – may adapt to a larger developmental approach to teacher education in organization, administration, lifelong teaching and learning, community life, and multivariate evaluation. Those levels include Programmatic Pre-Professional, Personal Professional, and Leader Professional.

In a 1976 doctoral dissertation, one of us (Darrell) initiated consideration of a applying these three stages to undergraduate education by developing a philosophy of institutional curriculum structure. His dissertation advocates that institutions, departments, majors and concentrations, minors, courses, and topics treated within courses apply this structure.

Slightly more than a decade ago, he also presented to KWC's Teacher Education Department the option of organizing its curriculum and program according to the three stages.

3.1 Conceptual Framework

First, we offer a few remarks about our conceptual framework. The term 'conceptual framework' refers to our blueprint for the educational process in KWC's Teacher Education Department. This *Framework* guides our program in many ways. It informs both design and sequence of coursework. It encourages integration of both procedural and declarative knowledge through inclusion of theory tested by practice. Our adoption and development of this approach receives encouragement as students work through the program and continue this work as educators. Our *Framework* also underscores the importance of relevancy; encouraging inclusion of issues such as diversity, equality, etc. This *Framework* demands we maintain a current knowledge and experience base with ever-increasing inclusion of technology (an ever-increasing factor in the real world of usefulness).

The *Conceptual Framework* for KWC's Teacher Education Department (for details see the appendix at the end of this paper) roots in a 'working understanding' of Whitehead. Our *Conceptual Framework* especially depends on the essay collection, *The Aims of Education*. In utilizing this collection, we certainly claim no originality. We do believe our *Conceptual Framework* advances the application of Whitehead to a new level in that we have attempted to apply Whitehead in a way more productive by providing both philosophical and practical direction for the Teacher Education Department and more productive in teacher preparation outcomes.

Our *Conceptual Framework* expresses itself programmatically as 'three gates': Admission to the program, admission to student teaching, and the exit presentation after student teaching. These three gates each address competences, dispositions, and knowledge expected of students at any point in our program. Students must demonstrate a growing understanding of the *Framework* and associated terminology. Moreover, knowledge and application of the *Framework* are assessed throughout the program of studies.

Although apparent from departmental documents posted on our College website that Whitehead's concept of "the rhythm of education" provides the main programmatic expression of Whiteheadian philosophy, a more basic Whiteheadian notion drives it. At the heart of the program resides the idea that "students are alive and the purpose of education is to stimulate and guide their self-development" (Whitehead 1967, 2). He continues: "It follows from this premise that the teachers should also be alive with living thoughts [.... This] is a protest against dead knowledge, that is to say, against inert knowledge" (Whitehead 1967, 2).

Whitehead speaks of education's cyclic nature. Education consists of cycles which in turn comprise stages. Education is a process of "cyclic reoccurrences"; "as we pass from cycle to cycle [...] the subordinate stages are reproduced in each cycle" (Whitehead 1967, 17).

In our approach, we attempt to allow usefulness to hold center stage. Inert ideas are "ideas that are merely received into the mind without being utilized, or tested, or thrown into fresh combinations" (Whitehead 1967, 1). For Whitehead, education is expressed in "the utilization of knowledge." In adopting the *Framework*," we discourage "the passive reception of disconnected ideas." Even the *Framework* proper must be useful, developing, and purposeful to be judged worthwhile. The *Framework* provides a structure for construction and connection and application of knowledge. According to Whitehead, "unless [knowledge] fits into a connected curriculum [...] there is no reason to teach it." (Whitehead 1967, 7). The same might be said of knowledge or facts in general.

3.2 The Three Stages in each Cycle

Whitehead speaks of each cycle comprising three stages: Romance, Precision, and Generalization. Each stage reprises, more richly incorporates, enlarges, and surpasses the previous stage(s). In the next few subsections, we provide Whitehead's term followed by our Department's equivalent with a brief description.

3.2.1 Romance/Exploration

Romance "is the stage of first apprehension" (Whitehead 1967, 17). The term implies playful, initial, passionate involvement. Passion is powerful at this stage, not shaped by serious commitment and knowledge and experience. Romance does not always develop into a permanent relationship. Directed by passion, the realities of the classroom may replace romance with indifference or possibly disdain. Romance also connotes a predisposition toward but not sufficient commitment to desire to become expert, to master the discipline or skill, to want to learn and apply all one can from that area, to commit oneself to a career in a given area. Rather, curiosity, subconscious predispositions, excitement, wonder contribute to shaping learning and performance.

At KWC, Exploration allows potential teacher candidates opportunity to explore the profession – its coursework, its teaching elements, its professional commitments, and associated general studies and obligations before selecting teaching as a career.

3.2.2 Precision/Precision

The second stage, Precision, encourages learners to seek "exactness of formulation" (Whitehead 1967, 18). Further, students learn the discipline – its content, methods, practices. Here, a basic mastery of specific knowledge and method particular to the student's selected area of emphasis is gained. Students, moreover, commit, for example, at conscious and subconscious levels, to teaching as a career.

They discipline themselves for high competence. They are becoming aware of what they wish to undertake to grow professionally and personally to become superior teachers. At KWC, precision consists of in-depth studies of learners, learning theory, teaching methodologies, discipline and classroom management, content studies, and additional guided field experiences.

3.2.3 Generalization/Synthesis

The third stage, Generalization, is one of synthesis. Synthesis enriches teaching and learning by drawing from other areas of knowledge and human experience and by applying one's own knowledge to wider areas of experience. Synthesis implies a creative 'putting together' of knowledge and skills, creating idiosyncratic pedagogy, professional commitment, performance, style.

At KWC, Synthesis helps students to connect previous learning – especially to the Precision stage – as they complete student teaching; create and present a summative portfolio; and, finally, establish an exit professional development plan helping them think through professional teacher roles in schools, communities, families, community service, the conditional or probationary employment year – indeed, those activities, events, and processes that encourage learning and teaching in large contexts.

Now, within each of these stages, the cycle will repeat in a smaller or more specific manner as students introduce themselves to specific areas, challenges, experiences, knowledge domains, and opportunities: They become again curious, choose to commit, and later seek to apply what they have gained to other areas of their lives – in and out of classrooms. "Education should consist in a continual repetition of [...] cycles" (Whitehead 1967, 18) comprised of the three stages, namely, romance, precision, and generalization.

In our program, our Teacher Education Program, referring to Lubbock's (1999) example of the 'Jewel Net of Indra', we see that each stage itself consists of a cycle comprised of all three stages, each forming a cycle. In this view, education is always a 'becoming' enterprise. Longer periods in the cycle form "starting-grounds for fresh cycles" where the process begins anew. Each stage is distinct, yet all cycles are included in any distinct stage.

At any stage, students will discover they explore once again; they search for more in-depth, useful knowledge; they apply what they know and who they are to deeper and richer circles within classrooms, schools, and external communities. Whitehead described the three stages cycle repeatedly, "each in itself a threefold cycle, running its course each day, each week, and each term" (Whitehead 1967, 38).

In coursework, for example, a student in an exploratory course will progress through exploration, precision, and synthesis related to that course content. The student expresses this progress in tentative grasp, tentative mastery, tentative enlarging vision of subject, self, profession. Though self-contained, this cyclical process points beyond that particu lar course to subsequent courses and experiences. In this light, students do not see an individual course as distinct or disconnected or the final examination on the subject.

3.3 An Appraisal

As a small department, we enjoy the advantage of being able to coordinate instruction and experiences, not only in terms of the catalog, but in terms of day-to-day learning goals. In our experience, that communication and cooperation among departmental faculty and students remains essential. Coordinated learning opportunities allow students to experience and reflect on ways to learn and to apply and to develop. They discover that their teachers live these cycles, too – an important identifying and communalizing of learning to live and living to learn that will enhance students' future professional relationships. Students receive in-the-field professional and professorial guidance in creating and refining a professional development plan to remediate limitations. Frequent student and advisor review of the plan remains essential to this element.

3.4 Stages: Unit-Creation Oriented

At KWC, student learning, both theoretical and procedural, is accomplished by means of unit creation. We cannot overemphasize the importance of creating, exploring, and searching for broader syntheses of interdisciplinary, thematic units. Units exemplify connected and applied knowledge, knowing and doing and expanding. Unit construction, field experiecne, and microteaching form the centerpiece of all methods courses. Transmission of disconnected bits of knowledge later recited through some typical examination is discouraged. The goal of instruction is student engagement in higher-level thinking demonstrated through analysis, synthesis, and evaluation.

National standards as expressed by learned societies, Kentucky state core content, and new-teacher performance standards as articulated by the Commonwealth provide guidance in defining content students are expected to master. Student ownership of the concept of the cyclic nature of education helps to ensure ever-increasing growth in this content, growth that will continue, we hope, long after they leave the College. It also contributes to students developing a perspective of life as dynamic, interconnected, all entities interdependent on each other for respect, knowledge, growth, health, wisdom.

As you likely already detected, we deem it important that college professors also accept the *Framework* as a way of approaching their own ongoing engagement in professional development and maintaining currency in theory, methodology, content, and service.

4. Three Levels

We propose three levels of application of Whitehead's philosophy that teacher educators may embrace profitably. Let us now turn our attention to these: Programmatic Pre-Professional, Personal Professional, and Leader Professional.

4.1 Programmatic Pre-Professional

In KWC's Education Department this stage includes the fullest application of the three-stage cycle – exploration, precision, synthesis – to the curriculum. This application applies to units within individual courses, to individual courses, and to course sequencing.

4.2 Personal Professional

The second level, we term the 'personal professional'. At this level, we expect students to achieve all outcomes listed above and pre-service teachers to possess a good, useful grasp of programmatic implications of Whitehead's thought concerning education. We deem essential that students understand and apply Whitehead education philosophy programmatically. Since the *personal professional* by definition implies a personal base or core from which *something more* may emerge, we doubt whether students can achieve this development of Whitehead thought without the programmatic base: Our anecdotal evidence confirms this doubt. Addition of aspects of Whitehead as outlined below as a *personal educational outlook* as opposed to knowing and practicing Whiteheadian educational theory in exclusively programmatic terms opens new vistas to thoughtful students.

In this personal professional perspective, pre-service – as well as in-service – teachers endeavor to examine the educational process of their own students from dual perspective under which their own education was directed and from under which they now direct their continuing education, theoretical and practical. These teachers will employ an unapologetic, determined, passionate, and purpose-directed, perhaps constructivist approach, to learning (Brooks 1999). Although the term *constructivism* as currently used employed was, no doubt, foreign to Whitehead, we consider it difficult to imagine how any contemporary approach to education based upon Whitehead could be severed realistically from constructivism. What we now term constructivist psychology inheres in Whitehead's process view of education. In many ways, Whitehead appears prophetic. Few persons will doubt that Whitehead's process philosophy anticipates the major themes of constructivist psychology, as evidenced by the brief examination of Whitehead's terminology above. Dominance of meaning; criticism of the discrete, useless, and disconnected knowledge; enthronement of active processing – all these elements surely anticipate the psychology of meaning and active learning. This system, now strongly suggested by brain research (Caine & Caine 1999; Sylwester 1995) and introduced long after publication of Whitehead's essays on education in *Aims,* presents itself with an uncanny connection to a philosopher who dates from Victorian days.

Certainly, Whitehead's approach would be friendly to the idea of discovery learning (Ellis 2002, 177-215). Yet, this congeniality does not in any sense, predict enslavement to discovery. When the teachable moment is obvious and the need present, why would a teacher hesitate to 'tell' if such 'telling' renders learning natural and efficient? Everything cannot and need not be discovered. In fact, such learning, especially in view of Gardner's comments on authenticity of apprenticeship (Gardner 1993) may well be called for. In mentoring the apprentice, the master demonstrates, guides, and undoubtedly tells. The test of appropriateness for the teacher is usefulness. Can this be 'thrown into fresh combinations'? 'Living knowledge' is the prize that which 'inert' and useless results in a collection of 'dead' facts, hardly a usable living knowledge base. Where is the romance? The precision? The generalization?

Teachers adopting such an approach would be compelled to encourage the same reflective stance to which *their* teacher educators guided them to formulate and embrace learning and teaching. Teachers would encourage process reflection in students under their care by employing many resources. Young children could learn to reflect on learning experiences through discussion groups such as literature circles (Hennings 2000, 137-140). Reflection might be encouraged in cooperative learning groups employing a jigsaw model (Aronson 1978). Reflection may occur through art. A literature-based classroom offers an ideal environment for such reflection to occur (Hennings 2000, 41-43).

Certainly many of the above reflection venues may be inappropriate for older children. At middle- and secondary-grade levels, cognitive processing may sound a more abstract note. With maturity, cognitive processes tend to become more formal and symbolic. Especially at this level, exploration and application of moral dilemmas as a method of expanding students' ethical reflection becomes a useful tool.

The point? We need to recognize the *nature* of education and encourage its *natural* progression. The cyclic process of exploration, precision, and synthesis informs teachers in designing curriculum as well as in adopting appropriate pedagogical approaches. What teachers had been guided by, those teachers now extend in dealing, in turn, with their students.

4.3 The Leader Professional Level

The third and final level of philosophically informed leadership suggested for teacher educators and their students we term the *leader professional level*. At this level, we refer to that larger philosophical scaffold offered by Whitehead, adoptable and adaptable by students who have mastered the two previous levels and applicable in such fashion as to expand and deepen their philosophical coherence informing *all* their thinking and behavior – indeed, providing an axiological, cosmological, and ontological process context in which to live and to understand themselves and their world and to mentor other professionals in teaching and other fields..

4.3.1 Questions, Considerations

If, primarily, we educate undergraduates, why should this level concern us? Students need not achieve this level to graduate from college or from graduate school. Students and teachers do not need to adopt this level to achieve career or personal success and happiness. The fact is that Whitehead's description of the educational process roots in a much larger understanding of reality. For better or worse, we have attempted to describe this cosmology in 'teacher-friendly' terms. Whitehead offers us at once both an appealing system, one apparently and compellingly requiring a 'yes', and a system full of complexity. Doubtless, life is richer if we understand at least some of the philosophical moorings supporting the edifice we describe here. Moreover, by introducing this level, we help students to think beyond improvised eclecticism and technocrat perspectives.

4.3.2 Process and Optimism

By introducing and preparing students for this third level, we may help them – as they mature in career and life – appreciate and appropriate the process perspective at progressively richer plateaus. Whitehead extends a view of the cosmos – of ultimate reality – that calls for fearless recognition (perhaps acceptance?) of process as a way of learning, understanding, believing, behaving – which otherwise can appear capricious, purposeless, amoral, unreasonable.

Process also calls us to a certain optimism concerning humanity; a direction, a "becoming," if you will, in which, like it or not, we all play – independently and interdependently essential roles. In process philosophy, creativity pilots the ship on which we all, passengers, travel. We are moving onward. We are all a part of the ensemble (Lubbock 1999) playing a tune we might title 'reality'. We may believe in an inherent rightness of it all, about the part each of us plays, even about the perfectibility of humanity and of the universe.

For educators, this perspective implies a child-centered, youth-centered, adult-centered outlook that refuses to embrace the despair that seems to fill our world. (Note: As we write – summer, 2004 – the world appears to be sinking deeply into the quagmire of retaliation, revenge, violence, and hatred.) Process philosophy calls all, no doubt, to nurture, to learn, to love. How can such optimism fail to influence all we do as educators? We think it difficult to imagine such a view, if truly held, not contributing to a general enthusiasm for life, productive commitment to the educator's mission, to advocacy for the child, to conviction that education should function to promote the common good, justice, and progress.

4.3.3 Life Journey

Initially, one may think what presumption to believe any teacher educator would adopt entirely a view such as that offered by White-head. First, the system he describes is complex even as it simply appeals. Second, in view of this paradox, the effectiveness of our attempt to describe the role of Whitehead's philosophy in constructing an effective teacher education program surely must fall short. Third, a philosophical system such as Whitehead's does not distill easily. Fourth, as one principal goal of this essay, we sought to offer teachers and future teachers a succinct summary of Whitehead relatively free of philosophical jargon; however, technical terms persisted.

Even, however, to aspire to achieve these objectives requires an honest attempt to understand and, ultimately, to point beyond rudimentary processing resulting in rudimentary knowledge and rudimentary comprehension – indeed, to signal Whitehead's invitation to journey toward a process understanding of our lives, our cosmos, and ultimate reality. Some educators will embark on this journey; fewer will travel this road sufficiently to attain meaningful tentative synthesis (after all, *what* ultimately, Whitehead calls for) that will result in a worldview offering consistency, coherence, adequacy, truthfulness about reality, and guidance.

A professional leadership application of Whitehead does not imply religious zeal or ardor of a 'true believer'. If anything, Whitehead points us away from such an absolute 'either/or'. To own this view is to accept lack of finality, welcome tentativeness, and embrace inclination toward becoming. Indeed, is this not the essence of it all? How many will enter this journey? Though difficult to say, let us remember, this journey we all travel by degrees.

4.3.4 An Occasional yet Persistent Problem

In attempting to introduce this third Whiteheadian way, that of the philosophically informed leader professional, we may encounter a challenge threatening to levels, cycles, and other opportunities inherent in Whitehead's application to education. Although we have discovered that students readily embrace Whitehead's concept of the rhythm of education, when they hear that Whitehead might provide a philosophical soil (specifically, the third level) in which students might root their thinking about education, their thinking about their lives beyond learning and teaching, a thinking ultimately connected to a larger view concerning the nature of things, an occasional student may become frightened at that deeper peering into Whitehead. Whitehead challenges our *ad hoc* or conventional ways of thinking and acting.

This phenomenon became apparent when one of us was collaborating with a student in creating promotional material for our Teacher Education department. During the project, the student encountered the word 'process'. Of course, she had met the word many times before. On this particular occasion, she asked for a definition of the term. When this student heard the Whiteheadian definition, she associated this term (correctly) with process theology. At that point, the student clearly remarked that she "had no use" for Whitehead's philosophy. In fact, she wanted nothing to do with it. Aha! A challenging 'teachable moment'! Seriously though, this almost 'knee jerk' reaction can render more difficult effective transmission of Whitehead's perspective.

5. Whitehead and Education: Additional Considerations

At least two topics dominant in teaching today deserve special attention: Constructivism and literacy education.

5.1 Whitehead and Constructivism

As mentioned, we return to constructivism. Constructivism can benefit from process philosophy. Whitehead presents us an epistemology both appealing and shocking. On the practical level, Whitehead is at home in modern education – or would be if he were not sitting on the front or back porches, overlooked and neglected! Educational psychology, educational philosophy, and teacher education program organization need the metaphysical applications Whitehead provides. Apparently, Whitehead's entire idea of process, – ever becomingness and progress – fits comfortably with constructivism. Whitehead can provide the philosophical base from which constructivism can emerge more effectively. Here we see science, empirical science, deeply rooted in a metaphysical view that denies modernity and its dependence on positivism.

In this constructivist framework, learners are always constructing reality: Making tentative judgments concerning the nature of things. The well-known Piagetian concepts of assimilations and accommodations imply ever-expanding reality. We see a certain undeniable recognition of the role of tentativeness in constructivism. In fact, such tentativeness we encourage, even celebrate! Our knowledge of the world is never carved in stone. It always changes, moves, becomes. Current teacher education needs the overall philosophical, ethical, organizational coherence Whitehead offers.

This Whitehead paradigm flourishes in many research areas and knowledge domains. Certainly, it is brain-research friendly (Jensen 1998). It fits well into developmental psychology. Since our program at Kentucky Wesleyan College deeply roots in constructivism, the Whitehead connection is 'natural'. As spelled out in KWC's Teacher Education program, usually students eagerly embrace Whitehead as the guru for educational practice and theory. Still, if a student desires to dig deeper, he or she may encounter a philosophy so foreign to conventional wisdom that he or she feels compelled to reject it. Apparently, Whitehead strikes deeply at what remaining certitude our postmodern world retains.

5.2 Example: Literacy Education

Consumers of educational theory, philosophy, and psychology rarely take much stock of the moorings forming the foundations upon which these enterprises may rest. Educators often form eclectic philosophies with scant attention to internal consistency, coherence, adequacy, etc.

Please note again the need for a comprehensive educational philosophy such as Whitehead's.

Consider, for example, literacy theories. The whole language approach (Goodman 1986), which gained wide acceptance in English-speaking countries in the 1970's 80's, and 90's, exemplifies these shortcomings. This approach is rooted firmly, wittingly or unwittingly, in a postmodern epistemology (Alexander 2000). Of course, it would verge on ridiculous to claim that literacy educators actually sat down with postmodernist writings (for overview see: Rosenau 1992)) and planned ways to include postmodernism in literacy instruction. We believe, however, that a postmodern outlook has reigned in the academy in such unchallenged fashion that it became simply a foregone conclusion that literacy theory would be influenced decisively by the subjectivity and relativity that comprise postmodernism. Moreover, Rosenblatt's views of transactional theory of text construction (Rosenblatt 1996), and the creation of whole language theory firmly rooted in individual text construction seems almost necessary, inevitable.

Yet most educators certainly do not, and at the time did not, think they are practicing a literacy approach deeply indebted to postmodernism. Being eclectic and influenced by the cultural climate in which they found themselves, literacy experts simply created a theory that might explain how children construct literacy.

5.3 Example: Postmodernist Pedagogy

Postmodernism deeply influences and shapes educators, although they may not be aware of it. Educators are subject to their own 'hidden curriculum'. Yet, when postmodernist tenets are articulated, educators, like many people, tend to protest those philosophical tenets. Our experience indicates undergraduate students react similarly to first encounters with novel ideas. When Whitehead's notion of process is 'thrown into the mix', students occasionally may react warily. At programmatic and personal levels, students readily accept Whitehead. Advancement beyond the leader professional level, however, may not be realistic for many undergraduate teacher education students. In view of this observation, we offer undergraduates 'Whitehead Lite'. 'Whitehead Lite' works well; students accept 'Lite' readily; students and faculty appreciate its outcomes. Our 'Lite'? – provide the first two levels – Programmatic Pre-professional and Personal Professional; add to both levels romance, precision, and generalization cycles. And stir! These elements certainly provide a recipe that will improve teacher education in ways we have referred to already.

As indicated earlier, it may be unusual to encounter students sufficiently curious to dig more deeply. In short, to arrive at the third level of application and utilization of Whitehead requires a sophistication and suspension of judgment born of maturity. On one hand, Whitehead is infinitely practical and down-to-earth. On the other, Whitehead is complex and requires much effort on the student's part to understand. Not many undergraduates willingly may invest the time and effort to discover deep meaning in Whitehead's offer of a new way of thinking systematically about their lives. For most students, programmatic pre-professional and personal professional levels – become the levels with which students will identify themselves.

We do not imply that it is without merit to 'push the edges' of student's comfort zones to discover deeper meaning in Whitehead's approach. We, however, do not demand conversion! After all, few of us are 'pure' devotees to any school of thought. We are not pure Whiteheadians. We are not purely proponents of whole language or skills instruction. Most of us are, as acknowledged earlier, eclectic. Students must learn to think outside their boxes. We help students catch glimpses of the third level through making the most of teachable moments (Stewart 1993). We directly teach and require accountability of Whitehead's thought as set forth in the conceptual framework. We encourage students to move to the second level. We hope we probe the third level sufficiently with our students so that they may grasp what it would mean to apply and think in terms of the *Conceptual Framework*; always constructing an unfinished, ever-changing knowledge of the world.

How far can we take it? That question is answered by the teacher educator's knowledge and conviction, the nature of the teachable moment, and the student's interest. Certainly, to explore such larger questions belongs in our mission as a liberal arts college. As teacher educators, our task is to assist students in constructing their own educational philosophy, to teach them to grow constantly, and to urge them to remain accountable to that philosophy or, if inadequate, to change it.

6. Summary

In our essay, we investigated A. N. Whitehead's philosophy and how a liberal arts college department of teacher education employed his philosophy as its *Conceptual Framework*. This foundation has proven highly useful and productive in directing the department's program and achieving its outcomes. Also, this long-term commitment to Whiteheadian thought as a guide in creating and implementing our foundational and guiding documents has proven highly productive. It has provided a way for students and teacher educators to think about education, to actualize that thinking in behaviors, and occasionally to apply that thinking to life's larger realms. For more than a decade, it has undergone accrediting agencies' scrutiny and been accepted by the College and school districts employing its students.

The question of how, when, or even if, our Department of Teacher Education might adopt a more inclusive Whiteheadian perspective remains open. In this essay, we described Whitehead's programmatic level and sketched two additional levels – personal professional and leader professional – dependent on the programmatic. We believe Whitehead's thought possesses wide implications and merits consideration in teacher education circles.

Bibliography

Alexander, J. (2000): Reading and postmodernism. *Balanced Reading Instruction* 7, 1, 15-24.

Aronson, E. (1978): *The Jigsaw Classroom*. Beverly Hills: Sage.

Brooks, J. G. (1999): *In Search of Understanding: The Case for Constructivist Classrooms*. Alexandria, VA: Association for Supervision and Curriculum Development.

Bruner, J.S. (1990): *Acts of Meaning*. Cambridge: Harvard University Press.

Caine, R. N. & Caine, G. (1994): *Making Connections: Teaching and the Human Brain*. New York: Addison Wesley.

Darrell, R. (1976): Theory of Curriculum Organization for American Undergraduate Education Leading to Baccalaureate Degrees. Ph.D. Dissertation. Nashville: Peabody College for Teachers.

Ellis, A. K. (2002): *Teaching and Learning: Elementary Social Studies*. Boston: Allyn and Bacon.

Gardner, H. (1993): *Multiple Intelligences: The Theory in Practice*. New York: Basic Books.

Goodman, K. S. (1986): *What's Whole in Whole Language?* Portsmouth, NH: Heinemann.

Hennings, D. G. (2000): *Communication in Action: Teaching Literature Based Language Arts.* Boston: Houghton Mifflin[7].

Jensen, E. (1998): *Teaching with the Brain in Mind.* Alexandria, VA: Association for Supervision and Curriculum Development.

Kentucky Wesleyan College Department of Teacher Education (n.d.): URL: http://www.kwc.edu/academic/educ/ (access: July 6, 2004).

Lubbock, R. (1999): Alfred North Whitehead: Philosopher for the Muddleheaded. URL: http://www3.sympatico.ca/rlubbock/ANW.html (access: July 6, 2004).

Rosenau, P. M. (1992): *Postmodernism and the Social Sciences: Insights, Inroads, and Intrusions.* Princeton, NJ: Princeton University Press.

Rosenblatt, L. M. (1996): *Literature as Exploration.* New York: Modern Language Association[5].

Sherburne, D. W. (1981): *A Key to Whitehead's Process and Reality.* (Reprint Edition) Chicago: University of Chicago Press.

Stewart, D. L. (1993): *Creating the Teachable Moment.* Blue Ridge Summit, VA: TAB Books.

Sylwester, R. (1995): A celebration of neurons: An educators guide to the human brain. Alexandria, VA: Association for Supervision and Curriculum Development.

Whitehead, A. N. (1971/1926): *Religion in the Making.* New York: World Publishing Company.

Whitehead, A.N. (1978/1929): *Process and Reality.* (Corrected Edition) New York: Macmillan.

Whitehead, A.N. (1967/1929): The *Aims of Education and other Essays.* New York: Macmillan.

Whitehead, A.N. (1958/1938): *Modes of Thought.* New York: Capricorn Books.

Appendix:

Conceptual Framework for Teacher Education at Wesleyan College, Department of Teacher Education, Kentucky

The conceptual framework for the Teacher Education Department at Kentucky Wesleyan College is derived from the philosophical writings of Alfred North Whitehead. Many of Whitehead's ideas concerning education are found in his collection of essays first published in 1929 as The Aims of Education and Other Essays. This short paper presents an overview of Whitehead's ideas and how they are utilized in our conceptual framework.

By the term conceptual framework, we are referring to a blueprint for how we view the educational process in the Teacher Education Department at

KWC. This framework guides our program in terms of what classes are taken and at what point in a student's program he or she enrolls in various courses, the three gates (admission to the program, admission to student teaching, and the exit presentation after student teaching), and what we expect of our students at any given point in the program. All Teacher Education students should be familiar with this framework and its terminology. Students are expected to accept accountability for demonstrating an understanding of the framework.

Whitehead's main notion is that "students are alive and the purpose of education is to stimulate and guide their self-development." He continues, "It follows from this premise that the teachers should also be alive with living thoughts. [... This] is a protest against dead knowledge, that is to say, against inert knowledge."

Whitehead defines inert ideas as "ideas that are merely received into the mind without being utilized, or tested, or thrown into fresh combinations." Education, for Whitehead is "the art of the utilization of knowledge." Education with inert ideas is useless and even "harmful". Education is not "the passive reception of disconnected ideas." Education must be useful or it is worthless. According to Whitehead, "unless [knowledge] fits into a connected curriculum [...] there is no reason to teach it."

At KWC, we attempt to put this notion into practice by having students constantly apply knowledge to actual experience in field and clinical settings, through opportunities to write and create in such a way that knowledge is used and applied, and by reflecting and improving upon a professional development plan to remediate weaknesses. We do not believe in discrete, disconnected bits of knowledge for the sake of passing a test. We are interested in all students attaining higher levels of cognitive processing involving analysis, synthesis and evaluation.

At the heart of our conceptual framework is Whitehead's concept of "the rhythm of education." He speaks of education being composed of cycles each comprised of stages. These cycles are manifested in "cyclic reoccurrences [....] as we pass from cycle to cycle [...] the subordinate stages are reproduced in each cycle."

Each cycle is comprised of three stages: The stage of romance which "is the stage of first apprehension"; the stage of precision, where the learner aims toward "exactness of formulation"; and the stage of generalization, which is a stage of synthesis. "Education should consist in a continual repetition of [...] cycles" comprised of the three stages, namely, romance, precision, and generalization. At KWC, we have entitled the stages exploration (romance), precision, and synthesis (generalization). All learning is a minor version of the complete cycle, including all three stages, and "longer periods form starting-grounds for fresh cycles."

During the exploration stage, pre-service teachers at KWC explore the field of education as well as general studies to see if education is indeed the field they want to pursue in their college studies. They also explore learners, learning theory, and participate in field experience. During the precision stage, students engage in in-depth studies of learners, learning, classroom management, teaching methodologies, content area studies, and gain additional field experience. In the final stage, synthesis, students have the opportunity to "put it all together" through student teaching, additional on-going assessment and seminar experience. At any stage, they may find that they are once again explorers or in search of more in-depth knowledge.

Although each stage is always present in each learning experience "there is an alteration of dominance". Sometimes we are more definitely in the exploration stage and sometimes more in the synthesis stage. If we represent a given cycle by one circle, containing all three stages of the cycle, we might get a picture of how this operates:

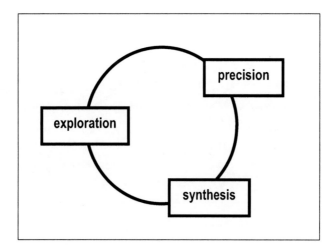

Now imagine each stage (exploration, precision, synthesis) as a cycle unto itself but at the same time containing all three stages progressing always onward to the next cycle. Then we end up with something like this:

In this example, each cycle is made up of the three stages and synthesis in one stage leads on to exploration in another stage. The long arrow demonstrates that this is an ever-continuing process. As Whitehead has stated, the three stages occur again and again "each in itself a threefold cycle, running its course each day, each week, and each term."

This conceptual framework is consistent with the overall mission of KWC as a liberal arts institution dedicated to constantly developing the whole person and preparing them for service and lifelong learning. It seeks to coordinate and integrate knowledge resulting in Teacher Education candidates becoming servant leaders in the school, community and the profession. It provides a coherent system to guide instruction, practical experience and assessment for KWC's Teacher Education Department. It is a framework not only for students, but also for the faculty whose aim is to be reflective practitioners interested in their own professional development. It is comprehensive and provides guidance for growth for both students and faculty.

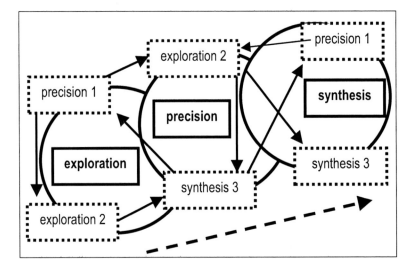

This framework provides guidance in several areas essential to education. It is a way to explore and continually value the diversity which exists among peoples and to reflect on personal commitment to valuing and embracing diversity. It reminds us that there is always more to learn about the human family. It encourages exploration of new instructional methods and technologies. As we gain proficiency with technology and methods, we find a starting place to learn more and apply what we learn. It is compatible with state and national standards encouraging on-going assessment.

It is important that the education students at KWC become familiar with this conceptual framework. Familiarity with the concepts it embodies will aid students in constructing knowledge concerning pedagogy, learner characteristics, and content knowledge during their time at Kentucky Wesleyan and in the years following their time here.

Prophetic Visions for Professional Teachers: A Whiteheadian Perspective on Designing University Courses

Robert Regnier

Abstract

Besides learning transmitted content, university students develop learning patterns through pedagogical processes designed into the structure of courses. When these courses are shaped within the assumptions of epistemologies and ontologies that only afford narrow learning patterns, they can reinforce processes that eschew learning as processes discernment and valuing. However, university courses can be conceptualized within assumptions that students should experience the freedom to respond to the lure for learning and that students ought to foster the discernment and valuation of importance that makes freedom possible. This paper provides an examination of two Whiteheadian notions upon which the pursuit of truth can become the lure for learning, and it illustrates how these notions can be the bases for liberating pedagogical processes. To do so, it conceptualizes learning as event processes through analysis of Whitehead's concept of event, and it examines learning as achieving strength of beauty in which contrasts are reconciled in patterns through harmonizing contrasts in the subjectivities of students. Through these concepts, the paper illustrates how university courses can be designed as learning events in which students create prophetic visions as a means of achieving strength of beauty.

1. Introduction

University students learn through pedagogical processes designed into the structure of courses. Because the hidden curriculum of these learning processes shape student practices while they convey content, one of my efforts is to design university courses with pedagogical processes that broaden student perspectives from narrow-gauged learning patterns. This effort takes into account Whitehead's educational commandments "do not teach too many subjects" and "what you teach, teach thoroughly" (Whitehead 1949, 14). My central pedagogical strategy follows Whitehead's idea of having students inquire into a single idea illuminated with "the spark of vitality" (Whitehead 1949, 14) to ensure that learning does not degenerate into "the passive reception of disconnected ideas" (Whitehead 1949, 14).

One of these course designs discussed here is intended to facilitate student discernment and selection of importance as a lure of freedom from one learning event into the next. Such discernment and selection separates considering importance and what one is interested in from what may be fascinating but trivial. To facilitate such constant valuation in some of my courses, I introduce to my undergraduate students in teacher education programs and to graduate master of education students the course project of having each student formulate a "prophetic" vision of teaching or learning which they could be committed. This prophetic visioning combines speculation about what the world should be with practical considerations about what it actually can be. To facilitate this project, each course is designed with the single prescriptive core assignment of having each student identify, propose, and research a policy proposal in which each advocates for educational development or change in relation to a social, cultural, economic, or political issue.

The course is designed to support each student's appropriation of their most fertile prophetic intuitions, to assist students critically assess and revise these intuitions to reflect what is of most enduring value in them, and to formulate these intuitions into compelling and defensible resolutions that address educational issues in a public manner. The central pedagogical feature designed to facilitate student hypothesis, criticisms, and revision of their initial ideal aims into compelling and defensible arguments demanded by this core assignment consists of three interrelated, learning events. These events consist of having each student consecutively prepare, present, and revise a Concept Paper, a Proposal Paper, and then an Advocacy Paper in the fifth, eighth, and twelfth weeks of a thirteen week course. This design has students identify and engage their own aesthetically-based intuitions of value, discern and select the most desirable of ideals from these values that they could advocate publicly, reconcile varieties of diversity and complexity that broaden and deepen their consideration notion of value, and provide a structure for advancing the organic evolution of their thinking.

This paper is constructed in two major parts. In the first part, I review the relation of four ideas from the work of A. N Whitehead to learning, and in the second part I review the pragmatics of a course structure that I have designed. The purpose of the first part is to demonstrate how the work of A. N Whitehead provides a broad conceptual framework for discussing the course design in part two. In part one, therefore, I draw upon Whitehead's notions of 'event', 'strength of beauty', 'importance', and 'creativity'. I construct the idea of learning as an event or learning event from Whitehead's notion of event. This idea serves as the primary concept of learning throughout my work and through which I explain the three focal learning experiences in the course. From Whitehead's notion of strength of beauty, I propose learning as strength of beauty to characterize learning achievement as the reconciliation of diversity in a harmony characteristic of prophetic visioning. I then analyze how importance is the lure for learning to show how the course is designed for students to discern and select what is important or most worthwhile to them in the assignment. Finally, I discuss how Whitehead's notion of creativity is a form of pursuing of the greatest good, the purpose at the base of the course's design. Following the general introduction to the course design in part two, this paper examines each of the three interrelated focal learning events of the course, then explains how the structure of the proposal and final advocacy paper facilitates student preparation of a compelling and defensible argument in the course that addresses recognition of diversity.

2. University Courses and Learning as Events

Because the greatest of learning possibilities reside in the creative subjectivity of each student, development of creative subjectivity is the achievement in which university instructors should be most interested. Many approaches to education have limited perspectives on human subjectivity and offer limited frameworks for university instructors to design pedagogies that seek morally perceptive and creative achievement in student learning. A. N. Whitehead's process ontology, however, offers a framework for conceptualizing learning as strength of beauty in shaping the self-creating, subjective character of students. Within Whitehead's ontology, achievement occurs as events of self-creative prehending, concrescence, and satisfaction. Each event is constituted by other events, the continuous interrelation of which constitutes the fabric of the world.

Within this ontology, learning as event consists of: 1) positive and negative prehending or valuation and gathering which includes and excludes influences and relations; 2) the concrescening or crystalization of influences and relations into defining patterns of individuality; and 3) completion or satisfaction which projects beyond itself. Within Whitehead's ontology, therefore, learning events can be conceptualized as subjectivities of discerning importance, of valuations which select and exclude. Each learning event is constituted by and emerges as the interrelation of events, including micro-learning events. Each learning event constitutes the subjectivity of learning and makes the progressive continuity of learning possible just as subatomic energies constitute atomic relations and shape the fabric of the world.

Learning micro-events occur in the smallest of possible units as students experience physical feelings, conceptual feelings, propositional feelings, and intellectual feelings through reading, listening, analyzing, and conversing. Learning occurs in the spontaneity and construction of university class events including story telling, jigsaw reading, collective improvisation, lecturing, and discussions to the extent that each is a self-creative of prehending, concrescence, and satisfaction in the creation of some novel value. Even whole courses can be learning events comprised as prehending, concrescing, and satisfaction durations constituting new value.

Just as each learning event is constituted by its specific history of relations that constitute it, each student *has* a perspective and *is* a perspective defined by the particular history of relationships which shape the vector forces orienting them into the future. The ultimate task of education is to inspire students into considering possibilities that enrich their perspectives and support wise decisions about how to proceed in their learning. Learning events, as processes of selecting, crystalizing, and projecting diverse influences and relations have the paradoxical potential of broadening student perspectives while channeling their attentiveness on what is important. They broaden student perspectives by engaging them in diverse experiential and theoretical contrasts, and they channel attentiveness by reconciling emerging patterns of relations in relation to ideal possibilities. University courses can be designed on the assumption that learning occurs as events and at least some learning events can be shaped and designed intentionally. The course design discussed below assumes that learning occurs as events and that particular learning events can be part of more encompassing learning events designed to assist students propose compelling and defensible resolutions.

3. Learning as Strength of Beauty: Perfecting Harmonies

> [H]armony is always an achievement, never something given. Harmony comes about as the result of a process of concrescence, a process in which the differences initially experienced in our encounter with a diverse world must be reconciled if our experience is to make sense and if our character as an enduring self-same entity is to be affirmed (Allan 1998, 91).

Harmony depends on the immanent relationality and interconnectedness of events through which prehending sustains differences of contrast while relating contrasts to one another in patterns. In a painting, for example, the harmony of patterned relationships created by artists on a canvas depends upon the possibility of relationships among color, of paint on canvas, of the artist with the paint brush, etc. Harmony in the world is this continuous interconnecting of differences in diversity which coheres diverse relations and entities into distinctive patterns. This harmony joins divergent influences through discerning selection to constitute the definiteness of realities with their distinct values. Each achievement of learning is a harmony comprised through valuations that combine selected relations into distinct patterns of value. Learners emerge from learning as an achievement of the creative interplay of patterns of feelings, emotions, thoughts, and directions that constitute their subjectivity.

Harmony in learning occurs through the reconciliation of contrasts which sustain and unify difference. Through these contrasts, "parts contribute to the massive feeling of the whole and the whole contributes to the intensity of feelings of the parts" (Whitehead 1969, 324).

Intensified feelings about particular aspects of some phenomenon affect student learning of whole phenomenon. For example, student insight into the meaning of 'limit situation' in Paulo Freire's process of conscientization contributes to understanding his whole pedagogy of the oppressed. The intensification of feelings on particular matters constitutes subjective valuations which create new contrasts and synthetic additions to knowledge and experience transform perceptions and conceptions of theory and reality. Likewise, feelings about the whole changes perceptions of the parts, learning proceeds through continuous reconciliation of contrasts which shape the whole and the parts.

Beauty is not just harmony, however, it is the perfection of harmonies. Such perfection is effected through the congruity of diverse prehensions that concresce with definition into value. Finer definitions of unity, rendered through broader ranges of diversity, require more harmonizing and are more beautiful. With less definition and less diversity, less harmonizing is required and is less beautiful. The same applies to learning. Teachers and students experience harmony among patterns of relations in practices and theories that decode difficult problems with variations of penetrating coherence. Beauty is not just harmony in relations, it is the fineness of achievement of harmony. The more penetrating the disclosure and the broader the scope, the more beautiful the achievement.

Some students achieve value through much more demanding academic initiatives than others by virtue of the complexity and problematic nature of such initiatives. The strength of beauty in these achievements relates to the 'comparative magnitude' of their intensity. Students who offer more elaborated and insightful accounts in position papers, for example, demonstrate strength of beauty in their appreciation of patterned relationships among various contrasts that give rise to conscious discrimination and discernment. This appreciation is distinct, for example, from students who offer less elaborated and discriminating accounts in their work. Such achievements reflect each student's subjectivity. Beauty in learning, conceptualized within a broad liberal notion of education, is this fineness of harmony attained through forms of aesthetically grounded appreciation of truth and moral goodness.

Whitehead defines beauty or the perfection of harmony of subjecttive form in terms of 'strength'. Strength consists of "variety of detail with effective contrast" (Whitehead 1969, 325) and intensity Just as, the different levels of complexity of dives in diving competitions and of figures in figure skating competitions require increasing dexterity and attentiveness or intensity to execute them, learning required to strengthen the capacity of these performers to achieve these levels of execution require patterns of contrasts in learning processes, or intensity, that meets the complexity which their performance demands. Strengthening the beauty in learning, therefore, consists in increasing student capacity to relate diverse notions to various themes and theories while developing insights that increasingly reveal cohering patterns of harmony in increasing complexities of diversity.

Education for strength of beauty in university course designs can enhance the subjective capabilities of students to perfect harmonies. To strengthen student capability to realize this harmony of harmonies requires challenging them with a "sufficient variety of detail with effective contrast" (Whitehead 1969, 325) so that their capacity to engage complexity and ambiguity expands. Teachers attend to complexity by teaching to goals, through pedagogical designs, and with instructions that intensify challenges which make it possible for students to emerge from limited learning structures and processes. University courses, therefore, can be events through which students 'intensify' their comprehension and appreciation of values. This intensification occurs as students discern and appreciate harmony in complex patterns of relations that disclose 'importance'. Achieving intensity is at the heart of learning, and making this intensity possible is at the heart of teaching. Through intensification, increasingly broad ranges and diversities of contrasting feelings, emotions, and thoughts become finely reconciled as self-creating subjectivities. The course design for having students propose prophetic visions as reviewed in part two reviews structure and processes designed to intensify learning and assist students achieve strength of beauty.

4. Importance as the Lure: Concentration as Intensity in Learning

"Morality consists in the control of process so as to maximize importance." (Whitehead 1958, 13)

While theorists and philosophers theorize and speculate about what constitutes the good and the greatest good and can suggest valuable guidelines about what might constitute moral and immoral human conduct under various conditions, and while any person can be influenced by and draw upon this theorizing and philosophizing, moral decision making only occurs in particular lives and in the particular contexts of those who make such decisions. Whitehead's ontology locates morality in particular historical emergences rather than in generalizations and schemes that abstract morality from particular occurrences and events. Morality is not theory about morality. Morality is life presenting itself to itself through itself for discernment those processes which in its broadest conceptualization constitute aim, creativity, and enjoyment. Human control occurs where humans discern and select options that influence and determine in varying degrees how importance is attended to. Morality is not simply control garnered by considering theoretical options. Nor is it just control garnered through openness to the aesthetics of experience expressed bodily as feelings. Rather morality is control garnered through the creativity of discernment that allows oneself to enhance or diminish experiences and influences that maximize importance.

Morality is key to bringing about intensity in learning because it focuses on maximizing importance. The continuous rediscovery of 'importance' is the lure to the self-creation, self-disciplining, and self-projection of learning. "We concentrate by reason of a sense of importance" (Whitehead 1958, 4). When students experience a sense of importance, they acquire an attentiveness that lures them to concentrate on those patterns of relation to which they are lured. This sense of importance, the insistent call through which one feels compelled to attend, excludes that which is not relevant, meaningful, or valuable. This attention and exclusion is evident, for example, in student discernment and selection of topics to research and in research processes that expand and focus inquiry and allows students to focus on emerging patterns of value. The judicious exclusion of focusing on what is important produces the intensification of concentration which allows for learning to evolve.

Concentration, for Whitehead, involves combining a sense of importance with matter-of-fact. In contrast to those empiricist epistemologies which focus solely on detailed analyses of qualities without taking into account the whole, concentration relates the specific to the whole. Concentration, paradoxically, engages the broad and vague. It affords experiences of "large, vague characterization indicative of some form of excitement arising from the particular fact" (Whitehead, 1958, 6). This vague characterization is constituted by the aesthetic experience of the whole and of patterns which open up at the edges of our conceptualizations. Although the tendency in modern course design is often to support learning detail, "we must shake ourselves free of it" (Whitehead, 1958, 8) to "keep our systems open" to "the vague 'beyond,' waiting for penetration" (Whitehead 1958, 8). Instead systemizing detail, learning for importance requires encounters with the particular which signal patterns of interconnectedness and relations within the whole. The course designed for learning as intensification, therefore, requires pedagogies structured to foster sense of importance. The course design reviewed in part two recommends such a design.

5. Prophetic Vision and the Call for a Compelling and Defensible Argument.

> The prophetic voice speaks most directly to issues of justice and righteousness; it is a voice that not only roars in protest at oppression, inequity, poverty, and hunger but cries out in pain and compassion. It is a voice that haunts us because it echoes our own inner voice which speaks to our impulse to nourish and care for others. (Purpel 1989, 81).

The central task in many of my undergraduate and graduate courses in the foundations of education is to have students create prophetic visions of education. These courses provide structures and processes to assist students theorize prophetic ideals in education by having them search for, hypothesize, and defend proposals for educational development to which they could potentially be committed. Through these structures and processes, each student focuses on, searches for, and penetrates a single issue they regard as of the most importance to them. The purpose of having students generate prophetic visions is to challenge them to search for what is most personally meaningful while determining what serves the greatest common good. The challenge to be prophetic, therefore, has each student be critical of perceived injustices and has them forge possibilities for achieving justice. As students begin from their own value experiences to discern importance, they assume authority over and responsibility for the ideals they codify.

Through this development of conscientious imaginations, students transform patterns of valuing in ways that make both their own and public ideals problematic and a lure to further investigation. Such transformation of patterns of value allow for the emergence of personal meaning and moral insight as students codify and analyze their experience.

The practice of hypothesizing what to value and strive for facilitates the organic growth of moral imagination within the aesthetic of student experience and language. This proposing takes up "[t]he moral dialectic between the actual and the possible" where "[i]deals are first perceived in the imagination before being poetically called into existence" (Garrison 1997, 22). By interpreting and calibrating the meaning of ideals in contexts, students create increasingly and purposeful finite expressions of value. When understated, ideals fail to recognize potential. When overstated, they fail to recognize feasibility and ring hollow. The art of theorizing ideals is measured in part through student efforts to select the best of possibilities which can achieve the greatest good in context of a given reality. By articulating ideals, students move beyond critique as a sufficient approach to addressing educational problems and they are challenged to propose creative possibilities.

Student efforts to formulate concise resolutions open pathways of imagination which link private intuitions to public issues. The resolutions are vehicles through which to *advocate* proposals for educational development at public forums such as school board meetings or teacher federation councils. The resolutions, then, become the means through which to transform assessments of need or importance into public artifact. The task of hypothesizing such resolutions has students clarify and express intuitions and convictions about what they consider most important and provides a form of rehearsal which protects one from the effects of actually advocating for an ideal in a public forum and having to live with its consequences.

Student formulation of satisfying resolutions can be very problematic undertakings which require discernment and selection. As new theory and analyses are progressively introduced through course content, and as student intuitions and convictions are held up to public discussion and scrutiny initial notions require revision, rejection, and/or improvement. Just as Socrates sought to determine what constituted his interlocutors' convictions so he could examine them through his elentic discourses, the formulation of resolutions has students articulate beliefs worthy of further examination. As students put their beliefs forward for examination by their peers and the course instructor, it becomes possible for those students to determine whether they are sufficiently committed to them as a means of giving definition to what they consider most valuable. As the course proceeds, new readings, lectures, and discussions bring new frameworks forward for experiencing the meaning and value of their interests, beliefs, and commitments.

To be compelling, resolutions appeal to the moral imagination in a persuasive way. To be convincing, students need to express themselves with clarity of insight and force of conviction which they hone and perfect through the discerning inclusion and exclusion of selected values and analysis. Arguments demonstrate their defensibility when they practically withstand the questioning of their peers and instructor who seek justification, coherence, definition, and consistency. Each engagement or challenge to student perception and analysis introduces new experiences of contrast to attend to and intensifies value experiences which students encounter as they inquire into the validity of their own beliefs and as they attempt to frame them. To helpstudent learning and ideas grow organically, courses are designed through three interlocking learning events designed to have students broaden perspectives, purge contradictions, spell out implications and assumptions, and discriminate among possibilities. Concentration on a single emerging focus through these three assignments supports a penetrating inquiry that intensifies from one learning event to the next.

6. Course Assignment Structure: Three Focal Events

The core course assignment to prepare a prophetic vision essentially builds through three focal events. Students initially develop a three page Concept Paper to select and propose an area of interest and importance to investigate. After in class presentation and peer and instructor review of this paper, students assemble a five page Proposal Paper which hypothesizes a formal resolution they could be interested in advocating publically for and proposes a four part argument to support the resolution. After an in class presentation, and peer and instructor review of this proposal, each student proceeds to research and write a compelling and defensible Advocacy Paper on public policy development in education. The first two assignments provide a basis for the emergence of the final assignment.

The distinctiveness and rigor with which each preceding assignment is completed projects into the work of subsequent assignments. These three events provide an increasingly complex framework for having students intensify their study. As the course progresses through these events, students are moved by their own and peer research, presentations, and criticism. Simultaneously, the assignments have students continuously determine which interests are most worth pursuing and can most feasibly be pursued.

6.1 The Concept Paper

The first section of the course is designed to have students overcome inhibitions or resistance to investigating what they consider worthwhile and inspiring. The assignment to prepare and present a three page Concept Paper to their peers provides students a forum to present tentative insights into an ideal in education or problem they believe is important. It also begins to create a public sphere within which to build student dialogical practice and solidarity through which to assess the value of their ideas. This assignment is deliberately short to give students the opportunity to explore an area of interest and to keep them from over-investing in an inquiry which they are not certain is of primary importance to them. It, nevertheless, provides a substantive and early occasion for students and instructor to express and discuss what may constitute a most worthwhile endeavor. Through this assignment, students begin to express and test the suitability of a topic. Peer and instructor responses provide early formative assessment.

The specific task of preparing a Concept Paper is preceded by various events designed to inspire students to investigate areas of interest, grasp what constitutes issues of public importance, and engage with one another as community. In one of the first course sessions, for example, each student surveys a range of Selected Student Essays written by students in previous sections of this course and kept in the reserve section of the library. Each reviews one essay and presents this review to a group of students with whom they discuss the papers merits. For many students, this occasion is a first time experience to see other student's papers made available in a library and a required reading for a course.

This exercise has them experience the public value of student work and each essay presents a standard of achievement they might aspire to. Just as importantly, this event tacitly shows how their work can be written as part of a democratic citizenship with other students, and it demonstrates moral role responsibility in broader professional and public policy development beyond simply teaching in classrooms or living through a private ethic. Furthermore, this exercise exemplifies how their own moral speculation and analyses of education can have purpose in the intellectual lives of future students. In other course assignments designed to improve learning practices, students teach assigned works to their peers as a means of increasing their own critical reading skill, engage in collaborative story telling to practice narrating significant educational experiences in their lives, engage in collective improvisations to affirm the value of intuitive and imaginative inquiry, and work cooperatively to build a spirit of solidarity in place of competitive individualism.

The preparation of the Concept Paper is an event comprised of several distinct but interrelated events designed to intensify their study. To prepare these papers, students 1) identify areas of interest and importance to research, 2) select and investigate a topic of importance and write their papers, 3) orally present their papers to a group of students in class, 4) receive and engage questions and comments about their papers from peers, 5) provide oral comments on the Concept Paper of some of their peers, 6) make their paper available to one other student in class for written comment, 7) read one other student's paper in class and write comments on it, 8) reread and revise their own paper then submit it to the instructor, 9) receive comments from the instructor, and 10) possibly revise and resubmit their paper to the instructor. These learning events intensify student engagement with their work beyond the simple requirement of writing a paper and submitting it for the instructors comments and grading by providing a range of contrasts through which their work is assessed.

6.2 The Proposal Paper

Once the Concept Paper is assessed and returned, students immediately begin a Proposal Paper in which they propose a resolution and argument for developing educational policy in their final Advocacy Paper. In this paper, students formulate a concisely worded resolution and they hypothesize the 1) problem, 2) context, 3) theory, and 4) practical response elements of a research investigation that could possibly justify the resolution. Most students elaborate and draw upon the insights from their Concept Paper. Others reject their initial paper in favor of another possibility. This proposal which differentiates inquiry into four contrasting sections reconciled in the resolution challenges students to imagine a compelling and defensible account. As students investigate, present, and discuss each part of the paper from the perspective of their initial, ideal aim and naive perceptions, new realities appear and new contrasts affect perceptions of the whole.

The four part design for the assignment has evolved partly from pragmatic concerns about the limitations in student research and writing. Some students find it difficult to move beyond deconstruction to propose ideals or practical responses to problems. Others recommend ideals for and solutions to issues which are not substantially defined or problematized. Some acknowledge problems in broad terms but do not sufficiently define or characterize them. In the absence of context and recognition of need, ideals are too easily regarded as inert abstractions and slogans of goodness applied here and there, external rallying cries to which one might adhere but not live through. Reconciliation of the four sets of contrasts in a resolution excite a creative self-reflexivity that refines proficiencies and through which self-discipline grows.

The challenge of arguing for a resolution is the primary disciplinary vehicle of the course. The resolution, like a zen koan, serves a fixed point that allows students to take up *their* own issues from *their* own perspective. Resolutions focus student attention on a single undertaking so they can plumb matters that most interest them. Compelling resolutions are to the point. They call directly for specific action or development. Vague and ambiguous resolutions are less compelling and more difficult to defend.. The requirement to forge a resolution acknowledges real agendas which students *feel* are important to attend to. It is one thing for students to attend to an ecological issue, for example, because it is written into a course outline or because some professor thinks it is worthwhile. The advocacy dimension implicit in the resolution forestalls preparation of position papers that merely document, prove, or declare some current state of affairs, or that are critical without being visionary. The focus on possibility and action forces students to assess whether their beliefs can be created into ideals that reflect what they value and it requires that students assess the feasibility of the resolution they might advocate. Student valuation and honing of a resolution is a means to cultivate their own moral perceptiveness not simply as an expression of private sentiment to a sympathetic professor but sufficiently valued to be publically advocated for.

6.3 The Advocacy Paper

Once students receive their Proposal Paper with peers and instructor comments, they complete their research for the final Advocacy Paper which they submit to the instructor after presenting it to a small group of students in the second last class of the course. Throughout, its preparation students adjust their perspectives on 1) the problem they see the resolution is a response to, 2) the context in which the problem could be explicated, 3) an ideal which they could theorize as the basis for their response to the problem, and 4) how challenges presented in the problem could be addressed practically through the theory. These four dimensions of the paper are discussed below.

6.3.1 Problematizing an Issue and Grieving Its Consequences

To make an issue problematic means to spell out its characteristics and explicate its grievous effects. The failure of environmental education programs in schools to directly address major environmental predicaments, for example, could be one such issue. Students problematize issues by examining contrasts and connections that disclose such problematic characteristics and by elucidating their consequences. The purpose of problematizing an issue is to provide a compelling case that the problem is not only real and located in the real social, political and/or cultural world but is part of our moral landscape and warrants a response. The task, therefore, is to investigate the grievousness of the problem to which the formulation of a prophetic vision can be responsive. The more penetrating and rich the definition of the problem, the more demanding and exacting are the requirements for an adequate ideal that will provide a sufficient basis for responding to the problem. The more coherent and supported the analyses of the problem, the more defensible the definition.

This task of problematizing an issue is a prophetic task. "Prophets were passionate social critics who applied sacred criteria to human conduct and, when they found violations in these criteria they cried out in anguish and outrage" (Purpel 1989, 80). The process of identifying an issue as important by explaining *why* and *how* it is important is a means for each student to thematize what they value from their perspective. From this thematization, they can dialogue about it with others and relate insights from literature and lectures to them. Disclosure of this perspective makes it possible for students to then critically assess whether their interest or desire is truly worthwhile to investigate more deeply or whether what they had once considered important is in fact trivial and or insufficiently relevant to examine. For example, one, who regards the environmental crisis as an issue and who believes that schools are not sufficiently addressing major environmental issues in society, could produce an account of why and how it is a problem worthy of one's attention. To make a compelling and defensible case that this issue is real and important, a student needs to discern the grievousness of the issue and make this problematization available for dialogue with others.

Learners, however, can problematize in ways that deny their own involvement, focus on the trivial rather than more profound characteristics, and avoid culpability. This denial makes it impossible to act forcefully with a compelling, prophetic vision that arises from our deepest convictions.

> When we deceive ourselves and our community, we undermine our efforts to act on our deepest belief. There is thus in self-deception a genuine subversion of personal agency and, for this reason in turn, a subversion of moral capacity (Finagrette 1968, 141, quoted in Purpel 1989, 63)

Increasing student capacities to envisage and formulate the significant consequences of a problem is a critical part of having them imagine an ideal to which they can be committed, for it is in response to limitations, deficiencies, and failures that high ideals are conceived and through which practical responses proposed. Likewise, interpretation of one's highest aspirations provides a framework for and insight into analysis of problems. The work of problematizing issues, therefore, is part of a hermeneutic which moves between fathoming the problematic nature of a situation and expanding one's moral insight. The more sufficiently and finely students hone a problem, the more they can propose an ideal and practice through which to address it. Formulation of the problem and its differentiation from other parallel problems can be done with varying intensity and magnitude to strengthen the beauty of each student's learning and character. This problematization is one of the four sets of contrasts that strengthen students.

6.3.2 Context: Exploring Interrelations and Causes

Students are challenged in their research to differentiate a *specific* problem from its broader problematic context. Often before students zoom-in on a precise problem to address, they are faced with the task of valuing and selecting one problem from a myriad of possible problems. This task arises from the profusion of relations and perspectives for differentiating problems and contexts in any situation. Distinguishing problems from one another then distinguishing *a* problem from the broader context requires that students identify and distinguish patterns of relationship. Defining lack of 'reverence' for the sacredness of creation in school curricula, for example, is similar to but distinct from defining lack of 'respect' or another apparently similar notion for the sacredness of nature. Furthermore, this lack of reverence may be only one among many perceived related deficiencies in schools. For students to pursue a question with any focus or ability to penetrate the unknown, it is necessary to delimit the quest. These delimitations make it possible to recognize how problems are related to and definable in broader contexts from which to assess their importance. Within what set of problems is this problem located? Why is it more important to address one problem than another?

De-contextualization cuts students off from discerning and pursuing the causes of problems and from seeing the full importance of addressing a problem. While one might, for example, be able to problematize how corporate hegemony causes a deficiency for environmental education in schools, it is not possible to address the problem of this hegemony unless one acknowledges how this hegemony relates to corporate power in society and corporate involvement in the environment. Viewed within the context of corporate involvement in society and the environment, it becomes clear that the importance of reverence as an ideal is more important than just for increasing student motivation in an environmental education program. Its importance extends beyond the school. The problem may reside in the fundamental notions which dominate a whole historic era of cultural relations and political power. Addressing the problem of lack of reverence might require acknowledging how the cause of this problem is embedded in corporate relations to the environment.

While it is one thing to define a deficiency in an approach to environmental education as a problem, for example, it is quite another to clarify how that deficiency persists in spite of several unsuccessful efforts to address it. The recognition of how unsuccessful efforts have failed, for example, further help delimit what exactly must be addressed in order to sufficiently consider the problem. Problems do not exist in vacuums or isolated from the rest of reality. Like other events and entities, they are constituted by the complexity of realities in which they are located. Students need to spell out contexts to clearly identify the elements of problems that need to be more throughly understood and addressed and through which adequate responses can be determined.

6.3.3 Theory and Ideals: Discerning Value

Following the problematization and contextualization of some important and interesting issue in their Advocacy Paper, students propose and justify an ideal from which to respond to the problem. To elaborate the ideal itself, students take up some primary conviction or intuition about 'why' some policy in education ought to be advocated and on what basis the advocacy can be justified. They strive to recommend elements of moral, political, and/or educational theory which can clarify the characteristics of an ideal which offers a basis for responding to the problem. In this process, students hypothesize the most adequate of ideals that will support their discernment and selection of the best of possibilities for action in response to the problem. To respond to some environmental issue in education, for example, students will need to determine what ideal can adequately provide a basis for responding to the problem in that context, and what account or theory provides a compelling and defensible basis for supporting that ideal.

It is this very practice of imagining and theorizing ideals, and selecting the most adequate ideal to respond adequately to some need or calling that teachers and educational researchers experience freedom to be most practically responsive to problems.

> The dialectic between the actual and the possible is the dialectic of freedom. Expanding freedom is as much a creative aesthetic adventure as it is a moral duty. Practical reasoning connects the actual to the possible. Inquiry transforms a needful situation into desired possibility (Garrison 1997, 22).

Even as students criticize the cause and effects of a problem they regard as grievous, they assume some assessment of value and importance which could be the basis for a compelling and defensible argument for addressing the problem. Students hypothesize their ideal by imagining and valuing their best possibility for responding. If a student sees some notion of respect for nature as an ideal which provides a good response to some environmental issue, for example, then that student could explore the possible meanings of respect as the foundation for a response to the problem. The more encompassing the ideal, the more it sorts out complex issues, contrasts, and possibilities. The more it concerns itself with questions about ultimate purpose and meaning, the more visionary the ideal is.

This assignment to formulate ideals is based upon the assumption that educators must create and recreate the precepts which they can intelligently advocate and with which they can defend educational policy and practice. Ideals in this case are not given. Ideals are not generic, stand-alone entities that exist in some independent conceptualization or other worldliness. They are not abstract forms detached from individual efforts to propose and justify them. One can not just take a definition of respect, justice, reverence, or compassion off the shelf, for example, and believe in it. Ideals have internal integrity and meaning as they are symbolically formulated and interpreted from the perspective and in the experience of each student. These ideals consist of creating, projecting, and selecting that which relates the actual to the best of possibilities for determining what constitutes importance. These ideals have the greatest intensity in meaning and can be sustained and maintained if the students who propose them apprehend and can publicly justify them. The achievement of intuiting, hypothesizing, and justifying compelling and defensible ideals transforms the subject who proposes them.

The pedagogical task of facilitating student formulation of ideals begins by creating conditions in which students can take up and express their intuitions about what constitutes their highest aspirations. While the presentation of theories of education and analysis of educational issues in courses provide frameworks through which students can express their intuitions and elaborate their aspirations, student exploration of ideals begin with their feelings about what is, can be, and should be. Pedagogical efforts in the course need to be designed, therefore, to assist students inquire into specific moral and/or political insights which offer some prophetic possibility for responding most adequately to problems they have elaborated. As students investigate some ideal, they become committed to searching for theories and accounts that can clarify their emerging interests. The ideals reflect the insights studied from each student's perspectives and codify their meaning and values. In the absence of this process, students find themselves espousing idealist rhetoric in slogans and tautologies disconnected from personal conviction and commitment. What they learn through processes of proposing ideals is that ideals are not given, they are recreated from occasion to occasion, event to event, and that to flourish in their teaching or research one of their primary tasks is to create and select ideals to strive for.

6.3.4 Resolving the Problem Through Practical Response

For the last part of their Advocacy Paper, students suggest practical responses to the issue they problematized within the context they explicated, and though the ideal they theorized. These practical responses culminate the process of reconciling each of the four parts of the proposal in the claim of the resolution. The resolution proposes policy development or action that makes a difference in the public sphere, and this section of the paper elaborates what that policy or action could be and how it constitutes an effective response to an issue. This response, therefore, takes up student insights into the meaning and importance of the issue as it is problematized and it focuses on the purpose for responding to the problem within the larger context of inter-related issues and possible frameworks.

Most importantly, students can propose practical responses by imagining and interpreting how the ideals they have theorized suggest worthwhile practices, and by presenting accounts of how practices they have discovered reflect the ideals they hypothesize. Students are inspired initially into prophetic visions through experiences which reveal insights about possibilities, realities, and ideals. These direct encounters offer synthetic experiences of variables which constitute ideal practices. The hermeneutic quest in these cases is to explore particular practices to appreciate what these practices accomplish and why they are so meaningful and valuable.

The interpretations of ideals in response to problems constitute a form of what Jim Garrison refers to as "outlaw logic" (Garrison 1997, 171). This logic emerges from experiences and conceptualizations formed through perceptions and intuitions inherent in the vector character of student experience and insight. Rather than consist of deductions from pre-cast categories, this logic comes from synthetic formulations of patterns of variables and relations. Since ideals are constructed from the aesthetic of each student's own value experiences and formulated in a manner unique to their creation, these ideals ground a logic and moral perception outside of standardized categorical meanings. Likewise, because these ideals are created through the projection and selection of possibilities outside dominating social, cultural, and epistemological norms, the *logos* for these ideals is based in the prehension, concrescence, and satisfaction of events through which they are created. The task of interpreting ideals into practice comes consequently from re-experiencing the meaning of the ideal and from imagining what the ideal implies for practice. To be compelling and defensible the practical responses need to illuminate the meaning of the ideal within context and definition of the problem. The achieved strength of beauty produced in the character of students who take up the challenge of attempting to formulate a prophetic vision through this assignment is reflected in the transparency of the problems they formulate, comprehension of the problem context, moral perceptiveness of the ideal, and tacitness with which they generalize the insights of the ideal in a practical response.

7. In Conclusion

University courses can be designed to have students achieve a strength of beauty that increases their scope of analysis and rigor in valuing importance. Such courses can be layered with challenges and experiences that have students learn to read with discernment, write and re-write with vision and logic, share perspectives openly, work collaboratively, and build solidarity. The layering of challenges in such courses is designed as a form of intensification to lure students into actualizing realizable possibilities. The lures of potential and possibility are the *sine qua non* of liberating and liberalizing education that broaden student horizons on the highest of human aspirations. These lures broaden student perspectives beyond their limitations at any point and they extricate students from the limitations of learning routines that reduce memory to memorization, imagination to mere fantasy, cognition to banking ideas, speculation to determining conesquences, and compassion to sentimentality.

In the design of this course, the Concept Paper, the Proposal Paper, and the Advocacy Paper are presented the crucibles of intensity, the refineries of insight into interest and importance that inspire students to prophetic vision. These three focal learning events, comprised of many learning events, constitute the learning event of the course as a whole. Each event broadens student perspectives by introducing new contrasts, and each event has students engage in a quest for importance. The resolution required in the concept and advocacy papers is designed to keep students focused on reconciling the best of possibilities for problematizing and addressing real issues. The four part structure of the papers insists that students address complexity. By designing these courses as processes of intensification which allow students to transform initial, ideal aims in solidarity with one another, students are assisted in achieving strength of beauty in their character growth not only as individuals but in the fabric of the commons they create with one another. The possibility creating the commons of the future is dependent not on abstract ideals but in its emergence in the classroom.

Acknowledgements
This chapter is a revised version of an article to be published in *Interchange* 36/1-2 (2005).

Bibliography

Allan, G. (1998): Harmony and Holism in Process Philosophy of Education. *Interchange* 29, 1, 90-99.

Garrison, J. (1997): *Dewey and Eros: Wisdom and Desire in the Art of Teaching.* New York: Teachers College Press.

Purpel, D. (1989): *The Moral and Spiritual Crisis in Education: A Curriculum for Justice and Compassion in Education.* New York: Bergin and Garvey.

Whitehead, A. N. (1949/1929): *Aims of Education,* New York: MacMillan.

Whitehead, A. N. (1969/1933): *Adventure of Ideas*, New York: MacMillan.

Whitehead, A. N. (1929): *Process and Reality*, New York: MacMillan.

Whitehead, A. N. 1985/1927): *Symbolism: Its Meaning and Effect*, Fordham University Press, 1985.

Whitehead A. N. (1958/1938) *Modes of Thought.* New York: Capricorn books.

Education as Process:
Why Engaging the Whole Person is Important and How to Do It

H. E. Thompson

Abstract

Part One: The largest goal of teaching is to "grow persons". Learning is a life-altering process, in which the whole person changes, for better or worse. The whole-person student is personally (not just, "intellectually") engaged with the learning process, and thus has all of his resources and energy available for the tasks of learning, and is the most likely to put the results to the true benefit of civilization. Education is optimal for both the student and the culture when all of the student's (and teacher's) creative resources are enlisted together. This is why "engagement" is important.

Part Two: I present a detailed "teacher's" narrative of my own five-stage process, showing how engagement can be created, step by step. I also exemplify Whitehead's stages of romance, precision, and generalization. The basic idea is: first, I make an immediate assignment to find/ create "your own" views in a task or project (appropriate to the course subject), due a week or so later. Second, I then have them compare their own results with a peer's. Third, we all reflect together on what we've learned (about both the subject and learning itself). Fourth, I invite them to use the rest of the course as an opportunity and aid in gradually developing their own personal, yet publicly defensible, view of the course subject. Students frequently tell me this approach has been "life-changing" for them. This process could be adapted or abbreviated for a wide range of courses and purposes.

Part Three: From reflecting on my own struggles to become a better teacher, I make recommendations under a number of headings. 1. Credencing feelings and concrete individuality; 2. Authenticity, mutuality and trust; 3. Leading responsibly and responsively; 4.Respecting limits and cherishing achievements; 5. Facilitating drama and zest; 6. Adapting to other disciplines and personalities; 7. Proper motivation and reward; 8. Relevance and protecting vulnerability. Ultimately, we must learn all this by doing it, so "eat the meat and throw away the bones".

1. Introduction

Hello, Reader. You will find that my style varies herein. That is because I wrote the middle part some time ago, when I was still teaching full-time, and class sizes were usually 20 to 40 students per class. Now, fifteen years later, having recently taken early retirement from my department, I still care deeply about teaching and want to convey some useful insights about its proper purposes and effective processes. This book offers me a chance to give my thoughts another and considerably wider circulation than at first writing. (A version of Part Two was published in the *Proceedings of the Association for Process Philosophy of Education Conference* held in 1991 at Cornell University.) Moreover, I find I now want to make some further and different points; and I find the earlier content, format and tone less suitable to my current aims. Parts One and Three create a rather different tone and focus that reflect changes in this teacher-author, for better or worse. And, like Whitehead, while I argue for universality in some points, I also feel that there is a personal, individual, and concretely unique aspect to teaching that must be acknowledged and borne witness to, if we are not to lose our way disastrously in this newer but less brave world. Put another way, an essential part of anything I can offer, here or anywhere else, is simply who I am (and have been and am becoming).

2. Why Engagement Is Important

The largest goal of teaching is to "grow persons". It is hard to imagine anyone being satisfied with saying, "since he produced class after class of highly efficient Nazi technicians and bureaucrats, he was a very good teacher." By contrast, a commonly accepted mark of the really good teacher, beyond merely competently presenting the subject-matter, is that she made a lasting positive difference in the *lives* of her students. Inspiration and support for their struggles, conveying a real understanding of the larger meaning and value of the subject matter, providing examples of worthy living: these are the sort of more general hoped-for results that make successful teaching both its own reward and the noblest of callings. *Lives are extended processes of growth and development (and perishing), authored and lived by persons. A "person" is a multi-layered concept, with dimensions ranging from the universally human (such as ethical or logical) to the relative, social (such as citizen or shaman or parent) to the concretely local and unique individual (such as you or I, and, perhaps, Willy the Dolphin).*

Over the course of human cultural evolution, we have discovered/ invented the institution/practice of *"education"*, in which we become self-conscious about *deliberately facilitating learning*, and so the correlative notions of *student* and *teacher* and *pedagogy* were born. Of course, "education" presupposes "knowledge" (however conceived; even the hate-filled incantations "learned" in the Wahhabi madrassas are thought to be "true" by the teachers therein). And there is a huge amount of pedagogy-theory concerned with such "truth-related" topics as, how to keep lessons up-to-date with the progress of knowledge, or how to most concisely organize and accurately present the maximum number of facts. But, as Whitehead asserts, in *Adventures of Ideas*, in the creative evolution of culture, it is more important that an idea be interesting than true. (see: 1967c, 244) (This is so even though an idea is generally more likely to be interesting if it is true than if it is false.) *Good learning*, thus, should be conceived of as *intrinsically interesting*, and a lack of interest should be seen as a sign of bad learning. (The same holds true for good/bad teaching; but I will say more on this in Part Three.) My forty years-teaching experience has confirmed what all good teachers eventually learn: *Learning is a life-altering process, in which the whole person changes, for better or worse. There are bad forms of learning.* Learning a subject-matter incorrectly (falsely or confusedly) is more or less inevitable and at least correctable, as knowledge progresses. More pernicious is when the "overall lesson" taught is that the subject is intrinsically boring, as Whitehead shows in his discussion of *"inert ideas"* (Whitehead 1967, Ch I), in which the subject is *not connected* to anything which is *live for the students*. Even worse can occur, as Ivan Illich shows in *De-schooling Society*, when students "learn", by repeatedly loathsome "schooling" experience, that learning in general is impossibly difficult and/or intrinsically unrewarding; or, the subjective form of this, that one neither can nor likes to learn. When learning goes badly in this deep, process way, the student is fragmented and disempowered, and becomes a burden to self and to society. *Ideally*, as necessary and beneficial for civilized living, we want students not only to learn the subjects but also to *learn how to learn*. History has shown that human beings have the capacity to become *integrally whole persons*, to become increasingly active learn-ers and knowledge-producers, autonomous and connected, profoundly responsible for self and community and our beautiful burning world. The whole-person student is personally engaged with the learning process, and thus has all of his resources and energy available for the tasks of learning, and is the most likely to put the results to the true benefit of civilization.

It is important to note that there is a further value-dimension to getting education right than the potential dis/benefit to the student; there is also the potential dis/benefit to the culture to consider. And, indeed, some wonder, *what about fanatics?* What of those who harness all they have been taught to the service of some hateful, partisan, taken-for-granted ideal, and murder us at our work or play? Does this extreme possibility not argue for the dangers of the whole-person approach, and recommend instead that we abjure "relevance" and "feeling" and all value issues in the classroom, for, after all, "Who's to say what's true benefit?" Sad to say I have heard this kind of what I call a "botox pedagogy"[1] a narrower, more dispassionate and sup-posedly "objective", and *safer*, approach to learning and teaching. The short answer here to such worries is, *each of us represents our culture internally, and the best learning and teaching of our culture is one that tests it, in order to improve it.*

Cultures incorporate, and function in terms of, basic views of reality (including views of fact, of value and of meaning), and they can get it more or less right or wrong (think of the Easter Islanders). As cultures evolve, they can develop tensions and contradictions between competing world-views (Thompson 1999). History is rife with exam-ples of long-term changes in living (e.g., from feudalism to market

---

[1] In "botox cosmetics", a diminished form of botulism toxin is injected into an area of skin which has wrinkles, and the body's disease-fighting process tightens the skin, leaving a smooth appearance. The effect is, of course, tem-porary.

capitalism) – and thinking (e.g., from absolute-value scholasticism to value-relativistic/nihilistic materialism) – in which the old harmonies were disturbed. The health and vitality of our culture depends in part on having a clear and confident sense of itself, as whole and consistent and hopeful, not deluded or hypocritical or morally bankrupt. This cultural self-concept may be called "the *cultural mind*" (Adams 1991 & 1997), and finds expression in all areas of a society, including its arts, religions and politics. Its study is the province of the humanities (especially, history and religious studies and philosophy), but it is no mere abstraction. Each of us feels it at the deepest level; more or less vaguely, and similarly or differently, according to our social and personal history. In the bustle of going and doing, each of us is guided or stymied by what it holds as possible and effective (compare voodoo and modern medicine and holistic health). In the quiet night or during a pause on a hill, it consoles or inspires or haunts us by what it holds as worthwhile and meaningful (compare Mother Teresa and Madonna and T. S. Eliot). Our smaller identities and roles are held in its hands, it is the ground from which I dare to seek to know and act and love. It is what makes me myself at bottom and in the large: an Arab or an American, or a member of Western Civilization, or a Human Being Today. It matters terribly, even while it is hard to grasp and shape (a good philosophy course can be of great help), and what are we to do when our culture goes wrong? We are all creatures of and hostage to our culture's evolution and development, but we are not totally help-less; rather, we are all also its authors. How well we author our-lives-in-our-culture is largely a function of knowledge and courage and (of course, "luck/grace").

Again, each of us represents the modern cultural mind internally, and the best learning of our culture is one that tests it, in order to improve it. What is wanted is for the whole person to get engaged and to *use the full range of tools of rational appraisal* – critical thinking, empathetic imagination, scientific method, and others – to *help sort out the false from the true, the bad from the good, the real issues from nonsensical ones*. For example, when students encounter "absolutism" or "nihilism" in their study of ethics, awareness of others' cultures as well as of the concrete complexities of their own lives is the natural allies of more modest and realistic lines of thought. The "fanatic" is not produced by whole-person education, but by the pedagogy of narrowness and deliberate ignorance and fearful repression of curiosity and compassion. Deranged or crippled cultures do tend to produce like individuals, who in turn tend to resist "liberalizing" education. Yet civilization exists, where once it did not, however much further we still have to go. Thus self-correction and progress in culture is possible and real. Human individuals, we whole and still-becoming persons, have inherent normative drives, for logical and ethical harmony, for breadth of vision and accurate fact, for concrete feeling of beauty and fellowship. These are powerful and enormously wide-ranging and sensitive forces inside us; and the most basic way we have of sensing them at work is to *feel* them. *Each student (and teacher) can and should become individual crucibles for the culture's working out of its challenges.* (Indeed, each course and university community can and should become supportive of this.) *Education is optimal for both the student and the culture when all of the student's (and teacher's) creative resources are enlisted together, through deliberate and explicit whole-personal engagement. This is why "engagement" is important.*

3. How to Get Them Engaged: the Five-Stage Process as an Example

This part is a structural and phenomenological description of a set of orchestrated praxes showing how I teach the first three weeks or so of any introductory philosophy course. It depicts the enactment of a five-stage process which I have developed over about ten years. *The general aim of the process is to significantly engage all of my students, from day one, as active and personally interested participants in the course.* I'll give specific examples presently, but the *basic idea* is as follows: *first, make an immediate and ongoing "no-fault" assignment to find/ create "your own" task or project* (appropriate to the course subject). *Second, during and after, have them compare their own struggles and results with a peer. Third, have them reflect together on what they've learned (about both the subject and learning itself).* The specifics of the stages are designed to help them concretely discover the power and value (and fun!) of autonomy, preparation through writing and reading, peer discussion, sympathetic critical debate, and reflective evaluation of their own learning. There is a semblance of careful precision, in the sequencing and timing of each detail, which is both real and phony. It is real in that I find it useful to have an ongoing, previously-tested framework for everyone to start with and fall back on. It is phony in that each individual must be encouraged to treat themselves as if they are the important point of it all, and adaptation is essential to authenticity of process. *The purpose of the process is to provide enough structure for free achievement of likely useful concrete results, which then can be revised as needed, in situ, as felt by those involved.* The point of my own highly individualized narrative is not to recommend that anyone do it exactly *this* way, but that anyone who creates such a "process of engagement" approach in their own teaching will necessarily develop *some* set of specifics, which, hopefully, they will then use in a flexible, adaptive manner.

Outline of the Five-Stage Process

Days	Event in Class (80 min., minus 5 min. for 'Adm.'	Stages
One	*A.* Meet a Stranger (5 min.) *B.* Call Roll (4 - 5 min.) *C.* Introduce and Assign First Reading (2 - 4 min.) *D.* Go through the course outline and Lecture on Philosophy of Education and Assign Stage One (35 min.) *E.* In-Class Writing of Your Philosophies (15 min.) *F.* In-class Discussion and Demonstration of Applied Logic Re: Your Philosophies (15 min.)	*One = Write Essay: "My Philosophy of* (for example*) Life".* (More generally, "Create and complete a small project appropriate to the course subject matter.")
Two	*A.* Call Roll While They Meet a Stranger (5 min.). *B.* Assign Topic of Reading and 2 pp. written response In Preparation for Stage Two (2 min.). *C.* Go Through Course Outline while Conveying My Philosophy of Education (38 min.). *D.* Lecture and Discussion on First Reading (30 min.)	
Three	*A.* Call Roll While They Meet a Stranger (5 min.). *B.* Introduce and Do Stage Two (Small Groups – 20 min.).	*Two* = Having Read and Written Briefly on the Topic, Discuss This in *Small*

	C. Discuss Assigned Topic and Small Group Results. Assign Third Reading (13 min.) D. Review Small Groups as Learning Process (7 min.) E. Lecture on Logic (30 min.)	*Groups*: Due: Day Three
Four	A. Call Roll While They Meet a Stranger (5 min.). B. Assign Stages Three and Four (5 min.) C. Lecture/Discussion on Third Reading (35 min.) D. Lecture on Logic (30 min.)	*Three = Exchange* "My Philosophy" *with Peer and* (at home) *Write a Response* to it. Due: Day Five
Five	A. Call Roll very quickly, so they can get to it! B. Do Stage Four (65 min.) C. Whole-Class Review of Stage Four "How was it?" (13 min.) D. Assign Stage Five as Topic of Writing. E. First Draft Ready for Small Group Discussion on Day Six. Final Draft Due: Day Seven (2 min.).	*Four = One to One Discussion* of Peer's and Own Essays and Responses – and – *Five = Write Essay "Evaluating My Learning* Through the Five-Stage Process."
Six	A. Do Stage Two (30 min.) B. Whole-Class Discuss Results (15 min.) C. Lecture on Logic (30 min.)	*Two = Small Groups* (again) Discussion of Your Learning and the Five-Stage Process.
Seven	A. Turn in Stage Five and Discuss Education. B. Assign, as follow-up a Philosophical Journal (30 min.) C. Introduce and Assign Reading (Optional B Assign Mini-Version*) for Next Section of Course (5 min.) D. Finish Lectures on Logic (40 min.)	*Follow-up* = Begin Keeping Your Own *Philosophical Journal*, throughout the Course.

Tab. 1 *Mini-Versions* of the Process (e.g., Stages One and Two, or One and Four) can be used subsequently to *introduce* major topics/ areas *within* the course (e.g., Philosophy of Religion, or Abortion).

I believe that *this process could be adapted to a wide range* of courses with specific contents and treatments, philosophical and political orientations, and personal teaching styles. *I invite readers from other disciplines to imagine, as you read, specific goals, tools, assignments, exercises, and satisfactions, which would be appropriate to your own courses.* Put aside, for now, "negative" thoughts, and *try to have fun*

with these ideas, as you did when you were a (relatively) carefree
student who found your subject *personally interesting*. Starting with
fears of difficulty or failure rarely lead you to new ideas, but once
something calls to your heart, the way forward to achieving (some
version of) it is much easier. (See also Part Three, in which I offer
some thoughts on what's needed and helpful for becoming a good
teacher.)

Of course, my methods of teaching are grounded in my own general vision of what is real and important. But I think every serious
teacher shares *three overall aims* with me. The *first* and most specific
aim is to *give my students access to the best knowledge and training
currently available* – theories, methodology, and skills of interpreting,
thinking, expressing, and discussing – plus public certification of their
acquisition of this material and skills.

As a *second* and more general aim, I *want my students to understand and feel that philosophizing (my subject/discipline) is a worthwhile and interesting activity naturally arising in response to fundamental human, social, and personal needs*. I want to give them the
vision to see that *we are all philosophers* (artists/ geologists/ animal
doctors/entrepreneurs/ social workers/ whatever is worthy of study).
And I want to *help each of them improve, as active creators and
critics*. I assume that the vast majority of introductory students are not
would-be "majors", but will take only this one philosophy course in
their whole lives. Consequently, the fundamental orientation of my
introductory philosophy course is towards a "one-shot" preparation of
ordinary students' abilities to deal wisely and competently with the full
range of philosophical issues they will face throughout the rest of their
lives. The reader may think that this approach would not work for
classes of "majors", who are presumably not to have fun but to buckle
down and grind through the next "brick in the wall" (Pink Floyd, *The
Wall*). But in fact, I have found that a large percentage of majors are
even more likely to like it[2].

---

[2] First, majors *need* to regularly *re-experience* the original *"romance"* with
which they enlisted in the subject; otherwise they become surly, and a real
burden to teach. Second, majors *already have some knowledgeable personal
engagement* with the subject, and an appropriately formulated project can
usually be found (and individualized) for each student, in which she can
exercise personal interest and creativity in extending their learning of this
further subject matter. It will take some teacher -preparation, but the projects

My *third* aim is the most general but also the most crucial: to *help students learn how to think for themselves, so they will take full responsibility for their lives and for our world*. I want to help them learn to *think independently of any coercion or seduction whatsoever –* including the taken-for-granted "authority" invested in me, my "expertise", and my control over their grades. Toward this aim, this process encourages students to talk and read and write and think independently of my "sanctioning" power. My experience has taught me that *if I can get them engaged in this manner at the outset, and follow up appropriately, they increasingly take active personal responsibility for their own learning. As a result, they work hard and creatively, they learn well, and our studies together seem vital and meaningful.*

In the following sections I give a blow-by-blow account of what I do and say in each "day" (class period).[3] The description is especially detailed (and lengthy) concerning the first day, because I do quite a number of different things by way of setting up the first and subsequent stages of the process. As the following outline indicates, only

---

need take no longer than a day to set up; thereafter, it can be like "office hours". *The professional colleges, especially, are likely to panic* at this point and lament the loss of even one precious day's' worth of "covering (ever) more subject matter"; *but*, in fact, the *gain in student interest more than compensates for time lost to apathy and dullness*. (Then one runs into the practice of chaining one course's objectives to the next in a virtual paroxysm of false efficiency. Why do not respected, protected faculties stand up against these emperor's clothes? The real problem is time and class sizes and cowardly, cheap, small-minded faculty, administrators, and politicians. The small-mindedness comes in thinking the status quo necessary, and then making a virtue of the self-repressing effort "success" requires in such conditions. No wonder the "learning motivation" becomes transformed into the external one, of the eventual "material" rewards to be gained upon graduation..) I do believe that a creative teacher can always find better ways of dealing with problems; but, *generally, as class sizes and "points to cover" go up and time allotted goes down, educational quality necessarilly decreases.*

[3] Although this particular account is tailored to a semester- or year- long course meeting twice a week in eighty minute periods, it can be adapted easily to the fifty-minute period, and, less easily, to the 150-minute period. I have tested both alternatives. The number of minutes allotted here is approximate and flexibility is very important. I have reserved five minutes for "administration" (roll-call, announcements, etc.).

about half of class or study time during these first three weeks is spent on process matters; the other half is spent on regular course content.

3.1 Day One – Stage One

On the first day I walk in and introduce myself and the course, and make some comment or joke as I unpack and look around the room, briefly making eye-contact with a few students. I want us to get working profitably as soon as we can, so I try to set a useful tone right away: interactive, respectful, and not too stuffy.[4] I usually say something like "My name is Ed Thompson, and this is Philosophy 110 – right? I hope so. You may call me 'Ed', if you like, or 'Professor', if the formality makes you feel more comfortable." I continue:

> "I have several things I want us to do today, which will use all of this class period, so let's get started. I will hand out a course outline and go over it with you, and tell you some of my philosophy of education and make some assignments. We'll do some writing and discussion at the end. Let's begin with a brief exercise. I'll say a few words about this first."
>
> "As a teacher, one thing that I think is terribly important to successful education is *atmosphere and attitude*. Learning is *helped* by feeling relaxed, and being able to operate from one's own personal interests, in an atmosphere of mutual respect and trust. By contrast, fear, compulsion, and impersonal isolation from other learners always *hinder* the educational process. So the first thing I want you to do is to take five minutes and *meet a stranger*. You can say "Hi, I'm so and so, and why are you here?' and then they get to ask you the same thing, unless they beat you to it! (Here I pause for tension-reducing laughter; if it doesn't come, I say, "That's a joke." At least a few always laugh by this point.) I'll keep track of the time for you, so go ahead and *start now*."

---

[4] They are often nervous the first day, and I know *I* am--even after 25 years of teaching! I have sometimes even *told* them I'm nervous, as an ice-breaker. See also footnote 7.

And they always get right into it. I look around for any "unmatched" person, and pair her or him up with another one or pair. You can literally *feel them relax* as a group with this exercise. When time is up (5-7 minutes), I rap on the desk for quiet and return to seats, and ask, "It feels a bit better now, doesn't it?" At least a few will nod or say, "Yeah." Teachers should note that *getting responses from them early helps establish an atmosphere of dialogue rather than monologue.* I continue, "We'll do this for the next three classes, and it will feed into a five-stage process we'll be doing over the next three weeks."

Then I start a bunch of course outlines circulating, during which time I call the roll, taking time to *make eye contact with each student in turn.* I say, "Please hold up your hand when called; it's one way I and the rest of the class can start getting to know who you are. And please correct me if I mispronounce your name." I usually roll-call every day for the first four or five weeks, by which time I've learned to recognize about half or two-thirds of the students by their faces (a seating chart is very useful.). Thereafter, I call the roll less regularly. I find this regular bit of personal contact and the individualized attendance record is well worth the time it takes, and the students use it as time to settle in and get ready to work. And *they really like coming to be recognized by sight.*[5]

So far we are about 15 minutes into the class. I plan to take 30 to 35 minutes on the next activity: presenting my philosophy of education while going through the course outline. There is the usual information to convey about routine administrative matters. I tell them at the outset that we will take time at the beginning of each class for any administrative matters, and especially during the second class for questions they may have only after reading the outline carefully at home. At this point I say,

> "I propose to spend a good bit of time today, and in the second class, sharing my views on the nature of education and worthwhile learning, and inviting questions and discussion. I will also give you some tips

---

[5] This way of calling the roll usually takes four to six minutes for forty students, during which time there is a low hum of private conversation and paper-shuffling. I should add that, in the introductory course, I require regular attendance, since class work goes well beyond the readings. This "gets the attention" of those students who attend university rather unseriously; and the "good" students often tell me they appreciate my emphasizing this value.

about effective study. These *process* topics will be part of what we will cover during the next three weeks. Most days we will also spend part of the period on substantive topics and readings which will introduce you to the typical *content* of this course. For example, if you turn to page four you will notice that assignment number one is to read pages 1-10 in the text. You should take notes on it and *think* about it and *be prepared to discuss it* next time. Also, *write* a paragraph (or more) in response to it, and bring that to class."

Here I *give a very brief "set-up" lecture on the reading*; I find a tiny bit of this very worthwhile, in terms of both what they subsequently get out of the reading and how they initially feel about undertaking it. Then I return to the five-page outline, discussing it page by page. I have a number of points to make to my students concerning my educational philosophy and approach. Some are briefly stated in the outline, and need expansion; others are not. On the first day, I usually cover some major points spontaneously and flexibly as I go through the outline. What I don't cover the first day I cover later. I find that *I can usually develop these points around live student questions and responses*. For example, when discussing required texts, I urge them not to be foolish by trying to "get by for a while" without doing the reading. I say,

> "If you're not sure you will want to stay with this course, you can buy only the first text used, keep the receipt, and don't mark the text up, so you can return it. But this leads us to some very important questions you should all be asking yourselves right now – viz, '*Am* I sure?', and '*Why* am I here?', and 'What is the *point* of being educated?', and 'Will this course be really *worthwhile* for me, or will I be wasting my time?'"

> I continue, "Surely some of you should not even be in university right now, despite what your parents might say. Perhaps you should work or travel for a while. And some of you should be at University, but should change your major to *what really interests you*, instead of opting for a good-paying but hateful career, in the hope that the money will buy enough fancy toys to make your *whole life* seem vital and rewarding. *And should you be taking this course, now*? Is this professor one you currently want to explore and learn with? *The professor-student match-up can be really quite important* if you are to feel dignity and excitement in your studies, because the professors and the students are the living concrete *witnesses* to the worthwhile ness of the discipline. If you and this course do not feel rightly suited at this time –

which need be no reflection against either one alone – I urge you to go elsewhere. *You're in charge now, because it's your life.* Are you responsible – that is, able to respond – to make choices which are worth your while? Or will you just go along with local pressures, like a leaf in the wind, until at last you die?"

To students, this often seems like fairly "heavy-duty stuff" for the first day, and since I plan to do a lot more of it, I regularly lighten up for a bit and then go back to it. Thus, *whenever the tension builds enough I will make a bit of space for relaxing and re-energizing.* I might say, *"Well! . . . Any questions so far?", and look around and wait for 15-20 seconds* – a lengthy wait, but I'm convinced of its usefulness. The students need such an interval in order to believe that I really want any questions, as well as to get their questions and their courage ready; meanwhile I "read the audience", and they can digest the arguments. Another space-maker is any semi-relevant joke; mild self-deprecation combats class defensiveness, and helps me not to get too ponderous or pompous. Comments which place professor and students on the same level can also help pace and mood.[6] I also find it useful to address student-teacher relations and attitudes explicitly. I may say,

"Let me say more about *mutual respect and trust.* In my view, we are all equally learners and all have an equal right to be here, and each can learn something from each. I have in fact learned from my students, and they have learned from me and from each other. Presumably, *I have some special skills and knowledge* which you are paying me to make available to you – in that sense I am more your employee than your boss. But *you can also learn things from and with your peers*

---

[6] For example, I may say "Incidentally, if we're mismatched, the reason you should leave and I should stay is not that I'm more important than you; it's just my *job* to be here to help those who really do *want* to pursue the work in this course – and there are other sections and other coursers and other instructors who will teach somewhat differently." As another example, I eventually introduce the term 'swine-pig-dog', in a clearly joking manner, to designate either myself or any others who have done some presumably bad thing – like students skipping class or not doing the assigned reading, or plutocrats stealing from widows and orphans, etc. This insult provides a light, mock-righteous egalitarian way of nevertheless seriously issuing a negative judgment. My intent is to always respect them and myself, by leaving psychic room for genuine excuse or dispute, or for accepting criticism without accepting domination, while still attending to real issues of value.

which I cannot give you directly – due both to time pressure and to our being at different stages of life – for example, actual working practice in clarifying and arguing live issues with a classmate. We are all learners here – and for all that *we need to cooperate and share, not compete and withhold.*"

"You will note that *I do not "curve" grades.* My reasons are, first, to promote this cooperative aspect of the learning attitude, and, second, because *knowledge and personal growth are not a fixed sum to be competed for – on the contrary, the more sharing, the more there is.* So I try to promote an atmosphere in which we are diverse equals, free to disagree among ourselves as individuals, while we explore and learn together."

I try to convey a number of "starting-up" points in this fashion about education. The half hour goes by very quickly, and I continue the discussion in the second day. There is one major point with which I always conclude this half hour. Stage One is assigned on p. 4 of the course outline as follows:

"Write an essay, 'My Philosophy of (for example) Sexuality and Two Different Sexual Issues', length – 5-6 pages (1,300-1,600 words), typed, double-spaced; and bring *two* (2) copies to class. DUE: fourth class. This *is required, but* will *not be graded.* Don't try to imitate or impress me (or anyone). The *purpose* is two-fold: to *get you started thinking for yourself,* and to *give you a "snapshot" of your own actual mind, to develop from during this year. Don't be late – we will use* this *in class. Just do the best you can now,* type it up, and bring it in."

I read it to them, and make comments expanding on it, somewhat as follows (though probably not so concisely).

"This is the first stage of a five stage process which I have worked up over the last ten years. I will tell you about the other stages as we get to them. You have nine days – just about enough time, and enough length, to really get something substantial, but not enough to get freaked out trying for perfection. *All you need to do is decide, O.K., I'll do it.* I'll come up with just *the best I'm able right now* for the fourth class' and your brain and heart will get to work on it, *and you'll succeed.* Now while this is required, it will *not* be graded on how you do it – in fact, you will notice that I'm not even giving you any guidelines. It's as if I tell you, 'paint a picture of life, but *you* have to create it'. *There's no one to imitate or impress because you are the authority here.*"

"But what is an authority? Often we think of an 'authority' negatively, as one who commands followers, and many students think of the professor that way – if only because they think she has the 'power' to force obedience by giving good or bad grades. But the root meaning of authority is positive; it's to *author*, to *create* something which then commands respect and devotion because people can see that it's true or good, that it's *worth* learning from, worth assimilating. And there is a double meaning to 'power' as well. In the negative meaning, it is the control of sanctions (like grades) which people want or fear enough to obey orders. People often don't realize the limits this has – for example, would any of *you* torture 20 babies to death with knives just to get a good grade instead of failing? (Pause) Or would you even refuse, perhaps, if I threatened to *shoot* you? (Pause) So you see, *we always seem to have some degree of freedom B we can author our own actions and values and form our own big picture of how things fit together.*"

"And there is a positive meaning to 'power', which is *ability or enablement* – like electric power which can help get things done, like the ability to think clearly, like knowledge. We are all more or less powerful in this sense – *and we can all empower ourselves further, in the sense of personal growth – as humans, as citizens, and as unique individuals.*"

"Now *that* is what I hope this course will help each of you with, in addition to mere academic knowledge – personal growth, empowerment, and real authority. But it will only happen if you are interested, willing to work hard, and willing to take the risks involved in exploration and deep personal learning. *If you write this paper two things will happen. First, you will have to think for yourself* – and it will be both fun and frustrating, as you get a point clear, or find you've contradicted yourself, or don't know where to go next. But you will necessarily be *active*, a *creator,* instead of a spectator, a sponge. And you will *learn by doing. Second*, rather than giving you a permanent end, *this paper will give you a beginning, a reference point to work from* (in fact, there are four more stages to come!) Have you ever looked at a recent picture of yourself – say, from a yearbook or a drunken party--and asked, 'My God! Is that how I look!' The answer, of course, is 'yes – it is *actually* one part of *you*'. When you have finished this essay, and look back at it you may decide you want to undertake radical surgery, or you may think you should just polish your fingernails – most of you will fall somewhere in between. But it will be your best statement during these nine days. *And the rest of this course can be a resource for your own growth project, or the continuing development of your own best philosophy.* (Pause) You may even learn to pronounce 'epistemological', which gets you a free drink at most bars. (Pause) So, there is one sense in which I think it is crucial to good learning that each of you takes the attitude that *you are the most important person in the room.* In this course I will try to present you with all the resources typically present in a university course in philosophy – the standard moral theories, the most advanced useful techniques and methodology, and my hands-on services as an experienced guide, sparring partner, coach, referee, judge and public certifier. And, instead of passively soaking up my pearls of wisdom, you will take the attitude of the active user, *with questions of interest to your own creative project.*"

"You know, if I go to parties and admit I'm a philosopher, some-one always asks 'So – *what's philosophy*?' or *'What's your* philosophy? (Pause) And the first thing I ask them is *'How long have I got?'* Right? Do you see that I'll put it differently depending on whether I have 30 seconds or 30 minutes or a semester? Well, *now you have nine days and 5 to 6 pages – so just do the best you can at this time. Feel free* to talk to others, read, whatever--but remember, it's your best philosophy and *you have the final say. So – go for it!* (Pause) Now, we'll talk more about education next time, and about the outline, and of course there's a reading assignment we'll discuss. There is one more exercise I want us to do today, so – are there any immediate questions on anything so far? If not, we'll go ahead."

(Experienced teachers will have noticed in the above how one can manage pace and mood with jokes, pauses, or even intonation. See further the paragraph on "drama and zest", in Part Three.)

Here I pause briefly. Obviously, eventually someone will ask *'What is* philosophy?' or even more blatantly, *'What are you looking for* in this paper?' In the interest of their doing the first paper on their own, *I always deflect such questions back to their own creative process.* If this comes up in Day One, I am very brief and definite about it; I give the students a longer reply in Day Two (see next section).

Now, I turn to the *last exercise of Day One* which takes 25-35 minutes. I say,

"Alright. Now I want you to take out some paper and *write an essay called "My philosophy of (course subject)*". We'll take *15 minutes* (12 is an absolute minimum) and I'll give you a half-time warning and a couple of writing tips. *Then* we'll get some of you to volunteer samples of your ideas and *do some work with these on the board.* So *let's begin now.*"

After 7 minutes I rap on the desk and say,

> "Everybody's different, but in my experience people tend to have two correlative strengths and weaknesses. Some of you may have written fairly concretely and specifically so far. And so *you might consider trying to put in some grand abstract generalizations, so that you connect everything into one big picture. Others* of you may have been writing mostly in this big picture fashion, and so it may be rather vague so far. So you *might consider* trying to get more specific about a point or two, and *give some concrete examples.* Anyway, let's now do another 7 minutes."

When the time is up, I *call for volunteers* to state some point they came up with. I make sure I *get in 3 or 4 for variety.* For each, I take from 2 to 4 minutes. I *put their names up* along with a *thesis statement that they agree is "fair enough".* Then I use fairly standard "applied-logic"(tools of the discipline) to *do personalized work with each volunteer's thesis.* I *clarify it,* by asking them for definitions and examples and contrasts and limits. I *reason with it,* by asking them for justifications and implications and objections, and *I encourage class responses* of rebuttal and support by suggesting *connections* between and *alternatives* to, different points and *"seed-philosophies".* In this exercise I am simply putting logic to use on their spontaneous input, which involves a certain amount of *thinking on my feet, sympathetically helping them to search for useful formulations.* (This is not always easy to do, if you are not used to it. It takes courage and practice to get good at this, but it is one of the most important of the teacherly skills for eliciting real engagement.) This *concretely demonstrates the value and power of logic and philosophical training,* but I do not begin to talk about logic as a systematic subject until Day Three. In this initial discussion a little bit of applied logic goes a long way in showing students how they can critically develop their own complex ideas – a major point we build on later. They are usually rather excited when the end of the period forces us to stop. *They leave wanting more, which is always a good way to finish the first class.*

Hello, again, Reader. If the above has stimulated your teacherly ambitions at all, may I *invite you to undertake a like experiment?* It is this. *Take 15 minutes and write out your own course goals,* what you would like to convey/have-them-learn, overall, in your favorite course. Pause, after 7 minutes, and see if you want the rest of your writing to be more specific, or perhaps, more grand (or perhaps, something else!); then carry on. *Next, take 15 minutes and talk to yourself out loud* (or write, if it please you) to *1. See if you can create several small exciting "beginner" projects* out of the various course goals you came up with, and *2. imagine,* using the concepts and tools of your discipline in an "engaging" manner, *how you would respond helpfully to better focus/-expand/ further the projects of students* who had come up with personal interests corresponding to any of your previous goals, or of those you now think of. *Then,* after making any immediate notes you might wish, *put this material away, and let the ideas percolate.* Promise yourself you will *look at it again in a day or so,* "just to see..." *All you have to do is, decide, "Ok, I'll do it", and do your best, and you'll succeed.* (Later, if you feel like it, you start a "teacher's journal", just for yourself, where you have an ongoing forum to reflect on one of the primary ways you spend your week. Or, you could show parts of any of this to a sympathetic colleague. But just do one step at a time.)

3.2 Day Two

On the second day I begin with "meet a stranger", call the roll, make announcements and assignments and tell late-entrants to the course to see me after class (when I do a five-minute group "catch-up" lecture). Then I review the previous day, preview the current day, and request and deal with clarifying questions from the previous day. All this becomes an expected standard procedure for subsequent days. On this second day the *assignment* for next class is to do another reading on the same topic as the current reading and writing assigned, and to write another paragraph (or more) on this topic, and to bring both to the third class to use as a basis for a small group discussion of the readings. Of course, *I choose these readings* for their relevance to students' likely initial concerns and *to be easily accessible and "juicy",* rather than ones that will seem remote, difficult, or dry. *I want the students to get "engaged" first and sophisticated later.*

Whitehead's discussion of Romance, Precision and Generalization, as the three stages of the *Rhythm of Education* (1967, Ch. II) is relevant here, especially in its criticism of the "false psychology" which conceives "the pupil's progress (as) a uniform steady advance undifferentiated by change of type or alteration of pace." On the contrary, he asserts, "Life is essentially periodic. [...] There are also subtler periods of mental growth with their cyclic recurrences. [...] The subordinate stages are reproduced in each cycle [...] Lack of attention to the rhythm and character of mental growth is a main source of wooden futility in education. [...]" .In relation to intellectual progress, Whitehead identifies three stages of mental growth.[7] "The stage of romance is the stage of first apprehension. The subject matter has the vividness of novelty; it holds within itself unexplored connexions with possibilities half-disclosed by glimpses and half-concealed by the wealth of material. [...] Education must essentially be a setting in order of a ferment already stirring in the mind; you cannot educate mind in *vacuo*." (1967a, 17f) (I will refer to the next two stages in due course.)

My plan for this second day is to use the first 25 to 30 minutes on presenting and discussing more "philosophy of education", expanding from the first day; and, to use the remaining part of the period (30-40 minutes) lecturing on and discussing the reading. In the "education" segment of the second day, I expand on the "process" model, repeating some points differently, and adding new ones. The pedagogic value of revisitation makes this worth doing, in addition to helping any late-entering students. The themes I work on first are: *"You are important; center yourself and use the course for personal growth; you can create and learn by doing, actively inquire and participate in the process; learning is arduous and fulfilling and risky and humbling and exciting; don't be afraid of making mistakes* or foolish-looking comments, since *we must risk that* – and occasionally expect that – in order *to maximize learning.*" I specifically emphasize that *we all have both the need and the capacity for philosophizing, and that this course should be seen as a major resource for their actively improving at this activity*, through acquiring both knowledge and skills (Theories and techniques of the discipline). When asked *what I am looking for* in their essays, I reply

---

[7] For distant scholarly interest, I think that Dewey might find that this corresponds roughly to his norms for Intelligence-in-action, viz, Feeling-Desire, Means-Ends Deliberation, and Wise-Choice-all-things-considered. More particularly, all non-routine activity begins with a "problem", a blockage of habit calling for satisfaction, and the impulsive formation of an end-in-view as a hypothetical "solution". Intelligence for persons involves the use of our ability to imagine, and to vicariously rehearse various actions with an eye to evaluation of their various consequences, both for the present problem and for any better self.

that *I want you to start* identifying *how* you look at "it all", *what* you are looking for by way of improvement, and *why*. I say, "*Start to find and express and work out your philosophy*." When asked 'What *is* Philosophy?' I usually reply, "That could be a very good question for you to work out, *if* it is genuinely important to *your* own search. For example, what do you think Philosophy *ought* to be, and why is that important to you? But is that really an urgent issue in your life – vs., say, a disguised desire for a *formula* to conform to, in order to do well on someone *else's* exam? *My advice right now is, deal with what really interests you, what seems really meaningful to you, and explore all that.*" I also ask them to start their own *personal philosophical journals*. I describe this as a *private notebook* for *regular writing*, and *review*, of whatever observations and ideas seem *personally interesting and significant for their own philosophical growth*. I emphasize that it can provide a centering locus to counter-balance the great variety of powerful ideas and arguments they will be encountering in the course, and that it may also be a resource when they write assigned papers. (I go over the idea of the journal again with them, at the end of the last stage, and help them to notice how its significance has changed, even in a relatively short time.)

In the segment of the second day spent on *the reading*, I have two equally important aims: first, genuinely *engaging the students' present beliefs and concerns* in an active dialogue with the text, with me, and among each other; and second, conveying a *useful and rigorous understanding* of the content and of the real issues the reading raises and of the correct lessons we may properly take from it. This requires that I seek that delicate balance between lecturing and facilitating dialogue – always a challenge, as any teacher knows. As Whitehead says, in the stage of *precision*, "width of relationship is subordinated to exactness of formulation. [...] A stage of precision is barren without a previous stage of romance; unless there are facts which have already been vaguely apprehended in their broad generality the previous analysis is an analysis of nothing. It is simply a series of statements about bare facts, produced artificially and without any further relevance." (1967a, 18) Thus, in these early days, I am more concerned with the engagement (romance); the sophistication (precision and generalization) proceeds faster, later, when that basis is well laid. Later in the term, I conduct some classes as set lectures; while in others, we put the chairs in a circle and go at it "town meeting"-style. Sometimes

I use small groups, preceded or followed by a lecture or by whole group discussion. But in the first few days of the course, I work hard to give them a variety of approaches, so that no one approach becomes "routine".

3.3 Day Three – Stage Two

In describing the next few days I will be much briefer. On day three we do the regular preliminary – "meet", "roll", assign a reading, administration, professor's review and preview, and catch-up questions. I *remind them that their essays are due next class, and encourage them* that my experience has shown that, while many students have not written a complete first draft yet, they still can, and will, come up with the essay on time.

Then I give a brief lecture *introducing the "small groups" process.* I re-emphasize the *value of peer-learning* and of the chance to actively practice oral expression and to try out one's own views, in a more private and personal forum. I strongly suggest a *size* of between 3 and 5, and warn against falling into talking about hockey instead of topics from the reading and their writing. I then chalk up a *precise* ending time (to return by if they leave the room) – usually about 20-30 minutes – *and say "O.K., do it now."* There are always a few who don't join a group at all, and some form as seven or eight. *I just wade in and say,* "Here – why don't you two join and let's have a couple from that big group come over here, too. That's right – you and you, o.k.? Fine – go ahead now, it's fun." When the time is up, I ask *each group in turn* for one or more reports on what they discussed and concluded. Then *I and the rest of the class respond dialogically.* This *reconnects* parts to whole and *acknowledges* the importance of the "private" discussions. I then take ten or fifteen minutes for *the whole class to comment on the nature and value of the small group process itself.*

Finally, I begin the first of several lectures on logic, which I continue next time. I begin with C. S. Pierce's story, in which the Bishop, arriving early at his retirement party, reminisces to the guests that his first confessant was a murderer. Later, the Mayor arrives and tells them that he was the Bishop's first confessant! The students always laugh, and I then say that their laughter at *this story proves that they all have some sense of logic, so they already have a purchase on what I'm going to talk about.* I tell them that "logic is your friend", that logic is basic to western philosophy, that we have already seen it used as a *technique* – for example, in the last exercise on Day One ("clarifying your philosophies"), and that I want now to present it to them as a *subject-matter.* I quote Whitehead's line (1967, 118), "Logic, properly used, does not shackle thought. It gives freedom, and above all, bold-ness." I say that this study of logic should give them both a general understanding of its nature (and importance for knowledge, civiliza-tion, and the good life) and also a discipline and skill which will help them to develop in their philosophizing (and even win some personal arguments). Eventually I cover validity, soundness, definitions, etc., as well as how to recognize and create logical clarity and structure.

3.4 Day Four – Stage Three

On day four, after the regular preliminary, I explain Stage Three. I say, "It's the big day, and I want to *congratulate you all on what you've already achieved.* You've done a lot of work and shown a lot of courage, too. I've had people drop out rather than come this far. *So, good for you!* Now let's go even further. You have met several people, and I want you to use this as a basis for Stage Three. I want you to *exchange one copy of your essay with another student who is not a friend* (a stranger will be more open for you to surprise your self with).After today's class, take your partner's essay home and read it carefully, and *write an essay for next class of two or three pages, called 'A Sympathetic Critical Response.' Next time, you will pair up for almost the whole class period for Stage Four: a one to one discussion of your two philosophies and responses.* I know this seems scary to some of you – and I will not coerce you into this. But I do *encourage you to go for it,* and I can tell you that over ten years almost all students do it and I haven't lost a patient yet! Remember, *you are each mutually vulnerable, so "do unto others" the way you'd like them to respond to you.* Do you want them to dump on you? No. Do you want them to just flatter you? No. *So read, think and respond carefully, honestly, and helpfully.* By the way, keep the extra copy so you can review for next time, and in case your partner runs off to Rio with the first copy to sell the film rights! (Any kind of tension-relieving laughter is helpful at this point, folks.) OK, then – *any questions* about all that? Then, *go ahead and move around and make a trade*." (I pause a while – 2 minutes or so.) *"Any unpaired people? Here, why don't you and you trade then?"* After this I spend half the period on the reading and the other half on more logic.

3.5 Day Five – Stage Four and Five

Day five is "a piece of cake". *First I pair them up for the one-on-one with minimum delay* – since some of them are nervous (another joke might help here, right?) – telling them we'll re-meet as a whole class for the last 10 (or 15) minutes. And off they go – usually about half leave the room for the one-on-one. When they return the predominant feelings are perhaps best described as *satisfaction and exhilaration*. In the *last ten minutes of whole-class discussion* of this stage, positive comments and dialogue come readily, and in great variety. At the end of the class I *assign the first draft of Stage Five* – a one to two pages *small essay , "Evaluating My Learning* – About Philosophy and About Learning Itself – Through the Five-Stage Process" – *to be used in the next class* (day six) as a basis for a small group discussion of the same topic. *And I assign the final draft* of Stage Five – 2-4 pages, typed, no grade, *to be given to me on day seven*, and we (almost) all leave feeling terrific. It's also very important, I find, to be clearly available to con- sole the occasional dissatisfied student, whose partner didn't show, or acted like a jerk. I tell them, "It's not your fault, etc.; why not try someone else, outside of class time?" And, in fact, a good number do voluntarily try an extra trade – and talk, because they found it so valuable the first time! It is surprising to many *how popular this exercise is*; but why should it surprise? *They are experiencing the joy of hard work, recognized by a peer, on that which is of real personal interest to them.*

3.6 Day Six – Stage Two (used to help Stage Five)

On day six we do the preliminaries and I review the "final draft" Stage Five assignment again, "merely suggesting" such specific aspects for evaluation as: the values and drawbacks of such features as: written, oral, one-on-one, small group, deadline, no grade, no guidelines, spe-

cific prior preparation, meet a classmate, this summary essay itself –
"and/or anything else you think worthy of comment". Then we form
small groups, followed by brief whole class discussion. Then my
lecture on logic fills the majority of the period to the end.

3.7 Day Seven – Follow up

On day seven I take some time early for *more discussion about the
five-stages, and about learning and education.* The students are usually
relaxed and reflective, and generally quite happy with what they've
achieved. They are active in criticizing passive impersonal classes, and
in pointing out the possibilities and virtues of autonomous engagement
as a productive learning attitude. Even reading, thinking and writing –
"homework"! – find support as "helpful" and "fun". After the scary
"opening" of Stage One, there is *now a sense of "closure" about education. At the same time there is an excitement about going on, opening up new areas and learning by exploration.* This fits Whitehead's
discussion of the third stage, *generalization*: "The final stage of
generalization is Hegel's synthesis. It is a return to romanticism with
the added advantage of classified ideas and relevant technique. It is the
fruition which has been the goal of precise training. It is the final
success." (1967a, 19) I always conclude this discussion by re-assigning
the personal philosophical *journal*, as the writing "backbone" of an
ongoing process of growth throughout the course. Then we go on to
more standard course fare – more logic, more reading.[8]

I have found that beginning with the Five-Stage Process sets the
tone for the rest of the course in a crucial way. Excitement, activity and
cooperative autonomy predominate over apathy, cynicism and whining
about assignments. I use Mini-Versions of this process throughout the
year and the final requires them to include and defend their own
current philosophical view of the course subject. For example, in
starting a new topic such as Religion, I usually assign a short essay
"My Philosophy of Religion", followed by either small groups and/or

---

[8] It's important to return the "evaluation" essays early and to give each student
some supportive comments on style and content. I make notes of points in the
process that seem to be good and points that need improvement, for my own
teacher's journal.

one-to-discussion. I have even found that small groups alone are very useful to insert between two lectures (or in even the middle of) one, if I wish them to discuss points I've just put forth). And I find that a number of students make serious use of their journals, and discussions outside class, to work-up intelligent questions and comments and essays. Virtually all of my students seem eventually to be seriously wrestling with the issues and authors we study, rather than merely memorizing arguments or just accepting this or that position or analysis. They like it, and, more importantly, *they value it!* Students frequently tell (and show) me that they've never worked so hard nor felt so engaged to real issues in their lives. Some have told me this during the course; others, several years later. Many affirm that this course, in a small but real way, changed their lives.

Since this is what I am aiming for, it seems that this process works.

4. What is Teaching?

These are reflections on education from the viewpoint of how to become a good teacher. Education is the process in which *"teachers" freely undertake the responsibility* of directly and deliberately facilitating the learning of "students". *Education essentially involves whole persons. There is something irreducibly individual and concrete about all learning and teaching,* which cannot be put entirely in general terms. The "Fallacy of Misplaced Concreteness" (Thompson, 1997) is particularly pernicious in education.

I want to say at the outset that I deeply believe that *we are capable of feeling more than we can immediately say or know.* I know that, as science and technology have increasingly become valued and taken for granted, there has arisen a movement (called "neo-materialism" in philosophy) to throw out and be done with "all that subjective stuff". (This movement, in psychology, has sometimes given the ludicrous result that the kind of attitude that "professionals" are supposed to take toward their subject matter – people – is the same wholly objective and disinterested attitude that is a defining characteristic of "psychopaths"!) But I don't mean to imply some transcendental dogmatic supernatural source of license to persecute or favor some group. *Feelings are an inextricable part of ordinary human experience.* In *Process and Reality,* Whitehead refers more than a dozen times to "bodily feelings", and has a much larger technical apparatus behind that.[9] (For example, he says, "[...] we have direct knowledge of the relationship of our central intelligence to our bodily feelings. According to this interpretation, the human body is to be conceived as a complex 'amplifier' [...] The enduring personality is the historic route of living occasions [...] The human body is thus achieving on a scale of concentrated efficiency a type of social organization, which [...] constitutes the orderliness whereby a cosmic epoch shelters in itself intensity of satisfaction.") (1978, 119) Neutrally to all that, and sticking to my own experience, what I mean is that *any of us can sometimes feel "something"* which may be important, in a very *particular and concrete situation*, (and perhaps always with some sense of the body), and in a way that can be quite vague or specific, and that is quite *fallible* (correctable by reference to other feelings of our own or of others), and *subject*, like any intuition, *to rational appraisal in the end*. Examples might be: feeling bodily discomfort; feeling "in (or out of) the zone"; feeling a group relax or become hostile; feeling "something wrong", or right, (or, perhaps, feeling indignation or gratitude) about what one or another is doing or saying; feeling that something is, or is not, of tremendous importance in one's or another's life; feeling that something is funny or beautiful (or not); feeling that the pace is right, or that a change in timing is needed. I *don't* think such feelings, *by themselves*, always, or even more often than not, give us "the whole truth", or sufficient direction for action. But deliberately ignoring them is a dangerous self-blinding. Asking others how they feel is sometimes an easy way to confirm (or not) that you're onto something; sometimes just looking or listening more carefully tells you what you need to know. Also, if what you're doing does/doesn't feel interesting and meaningful, consistently over a long time, that's probably how it is. *I do think, and feel, that it is very important for teachers and learners to pay attention to feelings, and to slow down and reflect a bit when the feeling is strong.*

---

[9] For example, he says, "[...We] have direct knowledge of the relationship of our central intelligence to our bodily feelings. According to this interpretation, the human body is to be conceived as a complex 'amplifier' [...] The enduring personality is the historic route of living occasions [...] The human body is thus achieving on a scale of concentrated efficiency a type of social organization, which [...] constitutes the orderliness whereby a cosmic epoch shelters in itself intensity of satisfaction." (1978, 119)

Teaching is personal. What I would first say to all teachers is, *Learn to be your own self.* We learn this by doing it. What I would say second is, *Learn to become a better self.* These two points are not separate or unrelated. They are related as What I Am (what exists) and What I Should Be (what calls to be realized). The third thing is, *Ask the same of your students. Trust among persons is essential to fruitful education, and it can only be based on mutual respect and risk.*

"Be your own self" means, don't be phony, and *don't hide your own individuality.* You are your basic resource in teaching. *You B your knowledge and passion, abilities and limitations B are the living core of what you have to offer them as you lead them to and through the course materials,* the subject matter, the "what" that you are teaching. *Let them see your genuine interest, as well as* a representative amount of your *struggle, as another student of* what you are teaching. We must always start from where and what we really are and try to do what's right – as best we can honestly judge it, together. "Becoming a better self" means, *always trying for good.* This means that the work is always being evaluated: how good was that, did we succeed, do we need to do more or to change direction, was that worthwhile or a waste of time, etc.? This *evaluation ought to be constant and spontaneous and shamelessly fallible,* as much so inside of each lecture or discussion as inside of the subsections and the whole of the course. *Bear witness* to all of this, as you *ask them to risk the vulnerability of authenticity. Help them, by reinforcing the good efforts* made by students, while extending *courtesy and respect to all.* For example, remember her name and refer back to, and make use of, her comment in the next class.(But don't fake it! If you have to, say simply, "I don't remember your name; what is it?" Then go on.)

Take responsibility for leading, for deciding what to try next. But unless it is *working for them* (and for you), it isn't working. *Get feedback* by noticing and by asking/testing, and *keep trying for good. Pay attention to how it all feels, always.* Whitehead reminds us to *teach fewer points* ("cover" less of innumerable isolated facts) *so that we can teach better* (treating a few important ideas with real depth and breadth of complex connection). There are times and places to be "inspiring" and issue pedagogic promissory notes like, assigning homework when you all are tired and feel like slacking off, and exhibiting confidence that this homework will bear fruitBbut then you should *monitor this and aid fulfillment or revision of plans, as appro-*

priate . You are, after all being paid and institutionally supported for all this, and owe it to them to give them what they need (without stupidly burning yourself or them out). And don't insist on too much at once; one can always hope, but we can only do so much. *Cherish what we do achieve;* it's what we work for, and it is always at least somewhat unique and surprising. *This is facilitating the growth of persons, and it is what makes teaching the noblest calling of all.*

Remember limits. Importantly, good teaching is always partly a matter of *good "match-up"*, between teacher and student. You are not the best teacher for every student, nor *vice versa.* Since you have to be "here, now" (teaching this section) and they don't, encourage each of them to ask, seriously, Is this teacher and course the best match-up for me this term? Is this the best use of my precious learning time? Is this *worthwhile*? Challenge each of them, "Respect yourself and decide – either to keep out of the way (drop the course), or to fully engage with what we're doing and to ask for what you need along the way. Equally, *don't fail to ask yourself, Am I getting what I need* to sustain good teaching Benough classroom space, or respect from the students, or enough sleep? And since you have diversity among the students, try to *offer a useful variety of pedagogic materials* (examples, tasks, perspectives, tools) to engage their own unique selves.

Aim for drama and zest, as you teach, and pay attention to expressiveness and rhythms! As I mentioned near the end of Day One, teachers will have noticed in my blow-by-blow account of the Five Stage Process how one can manage pace and mood with jokes, pauses, or even intonation. You can put in further explanatory comments, or leave them out for now; wander tantalizingly, or (wait for it) be ruthlessly concise and simple. I have even noticed how one remark can kindle a "romantic" phase for one student, while a second remark stimulates "precision" learning in her immediate neighbor, all in the space of a few seconds! In this sense *the classroom is a sacred space, and a good teacher is not unlike a good priest or actor or sculptor. You are responsible (able to respond) to engage your audience*, to give them the kind of "performance"-event that *enables them to grasp and enter most usefully into the material and issues at hand.* And there is another important similarity: *a good teacher* {or priest or actor or parent, etc.} *must develop a "feel" for the audience, in order to "lead" most effectively.* And there is an equal need for sensitivity in the individual interviews, after class or during office hours, as *our students differ as much as do our children. Learning (like worship or appreciating art) is a live and dramatic event.* "Delivery" goes well beyond mere logical organization of subject matter. The point never to forget is, *how they experience what is taught is as important as what is presented* (in some merely formal sense of "covering the material"). As Whitehead says: *"The justification for a university is that it preserves the connection between knowledge and the zest of life, by uniting the young and the old in the imaginative consideration of learning"* (1967, 93 my italics).

What about a reader from a very different discipline, or who has a personal style very different from this author? One such could still say, "these generalities may be well and good, so far as they go. But a philosophy essay is of *no relevance to* the kind of learning I want them to get from *my course. So what kind of assignment could I give them,* which would give them creative freedom and yet get them started in the right direction to *engaging with what I have to offer?* My answer to this utterly crucial question is, *"I don't know!"* I don't know your discipline; *but you do!* If any of my specific pedagogic examples inspire useful ideas for you, that's fine. But as an old traveling preacher once told me, "Just take the meat and throw away the bones." Again, we have all seen many examples of great teachers, with quite different personalities. *Each of us has different talents and flaws; everyone has to work with those facts of life.* Think about it. Surely your discipline is not so arcane that you couldn't give one or two or even three interesting lectures on it to a lay audience. Have you never served on your department's open-house committee for visiting high school students? You have studied, and, yes, loved your discipline for so long; have you never felt a sense of its real importance in the world, or shared stories from your lifelong passion with a friend or even an intelligent curious child? Of course you have; *you are a whole person, with your own rich and varied life.* Once you seriously ask what kind of engaging assignments you could start them with, you will *begin your own journey, one of both discovery and rediscovery.* Such an exploration will be frustrating as well as exciting. It will take some time get initial ideas, and then more time to think them through to manageable, communicable projects. But *surely you can do it,* surely you can. It will always be more or less a *work in progress,* so fears of not getting it perfect are irrelevant. But *starting this will make the course truly yours as well as theirs.*

I have argued that *whole-person engagement is crucial* to the best kind of learning and teaching; and I've given an example of a process aimed to facilitate that. I have also found my example confirmatory of Whitehead's notion of the three stages – romance, precision, and generalization – that make up the rhythmic cycles of good/bad learning. What I have to contribute here, perhaps, is the *promising possibility of using one's own past and present personal experiences as a learner and teacher to create an adaptable path to the engagement of all of the seeking-to-be-whole persons in the learning process*. In that spirit, I suggest that the promising, fascinating romance of vague but exciting ideas and possibilities which once lit up your own student heart and mind can likewise stir those of other young learners who are in your present charge. *All they need is the right kind of invitation, and they will find their own diverse manners of personal engagement.* And once they are begun, *you have all the course resources to offer them as and when they are ready and needful,* i.e., engaged and with their questions now capable of more focused answers. They can learn the precise disciplinary tools in due course, with some real appreciation of their significance; *and, eventually, achieve a meaningful closure* through some form of that maturer general understanding and appreciation that awaits a sufficient prior grounding in the preliminaries of the discipline, and that *satisfies the intellect and the heart in its own right,* in the time-honored fashion of truth, goodness and beauty. And, of course, for majors, more developments yet will beckon, as both practical applications and even grander theories lure further thought and study, in that endless journey of curiosity which all humans share. *Teaching in this "process" way is an "art" and can be a real joy* (as well as a real bitch) to practice and improve with. It is, after all, a teacher's question of "How much time do I have?" *And there is a lasting satisfaction in making this kind of difference in their lives.*

This, perhaps, is a good place to address the questions of *proper and improper Motivation and Reward, for teachers as well as for students*. There is no doubt that the rent must be paid, and a salary or other material means must accomplish that. Otherwise, no one will have time to teach or to study. This is why the Greek root of "school" is *"schola"*, meaning *leisure*. In ancient days, slaves made study possible for some others; today, salaries and loans accomplish the same *"free time"*. Let us agree that there must be relative freedom from external demands, (which, for example, sessional lecturers often do not have, or only barely have) and be done with that general issue. Unless I am paid enough, I *cannot* teach; but that does not mean that the pay is *why* I teach. Indeed, only a fool (I mean no disrespect here) would choose to make a career of that which was not fulfilling, merely for the means to "eventually" buy real life satisfaction elsewhere. One's work takes so much of one's time that one ought to *seek a sense of worthwhile ness* there first, and only then fiddle with the smaller extras. A second approach to the same conclusion is to remember the old distinction between extrinsic and intrinsic, and ask "*is teaching (and/or learning) rewarding in itself*". It certainly *can* be, if the match-up is right between the individual and the position. The argument of this whole paper further implies that the characteristic features of good education – the joys of discovery, the drama of effort and satisfaction, the beauty of curiosity and knowledge, the sense that one has significantly empowered the lives of oneself and/or others, – are their own proper reward. And it implies that extrinsic sanctions (punishments, rewards) are actually demeaning and deleterious to the proper functioning of learning and teaching. Imagine loving your spouse or best friend as you do, and then someone offers you "incentives" to adapt your own ever-growing loving relationship to some external demands. What you are being offered is a travesty of personal relationship. It is called "whoring" by the honest, and is peddled by evermore cynical others as "reality show" entertainment (e.g., "The Bachelor" and "the Bachelorette"). The current political drama about "rewarding good teaching" is first and foremost a protest against infringement of the freedom needed to teach, by the incompatible demands to spend ever more time publishing and serving on the right committees. Notably good and bad teaching *is* usually recognized informally, within the university community, far more than the bean-counters want to acknowledge. But the request to value teaching can all too easily turn into the demand to pin all teachers down to uniform, computer-graded lists of "client satisfactions". If all we get is just more general slogans and bureaucracy, that may be more damaging than simply agreeing to leave teaching not formally evaluated, alone and neutral (except for egregious cases of incompetence).

In conclusion, we need to always remember to ask, "*What is the goal of teaching?*" What do we want to foster, and what don't we? *We want to grow "persons"*, authentic selves constantly aiming to author goodness, constantly learning to become good selves in an improved world. This is a *process*, and the way must be consonant with the goal. *Teaching – being a teacher – is personal, and studying – being a student – is personal.* This is the real reason why the so-called "political correctness" issues, like racism and sexism, are relevant to the classroom, to pedagogy. It is true that *action is naturally connected to thought and understanding in the whole person.* As Whitehead said (1967b, 200), "impulse without sensitivity spells brutality; and sensitivity without impulse spells decadence." We are trying to grow persons, not merely produce technical skills or expertise. *But learning requires personal risk and development, which requires encouraging and supporting vulnerability.* As Whitehead says: "The initial discipline of imagination in its youthful vigour requires that there be no responsibility for immediate action. [...] You must be free to think rightly and wrongly, and free to appreciate the variousness of the universe undisturbed by its perils." (1967, 93) This is also the real reason why there is so much difficulty, and so much phoniness and resentment, in trying to merely "be complete", to act in a politically correct way (whatever the latest bureaucratically or ideologically established finished ideal is). The facts are, first, we all start out more or less racist and sexist (and much more) and are still growing, and, second, we are all concretely individual. Thus, *the only way to become authentically less impaired, and to learn how to deal with evolving understanding, is to grow to "there" from "here". The classroom is a microcosm of society, but it must be protected from external demands and forces, as a safe place in which to honestly risk and actually learn and grow.*

All things perish, and pass into their own "objective immortality". I hope that this writing will be of use to others. Goodbye, Reader, and good luck!

Bibliography

Adams, E. M. (1991): *The Metaphysics of Self and World.* Philadelphia: Temple University Press.

Adams, E. M. (1997): *A Society Fit for Human Beings.* Albany: State University of New York Press.

Illich, I. (1966): *Deschooling Society.* New York: Harper and Row.

Thompson, H. E. (1996): Pit-Collies in the Classroom: A Process Model for Teaching about Relativism in the Philosophy of Sexuality. In: G. D. Benson & Bryant E. G. (Eds.): *Process, Epistemology and Education, Recent Work in Educational Process Philosophy.* Toronto, Canadian Scholars Press Inc.

Thompson, H. E. (1997): The Fallacy of Misplaced Concreteness: Its Importance for Critical and Creative Inquiry. *Interchange* 28/2 & 3, 219-230.

Thompson, H. E. (2000): 'Feeling' Good: Knowing Value is More than Motivation. *Interchange* 31/1, 91-94.

Whitehead, A. N. (1967a/1929): The Aims of Education and Other Essays. New York: Macmillan.

Whitehead, A. N. (1967b/1925): Science and the Modern World. New York: Macmillan.

Whitehead, A. N. (1967c/1933): Adventures of Ideas. New York: Simon and Schuster.

Whitehead, A. N. (1978/1929): Process and Reality. New York: Macmillan.

Part II.3

EVANUATION –
A WHITEHEADIAN TURN

Evaluating University Teaching and Learning: Taking a Whiteheadian Turn

Howard Woodhouse

Philosophy, though unable to tell us with certainty what is the true answer to the doubts which it raises, is able to suggest many possibilities which enlarge our thoughts and free them from the tyranny of custom. (Russell 1984, 157)

Abstract
In this chapter I examine some of the evidence concerning student evaluations of teaching (SETS) based on research conducted with faculty and students at the University of Saskatchewan, Canada. My qualitative methodology emphasizes the need to avoid the 'Fallacy of Misplaced Concreteness'. The views of those interviewed are analyzed concerning the effectiveness of SETS, the extent to which they strengthen the ideology of 'students as customers', and the ways in which this undermines the goals of education. The skepticism of faculty and students towards SETS is supported by the literature, which I consider in depth. I conclude with suggestions about how teaching and learning could be evaluated from a Whiteheadian perspective that recognizes the dipolar nature of the process.

1. Introduction

The widespread use of *Student Evaluations of Teaching* (SETS) at universities in Canada and elsewhere has become a ritual. Faculty administer, and students routinely fill out, questionnaires towards the end of courses in the belief that they will improve teaching by providing accurate information about "teaching effectiveness". Students are largely unaware that SETS are used "for summative purposes" to provide "information used in decisions such as renewal of probation, tenure, promotion and right of first refusal." At the University of Saskatchewan (U of S), a policy has been approved by Academic Council for the adoption of a standardized questionnaire designed to make the university "more accountable to students and teachers alike" (Framework for Student Evaluation of Teaching at the University of Saskatchewan 2004, 3, 4, 1).

However desirable, SETS are beset with problems. I first encountered SETS almost thirty years ago when teaching courses with enrollments varying from thirty to one-hundred-and-eighty students. It was obvious to me even then that a uniform approach to teaching would not enable students to learn in such vastly different circumstances. Any attempt to evaluate teaching that failed to take into account the different content, goals, methods, and context of each course would not reflect the complexities of every classroom (McKeachie 1997, 1222). Yet, the introduction today of a standardized questionnaire for use by every department (in slightly modified form) presupposes that teaching and learning is the same in all disciplines. Even strong advocates of SETS like Herbert Marsh and Lawrence Roche concede that "SETS are difficult to validate because *no single criterion of effective teaching is sufficient*" (McKeachie 1997, 1189, my italics). Why, then, the rush to implement such a scheme at the U of S?

In this chapter I critically examine some of the evidence concerning the validity of SETS based on research conducted with faculty and students at the U of S. The views of those interviewed are analyzed with regard to three main issues: the validity of SETS as instruments for evaluating teaching and learning, the extent to which they reflect the view of "students as customers" seeking satisfaction in the market, and the ways in which SETS undermine the goals of education. In each case a summary of the views of faculty and students is followed by a critical examination of the literature. I conclude with some remarks about how teaching and learning might be more adequately evaluated from a Whiteheadian perspective (Woodhouse 2004a & b).

2. Methodology

Faculty and students were selected in a non-random manner for participation in this qualitative study. A faculty member from the College of Arts and Science and one each from the professional colleges of Medicine and Education were interviewed. They had all been recognized for the quality of their teaching on the basis of a teaching award or nomination for such an award. Two were women and one was a man, and they were all senior faculty members. Students from the Colleges of Arts and Science and Education, respectively, were interviewed in two focus groups. All were in the final year of undergraduate studies, and there was a balance between males and females. I had intended to conduct a focus group with students from the College of Medicine, but this proved impossible in the time frame set for this study. The students volunteered, knowing that their answers would be anonymous, as required by the U of S's Ethics Review Board.[1] Open-ended questions were used, with some overlap between those asked of faculty and those posed to students, enabling their different perspectives on key issues. The interviews and focus groups were conducted in the winter and spring of 2004, and each lasted for more than one hour. The transcripts amounted to almost eighty single spaced pages.

The same methodology was employed in earlier studies of women scientists in Cameroon (Woodhouse & Ndongko 1993), teacher educators in the Czech Republic (Safr & Woodhouse 1999), and students at the University of Waterloo (Woodhouse 1989). In their own study of Canadian universities, Tom Pocklington and Allan Tupper describe this approach to research as "a loose methodology". At the same time, they decry the fact that "the ideals and research models of modern science have been adopted, albeit with modifications, by other disciplines" (Pocklington & Tupper 2002, 199n, 83-84). They are right to point out that the research models of 17th century science predominate in the modern university. By characterizing their methodology as "loose" and hence less "scientific" than quantitative approaches, however, they weaken their own argument, since the two approaches can complement one another in reaching a critical understanding of the

---

[1] See University of Saskatchewan Behavioural Research Ethics Board (Beh-REB). (2003). *Format for Application for Approval of Research Protocol.* September 26, 4, 6-7.

human agent in an institutional context (Husen 1988, 11-13, Keeves 1988, 28-29).

Alternative methods capable of providing in-depth answers to questions of importance are worthy of adoption, precisely because they enable one to understand the rich complexities of human experience in ways not possible through survey research. As anthropologists David Young, Grant Ingram, and Lise Swartz argue:

> The need to collect data from large numbers of people means that only very superficial questions can be asked. The resulting generalizations may be well supported, but they are based on such a thin slice of reality that they run the danger of being trivial. (1997, 3)

In contrast, when engaged in prolonged conversation with participants one can pay close attention to their experience and strive towards a shared, interpersonal, and critical understanding of reality (Sullivan 1990, 17-19).

Alfred North Whitehead acknowledged the "astounding efficiency" of methods stemming from 17th century science "as a system of concepts for the organization of scientific research," but criticized them as "quite unbelievable" because they are "framed in terms of high abstractions". By systematically excluding human experience, quantitative approaches treat the abstractions composed of mathematical and statistical data as though they comprise the whole of reality. Whitehead, whose own work in mathematics was of the highest rank (1948), called this the "Fallacy of Misplaced Concreteness", which "arises because we have mistaken our abstraction for concrete realities" (Whitehead 1953, 54-55) or, to put the matter differently, because we mistakenly believe that abstractions are real while concrete human experience is not. The fallacy comprises a major flaw in the research methodology of the natural and human sciences, which has been adopted as "the guiding principle of scientific studies [... by] every university in the world" (Whitehead 1953, 54).[2]

The Fallacy is evident in the following statement about standardized questionnaires at the U of S. The Instructional Development Committee of Council, which developed the policy, "found that de-

---

[2] For further analysis of the 'Fallacy of Misplaced Concreteness', see Birch (1988), and the seminar by Flynn (1997), Regnier (1997), Thompson (1997) & Woodhouse (1997).

veloping a valid, reliable instrument to evaluate teaching takes expertise in statistics and psychological measurement" (MacPherson 2004, 12). Despite its "astounding efficiency" in quantifying "observable teacher behaviors", a statistical approach such as this rules out the experiential elements of the teacher-student relationship as irrelevant to its mode of inquiry. As a result, reality is construed exclusively in terms of what can be measured. "Teaching effectiveness" can then be quantified on a Likert scale, based on five alternatives ranging from "Strongly Agree" to "Strongly Disagree." This totalizing approach to teaching and learning is evident throughout a *Framework for Student Evaluation of Teaching at the University of Saskatchewan*, particularly in the final appendix where "reliability and validity" are reduced to "psychometric analyses" (2004, 23).

In a Whiteheadian framework, concrete experience is the basis for all abstraction which, in turn, is capable of reflecting the rich textures of human experience (Woodhouse 1999b, 331-335). Ironically, this conception of research stems from the new physics, whose "displacement of the notion of static stuff by the motion of fluent energy" (Whitehead 1957a, 362) suggests that material objects and human beings are better understood in terms of a more primitive fluidity existent throughout the universe (Bachelard 1995, 87, Capra 1996, 30-31).

3. Do SETS Help Us to Understand Teaching and Learning?

3.1 Professors' Views

While all three faculty members believed that students should have the opportunity to evaluate their teaching, they recognized the limitations of SETS as summative forms of evaluation. None of them believed that SETS alone were an adequate instrument for determining the quality of teaching and learning.

The professor of medicine was the most supportive of SETS based on a Likert scale. They helped her to improve her teaching by bringing "stuff out that you would never have thought to ask." At the same time, she acknowledged that "direct feedback from people in the classes [...] is more helpful than all the Likert scales in the world." She regularly used formative evaluation of this kind to determine the strengths and weaknesses of her teaching, especially when trying something new in her classes. Similarly, the faculty member in arts and science would use a formative evaluation process to ask about specific works used in a course or "probe a dynamic in the class that I'm unhappy about." The professor of education found that "open-ended questions are far more helpful" than standardized answers on a Likert scale, because "they give a more detailed account of how well I am presenting knowledge." Students' comments had led him to de-emphasize lectures in light of an approach to learning which emphasized "its alternating rhythms of freedom, discipline, and freedom."

All three faculty members were skeptical of the introduction of a standardized evaluation form approved by University Council. The professor from arts and science believed that it would be skewed in favour of the natural sciences, while the faculty member from education thought it would "tend to measure the professor's popularity with students, not what they had learned." As a result, he did not believe such forms should be used in decisions about tenure and promotion. The professor of medicine disagreed, because standardized forms would "certainly make the work easier" for committees making judgements about tenure and promotion. But she hoped that such forms would contain "unique" questions peculiar to each discipline in order to ensure that they were "comparing apples to apples" and did "not skew the way those scores happen."

Significantly, none of the faculty believed that SETS enabled them to understand what their students actually learned. The professor in arts and science thought that learning "takes place best when students are getting pleasure from what they are reading," but balanced this approach with a conviction that there were some things students needed to learn. Those who complained initially about the required readings "might have a totally different appreciation by the time we have finished discussing them." It was not the use of SETS, but "their assignments and what is going on in the class that let me know what they are learning." The faculty member in education went further, stating that SETS were fundamentally flawed because they did not provide any evidence of what students learned, but only their "attitudes towards teachers' observable behaviors", which are an "inadequate and unjust assessment of teaching and learning." While the professor of medicine believed in the reliability of SETS as a means of assessing "teaching effectiveness", she supplemented it with formative evaluations in the manner already described.

3.2 Students' Views

Similarly, none of the students found SETS to be effective tools for improving the teaching of those professors most in need of ameliora-tion. This view was shared by students in both arts and science and education: "I wonder if those professors who just show up could really learn from the evaluations. Are they just hardwired to not care about teaching?" said one, while another added, "I don't think that a lot of teachers take feedback seriously or look at it at all." Too often, "the only thing that mattered was their research", and professors made it clear that students were a hindrance preventing them from "getting back to their laboratory."

On the other hand, both sets of students really appreciated faculty who used formative evaluations in an attempt to improve their teaching "because it was important to them." They also respected those who cared deeply about their subject and conveyed their enthusiasm to students. Professors of this kind took the time to find out about students' interests in order to incorporate them into their courses. One student gave the example of a literature course in which the faculty member built the curriculum around those plays with which students were less familiar, making the class "one of my best experiences". The ability to relate teaching and learning to the needs of students had little or nothing to do with SETS, however. Rather, it stemmed from the ability of professors to engage in dialogue with students about matters of mutual concern.

Moreover, the students in education did not believe that SETS reflected what they learned in courses, or how they had learned it. This was largely because of the way in which SETS were constructed on the basis of three basic questions: "evaluate the content of the course, evaluate whether the professor has given you time to meet outside class time, and evaluate whether the professor has made the subject matter interesting." In the words of another student, "they never allow you to put a comment in about what you learned. It's always just about the professor's methods." Another student pointed out that learning should be considered as an integral part of the process: "and it should be valuable, something we can take with us [...] we should be able to apply it, especially in a College of Education." Yet, the intimate connection between teaching and learning was largely absent from SETS.

None of the students was aware that SETS were used in decisions about tenure and promotion. They thought faculty should explain this process clearly before administering the questionnaires. Interestingly, one student in arts and science questioned the validity of SETS as part of the decision-making process on tenure. She believed they simply reflected "students' attitudes and work habits" and should not be taken as a serious guide to professors' teaching ability. "If they are used to determine tenure," she explained, "I think that they are probably a little out of whack" and "should not necessarily have any weight."

3.3 Reflections on the Data

This general skepticism towards the validity of SETS reflects four central points in the literature. First, the use of a standardized questionnaire based on a Likert scale in no way guarantees scientific validity. The numerical tabulation of scores, which are then shown as means, standard deviations, or distributions is not a sufficient condition for validity. A prior question has to be asked; namely, are the student judgements upon which these numbers generated accurate? Some of the questions used to elicit these judgements are unproblematical ("Was the professor on time?" or "Were course requirements clearly stated?") but, as Stanley Coren argues, others such as "Did the professor demonstrate a clear understanding of the material" or "Was the material covered in the course appropriate?", cannot be validly answered by students. The reasons for this are clear:

> Both [questions] presuppose prior knowledge and understanding of the substantive material from which the course was drawn as well as an understanding of how that content relates to other aspects of the discipline [...] Remember that experts in any field often have different views about which course material is appropriate. (Coren 2000, 105)

Coren's conclusions are based on a study of several hundred students in introductory courses at the University of British Columbia, while my own qualitative research was conducted with final year students at the U of S. While these latter students may be more knowledgeable than their younger counterparts, one can still question whether or not their opinions provide a scientific basis for evaluating the content of a course. The professor of medicine in my study was insistent on this point even though she supported the idea of a standardized question-naire.

Second, if this is true, what *do* SETS measure? Evidence compiled by the Canadian Association of University Teachers (CAUT) suggests they simply reflect students' attitudes towards a course, or a professor, rather than what they have learned. The CAUT policy begins as follows:

> It cannot be emphasized strongly enough that the evaluation question-naires of the type we are discussing here measure only the attitudes of the students towards the class and the instructor. They do not measure the amount of learning which has taken place [...]. (1998, 1)

Ratings given by students to their professors on the anonymous SETS analyzed in the policy tend to reflect their perceptions of the instruc-tor's personality. They have little relationship to student learning or achievement (Damron 1994), and are "somewhat blunt instruments" (Campbell 1991, 9) for determining what students actually learn. Marsh and Roche admit that "historically, researchers have emphasized a narrow definition of students' learning" (1997, 1189). Their own attempt to broaden its scope along behaviorist lines is inadequate for reasons I provide in section 4.3 of this chapter. Moreover, a recent survey of the variety of SETS used at the University of Regina, Canada, showed that they do not ask students to judge if, and in what ways, their professors' teaching has helped them to learn (Fries & McNinch 2002, 73). A questionnaire used by the department of psy-chology at the U of S fares only slightly better, containing one question our of forty-eight that asks: "What one thing was done in the course that facilitated your learning?" (Framework for the Evaluation of Teaching at the University of Saskatchewan 2004, 18).

Third, proponents of SETS respond to this criticism by arguing that they are primarily designed to measure "teaching effectiveness," not student learning. Teaching effectiveness is then defined in terms of "observable teacher behaviors" which are, in turn, related to student performance (Murray 1994). A widely used model for SETS, known as the 'Teachers Behaviors Inventory' (Murray 1988) lists the following "observable teacher behaviors" as items for evaluation by students on a Likert scale: "answer[s] students questions thoroughly", "explain[s] subject matter in familiar colloquial language", "encourage[s] students to ask questions", and "incorporate[s] students' ideas into lecture" (Murray 1988, 97-98). So far, so good. But the inventory goes on to list the following: "speaks in a dramatic or expressive way", "gestures with hands or arms", and "tells jokes and humorous anecdotes". By classifying these appealing "behaviors" as integral parts of teaching, the inventory misleads students into believing they are *necessary conditions* for the dissemination of knowledge. Moreover, the inclusion of "stutters, mumbles, or slurs words," "says 'um' or 'ah'", and "covers very little material in class sessions" (Murray 1988, 98-100) discriminates against professors, who are nervous, foreign, thorough, or who present ideas students don't like (Coren 2000, 117).

Fourth, even a strong advocate of SETS like Bill McKeachie believes that the interpretation of SETS for the purposes of tenure and promotion is "the major validity problem" (1997, 1222). He argues that tenure and promotion committees often do not understand how to interpret the data presented, especially when SETS are tabulated statistically and used in different contexts. McKeachie shows how mistaken it is to suppose that a standardized questionnaire "with demonstrable reliability and validity in one academic setting can be assumed to have reliability and validity in similar settings for other academic units" (A Framework for Student Evaluation of Teaching at the University of Saskatchewan 2004, 7). This point was made most forcefully by the student in arts and science who believed that, while SETS should be included in decisions about tenure, they should not be weighted too heavily for fear of putting the whole process "out of whack" (Elton 1998, 8-9).

4. Do SETS Support the View of 'Students as Customers'?

All of the participants in my study agreed that students increasingly see themselves as "customers" in a market for education services. This conception reflects the market model of education which has come to dominate universities in Canada and elsewhere (McMurtry 1991, 1998, Woodhouse 1991, 2001, 2002).

4.1 Professors' Views

All three faculty members believed that the conception of 'students as customers' was mistaken because, unlike customers in the market, students lack the very knowledge they are seeking. The professor of education found the view that "the customer is always right" misconceived, because the job of teachers is to challenge students' beliefs, not to satisfy their wants as customers: "students do not always have the appropriate knowledge, and it is counterproductive to behave as though they do." This was reiterated by the faculty member in medicine, because "the truth is when you are a first year medical student, you don't know what you need to know." Faculty in a position of authority "have learned a thing or two", suggesting that "students need to trust our wisdom, and our judgement, and our experience." Moreover, since the goal of medical education is to improve the health of future patients, it necessarily involves the common good of society. Health care in Canada "is not truly a private enterprise but exists by virtue of society determining it's a common good that we will build together."

The professor in arts and science saw the view of 'students as customers' as "a problematical model", because "it commodifies education and I definitely don't think education should be a commodity." There is, she explained, "some form of contradiction between the market and education", because "if you are a customer and you don't like what you are getting, you should be able to return the product." This is far different in the case of education. Unlike the market, which deals exclusively with private goods, education by its nature involves "the public good", which means that "what society needs a student to hear, to learn, to be exposed to, are things that the student may not find at all comfortable, or make them happy." If education is to serve the common good, "some people's minds need to be opened and there must be classroom discourse" about controversial issues which "are challenging various kinds of hegemony." As a result, "there is a real potential conflict between the idea of the 'student as customer' and the public good" because "sometimes what the individual may perceive to be in their best interest is not."

The professor of education also believed that once students are treated as customers, academic freedom is undermined. "Faculty who teach only what customers want", he said, "end up abandoning their own views if they run counter to those of students, or to those of society at large." The freedom to express well researched opinions based on theories unpopular with those in power is thereby endangered. Even though SETS tended to reflect the view of 'students as customers', he did not feel they inhibited his own academic freedom in the classroom. In contrast, the faculty member in arts and science recognized that, "if I started to get a lot of negative student evaluations", SETS would compromise her freedom to express unorthodox views challenging hegemony in its various forms.

4.2 Students' Views

The two groups of students had different, sometimes contradictory, views about their being customers in an educational market. Students in education had reluctantly come to see themselves as customers buying a product because of the growing cost of their education. Escalating tuition fees and greater indebtedness had forced them to abandon their initial enthusiasm for learning as having a value in itself. "When I came to university", one student exclaimed, "I made myself a promise that I didn't come here to get a degree, or a job, or anything. I just came here to learn." But all that had changed "because I am so far in debt now" – a theme reiterated by another student, who made sure that "every class I take I want to be worth the money. This was never an issue before, and I thought everything I was taking was valuable." Without being prompted, these same students criticized the U of S for encouraging the view of "students as customers" by behaving like a business corporation, constantly trying to sell them clothes, expensive food, and other commodities: "every which way you turn, [the U of S] pressures us to buy their merchandise, Buy this, buy that." As a result, "I think it is really difficult not to feel like a consumer with the university being so corporate."

However, some of the students in arts and science felt that being a customer not only enabled them to "shop around" for the best professors, but was actually conducive to their education. One student saw herself "as a customer out to purchase the best education possible." Nor did she think this diminished the value of her education, since "I have really high standards for myself. I rearrange courses to get the hard ones, because I want them to challenge me." As a result, she felt she could "share [in the] wealth of knowledge and come out a better person, one who feels really satisfied and well rounded, and has a new way of thinking, a deeper way of thinking. So that is what I am shopping for." A second student went further, saying "I think we should be viewing ourselves more as customers getting a service from our professors and paying them for it." The problem was that, "unlike customers, who have the power to demand things, students were afraid to return a crappy product." She concluded that there was a need at the U of S for "customer service just like at Future Shop."

The growth in the popularity of the view of 'students as customers' among those in arts and science (and probably elsewhere) is directly related to the rise in tuition fees of more than one hundred per cent at the U of S during the past few years. Like their colleagues in education, they expressed the fear that "when I think of the debt I am incurring, it's like a large cloud moving over my education." To which another added, "it makes me feel like I need to get certain things out of my education or I'll feel cheated", and another, "if we are to endure this debt for at least four years, it does add up, and even at the end we have no guarantee of getting a job, so we have to be consumers."

4.3 Reflections on the Data

In what ways, then, do SETS contribute to the view of "students as customers"? The connection between rising tuition fees and the need to provide greater "customer satisfaction" is reflected in the following statement from the *Framework for Student Evaluation of Teaching at the University of Saskatchewan*: "As students at the national and local level are experiencing rising tuition fees, they want to know that the evaluations they complete will improve the classroom experience" (2004, 2). In order to "improve the classroom experience", the Framework advocates the adoption of a standardized questionnaire so that students feel they are getting their money's worth for the high costs of tuition. This supports the view of 'students as customers' seeking satisfaction in the market for the private good of a university education which can be measured on a scale. Rather than suggesting that more faculty be hired to replace one hundred and thirty positions lost during the 1990s, reducing the student-faculty ratio, and thereby improving the standard of undergraduate education, the Framework provides a technical solution to an educational problem in the form of a 'scientific' questionnaire based on flawed research.

While skeptical of the efficacy of SETS as instruments of assessment, the students in both education and arts and science had succumbed to the view of being 'customers', mainly because they were so deeply in debt. The main difference between them was that those in education still resisted this approach, while some of those in arts and science welcomed it. However, while one such student spoke of her "satisfaction" in "shopping around" for courses, she made sure they were intellectually challenging, and not just courses in which she would get high marks with little or no effort. In other words, she was not merely satisfying her wants by purchasing a private good with money, as in the market (McMurtry 1998, 189), but was seeking a deeper fulfillment in which she would "come out a better person." This was very different from the student who wanted a system of customer service to be put in place so that she and others could return goods (in this case, "crappy courses") in the same manner as at Future Shop.

This desire for "customer satisfaction" on the part of students is closely connected to the use of SETS. If, as was argued in the previous section, SETS only measure attitudes towards their classes or their professors, then they do reflect "student/customer satisfaction". This is an inadequate criterion for determining whether or not a professor has taught a course well, or students have actually learned something. Dissatisfaction may well arise from students being asked to question their own presuppositions in ways that foster learning. If such dissatisfaction is excluded by considerations of customer satisfaction, the process of teaching and learning becomes distorted in a fundamental way, and the academic freedom of both faculty and students threatened by market-oriented expectations (McMurtry 1991, 39, Woodhouse 1991, 50, 2001, 111-113). The Framework's desire to "improve the classroom experience" on the basis of "customer satisfaction" may actually undermine a professor's capacity to pose questions critical of her students' preconceptions (Marchak 1996, 31). This problem has been largely neglected by advocates of SETS, because they have "seldom criticized [SETS] as measures of student satisfaction with instruction" (Abrami, Perry & Leventhal 1982, 119).

5. Do SETS Undermine the Goals of Education?

None of the professors or students I interviewed believed that SETS enabled them to understand what was learned in their courses. If this is true, then SETS tend to undermine the goal of education as the advancement and dissemination of shared knowledge.

5.1 Professors' Views

As mentioned, the professor of education believed that SETS were fundamentally flawed because they only reflected students' attitudes towards professors, not what they actually learned. While some relevant information was available from SETS, they were an inadequate instrument for assessing teaching and learning, especially when based on a Likert scale. He believed they undermined the goals of education by blocking other flexible, open-ended, and inclusive forms of evaluation capable of providing a more accurate picture of what took place in the classroom. The faculty member in arts and science agreed. A standardized questionnaire was inconsistent with the goals of education, because 'objective questions' ruled out the very 'discipline-specific questions' required for any rigorous assessment of teaching and learning. In order to avoid this problem, she designed her own instruments to replace SETS. Although summative evaluations based on SETS were not required in her department because she was a full professor, she always used an informal process that provided her with ongoing feedback about her teaching. Moreover, it was not the use of SETS, but "students' assignments and what is going on in class that let me know what they are learning." The professor of medicine, who strongly supported the use of SETS, also recognized that "direct feedback from people in classes from a formative point of view is more helpful than all the Likert scales in the world," because it enabled professors to understand what their students were learning and, in conjunction with assignments, whether or not they were successful in achieving the stated goals of their courses.

All three professors agreed that the goal of education was to serve the public good. For the professor of medicine, the goal of medical education was to improve the health of future patients as an integral part of the common good of society. As "health care providers", the status of physicians was based on "a covenantal relationship, which cannot be reduced to a contractual/customer one without distorting its distinctly public character." The professor in arts and science believed that the common good was best served when educators raised questions which challenged both the hegemony of those in power and the assumptions of students, precisely because "some peoples' minds need to be opened." Similarly, the professor of education criticized those educators who pandered to their students by not providing opportunities for them to question their own assumptions. Without this process of critical and reflective inquiry, neither the goal of education nor the public good could be served.

The U of S, however, was becoming more "research intensive", and its contribution to the public good was being undermined. "A more research intensive university" is one where "what really matters is getting research grants" according to the professor in arts and science. As a result, teaching suffered and whereas "teaching and research at the university should go hand-in-hand", the connection between the two was being severed in favour of grant maximization. The result, she argued, is a palpable decline in the quality of undergraduate education which, combined with higher tuition fees, strengthened the view of 'students as customers'.

All three faculty members were skeptical of the university's attempt to rejuvenate teaching in the form of the "Teacher-Scholar Model" (Boyer 1990, 17-24). The professor of education believed it was simply "an attempt to make it seem as though teaching matters when the real emphasis is on 'research intensiveness,' which means getting more and larger grants." His colleague in arts and science felt that the university's emphasis on so-called 'excellence' in research was not matched by "a corresponding discourse around the importance of teaching [...] In theory, this university supports the 'Teacher-Scholar Model.' In theory. Does it do so in practice?" She had found little evidence of this. The professor of medicine believed that any real recognition of "the scholarship of teaching" was confined to "isolated examples of some of us who have been promoted largely on the strength of our teaching record." In general, however, "the mediocre teacher whom everybody acknowledges is a catastrophe, as long as they are a competent researcher, continues to rise through the ranks."

The promise of the 'Teacher-Scholar Model' to strengthen the role of teaching and learning was not being fulfilled (Flynn 2002, 1, Scarfe 2004, 6, Woodhouse 2002, 17-20).

5.2 Students' Views

Students also found SETS did not help them to understand what they learned in a course, and did little or nothing to further the goals of education. They recognized that the process of education was broader than vocational training even though they had come to see themselves as 'customers'. The students in education believed that the goals of education were thereby undermined for three related reasons: higher tuition fees meant they were constantly thinking about how to pay for their education; they tended to concentrate "mindlessly" on the marks needed for scholarships and bursaries; and they competed for grades rather than valuing what they learned. In the words of one student, "marks and money play a huge role in our being programmed to think in this way." The students in arts and science were largely in agreement. They felt deprived of the opportunity to pursue a "broader based liberal arts education", because of the costs involved, and one of them questioned the tendency of the university to "create employable people rather than better people. Is that the true aim of education?" he asked.

5.3 Reflections on the Data

If, indeed, the goal of education is to advance and disseminate shared knowledge (McMurtry 1998, 188-189) then freedom of inquiry is a precondition for this process. Yet SETS are based on a behaviorist framework at odds with the notion of free inquiry. "Observable teacher behaviors" are, as I have shown, the main criteria for determining "teacher effectiveness" (Murray 1994). These "behaviors" form part of "a scientific analysis and hence an effective technology [...] of behavior", whose goal is the "reinforcement" of "operant behavior." According to B. F. Skinner, a repertoire of behaviors can be established through a process of rewards, or "reinforcers," in which "a bit of behavior is followed by a certain kind of consequence" so that "it is more likely to occur again" (Skinner 1972, 7, 5, 147-148, 27). For example, professors whose "observable behaviors" are reinforced on the basis of student preference are more likely to repeat them. Improvements to their teaching can then be made by adopting the behaviors which appeal to students and avoiding those which do not. Even those "personality types" who have greatest difficulty in adapting to the demands of "effective teaching" can improve their performance, which "is composed of learnable skills and behaviors" (Lawall 1998, 6 cited in: Framework for Student Evaluation of Teaching at the University of Saskatchewan 2004, 4). The idea that teaching is reducible to a set of skills, which can then be measured, reinforced, and assessed as "observable behaviors" (Murray, Rushton & Paunonen 1990, 250), forms a common theme among those who advocate SETS.

While the corrective mechanism of SETS appears to afford students pride of place as the arbiters of "teaching effectiveness", paradoxically it also ensures their control by faculty. Skinner insists that a teacher should use "the most effective methods" to "improve his [sic] control of the student" by creating "behavioral processes" that result in "useful productive repertoires" and "successful work" (1973, 6). In other words, s/he must reinforce those behaviors which meet the well defined, task-oriented objectives s/he devises in order to ensure control over her students. Skinner goes further, asserting that freedom, like dignity, is an antiquated notion to be expunged. By "dispossessing man [sic]" of the "particularly troublesome" view that "a person is free", he shifts "the credit as well as the blame to the environment" in the form of consequences that reinforce behaviors. "Sweeping changes" can then be made to the "traditional practices" of education so that "a certain amount of control can be tolerated" (Skinner 1972, 19-21). How much control depends on the efficiency with which a teacher constructs environments capable of eliciting operant behaviors from their students.

Skinner's technology of behavior, of which SETS are an integral part, is inconsistent with the very notions of teaching and learning (Woodhouse 2004b, 4). Only where the pedagogical relationship enables students to think autonomously, critically, and imaginatively by examining commonly held presuppositions, can it be truly educational (Whitehead 1957a, ix, 21). Without the opportunity to question knowledge claims on the basis of the broadest experiential evidence, teaching reduces to indoctrination and learning becomes no more than the regurgitation of "inert ideas" (Whitehead 1957a, 5-6, 399; 1957b, v, 1-5).

5.4 Conclusion

Having examined the evidence from my interviews with faculty and students, as well as a good deal of the literature, I believe it is reasonable to conclude that SETS are inaccurate instruments for evaluating professors' teaching (d'Appolonia & Abrami 1997, 1205). I have looked not only for the evidence confirming this conclusion, but have conscientiously considered the evidence disconfirming it. SETS also provide little or no information about what students learn, and they contribute to the view of "students as customers", thereby undermining the goals of education.

These conclusions are hardly novel, for "there is clear evidence that information gathered from student evaluations is often biased and inaccurate" (Coren 2000, 117).[3] The idea of a standardized questionnaire is flawed because "it is virtually impossible to design a single student questionnaire that is equally effective for a large lecture, a seminar, and a laboratory course" (Seldin 1997, 336). Yet, the U of S is poised to adopt just such a questionnaire to be used *in all courses in every department on campus*. Significantly, the university policy ignores all counter-evidence in its zeal to adopt "a common questionnaire."

6. Taking a Whiteheadian Turn

A Whiteheadian approach to the evaluation of teaching rejects the behaviorist assumptions embedded in SETS. Teaching can only be understood in relationship to the process of learning, where each partner is capable of growth and the sharing of imaginative ideas (Wood

---

[3] See also Bulman-Fleming (2003, 1), CAUT (1998, 2-3)& Scarfe (2004, 4-5).

house 1995, 359). The pedagogical relationship is imbued with aesthetic value capable of creating a sense of beauty which, in turn, elicits action (Whitehead 1957b, 30, 57-58; Cobb 1998, 108).

6.1 Learning and Teaching

Unlike the mechanistic paradigm according to which learning, like teaching, comprises so many 'bits of behaviors' measured in static terms and quantified mathematically for the purposes of evaluation (Regnier 1997, 246-250), learning is a process in which human beings pass through overlapping, rhythmic cycles of growth that culminate in more fully expressed feelings and inclusive forms of understanding. The curiosity that sparks a rather vague apprehension of reality guides the learner through a phase of mastering details, enabling her to appreciate relationships among concrete details and broader abstract principles (Whitehead 1957b, 17-19, 26, 34-37). At its base, learning is a process in which a "wider generalization of integral feeling" (Whitehead 1957a, 244) is made possible through organic connections created between the student's experience and abstract ideas (Whitehead 1957b, 3).

Unless the imagination of both students and faculty is engaged, these goals will not be achieved (Scarfe 2004, 4). A university, for Whitehead, should be a place where there are "faculty whose learning is lighted up with imagination [...] a band of imaginative scholars" capable of "illuminating the facts by eliciting the general principles which apply to the facts, as they exist, and then by an intellectual survey of alternative possibilities which are consistent with those principles" (Whitehead 1957b, 97, 100, 93). This process of providing an integrated understanding that flows from the relationship between concrete facts and the general principles to which they apply lies at the core of the pedagogical relationship. Only where a full fledged intellectual freedom is guaranteed and "the heart of the matter lies beyond all regulation," can such a vision arise. Since "the learned and imaginative life is a way of living, and is not an article of commerce," learning is not a marketable commodity, nor its pursuit reducible to any exchange value. Rather, ideas are to be freely and openly shared in a manner quite alien "to the rules and policies which apply to the familiar business corporations" in which secrecy is required for the purposes of competitive advantage in the market. By working together on intellectual problems in collaborative ways that combine the vigour of youth with the experience of the more mature, students and teachers can "wear their learning with imagination" (Whitehead 1957b, 97-100).

Imaginative expression gives vent to the creative and aesthetic impulses of students and professors alike. Teaching becomes a craft in which a professor cares for her performance in the classroom as a process of dialogue creative of a beauty that links her with both students and the subject matter. Learning, as we have seen, broadens and deepens students' appreciation of reality and of the ideas they are studying. Together, faculty and students strive for knowledge that has value beyond the "apparently useful" (Whitehead 1958, 100). While appreciative of the intrinsic value of knowledge, they also recognize practical ways in which knowledge can be used to meet human needs without destroying the ecological balance of nature (Ford 2002, 124).

Teaching and learning become a shared, transformative experience in which the inner and outer lives of both partners change fundamentally. As John Cobb puts it, the aesthetic value of education is capable of "increasing 'strength of beauty'" in the sense of "beauty of the soul rather than of art objects." This inner beauty fortifies imaginative thought, prompting students to engage in practical action as they become aware of the kind of person it takes to achieve their goals. Imaginative expression provides a basis for "acting to realize what students have perceived as possible in their own lives or in the wider world" (Cobb 1998, 106-108). Only where they recognize that their lives have the potential for creative thought and action will students begin to transform themselves and the world. Aesthetic expression as the primary source of value sustains purposive activity by enabling students to grow in constructive ways that provide them with a source of hope.

6.2 Evaluating Teaching and Learning

The complexity of teaching and learning requires an evaluation process far more subtle than either SETS or the 'Teachers Behaviors Inventory' (Murray 1988), which are blunt instruments incapable of doing justice to the issues I have raised. What, then, might a Whiteheadian evaluation of teaching look like?

The use of questionnaires based on a Likert scale would be limited for the reasons given by the professors in my study. The 'scientific objectivity' of this approach is questionable, its tendency to measure student attitudes rather than teaching ability is apparent, and the homogenizing effect on teaching in different disciplines undermines academic freedom. The overriding justification for its use as an instrument for making decisions about tenure and promotion ignores the fact that "personnel committees and administrators" (McKeachie 1997, 1222) too often do not know how to interpret statistical data from different contexts. At the same time, there may be occasions on which recourse to a Likert scale is justified. The professor of medicine found this approach useful in determining whether or not certain things worked for her personally. Any dogmatic stance that rejected such a view would be out of keeping with the spirit of the philosophy of organism (Whitehead 1957a, 11).

In general, however, open-ended questions about what students find valuable for their learning are to be favoured. Suggestions about how course content can be more closely related to students' own experience enable faculty to understand how learning can be enhanced to develop the 'strength of beauty' required for appreciation and action. These questions can be used on formative evaluations, as was the case with the professors in both arts and science and medicine, and on summative evaluations. It was on the basis of the latter that the professor of education changed his teaching style from lecturing to one that paid greater attention to the rhythms of learning of his students.

In light of Whitehead's insight that "it is more important that a proposition be interesting than that it be true" (1961, 244), students should be invited to speculate on how professors might improve the learning process. Provided that there is no fear of censure, students can propose novel ways of engaging their interest through anonymous formative evaluations during any course. I have used this approach and found it to be a rewarding, if at first slightly daunting, experience that allows for insights that would otherwise be suppressed. It enables greater understanding of what students appreciate and how to strengthen their sense of aesthetic value. At the same time, a respect for truth on the part of students is necessary, since "of course a true proposition is more apt to be interesting than a false one [... and] action [...] is more apt to be successful if the proposition be true" (Whitehead 1961, 244).

Student complaints based only on a personal dislike of the professor, showing little regard for what actually takes place in the classroom, block the entire process. This has happened only once during the time I have employed this method and, like the professor of education, I took it 'with a grain of salt'.

The goal of evaluating teaching and learning as integral parts of a dipolar process is to enable freedom of thought and action for both professors and students. Freedom of expression is, as Whitehead makes clear, a prerequisite for critical and imaginative inquiry capable of taking into account the breadth of human experience (Whitehead 1957b, 99; 1957a, ix). However, the crucial goal of strengthening both partners' capacity for educational *praxis* cannot be ignored. Unless students can act in ways that embody a 'practicability of purpose', they are likely to remain frustrated about the value of what they are learning and cynical about the efficacy of the evaluation process ("Are they [i.e. professors] just hardwired to not care about teaching?"). The opportunity to put students' ideas into practice enables their self-development as free and responsible beings. For "freedom of action is a primary human need" (Whitehead 1961, 66) and without it they, like the majority of humankind, remain mere cogs in a bureaucratic machine.

A balance between the inner and outer aspects of students' lives can be achieved that enhances the beauty of their souls. By allowing students to "contribute to the complex pattern of community life" (Whitehead 1961, 67), a real collegiality would be enacted and the imaginative pursuit of knowledge, which Whitehead believed to be the heart of the university, rejuvenated. Rather than becoming 'customers' for the private good of a university degree, students would be active members of the many "bands of scholars who [have] treated learning imaginatively" (Whitehead 1957b, 100). Together with faculty, they could then sustain the goal of education to advance and disseminate shared knowledge as a public good.

Acknowledgements
I wish to thank my colleagues in the University of Saskatchewan Process Philosophy Research Unit–Mark Flynn, Bob Regnier, Ed Thompson, and Adam Scarfe for their collegiality, which informs my understanding of all matters educational. Eileen Herteis, former Programme Director of the Gwenna Moss Teaching and Learning Centre, assisted in the design of questions used in my interviews and provided important references for my research.

The research for this chapter was made possible by a McIntosh Research Release Stipend Award from the College of Education, University of Saskatchewan.

Without the ongoing support of Viola Woodhouse, I would not have completed this work.

Bibliography

Abrami, P. C., Perry, R. P. & Leventhal, L. (1982): The Relationship between Student Personality Characteristics, Teacher Ratings, and Student Achievement. *Journal of Educational Psychology*. 74, 1, 111-125.

A Framework for Action: University of Saskatchewan Integrated Plan. (2004): May 14.
    URL: www.usask.ca/vpacademic/integrated-planning

Bachelard, G. (1995/1934): *Le Nouvel Esprit Scientifique*. Paris: Quadrige/ Presses Universitaires de France.

Birch, C. (1988): Whitehead and Science Education. *Educational Philosophy and Theory* 20, 2, 33-41.

Boyer, E. L. (1990): *Scholarship Reconsidered: Priorities of the Professoriate*. Princeton, N.J.: The Carnegie Foundation for the Advancement of Learning.

Bulman-Fleming, B. (2003): Evaluation of Your Teaching: Don't Leave it Entirely in the Hands of Students. *TRACE Teaching Matters*. 13, 1, 4. Waterloo, ON: University of Waterloo. Available at:
    URL: www.adm.uwaterloo.ca/infotrac

Campbell, D. (1991): *A Guide to Student Evaluation of Teaching: A Sesquicentennial Project of the Queen's University Alma Mater Society*.

CAUT (Canadian Association of University Teachers Policy on the Use of Anonymous Student Questionnaires in the Evaluation of Teaching) (1998): Ottawa, Canada: May, 1-14. Available at:
    URL: www.caut.ca/english/about/policy/questionnaires.asp

Capra, F. (1996): *The Web of Life: A New Understanding of Living Systems*. New York: Doubleday.

Cobb, J. (1998): Beyond Essays. *Interchange* 29, 1, 105-110.

Coren, S. (2000): Are Course Evaluations a Threat to Academic Freedom? In: S. E. Kahn & D. Pavlich (Eds): *Academic Freedom and the Inclusive University*. Vancouver: University of British Columbia Press, 104-117.

d'Appolonia, S. & Abrami, P.C. (1997): Navigating Student Ratings of Instruction. *American Psychologist* 52, 11, 1198-1208.

Damron, J. C. (1994): *Instructor Personality and the Politics of the Classroom*. Unpublished manuscript. (Available from the author at the Social Sciences Department, Douglas College, P.O. Box 2503, New Westminster, BC, V3L 5B2).

Elton, L. (1998): Dimensions of Excellence in University Teaching. *International Journal for Academic Development* 3, 1, 3-11.

Flynn, M. (1997): The Concept of Intelligence in Psychology as a Fallacy of Misplaced Concreteness. *Interchange* 28, 2/3, 231-244.

Flynn, M. (2002): Learning In The Process of Teaching. In: *What Is A Teacher-Scholar?: Symposium Proceedings*. Saskatoon, SK.: Gwenna Moss Teaching and Learning Centre, University of Saskatchewan, 1-10.

Ford, M.P. (2002): *Beyond the Modern University: Towards a Constructive Postmodern University*. Westport, Conn.: Praeger.

Framework for Student Evalation of Teaching at the University of Saskatchewan. (2004): Saskatoon, SK.: University of Saskatchewan Council, January 29.

Fries, C. & McNinch, J. (2002): Signed Versus Unsigned Evaluations of Teaching – An Example of How Research Informs Teaching and How Teaching Informs Research. In *What is a Teacher-Scholar?:* Symposium Proceedings Saskatoon, SK: Gwenna Moss Teaching and Learning Centre, University of Saskatchewan, 71-80.

Husen, T. (1988): Research Paradigms in Education. *Interchange* 19, 1, 2-13.

Keeves, J. (1988): The Unity of Educational Research. *Interchange* 19, 1, 14-30.

Lawall, M. L. (1998): *Students Rating Teaching: How Student Feedback Can Inform Your Teaching*. Winnipeg, MB: University of Manitoba.

MacPherson, C. (2004): Council Supports Student Evaluations of Professors. *On Campus News*, 12.

Marchak, M. P. (1996): *Racism, Sexism, and the University: The Political Science Affair at the University of British Columbia*. Montreal & Kingston: McGill-Queen's University Press.

Marsh, H. W. & Roche, L. A. (1997): Making Students' Evaluations of Teaching Effectiveness Effective. *American Psychologist* 52, 11, 1187-1197.

McKeachie, W. J. (1997): Student Ratings: The Validity of Use. *American Psychologist* 52, 11, 1218-1225.

McMurtry, J. (1991): Education and the Market Model. *Paideusis* 5, 1, 36-44.

McMurtry, J. (1998): *Unequal Freedoms: The Global Market as an Ethical System*. Toronto: Garamond Press.

Murray, H. G. (1988): Teachers Behaviors Inventory. In: M. Weimer, J. Parrett & M. Kerns (Eds.): *How Am I Teaching? Forms and Activities for Acquiring Instructional Input*. Madison, WI: Magna Publications, 97-100.

Murray, H. G. (1994): Student Evaluation of College and University Teaching: A 25-year Retrospective. Paper presented at the meeting of the Canadian Society for the Study of Higher Education, University of Calgary, Calgary, AB.

Murray, H. G., Rushton J. P. R. & Paunonen, S. V. (1990): Teacher Personality Traits and Student Instructional Ratings in Six Types of University Courses. *Journal of Educational Psychology* 82, 2, 250-261.

Pocklington, T. & Tupper, A. (2002): *No Place to Learn: Why Universities Aren't Working*. Vancouver: University of British Columbia Press.

Regnier, R. (1997): Mathematics as the Metaphysics of Education: A Misplaced Foundation. *Interchange* 28, 2/3, 245-252.

Russell, B. (1984/1912): *The Problems of Philosophy*. Oxford: Oxford University Press.

Safr, V. & Woodhouse, H. (1999): Eastern, Western, or Pan-European? Recent Educational Reform in the Czech Republic. *European Education* 31, 2, 72-94.

Scarfe, A. (2004): An Historical Overview of Instructional Development in Canadian Higher Education. *Bridges* 2, 4, 2-6.

Seldin, P. (1997): Using Student Feedback to Improve Teaching. In: D. De-Zure (Ed). *To Improve the Academy*. 16. Stillwater, OK: New Forums Press, 335-346.

Skinner, B. F. (1972): *Beyond Freedom and Dignity*. New York: Alfred A. Knopf.

Skinner, B. F. (1973): The Free and Happy Student. *New York University Education Quarterly* 4, 2, 2-6.

Sullivan, E. V. (1990): *Critical Psychology and Pedagogy: Interpretation of the Personal World*. Toronto: The Ontario Institute for Studies in Education Press.

Thompson, H. E. (1997): The Fallacy of Misplaced Concreteness: Its Importance for Critical and Creative Inquiry. *Interchange* 28, 2/3, 219-230.

University of Saskatchewan Behavioural Research Ethics Board (Beh-REB) (2003): *Format for Application for Approval of Research Protocol*. September 26, 4, 6-7.

Whitehead, A.N. (1948/1911): *An Introduction to Mathematics*. London: Oxford University Press.

Whitehead, A.N. (1953/1925): *Science and the Modern World*. New York: The Free Press.

Whitehead, A.N. (1957a/1929): *Process and Reality*. New York: The Free Press.

Whitehead, A.N. (1957b/1929): *The Aims of Education and Other Essays*. New York: The Free Press.

Whitehead, A.N. (1961/1933): *Adventures of Ideas*. New York: The Free Press.

Woodhouse, H. (1989): *Independent and Traditional Learning: Are They Compatible?* A Report for the Office of Teaching Resources and Continuing Education, University of Waterloo, June.

Woodhouse, H. (1991): Contradicting the Market. *Paideusis* 5(1), 50-52.

Woodhouse, H. & Ndongko, T. (1993): Women and Science Education in Cameroon: Some Critical Reflections. *Interchange* 24, 1/2, 131-158.

Woodhouse, H. (1995): Towards a Process Theory of Learning: Feeling the Beauty of the World. *Interchange* 26, 4, 347-364.

Woodhouse, H. (1997): Tradition or Modernity? The Fallacy of Misplaced Concreteness Among Women Science Educators in Cameroon. *Interchange* 28, 2/3, 253-262.

Woodhouse, H. (1999): The Rhythm of the University: Part Two – Whitehead's Break with the Mechanistic Materialism of 17th Century Science. *Interchange* 30, 3, 323-346.

Woodhouse, H. (2001): The Market Model of Education and the Threat to Canadian Universities. *Encounters on Education*. 2, 105-122.

Woodhouse, H. (2002): The False Promise of the 'Teacher-Scholar Model'. In: *What Is A Teacher-Scholar?: Symposium Proceedings*. Saskatoon, SK: The Gwenna Moss Teaching and Learning Centre, University of Saskatchewan, 17-22.

Woodhouse, H. (2004a): Why Standardise Student Evaluations of Teaching? *On Campus News*. March 5, 4.

Woodhouse, H. (2004b): Evaluating Teaching Means Evaluating Learning: Taking a Whiteheadian Turn. A Paper Presented at the 5th International Whitehead Conference, "Process Thought and East Asian Culture," (The Whitehead Society of Korea and International Process Network), Seoul, South Korea, May 24-28.

Young, D., Ingram, G. & Swartz, L. (1997/1989): *Cry of the Eagle: Encounters with a Cree Healer*. Toronto: University of Toronto Press.

A Whiteheadian Approach to Self-Evaluation in Schools

Franz Riffert

Abstract

First an overview is given about the actual national and international situation concerning standardized testing. Two reasons are presented why accountability systems based on standardized testing have become so wide spread: (1) the missing reliability of teachers' assessment of students' achievement and (2) the important role standardized testing plays for out-put management in educational systems.

On the basis of these considerations Alfred North Whitehead's critical remarks on external standardized testing are presented. Whitehead's main point is that external standardized testing undermines the freedom of teachers to adapt to the complex, situation specific circumstances in order to obtain the maximum of a creative learning process for students who are conceived as 'specialists'. Instead external testing leads to 'teaching to the test'. As a consequence, the attitude of creative, adventurous exploration is undermined and substituted by simple pattern recognition, narrow visions, and even boredom.

Finally the question is raised if there is any possibility to develop a measurement tool which on the one side meets scientific test criteria, and on the other side still is flexible enough to be adapted to needs of single schools and not vice versa, as it is the case at present with external standardized testing. That such a flexible approach to evaluation is possible is demonstrated by the presentation of the basic ideas of the MSS (Module Approach to Self-Evaluation of School Development Projects) which was developed and examined so far in 10 schools by the author and his collaborators.

1. Status Quo: An Overview

Today the results and conditions concerning the effectiveness of schools and the educational system as a whole are examined by use of standardized tests in many countries. In the USA the *Educational Test Service* (ETS) is responsible for conducting such evaluations; in Great Britain it is the SEAC (*Schools Examinations and Assessment Council*), in France it is the *Ministry of Education,* in Sweden it is the *Council for Educational Research*, in the Netherlands it is *Institut voor Toetsontwikkeling* and in Austria it is the *Ministry of Education and Cultural Affairs* which authorizes different scientific institutions such as for instance the Austrian PISA-Center at the Department of Education at the University of Salzburg to conduct such evaluation studies. In Germany the Max Planck *Institut für Bildungsforschung* (Max Planck Institute for Educational Research) conducts the PISA studies. All these studies are, of course, based on standardized tests.

In the USA since 1969 periodical measurements of student achievements in mathematics are conducted by the NAEP (=National Assessment of Educational Progress). These studies are based on samples of 9, 13 and 17 year old students. They are repeated every four years. The results offer possibilities for comparisons of classes, schools, regions and federal states. Usually ranking lists are calculated on the basis of these results.

In the last 10 to 15 years a growing interest in national and international school achievement studies on the supra-national level can be observed. First steps in gathering international data on education have been undertaken already for a much longer period: The *International Bureau of Education* and the *United Nations Educational, Scientific and Cultural Organisation* have already been collecting data for decades. Probably the best known institution organizing and conducting international evaluation studies is the IEA (International Association for the Evaluation of Educational Achievement[1]); since the 1950s it periodically conducted such international studies. A few years ago the OECD (Organization for Economic Co-Operation and Development) started to coordinate the well-known international PISA (Programme for International Student Assessment) studies.

---

[1] It is an organization consisting of scientists and of government authorities of the 32 OECD countries.

The PISA study conducted in 2000 was designed to address literacy competences of 15 year olds in the fields of reading, mathematics, science. Also, first steps towards the evaluation of so-called "cross-curricular" competences such as self-regulated learning (2000), team-work and problem solving (2003) have been undertaken. 32 countries took part in the 2000 PISA study and almost 17 million students were assessed. In 2002 another 13 countries have administered the same assessment. The results – the unexpected bad results – led to a heating discussion on standardized testing in Germany which is still going on in the media and the public.

In some countries, which have a uniform school system, the results of these evaluative tests are ranked and published. We find such ranking lists even on the World Wide Web. This is the case, for instance, in GB where the results are published by the *Department of Education and Employment*. In France the national results are annually published in book form or in a journal. Such is the situation.

There is yet another type of standardized testing the so-called exit tests, entrance examinations and placement tests. These tests, contrary to the before mentioned tests, evaluate the achievement of *single students* and on the basis of the results of these tests far-reaching decisions, so-called "high stake" decisions, concerning their further educational development and – indirectly – economical and financial future are made. During the last twenty years such standard-based testing has increased enormously in the USA. In many states of the USA the graduate schools require that applicants submit scores of at least one general standardized test, mainly the GRE (Graduate Record Examination) or, more infrequently, the MAT (Miller Analogies Test).[2]

---

[2] Specific standardized admission tests are usually required in the USA for professional schools such law colleges (LSAT: Law School Admission Test) or medical schools (GMAT: Graduate Management Admission Test). India and China, to name but two more countries, also use standardized testing to select students for university education. In India the JEE (Joint Entrance Examination) is a standardized admission test conducted jointly by the six Indian Institutes of Technology. Beijing authorities have launched the "3 + X assessment system": "3" means that there are three compulsory subjects, namely Chinese, mathematics and one foreign language; "X" does refer to additional tasks, either art-centred or science-oriented depending on the application of the student.

More recently the so called "No Child Left behind Act", signed by President Bush on January 8th 2002, has lead to a tremendous increase of standardized testing in all US-states: while in 1998 thirty-nine states had adopted some form standard-based tests or accountability systems (twenty four of them attaching high stake decisions in the form of student recognition, promotion or graduation) the number had risen to forty-nine in 2001 (Goertz & Duffy 2001). States must bring all students up to the "proficient" level on state tests by the 2013-14 school year. Despite this ambitious target the problems raised by such high stake testing has since been addressed in many publications. Carnoy, Elmore and Siskin (2003), for instance, after having investigated in detail the accountability systems of four US-states – Kentucky, New York, Vermont and Texas – for two years have come up with thought-provoking results. Some of the results can be summarized in the following way: assessment based accountability systems lead to (1) "teaching to the test" and thereby are neglecting the broader scope of education, (2) changes in evaluating subjects – untested subjects such as music are de-emphasized, (3) handicap schools which start with a lower of internal accountability systems (= usually schools with a high percentage of students from low income families) because young teachers (especially in subjects such as mathematics and physics) try to get employed in well-performing schools, (4) lead to a shift from performance based testing (school band competitions, physics competitions,[...]) to multiple choice oriented paper and pencil tests; and finally (5) the fact that state officials, despite verbally maintaining the opposite, do hardly financially support the schools by improving their staff and resources.

To sum up: Fact is that regional, national and even international standardized testing for the use of policy makers and also for high-stake decisions (for instance in exit, entrance/admission and placement tests) has become very wide spread and is conducted periodically in a great number of countries.

2. Why has Standardized Testing Become so Widespread?

Let me, at this point, make one thing clear: The school system always has always been directed and modulated by the governments; and it can be no doubt that in democracies the democratically legitimated government should not only be allowed to do so, but has the undeniable responsibility to observe, evaluate and, if necessary, modify and change the school system. And it is hardly disputed that one major aim of democracies in respect to education can only be to secure (1) a fair, just and (2) an effective educational system: Everybody, no matter of one's social, religious, racial or any other status must have equal access to *good* and *fair* (public) education for the benefit of this person and for the benefit of the society in which s/he lives and works. It cannot be the case that schools are islands of absolutism within the sea of democracy, uncontrolled by democratically legitimated (elected) authorities. Without standardized tests low-performing students and schools could remain "invisible" and as a consequence no necessary extra resources or remedial help could be implemented.

Now, in order to understand, why evaluation based on standardized testing has become so important during the last decades one must draw ones attention to the role evaluation plays in directing and modifying schools.

In the past the major instrument for directing and modulating the school system was the government's influence on the curriculum. This kind of influencing and directing the development of the school system today is called "management by in-put" and proceeds in a top-down fashion from ministry of education to the single school and the single teacher. Government officials lay down the contents of the curriculum. Then in a top-down process – from government, to educational administration, to head masters – these contents finally have to be implemented by the single teachers in their everyday work of teaching.

Now, the results of national and international studies bring to the light, that (1) this top-down process is *very slow* and *very inflexible*, it may take years (if not the time span of a whole generation) until the new contents are implemented thoroughly and lead to positive results and (2) that the new contents get – let me say – 'transformed' along the way from the top of the government down to the single school and the single teacher. It has been demonstrated that one cannot hope that all contents or aims are implements and realized in the original spirit.

This, so it is argued, together with the necessity for ever more and quicker changes because of rapid developments in the sciences, technologies (let me only mention the PC and the Internet) and economics as well as political affairs such as the accelerating trend of globalization (in Europe, of course, the ongoing expansion of the European Union) has led to a change of instrument for directing and modulating the educational system. The former "in-put" oriented approach now is more and more replaced by "out-put management" techniques. That is: On the one hand the schools are given more liberty and possibilities to adapt their curriculum to the technological, economical and social/political developments and the schools' specific regional challenges. Now evaluation by standardized testing gains an indispensable function in "out-put management": it makes the out-put explicit or visible. And according to the quality of this output the system has to be changed or not. So evaluation by standardized testing is a major tool for keeping the school system effective and fair.

A further point, why standardized testing has become so important, is because many studies have shown that the teachers' testing is neither very objective, i.e. independent of the particular teacher evaluating the student, nor highly valid and reliable. If one and the same test (which was conducted by a certain student) is given to different teachers to evaluate them and to give marks, very different evaluations will be obtained form different teachers. (Studies demonstrating this were already conducted in the 1960s and 1970s. See for instance: Weiss 1965, Ingenkamp 1977, see also: Birkel & Birkel 2002.) This means that the teachers' evaluations and marks don't give us a very reliable picture about the students' competences and skills. So in order to direct the school system by out-put management one needs better, more reliable data on student achievement. Evaluation by standardized testing is to provide such data.

3. Whitehead on Standardized Testing

After this general introduction let me now turn towards Whitehead's position on standardized, or as he calls it 'external' testing. We can find a few critical remarks on standardized external testing in Whitehead's educational writings.

Whitehead's critique of standardized testing of student's achievement is intimately connected with his theory of learning and teaching. Whitehead's major point seems to be that standardized testing has negative impacts on the teaching and learning process.

Teaching, according to Whitehead, is a complex process in which a number of factors play a crucial role and which all must fit together in order to achieve the best result obtainable: "The best procedure [of teaching] will depend on several factors, none of which can be neglected, namely, the genius of the teacher, the intellectual type of the pupils, their prospects in life, the opportunities offered by the immediate surroundings of the school, and allied factors of this sort." (Whitehead 1967, 5) And Whitehead continues: "It is for this reason that the uniform external examination is so deadly." (Whitehead 1967, 5)

So Whitehead argues that in order to achieve the best possible results in education situation specific aspects, such as the teachers, the students, school equipment, etc. play a crucial role. And standardized testing cannot do justice to these situation specific factors and their unique combinations. "With this educational ideal nothing can be worse than the aimless accretion of theorems in our text books, which acquire their position merely because the children can be made to learn them and examiners can set neat questions on them." (Whitehead 1967, 80)

Another point of Whitehead's critique concerns what today is termed "test validity". Test validity concerns the question whether a test does in deed measure what its developers intend or maintain to measure: Does an intelligence test measure intelligence or does it measure school career? If a test fails to provide an acceptable level of validity (for a certain purpose) it is worthless. Now standardized tests can be based either on so-called concept of "curriculum validity" or according to a non-curricular standard usually termed "criterion validity". "Curriculum validity" is achieved if the test tasks have been taught before by the teachers so that the students had a fair chance to learn how to cope with presented types of tasks. It is beyond dispute that such "curriculum validity" is difficult to obtain in international studies and even at the national level, if the national educational systems has a high degree of diversification. So in the PISA studies the concept of "curriculum validity" was substituted by the "criterion approach". The non-curricular criterion in the PISA studies was the concept of literacy: reading, mathematical and scientific literacy. (For the definitions of these three literacy concepts see Table 1.)

Let me first turn to curriculum validity: In this case standardized testing cannot do justice to the unique learning processes which according to Whitehead is of essential importance and primacy. Whitehead for instance stresses the obvious fact that people are unique or as psychologists put it: idiosyncratically organized. Whitehead says that they are "specialists" and that a good teacher does adapt to his students' special capacities: "Now the essence of getting pupils through examinations is to give equal weight to all parts of the schedule. But mankind is naturally specialist. One man sees the whole subject, where another can find only a few detached examples. [...] But I am certain that in education wherever you exclude specialism you destroy life." (Whitehead 1967, 10) So standardized testing based on the concept of curriculum validity does away with the teacher's freedom to adapt to the students and to the situation in order to achieve the best possible result.

PISA definitions of literacy

Reading literacy
The capacity to understand, use and reflect on written texts, in order to achieve one's goals, to develop one's knowledge and potential, and to participate in society.

Mathematical literacy
The capacity to identify, to understand, and to engage in mathematics and make well-founded judgements about the role that mathematics plays, as needed for an individual's current and future private life, occupational life, social life with peers and relatives, and life as a constructive, concerned, and reflective citizen.

Scientific literacy
The capacity to use scientific knowledge, to identify questions and to draw evidence-based conclusions in order to understand and help make decisions about the natural world and the changes made to it through human activity.

Tab 1: PISA - Literacy Concepts in Reading, Mathematics and Science

The concept of criterion validity based on the concept of literacy seems to be more acceptable for Whitehead. He himself stresses the fact that education must be helpful for participating in society and to appreciate its fruits: "But the law is inexorable that education to be living and effective must be directed to informing pupils with those ideas, and to creating for them those capacities which will enable them to appreciate the current thought of their epoch. There is no such thing as a successful system of education in a vacuum, that is to say, a system which is divorced from immediate contact with existing intellectual atmosphere." (AE 77) But despite this general similarity of the literacy concept and the aim of education according to which Whitehead thinks education has to be conducted, there remains the fundamental problem that a standardized test is based on a certain operationalization of literacy. In the PISA study the concept of mathematical literacy, for instance, is operationalized according to Freudenthals's concept of "realistic mathematics" (Freudenthal 1977 & 1983). And since this specific kind of operationalization either places those students who are not taught according to this concept on a disadvantage, or again does not allow teachers to select this concept of mathematical teaching which seems to be best appropriate for their students.

Standardized testing can have even further unfortunate consequences: If the test is important i.e. if high stake decisions are based on its results, and entrance tests for instance, certainly are important for the students and their parents, then of course there is a strong urge towards teaching, even cramming to the test. Such *teaching to the test* has but one aim: passing the (entrance) test. It is not aimed at clarifying general concepts and creatively applying them to new problems. It also does not stimulate the spirit of adventurous research. Instead it relies on simple pattern recognition: Do enough test specific problems so that when you see a problem in the examination, you can recall the specific trick, the special integrating factor, the substitution or whatever else may be required to obtain the correct answers.

Further this specialized training usually is done on the expense of teaching and learning other contents: If you need much of the available time for cramming test relevant contents this time is missing for other tasks. So important time is lost which could otherwise be used to inspire curiosity and encourage adventurous exploration.

Such one-dimensional learning to the test further tends to create unfortunate attitudes as well: The practice of drilling affects the students' general attitudes towards the education process. Such attitudes are reflected in their performance, in the narrowness of vision, in passivity and finally in boredom: There is no more love for creative learning and spontaneous curiosity. The students wait in the lectures for the formulae they can learn by heart or the recipe they can follow automatically for solving the examination problem. And so Whitehead warns: "The evocation of curiosity, of judgement, of the power of mastering complicated tangle of circumstances, the use of theory giving foresight in special cases – all these powers are not to be imparted by a set rule embodied in one schedule of examination" (Whitehead 1967, 5).

So Whitehead's criticism of standardized testing concerns the unfortunate effects such testing has on the learning process and on the attitudes of the students towards creative learning. That Whitehead is not alone with his criticism shall be substantiated only by one further quotation. About half a century after Whitehead's criticism of external testing – in the 1970s – Jerome Bruner, one of the leading psychologists, made the same point: "A method of instruction should have the objective of leading the child to *discover for himself*. Telling children and *then testing them on what they have been told* inevitably has the effect of producing *bench-bound learners* whose motivation for learning is likely to be extrinsic to the task – pleasing the teacher, getting into the College, artificially maintaining self-esteem. The virtues of *encouraging discovery* are of two kinds. In the first place, the child will make what [s/]he learns his [her] own, will fit his [her] discovery into the interior world of cultures that [s/]he creates for [her]himself. Equally important, discovery and the sense of confidence it provides is the proper reward for learning" (Bruner 1971, 123f italics added).

But never the less it is just as true that, according to Whitehead, standardized testing and evaluation cannot be abolished altogether. Before dealing with this question, however, it is necessary to mention that Whitehead defined the *single school* as the *essential educational unit:* "When I say that the school is the educational unit, I mean exactly what I say, no larger unit, no smaller unit." (Whitehead 1967, 14) Therefore, Whitehead could also write without contradiction to the before mentioned critique on standardized testing, that the "classifying of schools [...] is necessary" (Whitehead 1967, 14). But such classifying of schools cannot be done by external standardized instruments, applying *one* single standardized test for *all* schools. In order to understand this point fully, we must remember that Whitehead opts for a great liberty for schools to develop according to their specific circumstances and possibilities. He complains about the fact that "[n]o headmaster has a free hand to develop his general education or his specialist studies in accordance with the opportunities of his school, which are created by its staff, its environment, its class of [pupils] (boys), and its endowments." (Whitehead 1967, 13)

But this liberty for Whitehead is essential to secure an optimal situational frame for creative learning processes. So the most important step in educational reform according to Whitehead is to grant liberty to the single schools: "[...T]he first requisite for educational reform is the school as a unit, with its approved curriculum based on its own needs, and evolved by its own staff. If we fail to secure that, we simply fall from one formalism into another, from one dung-hill of inert ideas into another." (Whitehead 1967, 13) Only the liberty to adjust the curriculum to the needs of a particular school with its specific constellation of teachers and the unique potentials of its students and equipment can provide the basis for a flexible creative learning process. So he argues that "[e]ach school should grant its own leaving certificates, based on its own curriculum." (Whitehead 1967, 13)

But Whitehead is well aware that such liberty on the other side has to be counter-balanced by evaluation: "The standards of these schools should be sampled and corrected." (Whitehead 1967, 13) That is that the particular developments of the schools based on the liberty to develop its own curriculum have to be the object of evaluation. "Each school must have the claim to be considered in relation to its special circumstances. The classifying of schools for some purpose is necessary. But not absolutely rigid curriculum, not modified by its own staff, should be permissible. Exactly the same principles apply, with proper modifications, to universities and to technical colleges." (Whitehead 1967, 14) So evaluation is necessary but evaluation has to adapt to the specific curricula of the single schools and not vice versa: the schools having to adapt to a single standardized test applied to all schools. So if external tests are conducted for some purpose – and Whitehead explicitly accepted such necessities for external tests – they have to be adjusted to the situation specific conditions of the school in question: "The external assessor may report on the curriculum or on the performance of the pupils, but never should be allowed to ask the pupil a question which has not been strictly supervised by the actual teacher, or at least inspired by a long conference with him." (Whitehead 1967, 5)

But, so one may well ask, is this possible? How can tests on the one hand meet scientific test standards such as objectivity, validity and reliability and on the other hand do justice to the unique situation of the single school in question? In answering this question I will turn to the final section of my paper.

4. Evaluation in a Whitehedian Spirit:
The Module Approach to Self-Evaluation
of School-Development Projects (MSS)

The concept of the MSS (Module Approach to Self-Evaluation of School-development Projects) was developed by the author together with his colleague Dr. Andreas Paschon at the Department of Educational Science at the University Salzburg, Austria. The development of this concept was made necessary by an educational reform which had taken place a few years ago in Austria: congenial to Whitehead's call for more liberty and flexibility for the single school as the essential educational unit, but of course in complete ignorance of it, the Austrian Ministry for Education and Cultural Affairs allowed the single schools to develop their own profile according to their own unique situation. The single schools, i.e. according to the Austrian law: the so-called school-partners, namely the teachers, parents and students, have been granted the possibility to change *one third* of the curriculum and adjust it to their own needs and potentials. The other two thirds of the teaching contents are still prescribed by an obligatory curriculum in order to secure a basic standard in education. These so-called core contents aim at securing a common basic standard for all Austrian schools and thereby keeping open the possibility for students to change schools without major problems. The curriculum of each subject can be modified to this extent and even new subjects can be introduced. So Whitehead's vision of a flexible, self-determining school is at least realized to some extent in Austria. To some extent priority can be given to certain aspects of the curriculum and even new contents can be introduced, while others may be reduced or even abolished. This liberty, of course, is counter-balanced by the necessity to make sure that the implemented changes indeed reach or at least approach the intended goals and to identify possible negative side effects, not foreseen when the implementation took place. In order to meet this requirement, evaluation has to be conducted with measurement tools which meet the scientific criteria of objectivity, validity and reliability i.e. they have to be standardized. Now, teachers are not – neither in Austria, nor elsewhere in the world – trained to develop on their own measurement instruments according to these standards, nor do they have the time to do so. The great majority of them also lack the theoretical and statistical background knowledge necessary for such developments. Also, they usual-

ly do not have a comprehensive knowledge of already existing measurement tools, nor do they have the necessary expertise to judge reliably if the available instruments fit their purpose or the skill to conduct
such testing according to scientific standards and so most of them will
not be able to reliably interpret the results obtained by such tests.

So we seem to arrive at a basic dilemma: on the one side external
standardized testing does not do justice to the unique situation of
schools which have developed their own profiles; it provides objective,
valid and reliable data which are irrelevant to the unique situation of
the single school. On the other side those who know their school – the
teachers, but also the parents and the students – are not able to elaborate adequate measurement tools for this unique school; their 'self-
made' measurement tools would provide relevant but invalid and un-
reliable data.

Now, the MSS-concept was developed to overcome this dilemma.
In what follows I shall briefly outline the basic concept of the MSS. By
doing so I hope to make evident that Whitehead's insistence that single
schools can only be evaluated by their own standards is possible on a
scientific level of measurement.

However, time will only permit a very short description of the basic
ideas of this concept and will not allow going into any detail of this
elaborated concept.

4.1 The MSS Concept

The MSS takes serious Whitehead's point that the school is the essential educational unit! And it is designed to be flexible enough to do
justice to the different developments possible in single schools (i.e.
their statements of mission and school programs). Even further the
MSS is based on an intimate cooperation between the school-based experts (the teachers, parents and students) and the scientists. According
to Whitehead no standardized testing of students should take place
without being „either framed or modified by the actual teacher"
(Whitehead 1967, 5). So far the MSS has been conducted in ten
Austrian schools and its concept has been permanently optimized on
the basis of the feedback from the expert-practitioners of the involved
schools.

In what follows, I will briefly[3] explain the major elements of the MSS-concept as they are presented in Table 2.

The core idea of the MSS-approach is to solve the dilemma, indicated above, by a *module conception*. A so-called module-pool was created which contains modules ranging from single statements up to elaborated inventories and validated, reliable scales as for instance on test anxiety, self-efficacy convictions, social and moral competences, tasks of international achievement studies such as TIMSS and PISA, leadership practice inventory, teacher-parents interaction, metaphor module, ... At the moment the MSS consists of more than 150 modules and even many more sub-modules.

Module Approach to Self-Evaluation of School Development Projects

© 2000 *University Salzburg Riffert&Paschon*

- **Module Approach** (Module-pool – Items/Statements - Scales – Questionnaire)
- **Self-Evaluation** (Motivation, STP-Consensus)
- **School Development** (Individuality/Schoolspecificity)
- **Multiperspectivity** (Students, Teachers, Parents – School Partnership)
- **Anonymity** (Individual Persons, Single Schools)
- **Full Data Collection** (Everybody gets the Oportunity to Contribute)
- **Analysis of Discrepances** (Is[fact]-Ought[ideal]-Comparison, Strengths-Weaknesses-Profile)
- **Aims** (Definitions and Evaluation of Achievement (Interventions))
- **Quantitative & Qualitative Aspects** (empirical Facts)
- **Cross Section Analysis** (Flashlight)
- **Longitudinal Analysis** (Measurement of Changes)
- **Comparison between Schools** (System Level)
- **Expert Knowledge** (University – School - Family)

Tab 2: Basic Elements of the MSS-Concept

---

[3] A more detailed presentation of the MSS-concept is given in: Paschon & Riffert 1997 and Riffert & Paschon 2004.

The MSS is an instrument for *self- or internal evaluation* and not for external evaluation (i.e. initiated and conducted from outside the school). This means: (1) the initiative for an evaluation must come from the single school (without any external pressure); (2) The expert knowledge of the school-partners (teachers, parents, students) is highly valued and reserved primary importance! The school-partners are the experts concerning their own school and their knowledge has to be taken serious! And since the schools are defined as the three groups of school partners it is obligatory for the MSS team that all three groups (T, S, P) must able to freely accept a MSS study. All three groups also must come to a freely reached conclusion concerning the modules selected.

A virtual example may help to illustrate this point (see PICTURE 1):

1. The school partners want to examine the field of educational aims. In particular they want to know how all three school partner groups experience the aims which are in fact realized in their school and want to compare them with the ideal, i.e. with those educational aims which should be aimed at. That is, they want to undertake an Is-Ought comparison on the specific aims of education of their school.

2. Further some parents and the school-psychologist report that there has been an accumulation of test anxiety during the last school year, while other parents and some teachers cannot confirm this impression. So the school partners discuss if they should not select a scale, for instance the AFS (Anxiety Questionnaire for Students; Wieczerkowski et al. 1980), for examining this issue of test-anxiety.

3. The math teachers have implemented a new method for teaching mathematics (for instance: Freudenthals method (1977, 1983)) and they now would like to know how their students are doing on PISA-tasks (which are operationalizations of Freudenthals theoretical concept of "realistic mathematics").

4. Since it is known that self-efficacy convictions are of major importance for achievement in the future, for physical, psychical and social health etc. (see: Bandura 1994) the school partners want to know how well developed these convictions are in their students and if there is any need to set forward steps in order to improve them.

Creating a „Schoolspecific" Measurement-Tool

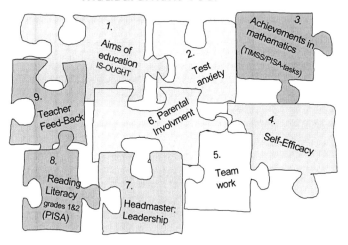

Picture 1: Creating a "School-specific" Measurement Tool - Possible Module Selection for School Developmental Purposes

5. Social competences acquire more and more importance in business and at university. The school partners decide to evaluate one aspect which is especially stressed at their school's statement of mission, namely team-work.
6. The parents want to know how teachers and students evaluate their involvement in school activities.
7. The headmaster wants to improve his competences on leadership practice and because he conceives himself as a moderator between the three groups of the school partners he wants a diagnosis from all three groups: colleagues, parents and students.
8. Since reading literacy belongs to the key competences in life and the school has a high percentage of non-native speakers the schools partners discuss the possibility to diagnose the situation in their school in order to be able to draw more reliable conclusions for future changes in this field.

9. The language teachers want to get individual feedback from their students on their teaching and on their „Learning Abroad". They insist that the results are reported only the individual teachers but that they get the average percentage on each statement for (social) comparison to their colleagues.

It is important at this point to notice that within the MSS standardized testing of students' achievement, although possible, is *only one* aspect of the wide range of possibilities of the MSS. The scope of the MSS is much broader: in principle all activities relevant the school development in its full complexity can be subject of an MSS study. So narrow concentration on student achievement output is avoided, and all kinds of aspects of the broad spectrum of school-life can brought into focus by the MSS.

In principle, any of the more than 150 modules (and their even more sub-modules) can be chosen and combined to form a school-specific measurement tool. Usually the process of discussing what topic should be selected in itself is already a very important activity within the school development process. The school partners at the beginning of this selection process often want to choose many topics and it is one major task of the MSS-team to warn the school partners not to select too many topics/modules but to focus on those contents highly relevant for their school at this time.

School-specificity: School partners normally are not able to conduct standardized testing (i.e. scientific-technological evaluation) according to scientific and technological standards. So the MSS-team offers help for this help: (1) The MSS-team provides a great number of different modules; each module concerns a special topic which *might* be of interest for a specific single school and its school development program based on its statement of mission. The school partners on the basis of their expert knowledge of their own school can select whatever module is relevant for their purposes; to a certain extent the MSS-team even offers the possibility to create new modules which do not yet exist but are relevant for this particular school and may later also become relevant for one or another schools as well. So the module-pool is constantly expanded to new areas of factual and possible interest. (2) The MSS-team provides help in selecting the modules from a methodological (technological) and theoretical (scientific) point of view: What does a certain scale measure? What are its limits? What further independent variables could be of interest if a certain scale, has been chosen?

Multiperspectivity: The MSS allows for multi-perspective data collection; the different perspectives of all three groups of the school partners are taken equally into account – teachers, parents and students. So the school – its strengths and deficits – can be looked at from different perspectives.

Anonymity is granted to each single person taking part in the evaluation and to the school as a unit. This secures that everybody (especially the students, but also parents and teachers) can answer without any fear of meeting negative sanctions (for instance students from teachers or teachers from colleagues). Exceptions are the headmasters since there is only one in each school. Further, *individual* anonymity can be granted concerning the way the collected data are presented. Only aggregated data (mean values) will be presented. If the teacher-feedback module was selected it is possible that each teacher gets only his feedback; but of course there are more possibilities if this should be wished: so for instance the mean value about all teachers of the same subject can be calculated in order to give the single teacher (teaching this subject) a social frame of reference for social comparison.

Comprehensive data collection: In order to give each person the chance to contribute his/her opinion to the school development process, the collection/measurement is not based on a sample; this also offers a possibility to analyse the selected data down to single classes! The detection of, for instance, sources of violence is possible and preventive initiatives can be placed with great accuracy.

Further, the MSS allows for *analysis of so-called discrepancies*: (1) Discrepancies between 'Is' and 'Ought' (existing fact and aimed at ideal) can be calculated; for instance concerning the educational aims of a school; or (2) discrepancies between strengths and weaknesses of the school as viewed from each perspective of the school partners can become the subject of the measurement.

Thereby the MSS makes the formulation of aims of the school development process easier: all three *perspectives* of the person groups are available on IS-OUGHT dimensions; no more guessing is necessary (of what others *might* want or how they *could* see the situation etc.); so many possible sources of frustrations can be avoided. Further, the analysis of discrepancies shows, on what topic there is high agreement between the three groups and therefore lends itself easily to change processes. It also shows, on what topics the people disagree. More discussions are necessary before any steps towards changes in these fields are meaningful.

The MSS collects *quantitative* as well as *qualitative data*. In the context of the MSS "quantitative" means: answers to closed (=pre-formulated) questions; "qualitative" on the other hand means: answers to open questions which allow a free response. Both types of data are presented to the school.

Cross section analysis: By any single measurement – and the MSS here is no exception – one can only obtain a kind of 'snap shot' of the 'measured' situation at a certain point in time. This certainly is a disadvantage. The distortion to which such cross-sectional 'snap shot' data collections may give rise, however, can and must, in fact, be counter-balanced by the experts of the school partners. To give but one illustrating example: a good and competent teacher has been given a 'difficult' class a few weeks before the MSS measurement takes place and now gets a 'bad' feed back from his 'difficult' class. The specific situation of this teacher is well known to his colleagues, to the head-master and to the parents; and this knowledge must counter-balance the results obtained by a cross single measurement at a certain point in time.

A *longitudinal analysis* is possible with MSS; the MSS-question-naire etc. only has to be conducted repeatedly to gather data along dif-ferent points in time. Such repeated measurements also contribute to correction of the possible distortions of a single measurement ('snap shots').

The MSS further allows, in principle and to a certain extent, for a *comparison between schools*. However, such comparisons were *not intended* by the developers of the MSS and are by no means of any primary importance: the MSS never was nor is aiming at school rankings of any kind; comparisons may, however, be of some value in particular cases. For instance: in order to locate one's own school in respect to other schools concerning 'aggressive behavior' etc. (= social criterion) a comparison with the average mean (not with another *individual* schools!) may be of some help. However, whether the MSS is used for a comparison, remains solely to the decision of the school-partners of each single school. Comparisons between single schools are refused by the MSS team because of its inherent dangers in respect to a constructive school developmental process. A further problem of such comparisons concerns the fact, that the referent for comparison, i.e. the mean value of those schools which have chosen the same module, does not representative (based on a representative sample). On the contrary, the sample is biased by the fact that maybe just those schools selected the, say module on aggression, which found this module to be relevant to their situation because they experienced a high rate of aggression! So comparisons with aggregated average results are dangerous and have been executed with great caution!

The MSS, finally, was developed in order to gain *synergy effects* by combining the advantages of two rivalling research paradigms: 'analytico-empirical approach' and 'action research' paradigm.[4] While the strengths of the analytico-empirical approach lies in its objective, valid and reliable instruments, action research stresses the importance of the knowledge of the practitioners in the field: teachers, parents and students. By developing the MSS concept an attempt was made to combine the advantages of both paradigms, together with an immense flexibility towards situation specific measurement.

4.2 Conducting an MSS-Study: The Major Steps

Besides the basic elements of the MSS-concept the way a MSS-study is conducted is also of major importance. This is so because it is the essential aim of the MSS-concept to bring together the expert knowledge of the scientists and of the practitioners (teachers, parents and students). In order to achieve this goal the way an MSS-study is conducted plays an important role.

In the following sections the major steps will be briefly described step by step (see Picture 2):

First Contact: The MSS-team usually is contacted by a school (by the headmaster or the chair of the school-development group). Since the MSS is an approach for self-evaluation the first step normally has to come from the school. Exceptions can be research projects.

---

[4] For a discussion of the MSS-concept with special emphasis on the underlying idea of combining two educational paradigms, which so far have been conceived as competing see: Riffert & Paschon 2001.

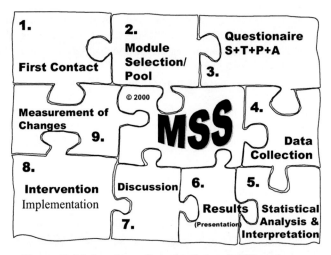

Picture 2: Major steps of conducting an MSS-study

Second, *module selection*: The invited MSS-team visits the school and presents the MSS-conception, its strengths and limitations, and the way the MSS is implemented before each group: teachers, students and parents. (This usually takes about two hours for each group.)

After a discussion of the concept, the process of module selection starts. This discursive process can be quite time consuming and is an important work, since the school partners have to discuss the situation of their school in order to be able to select the relevant modules! At the end the final questionnaire will be produced.

The next step consists of *data collection*. Usually teachers and parents have one week to fill in the questionnaire; the students do this during one or two lessons, depending on the length of the questionnaire. The questionnaires are sent to the MSS-group at the university.

There *statistical calculation* of the data and an analysis as well as a first interpretation of the results takes place at the university.

Data presentation: The results are presented by the MSS-team separately for each group so that a free discussion and feedback can take place.

The next step consists in the *discussion* of the results and of the interpretation offered by the MSS-team. All three groups of the school-partner take part in this discussion. Sub-groups can be built in order to distribute the work.

On the basis of these discussions *changes* are planned, initiated and realized.

Finally another *measurement* concerning these implementations has to take place in order to secure that the change go into the right (intended) direction and that no unforeseen side-effects occur.

5. Concluding Remarks

Standardized testing is wide spread today. And it fulfils some important functions. However, its effects on the creative learning process can be disastrous as Whitehead has pointed out. If evaluation and standardized testing has to take place, it has to be adapted to the single schools and their unique curricula and not vice versa. That such a flexible evaluative approach, despite the seeming dilemma, is possible, has been proven by the development of the MSS.

Acknowledgements:
This chapter is a revised version of an article to be published in *Interchange* 36/1-2 (2005).

Bibliography
Bandura, A. (1994): *Self-Efficacy- The Exercise of Control* New York: Freeman.
Birkel, P. & Birkel, C. (2002): Wie einig sind sich Lehrer bei der Aufsatzbeurteilung? In: *Psychologie in Erziehung und Unterricht* 49, 219-224.
Bruner, J. (1971): *The Relevance of Education* New York: Norton.
Carnoy, M., Elmore, R. & Siskin, L. S. (2003): *The New Accountability: High Schools and High Stake Testing.* New York: Routledge Falmer.
Freudenthal, H (1977): *Mathematik als pädagogische Aufgabe* (vol I & II) Stuttgart: Ernst Klett.
Freudenthal, H. (1983): *Didactical Phenomenology of Mathematical Structures* Dordrecht: Reidel.

Goertz, M. E. & Duffy, M. C. (2001): *Assessment and Accountability Systems in Fifty States: 1999-2000.* CPRE Research Report.

Ingenkamp, K. (1977): *Die Fragwürdigkeit der Zensurengebung* Weinheim: Beltz.

Paschon, A. & Riffert, F. (1997): Der Modulansatz zur Selbstevaluation von Schulentwicklungsprojekten. (english title: The Module Approach for Self-Evaluation of School-Development Projects) In: J. Thonhauser & F. Riffert (Eds.): *Evaluation Heute – Zwölf Antworten auf aktuelle Fragen* Braunschweig: Braunschweiger Studien, 199-213.

Riffert, F. & Paschon, A. (2005): *Selbstevaluation von Schulentwicklungsprojekten – Der Modulansatz zur Selbstevaluation von Schulentwicklungsprojekten (MSS)* Lit: Göttingen.

Riffert, F. & Paschon, A. (2001): Zur Kooperation zweier rivalisierender Paradigmen – der Modulansatz zur Selbstevaluation von Schulentwicklungsprojekten *Pädagogische Rundschau* 55, 335-356.

Weiss, R. (1965): Die Zuverlässigkeit der Ziffernbenotung bei Aufsätzen und Rechenarbeiten. In: R. Weiss: *Zensur und Zeugnis.* Linz: Haslinger.

Whitehead, A. N. (1967/1929): *The Aims of Education* New York: Macmillan.

Wieczerkowski, W., Nickel, H., Jankowski, A., Fittkau, B. & Rauer, W. (1980): *Angstfragebogen für Schüler* Braunschweig: Westermann.

List of Contributors

James Alexander, PhD. is Associate Professor of Elementary Education at Kentucky Wesleyan College in Owensboro, KY. He has responsibility for maintaining documents related to the Departmental Conceptual Framework, based on the philosophy of A.N. Whitehead. He earned his doctorate in Curriculum and Instruction at the University of Arkansas. He also holds a masters degree in historical theology. He has published articles in both educational and theological journals and is an ordained Cumberland Presbyterian minister. His educational interests include literacy acquisition and philosophical foundations. His theological interests include the Jewish roots of Christianity and Second Temple Judaism.

George Allan is Professor emeritus of Philosophy at Dickinson College. He was on the Dickinson faculty from 1963 to 1996, and was academic dean from 1974 to 1995. He has published three books exploring the ontological foundations for social value (most recently,The Patterns of the Present: Interpreting the Authority of Form, 2001) and two books on philosophical and educational issues regarding the liberal arts (most recently, Higher Education in the Making: Pragmatism, Whitehead, and the Canon , 2003). Allan has published numerous articles in metaphysics, social philosophy, philosophy of history, education, and philosophy of education, usually from a process or pragmatic perspective.

Robert Chia is Professor of International Management at the Graduate Business School, University of St Andrews. He holds a PhD in Organisation Studies and is a Fellow of the Royal Society of Arts. For several years he was a regular contributor to a leading-edge International Masters in Practice Management programme chaired by the renowned organizational strategist Henry Mintzberg. Well-established within the United Kingdom and Europe he is highly respected for his intellectual flair and penetrating insights into the fundamental nature and process of organising, leading, influencing and managing complex organisations within the context of a global economy. His research interests revolve around the issues of strategic foresight and leadership, complexity and creative thinking, contrasting East-West metaphysical mindsets and critical cultural studies. He is the author of three books and numerous international journal articles as well as book chapters in a variety of management sub-fields.

John Boswell Cobb Jr., Founding Director of the Center for Process Studies is Professor emeritus from Claremont School of Theology and Claremont Graduate University. He continues active as a co-director of the Center for Process Studies. He has held many positions includeing Ingraham Professor of Theology at the Claremont School of Theology, Avery Professor at the Claremont Graduate School, Fullbright Professor at the University of Mainz, Visiting Professor at Vanderbilt, Harvard, and Chicago Divinity Schools. His writings include: *Christ in a Pluralistic Age*; *God and the World*; and co-author with Herman Daly of *For the Common Good* which was co-winner of the Grawemeyer Award for Ideas Improving World Order.

Paul D'Arcy, PhD is Executive Vice President of the *Sanyo Fisher Company*, a division of Sanyo North America Corporation, a subsidiary of Sanyo Electric Co., Ltd. In addition to significant graduate study under Dr John B. Cobb, Jr., he gained his Doctorate in process philosophy and theology at the Claremont Graduate University. He is a member of the Board of Directors of the Consumer Electronics Association and serves on the Board of Governors of the Electronic Industries Alliance. In November 2001 he received the S. David Feir International Humanitarian Award from the Anti-Defamation League in recognition of his services to management for the promotion of ethical business practice.

Bob Darrell is Professor of English emeritus (Kentucky Wesleyan College where he still teaches occasionally), former department chair, former director of Wesleyan Writing Workshops, and funding director of KWC's PLUS Center, Bob Darrell, Ph.D., is communications and leadership consultant for businesses and professions (including several Fortune 50 companies); co-author of *Every Number Counts I* and *II;* editor of several books, including *The Health Explosion;* former assistant editor of the *Peabody Journal of Education;* founding editorial Board member, managing editor, and senior editorial board member of *Cumberland Poetry Review;* Bob's dissertation presented a Whiteheadian theory of curriculum organization for liberal arts institutions. Following a presentation on organizing undergraduate education depart-

ments in light of Whitehead's philosophy, KWC's education department adopted and maintains (with adaptations) this structure. Bob
studied process philosophy and process theology at Drew University
and SMU where he obtained his master's in theology.

Mark Dibben, PhD is Senior Lecturer in Management at Lincoln University. His doctorate used Whiteheadian metaphysics to unpack the
processual nature of trust and co-operation in organizational development. He is the Founding and co-Director (with Thomas Kelly) of
the Chapter for Applied Process Thought at the National University of
Ireland, Maynooth, and is Chair of the Learning and Teaching Development Committee, and Governing Board member, of the International
Process Network. He serves on the editorial board of *Philosophy of
Management* and is a co-editor of *Concrescence – the Australasian
Journal of Process Thought*.

Mark Flynn, Ph.D. (Dalhousie), is a Co-Director of the University of
Saskatchewan Process Philosophy Research Unit. He is also a Professor of Educational Psychology at the University of Saskatchewan,
Canada. His research interests include; the philosophy of science, epistemology, process theories of learning, systemic constraints on learning in schools and universities, and the critical analysis of tacit assumptions in the theoretical foundations of psychology, educational
psychology, and 'special' education. He has published a number of articles and book chapters in these areas and is presently involved in
research projects with colleagues at the University of Oulu, Finland.

William J. Garland is professor of philosophy at the University of the
South in Sewanee, TN, USA. His intellectual interests include traditional metaphysics, American philosophy, value theory and (more recently) virtue ethics, the ethics of care, and business ethics. Garland
has published articles on Plato, Whitehead's metaphysics, Whitehead's
philosophy of education, the ethics of care, and the social philosophy
of Richard Rorty. He is currently doing research on trust and trust-
worthiness in the business community.

Ronald Preston Phipps was the personal research assistant for 7 years
to University Professor Henry S. Leonard, former President of the
American Philosophy Association. Leonard served as Alfred North

Whitehead's personal assistant at Harvard during the period when Whitehead wrote Process and Reality and other major philosophic works and later was a colleague of Kurt Gödel at the Princeton Institute of Advanced Studies. Phipps taught Whitehead's metaphysics and mathematical logic. He was recipient of a National Science Foundation fellowship in the philosophy of theoretical physics, developing a philosophy of an Infinite and Open Universe. He is a founding member and former Chairman of the US/China Friendship Association, Seattle, and President of CPNA International, Ltd. He is a founding member and Advisor to the China Project of the Center for Process Studies.

Robert Regnier is a professor of Educational Foundations in the College of Education at the University of Saskatchewan who is interested in process philosophy and education, ecological education, critical pedagogy and critical educational theory, and Indigenous education. He is currently a board member of the International Process Network and a co-director of the University of Saskatchewan Process Philosophy Research Unit.

Franz G. Riffert has studied philosophy, theology, psychology and education at Salzburg University, Austria. He received grants to study at the Catholic University of Eichstätt and at the Center for Process Studies. Since 1995 he has been working at the department for educational research at Salzburg University. His interests focus on studies in emprical education (diagnosis, intervention, methods of instruction, teacher training, school development, and self-evaluation) and philosophical foundations of education (with special emphasis on the works of A. N. Whitehead and K. R: Popper). He serves on the editorial board of *Cosmos and History: The Journal of Natural and Social Philosophy* and co-editor of the journal *Salzburger Beiträge zur Erziehungswissenschaft*.

Adam C. Scarfe received his Ph.D. in Philosophy from the University of Ottawa, Canada in 2001, having written a dissertation on the role of scepticism in Hegel's and Whitehead's respective speculative philosophies. Dr. Scarfe is currently pursuing post-doctoral graduate work on Whitehead's Philosophy of Education with the University of Saskatchewan Process Philosophy Research Unit (U.S.P.P.R.U.). He is a sessional instructor for the departments of Educational Foundations and Philosophy.

Howard Edward Thompson has studied at the University of North Carolina at Chapel Hill, obtaining a B. A. in psychology and an "A. B. D." (All courses and exams passed for the Ph. D., but dissertation unfinished) in philosophy. He was a member of the philosophy Department at the University of Saskatchewan from 1967 until 1999 and has received several awards for teaching excellence. Inter alia, he created both academic courses and several non-academic discussion/action groups, in Mysticism and in Sexuality and in Men's Liberation. In 1998, he co-founded, and has since co-directed, the University of Saskatchewan Process Philosophy Research Unit He has recently taken up sculpting, and has had works exhibited in two local shows.

Martin Wood is Research Director and Senior Lecturer in Social Theory and Organisation, Department of Management Studies, University of York, UK. Previously a member of faculty in the Centre for Leadership Studies, University of Exeter and before that as Research Fellow at Warwick Business School. He earned his PhD for work on the production and consumption of knowledge in the public sector area of health care. An enduring theme across his researches is a comitment to an epistemology of *process*, *immanence* and *difference*, for which he draws substantively, though not exclusively, on the work of Alfred North Whitehead, Henri Bergson, and, amongst others, Friedich Nietzsche and Gilles Deleuze. Martin has published in academic journals of the highest international standing. He is currently preoccuied exploring management and leadership in relation to issues of idenity and difference, and digital technologies and the perceived acceleraion of events in contemporary life.

Howard Woodhouse is Professor of Educational Foundations at the University of Saskatchewan, Canada, where he teaches philosophy of education and international education. He has a Ph.D. from the University of Toronto in educational theory, and has taught at several universities in Canada and Nigeria. He has published extensively in books and refereed journals on the educational philosophies of Alfred North Whitehead and Bertrand Russell, on African education and cultural dependency, and on the importance of critical thought to education, and is currently writing a book titled Academic Freedom and the Corporate Market for McGill-Queen's University Press. In addition to being Co-Director of the Saskatchewan Process Philosophy Research Unit and Consulting Editor for the journals *Interchange* and *Journal of Public Administration*, he is a Research Associate for the *Canadian Centre for Policy Alternatives*.

Index of Names